Y0-DVY-013

DATE DUE			
GAYLORD			PRINTED IN U.S.A.

# REVIEW 3

REVIEW

Volume 3   1981

Edited by

James O. Hoge and
James L. W. West III

University Press of Virginia
Charlottesville

THE UNIVERSITY PRESS OF VIRGINIA
Copyright © 1981 by the Rector and Visitors
of the University of Virginia

First published 1981

ISBN 0190–3233
ISBN 0–8139–0910–4

Printed in the United States of America

Contents

Slips, Sacred Commodities, and Broadway Bladder   1
  by Robert L. Patten
    Review of Victor Bonham-Carter, *Authors by Profession*; Philip Gaskell, *From Writer to Reader: Studies in Editorial Method*; June Steffensen Hagen, *Tennyson and His Publishers*; Edgar F. Harden, *The Emergence of Thackeray's Serial Fiction*; J. A. Sutherland, *Thackeray at Work*; J. A. Sutherland, *Victorian Novelists and Publishers*; J. A. Sutherland, *Fiction and the Fiction Industry*; Siegfried Unseld, *The Author and His Publisher*

Pound and Around   25
  by Hugh Kenner
    Review of Michael Alexander, *The Poetic Achievement of Ezra Pound*; Peter Brooker, *A Student's Guide to the Selected Poems of Ezra Pound*; Ronald Bush, *The Genesis of Ezra Pound's* Cantos; Barbara Eastman, *Ezra Pound's* Cantos: *The Story of the Text*; George Kearns, *Guide to Ezra Pound's Selected* Cantos; Peter Makin, *Provence and Pound*; Frederick K. Sanders, *John Adams Speaking: Pound's Sources for the Adams Cantos*; Richard Sieburth, *Instigations: Ezra Pound and Remy de Gourmont*; Carroll F. Terrell, *A Companion to the* Cantos *of Ezra Pound*

The Carroll Connection   45
  by Peter Heath
    Review of Morton N. Cohen with R. L. Green, eds., *The Letters of Lewis Carroll*; Denis Crutch, ed., *The Lewis Carroll Handbook*, rev. ed.; Anne Clark, *Lewis Carroll: A Biography*; William Warren Bartley III, ed., *Lewis Carroll's Symbolic Logic*

The Kenneth Burke Problem 63
  by William E. Cain
    Review of Kenneth Burke, *The Philosophy of Literary Form*

Tom Sawyer Once and for All 75
  by Robert C. Bray
    Review of Paul Baender, Terry Firkins, and John C. Gerber, eds., The Adventures of Tom Sawyer, Tom Sawyer Abroad, *and "Tom Sawyer, Detective,"* vol. IV of *The Works of Mark Twain,* Iowa-California Edition

Constructing and Deconstructing Autobiography 95
  by Jerome H. Buckley
    Review of George P. Landow, ed., *Approaches to Victorian Autobiography*

Buns and Butter: A Taste of the Afro-American Cultural Canon 103
  by John Oliver Perry
    Review of Michael S. Harper and Robert B. Stepto, eds., *Chant of Saints: A Gathering of Afro-American Literature, Art, and Scholarship*

Expatriate Lives: First Biographies of Maugham and Auden 115
  by Stanley Weintraub
    Review of Ted Morgan, *Maugham: A Biography;* Charles Osborne, *W. H. Auden: The Life of a Poet*

For Mark Schorer with Combative Love: The *Sons and Lovers* Manuscript 129
  by Mark Spilka
    Review of D. H. Lawrence, Sons and Lovers: *A Facsimile of the Manuscript,* ed. Mark Schorer

Contents

American Serials   149
   by Martin Roth
     Review of Bruce Granger, *American Essay Serials from Franklin to Irving*

Pope: "Practical Poetry" and Practicing Poetry   155
   by John Dixon Hunt
     Review of Morris R. Brownell, *Alexander Pope and the Arts of Georgian England;* Dustin H. Griffin, *Alexander Pope: The Poet in the Poems;* Miriam Leranbaum, *Alexander Pope's "Opus Magnum," 1729–1744;* Howard Erskine-Hill and Anne Smith, eds., *The Art of Alexander Pope*

Dreiser in the Making   175
   by Thomas P. Riggio
     Review of Yoshinobu Hakutani, *Young Dreiser: A Critical Study*

Eliot upon the Rood of the Times   181
   by Ronald Schuchard
     Review of Keith Alldritt, *Eliot's* Four Quartets: *Poetry as Chamber Music;* George Bornstein, *Transformations of Romanticism in Yeats, Eliot, and Stevens;* Ann P. Brady, *Lyricism in the Poetry of T. S. Eliot;* Lyndall Gordon, *Eliot's Early Years;* Nancy Duvall Hargrove, *Landscape as Symbol in the Poetry of T. S. Eliot;* James E. Miller, Jr., *T. S. Eliot's Personal Waste Land: Exorcism of the Demons;* A. D. Moody, *Thomas Stearns Eliot: Poet;* David Newton–De Molina, ed., *The Literary Criticism of T. S. Eliot: New Essays;* A. C. Partridge, *The Language of Modern Poetry: Yeats, Eliot, Auden;* Balachandra Rajan, *The Overwhelming Question: A Study of the Poetry of T. S. Eliot;* M. L. Rosenthal, *Sailing into the Unknown: Yeats, Pound, and Eliot;* Stephen Spender, *T. S. Eliot;* Stanley Sultan, Ulysses, The Waste Land, *and Modernism: A Jubilee Study;* Derek Traversi, *T. S. Eliot: The Longer Poems*

The Literary Scholar Faces the Computer 209
  by Philip H. Smith, Jr.
    Review of Robert L. Oakman, *Computer Methods for Literary Research*

Chaucer Manuscripts and Texts 219
  by N. F. Blake
    Review of P. G. Ruggiers, ed., The Canterbury Tales: *A Facsimile and Transcription of the Hengwrt Manuscript;* Troilus and Criseyde, *Geoffrey Chaucer: Facsimile of Corpus Christi College Cambridge MS 61,* intro. by M. B. Parkes and Elizabeth Salter

Bishop Bibliographed: The New Descriptive Bibliography? 233
  by Craig S. Abbott
    Review of Candace W. MacMahon, *Elizabeth Bishop: A Bibliography, 1927–1979*

Green Thought and Ideology 243
  by Annabel Patterson
    Review of James Turner, *The Politics of Landscape: Rural Scenery and Society in English Poetry, 1630–1660*

The Lees of Happiness: More Fitzgerald from Bruccoli 249
  by Veronica A. Makowsky
    Review of Matthew J. Bruccoli and Margaret M. Duggan, eds., *Correspondence of F. Scott Fitzgerald*

Virginia Woolf and the Creative Critic 265
  by Harvena Richter
    Review of Maria DiBattista, *Virginia Woolf's Major Novels: The Fables of Anon;* Leon Edel, *Bloomsbury: A House of Lions;* John Lehmann, *Thrown to the Woolfs;* Perry Meisel, *The Absent Father: Virginia Woolf and Walter Pater;* Roger Poole, *The Unknown Virginia Woolf;* Phyllis Rose, *Woman of Letters: A Life of Virginia Woolf;* Beverly Ann Schlack, *Continuing Presences: Virginia*

Contents

> *Woolf's Use of Literary Allusion;* Leonard Woolf, *The Wise Virgins;* Anne Olivier Bell, ed., *The Diary of Virginia Woolf,* vol. III; Nigel Nicolson and Joanne Trautmann, eds., *Letters of Virginia Woolf,* vol. VI; Ralph Freedman, ed., *Virginia Woolf: Revaluation and Continuity*

The Development of Hawthorne Primary Bibliography   285
  by Joel Myerson
> Review of C. E. Frazer Clark, Jr., *Nathaniel Hawthorne: A Descriptive Bibliography*

Foison Plenty: Nine Studies of Shakespeare   301
  by Thomas McFarland
> Review of Robert Grudin, *Mighty Opposites: Shakespeare and Renaissance Contrariety;* Bertrand Evans, *Shakespeare's Tragic Practice;* Susan Snyder, *The Comic Matrix of Shakespeare's Tragedies;* Lawrence Danson, *The Harmonies of* The Merchant of Venice; Darryl J. Gless, Measure for Measure, *the Law, and the Convent;* James L. Calderwood, *Metadrama in Shakespeare's Henriad:* Richard II *to* Henry V; Joseph A. Porter, *The Drama of Speech Acts: Shakespeare's Lancastrian Tetralogy;* Alice-Lyle Scoufos, *Shakespeare's Typological Satire: A Study of the Falstaff-Oldcastle Problem;* Alvin B. Kernan, *The Playwright as Magician: Shakespeare's Image of the Poet in the Public Theater*

Subtlety and Sabotage in *Piers Plowman*   323
  by Britton J. Harwood
> Review of David Aers, *Chaucer, Langland, and the Creative Imagination;* Priscilla Martin, Piers Plowman: *The Field and the Tower;* Daniel Maher Murtaugh, Piers Plowman *and the Image of God*

Correspondence   341

Contributors   345

Editorial Board

Felicia Bonaparte
City College, CUNY

Jerome H. Buckley
Harvard University

Paul Connolly
Yeshiva University

A. S. G. Edwards
University of Victoria

Robert L. Kellogg
University of Virginia

James R. Kincaid
University of Colorado

Cecil Y. Lang
University of Virginia

James B. Meriwether
University of South Carolina

Hershel Parker
University of Delaware

Martin Roth
University of Minnesota

George Stade
Columbia University

John L. Sharpe III
Duke University

G. Thomas Tanselle
*John Simon Guggenheim
Memorial Foundation*

Stanley Weintraub
Pennsylvania State University

Slips, Sacred Commodities, and Broadway Bladder

Robert L. Patten

Victor Bonham-Carter. *Authors by Profession, Volume One: From the Introduction of Printing until the Copyright Act 1911.* London: The Society of Authors, 1978. 252 pp.

Philip Gaskell. *From Writer to Reader: Studies in Editorial Method.* Oxford: Clarendon Press, 1978. xiii, 268 pp.

June Steffensen Hagen. *Tennyson and His Publishers.* University Park: Pennsylvania State University Press, 1979. xv, 233 pp.

Edgar F. Harden. *The Emergence of Thackeray's Serial Fiction.* Athens: University of Georgia Press, 1979. x, 385 pp.

J. A. Sutherland. *Thackeray at Work.* London: Athlone Press, 1974. ix, 165 pp.

J. A. Sutherland. *Victorian Novelists and Publishers.* London: Athlone Press, 1976. iii, 251 pp.

J. A. Sutherland. *Fiction and the Fiction Industry.* London: Athlone Press, 1978. xxvii, 231 pp.

Siegfried Unseld. *The Author and His Publisher.* Trans. Hunter Hannum and Hildegarde Hannum. Chicago: University of Chicago Press, 1980. xi, 300 pp.

When I first studied literature, books had no authors, no editors, no publishers, no textual cruxes, no early reviews, no revised editions, no relevant historical or cultural context. My philosophy professor was coauthor of the theory of the intentional fallacy; my psychology professor dismissed all Freud (the intentional phallus?) by intoning in Kissingerman, "All things are either round or pointed." In such an atmosphere, exclusively New Critical, it was difficult to conceive of a personality that created a text or of conditions extraneous to the theme that might impose on it without loss of unity or effect. Works so deformed by external circumstances were left out of anthologies; what we read, we confidently assumed, were masterpieces which worked, which were wholes, which were unviolated by any necessity besides Art.

From such a beginning graduate school came as a great shock. The mandatory Introduction to Graduate Study seemed wholly beside the point—it certainly didn't touch on any of the issues that made the study of literature satisfying. Edition, issue, state; paleography; quartos and folios and forms; bibliography of all sorts; watermarks; McKerrow and Bowers; incunabula; *Dissertation Abstracts* and the *BM Catalogue* and *PMLA* —all of these were such depressing and irrelevant facts of life for us that we "collaborated" on the homework and skimmed the reading assignments. A few wayward souls got interested in editing and compiling indexes; one enterprising bibliophile paid his tuition by buying and reselling the library's duplicates; but for most of us most of the time in the early sixties, literature stood apart from the circumstances of its creation and dissemination, a Platonic form visible through type and ink on paper.

Our professors knew better, of course, but the more they taught of the circumstances surrounding a text the more dismissive we were inclined to be: "He lectures for hours about theatrical companies (or eighteenth-century sermons, or vowel shifts), but he doesn't know anything about thematic development or point of view!" we would complain to one another in private. Leavis made scarcely a dent in our consciousness, and Poulet was out of sight: James and Stevens were our aestheticians, Dorothy Van Ghent quizzed us on fiction. The closest we came to considering external factors was *The Elizabethan World Picture* and Freudianism: Ernest Jones psychoanalyzed Hamlet and Edmund Wilson psychoanalyzed Dickens.

It was therefore another shock to come across John Butt and Kathleen Tillotson's now famous *Dickens at Work* (1957). For (at least as I then understood their purposes) they set out to defend the integrity of Dickens's artistry against his detractors by looking at the circumstances affecting the composition and publication of his serials. In other words, their defense of his art came from examining his craft, not from dwelling on imagery and symbolism and irony and ambiguity and tone. Doubtless there were other books about other authors, earlier and perhaps even more major, that took the same tack: but for me *Dickens at Work* was revelatory. It proved that criticism written in ignorance of the circumstances affecting publication often proceeded from implicit biases that skewed the "disinterested" interpretation of the text, and it demonstrated again and again that although Dickens wrote rapidly and for serial publication, he could still be shown to have unity of purpose and effect. For the succeeding decade, I labored on footnotes to that discovery.

But rescuing Dickens didn't automatically entail rescuing other novelists, especially Victorian novelists, from charges of careless writing. Henry James, after all, aimed his famous attack on Victorian fiction as "large loose baggy monsters" in response to a reading of *The Newcomes*.[1] Trollope, thought to be a dismal example of the substitution of assiduity for art, was despite his ardent partisanship our authority for believing that Thackeray was "unsteadfast, idle, changeable of purpose": "Though he can settle himself down to his pen and ink,—not always even to that without a struggle, but to that with sufficient bursts of energy to produce a large average amount of work,—he cannot settle himself down to the task of contriving a story."[2]

The very title of John Sutherland's *Thackeray at Work* (1974) indicates his intent to defend Thackeray by the same kind of scrutiny to which Butt and Tillotson had subjected Dickens two decades earlier. Dickens himself, in his obituary tribute to Thackeray, thought his fellow novelist too much *feigned* a want of earnestness in his application to his art.[3] Bolstered by that slight benefit of the doubt, Sutherland goes on, not to excuse the rather trivial errors of dates and names present in every one of Thackeray's texts, but to reconsider how Thackeray's "touches of genius" and his "touches of vagueness" are parts of the same sensibility (p. 8). The theme running through his book, he announces at the beginning, is that Thackeray "is a novelist of genius, but one whose genius is of a peculiarly spontaneous and easy-going nature" (p. 10).

Sutherland is not blind to Thackeray's apparent sloppiness, but he does show how brilliantly, on occasion, Thackeray could improvise, and he argues (with respect to *Henry Esmond*) that part of his art derives from a refusal to revise. The place of *Esmond* in a defense of Thackeray's art is reexamined by Sutherland in his important second book, *Victorian Novelists and Publishers* (1976). There he broadens the implications of his and Butt and Tillotson's earlier work to embrace the whole of Victorian fiction: "The great novels of the period which appear to be the unaided product of creative genius were often . . . the outcome of collaboration, compromise or commission. Works like *Henry Esmond*, *Middlemarch* or *Framley Parsonage* cannot be fully appreciated unless we see them as partnership productions. . . . There is, I would maintain, no Victorian novel (and I would include even literary eccentricities like *Wuthering Heights*) which was not materially influenced by the publishing system, for good or ill" (p. 6). In the case of *Esmond*, Sutherland believes that some of the credit for that novel's unity of tone and effect should be given to Thackeray's publisher, the twenty-six-year-old George Smith, whose flexibility in offering and modifying the contract for the book allowed Thackeray the elbowroom, time, and money he needed to bring a three-decker, not a serial, into wholeness. Smith helped create "a rational economic framework for its composition" (p. 112).

Implicit throughout Sutherland's two studies—even explicit at times—is the assumption that the "hand to mouth" existence of serial composition "aggravated the tendency of Thackeray's fiction towards shapelessness."[4] According to Sutherland, there was little opportunity for revision during or after publication, the writing was subject to all the quotidian distractions of human existence from illness to infatuation, and commercial pressures inevitably deflected the writer from his purposes. *The Virginians* seems an object lesson in everything that can go wrong with serials, on the whole deserving the opprobrium of

Douglas Jerrold's apocryphal quip that it was "the worst novel anyone ever wrote."

Edgar F. Harden mounts a more uncompromising defense of Thackeray in his weighty study of the emergence of Thackeray's serial fiction. After examining all the surviving evidence for Thackeray's composition—manuscripts, letters, proofs, editions—Harden concludes that even in the loosest of the monthly novels, Thackeray was the reverse of an idle dilettante: "Neither a careless nor a hasty worker," Thackeray continuously revised his texts and proofs, "making simple deletions, changes, and additions, but also reshaping, providing new interpretive contexts, refocussing perspectives, modulating tones, shifting emphases, anticipating future developments, and embodying new artistic discoveries" (pp. 12, 15). Harden greatly admires Thackeray's spirit: "Thackeray—amid all his distractions—was indeed possessed by a sacred rage that could not be extinguished except when he was overcome by waves of intense physical suffering. To study the composition of his major serial novels is, increasingly, to feel something of that anguish and to be deeply moved by the narrowing but invincible gaiety with which that central flame continued to burn" (p. 15).

This is not an easy book to read, nor an enjoyable one, despite Harden's efforts to infuse his meticulous scholarship with the warmth of the earned enthusiasm; but it is one of the most important studies of the composition of fiction ever produced. So painstaking is Harden in his treatment of all the evidence (inconsistent, scattered, but abundant) for Thackeray's compositional strategies, so delicately appreciative is he of the motives for visions and revisions, that I am inclined to grant assent well before he has finished his argument. Thackeray emerges from this study so inventive, rich, sophisticated, and arduous a writer that we should not be able any longer to perpetuate the myth of idleness. The dismissive verdict of a century, repeated even in Gaskell's *Writer to Reader* ("a dilatory author who did not give himself time to be meticulous" [p. 156]), cannot withstand this massive demonstration of Thackeray's literary integrity. We have come to the threshold of a new era in Thackeray studies, which should be confirmed by the eventual publication of a critical edition of all the texts under the general editorship of Peter L. Shillingsburg.

Evidence does not, of course, preclude differences in interpretation. From the first 113 manuscript leaves of *Vanity Fair*, written by Thackeray in both his slanted and his upright script, scholars have drawn very different conclusions. Gordon Ray's biography infers a fairly neat chronology, wherein Thackeray shifts his purpose and strategy through alterations inserted in his upright hand during late 1846. At that time, Ray believes, Thackeray changed a detached, noncommital narrative marked by misanthropic nihilism into an expansively hortatory direct address that was also gentler, more reasonable, and more human. The Tillotsons, in their edition of the novel, discuss Thackeray's search for an appropriate voice, his use and parody of other styles in previous fiction and criticism, and conclude that when he cancels the parodic opening to the Vauxhall chapter (postponed from Number I to Number II), he defines his own particular vision. Sutherland thinks that Thackeray's mimicking the style of the then manager of Drury Lane, Alfred Bunn, in his direct address to the reader ("I warn 'my kyind friends,' " inserted at the end of Chapter 8), far from indicating a new confidence in his role as showman, lands him "in an artistic impasse which . . . he could only blur with a distractingly virtuosic display" (p. 31). Harden, on the other hand, concludes that the handwriting "does not offer persuasive evidence for dating Thackeray's additions and corrections to the manuscripts of the first two installments" (p. 29), and sees in the changes Thackeray's discovery of a structural pattern of alternation and contrast (not only Becky to Amelia and George to Dobbin and Jos, but also George/Becky to Dobbin/Amelia and George+Amelia to Jos+Becky) that shaped the entirety of his masterpiece.

Harden is restrained in his conclusions and temperate in correcting others. Nonetheless, one can see that he differs from Sutherland in virtually every case where they treat the same material. Whereas Sutherland believes Thackeray was essentially a "one draft writer" (p. 9), Harden stresses the lapidary *process* of composition whereby one version is superimposed upon another, as second (third, fourth) thoughts modify the original draft. Sutherland calls these changes "running repair work" (p. 32) and tends to see later interpolations as "narrative upholstery" (p. 25); Harden points out that Thackeray made extensive cuts as well as additions, that the augmentations often enhanced the dramatic artistry and complexity, and that he carried the folded leaves of manuscript around in his pocket so that he could note down revisions and interlineations that occurred to him away from his desk.

Differing in their assessment of the degree of control Thackeray imposed on his texts, they consequently interpret the surviving evidence differently. Thus Sutherland believes Thackeray drafted the plan for the final nine numbers of *The Newcomes* "because he was exhausted, depressed and distracted. It served as a crutch to sustain a limping imagination" (p. 78). Not so, contends Harden, at pains to note how meticulous Thackeray was to the end in scrutinizing proof (p. 246), despite his "attacks of illness wh. are now so frequent."[5] In these plans Thackeray "was sketching the final curve of his narrative, not outlining the structure of individual installments," and through a complex interweaving of lateral parallel incidents he brought to a successful conclusion his "vast and complex design" (pp. 132, 137). Moreover, *The Virginians,* according to Harden, is not a failure, but rather the serial "that most extensively integrated personal history with political events" (p. 219).

Even on the significance of details the two authorities clash. They disagree about Thackeray's motive for altering Becky's character in her letter to Amelia (Sutherland, pp. 33–34; Harden, pp. 46–47) and quarrel once more about the leaves of *Philip* X now housed at Yale (see Harden, pp. 274–76 and n. 39). One particularly illuminating difference occurs in their treatments of a small revision to *Vanity Fair* IV. In Chapter 13 Thackeray recounts a dinner party at the Osbornes to which Amelia is invited at a time when her prospective father-in-law has become uneasy about rumors of Mr. Sedley's insolvency. Originally Thackeray, partly intent on emphasizing George's tardiness to dinner and neglect of Amelia, wrote of the "great

French Clock" on the drawing room mantelpiece (present too in the illustration Thackeray supplied) that it "tolled five in a heavy Cathedral tone," and that "it had a cheerful brass groupe of Jepththah sacrificing his daughter" (see facsimile, Sutherland, plate 2). Revising, he changed "it had" to "wh was surmounted by," and Jephthah, which he couldn't spell, to what Harden calls "the more grimly purposeful" "sacrifice of Iphigenia." A small change, one of many in the passage which Harden believes add "to the tone of dark comedy" (p. 70).

Sutherland has a good deal more to say about this change (pp. 11–17). First, old Osborne has reason to look askance at the girl he once arranged as fiancée for his son, and he makes no effort to disguise his disfavor: "Sacrifice is predicted by the very furniture around Amelia." Second, while aptly foreshadowing Amelia's fate, the brass clock contrasts "her as the passive Iphigenia victim and Becky as the active Clytemnestra: an opposition which is sustained until the murderous last chapter and 'Becky's second appearance in the character of Clytemnestra.'" Sutherland believes that the change was inspired in part by Thackeray's reflections on the original sentence, commencing "When that chronometer tolled five in a heavy cathedral tone. . . ." The intimations of religious ritual suggested Jephthah, "but the overtone of biblical severity was not entirely appropriate to the old pagan Osborne, and the decoration was eccentric and extremely unlikely." Furthermore, the associations were inappropriate, since Jephthah sacrificed his only child because of a rash vow to God. The switch to Iphigenia, another sacrificed daughter, supported both the Grecism "chronometer" and the Frenchified interior of an upper-class house; the allusion to Racine's *Iphigénie* is possible. So a future theme that swells into vital significance derives from Thackeray's inspired improvisation; and the result was so effective that Trollope openly copied it in the famous "Iphigenia" chapter of *The Warden*. I find Sutherland's expansive discussion of this detail brilliantly persuasive.

One piece of evidence frequently used against Thackeray was his practice of dictating to an amanuensis, either his daughter Anne or Eyre Crowe. How could he possibly be a careful author when he lounged about all day in bed, whiffing a cigar and desultorily uttering the pastiche Georgian of *Henry Esmond* to an attendant scribe? Few have considered that Thackeray may have been dictating from notes or earlier drafts, that the very periods of inactivity before composition were times of intense mental effort and planning, as Dickens's were, or that, like Tennyson, Thackeray could keep large portions of his script in mind, revising prior to committing himself to paper. "For the last ten days," he wrote as he was beginning *Denis Duval*, "I have been almost *non compos mentis*. When I am in labour with a book I don't quite know what happens. I sit for hours before my paper, not doing my book, but incapable of doing anything else, and thinking upon that subject always, waking with it, walking about with it, and going to bed with it. Oh, the struggles and bothers—oh, the throbs and pains about this trumpery!" (*Letters*, IV, 292; quoted also in Sutherland, pp. 127–28).

All who write know the agonizing periods preceding composition, when ideas swirl in one's head and painful choices about strategy, tone, range, and judgment have to be made. But, prisoners of the document, we scholars tend to employ for reconstructing others' efforts only those *disjecta membra librorum* we can see or infer from surviving texts. One of the ironies of efforts like Sutherland's and Harden's is that we may have to reinterpret Thackeray's bouts of laziness as bouts of strenuous, though unwritten, activity, and discern in the very absence of evidence a greater fidelity to art than his studied amateurism would lead one to suspect.

June Steffensen Hagen doesn't look closely at Tennyson's extended process of composition in her book on Tennyson and his publishers (though Philip Gaskell does, in a chapter on the many revisions from 1830 to 1842 of the opening of *Oenone*). Indeed, it is not quite clear what she does intend by her title, since the focus of the book wavers between Tennyson's social relations (especially with Edward Moxon), his contracts and receipts, his public reception, criticism of the poetry, and accounts of later and collected editions. All these are, quite properly, part of the story of Tennyson's lifetime of professional authorship; in writing such a narrative, one is inevitably constrained by the surviving documents, dealing more fully with finances where publishers' records or bank accounts exist, or with "conviviality" (Sutherland's term, *Victorian Novelists and Publishers*, p. 85) if the letters are particularly explicit, or with reception, if the reviews prove numerous and influential. Here, however, my sense of wavering focus is occasioned less by believing that she has wrung every inference from the scarce facts than that she has dipped shallowly in too abundant documentation.

There are three areas in which she uses evidence oddly. The first concerns her efforts at original research. "Much of the primary material for this study is in the Tennyson Research Centre, Lincoln, England," she informs us at the start (p. xiv). The documents housed there are not easy to use: No comprehensive index has been compiled, and they can shift their location (or their ownership, as a recent Sotheby auction proved) unpredictably from one week to the next. But if a work aims to incorporate original research, it ought to do so straight through. Hagen relies too heavily on H. G. Merriam's outdated study *Edward Moxon* (1939), on P. F. Jamieson's 1952 account of Tennyson's 1832 audience, and on Sir Charles Tennyson's unpublished typescript "Tennyson's Dealings with His Publishers." She tends to quote others about matters on which she should be authoritative and to use others' transcriptions of letters or reviews instead of going directly to the original.[6] Why quote Christopher Ricks's transcription of a letter in the Tennyson Research Centre (p. 30) or Marcia Allentuck's transcription of a passage from William Michael Rossetti's biography of his brother (p. 105)? Why, in naming the contributors to *The Tribute*, where Tennyson first published "the germ" of *Maud*, quote the list given by E. E. Kellett in G. M. Young's *Early Victorian England* (p. 46)? And why quote Hallam Tennyson's *Memoir* when it is wrong (p. 91)?

A second problem of focus comes with her incorporation of criticism. Granted Tennyson's poetic career was significantly affected by the early reception of his works; granted too that he was throughout his life abnormally sensitive to censure. Edgar F. Shannon, Jr., looked into this subject over a quarter century ago; John Jump has assembled the critical heritage; Christopher Ricks and others have done significant further work. The essential thing for Hagen's purposes is to document the extent to which reviews affected Tennyson's publishing practices, either by "silencing" him or by encouraging a new, cheaper, expanded, illustrated, or collected edition. Much of the time Hagen provides a useful narrative tracing the effects of reception on publication and composition, and vice versa; but there are pages devoted to an assessment of Tennyson's poetic achievement that are both irrelevant and trite. For instance, we are told that *In Memoriam* "has themes of unity, identity, and the affirmation of faith, with a principle [*sic*] aesthetic theme operative throughout" and that the poem "remains alive most notably as a re-creation of grief and doubt, and a tentative exploration of the artistic spirit's response to both" (pp. 81, 83).

A third wavering focus derives less from the abundance of tangential evidence than from her insufficient understanding of the evidence to hand. About the physical form of books, the complex legal provisions of contracts and copyright, and the enormously complicated mechanical processes of printing and distribution she simply doesn't know enough. The evidence she uncovers can be less revealing, or more, than she realizes. For instance, on pages 26–27 she discusses Moxon's publishing practices, leading up to an analysis of the agreement for the 1832 *Poems*, the first of ten titles that Moxon and his firm would publish. She cites, to demonstrate Moxon's conservative advertising practice, his "running four- or eight-page listings of his publications on the flyleaves" (p. 26). Physically impossible as stated, it was standard practice to insert advertisers after the front flyleaf or before the back one; Moxon's is *not* an example of especially prudent practice.

Hagen then goes on to consider Moxon's business arrangements: "He usually took the financially conservative tack of encouraging the 'half profits' agreement whereby the publisher paid all costs of production and advertising, and then, after reimbursing himself for these costs, shared whatever profits remained with the author" (p. 27). "Financially conservative tack" is a misleading description of what Moxon effected, for

Hagen fails to distinguish between the purchase of copyright and the costs/profits of publication. Apparently what Moxon did (the actual agreement has not survived) was to lease half the copyright, for an unspecified time and number of editions, for no outlay at all. He then agreed to publish an edition of the poems and to set all receipts against his publication and advertising costs. (No wonder he was conservative in his advertising: those payments went out of the firm, whereas all the rest went to recoup his own expenses.) Anything left over, after his fixed costs and outlays for paper, ink, composition, pressing, and binding were covered, he shared with Tennyson fifty-fifty. Merriam, Hagen's authority here, is surprised that Moxon prospered "with few histories on his list of publications, few religious books, no textbooks, few biographies, little fiction, practically none of the classics, no foreign books, and with the sale of poetry exceedingly slow" (p. 25). But Moxon could wrest from poets terms that no novelist would have accepted, and he published books that were on the whole, despite Tennyson's infuriating delays over proof, much less expensive to manufacture than a three-decker.

Another point about Moxon's practice is worth mentioning. In the agreement with Leigh Hunt to publish a new edition of his *Poetical Works* which Hagen offers as "typical," Moxon reserves to himself the right "from time to time . . . to print and publish any further such edition or editions of the said Poetical Works (to consist of 1000 copies) as by him shall be deemed advantageous" (p. 27). From early on, Dickens leased his copyrights for a limited period rather than selling a share outright: that way he could exercise some control over his market and his publishers. It is evident from Hagen's subsequent narrative that Tennyson also leased his copyrights and that he had much to say about the format, timing, and content of new editions. Thus in this important particular the Hunt agreement does *not* provide a precedent for Tennyson. And it is an important particular, for as Hagen demonstrates convincingly Tennyson ceaselessly revised his published poems (especially the early ones, but even the *Idylls*) in new editions carefully tailored to meet some new market or aesthetic requirement. Few writers exhibit a more complicated history of published revision: like the novels Sutherland discusses, Tennyson's poems too were "materially influenced by the publishing system, for good or ill."

On the matter of copyright, Hagen makes other mistakes. Regarding the Ticknor American edition of the 1842 *Poems*, she writes: "Tennyson ended up with a $150 payment for copyright, 'possibly the earliest copyright payment by an American publisher to a foreign author.'" The statement is repeated, without the "possibly," on page 180. The authority quoted here is John Olin Eidson's 1954 essay in the *New England Quarterly*. He is incorrect: Dickens was receiving payments from American publishers, either gratis or for advance proofs, in the late 1830s, a fact that has been noted many times. Nor was it a payment for *copyright*, since none existed in the United States for works written by foreigners and first printed abroad. In the absence of reciprocal copyright, American editions cannot be called "pirated" or "*sub rosa*" (p. 131): they may have been infuriating to English authors, but they were legal.

One further confusion with respect to the 1832 *Poems* agreement: if the Hunt contract *is* typical, Moxon agreed to risk "the costs and expenses to be incurred . . . in printing, stereotyping, publishing, and advertising." On page 66 we are told that Tennyson agreed to bear all the expenses of publishing the fifth edition of *Poems* (1848) and that these terms "duplicate those for the 1832 *Poems*." Then on pages 83–84 Hagen implies that with the agreement for *In Memoriam* Tennyson for the first time accepted the liability for any publishing costs not reimbursed from sales. The point Hagen is making—that because of this change Tennyson felt freer to demand revises and trial printings—is important. I wish I knew *when* the altered arrangement began.

Eventually Tennyson made a lot of money from his poetry —from single poems commissioned for magazines in England and America, from new volumes, and from collected editions. For instance, the half-yearly receipts totted up by Emily Tennyson show that *Enoch Arden,* published by Moxon in August 1864, earned £6,664.4.2 through December 1864, and a further £1,410.17.8 through June 1865.[7] That was nearly double what the first *Idylls* made in a similar period, and a high point of his earnings. "My whole living is from the sale of my books," Tennyson boasted, forgetting that he was also in receipt annually of a £200 Civil List pension and a further stipend of £200 as Laureate. But the boast expressed an important truth, nonetheless: Tennyson's income essentially derived from his writing alone—even the pension and salary were tributes to him as a writer—and on the receipts from that writing he could live quite comfortably. Indeed, unlike Carlyle, Thackeray, Dickens, and Wilde, Tennyson refused to supplement his income by lecture tours.

Historians and sociologists have been much preoccupied in the past twenty years with studying "professionalization" in the nineteenth and twentieth centuries.[8] To apply the concept to writers may seem absurd, for seldom have authors displayed the kinds of regular habits, disciplinary self-regulation, "monopolistic privileges," and "public service ideals" characteristic of professionals.[9] But Victorian writers *aspired* to professional status and rejoiced in those complex circumstances that delivered them from subservience to a patron or dependence on legacies or sinecures. Victor Bonham-Carter traces the economic emancipation of writers from the time of Caxton to the English Copyright Act of 1911 in the first of two volumes published by the independent trade union, the Society of Authors. (At the time the society was considering joining the TUC, some members took to the letters columns of the papers to scoff at the idea of a writers' strike; one wonders whether the success of the actors' strike in Hollywood has changed any minds.) Bonham-Carter spends little time wrestling with definitions; a professional author is for him simply one who earns his living from writing. Instead, he surveys the efforts writers have made over the past four centuries to survive as writers, concluding that "authors' best aid sprang out of their own efforts" (p. 9). Though collective action came late in the history of authorship and though the first efforts (by Dickens, Bulwer, and others) were unsuccessful (indigent authors disliked being patronized by their fellows even more than they disliked receiving pensions from the crown), significant steps have been taken in the last hundred and fifty years to recognize in law the author's right to exercise control over, and to receive an income from, the productions of his pen.

Much of Bonham-Carter's rich history of authorial penury derives from the records of the Society of Authors, founded by Walter Besant in 1884, with Tennyson as first president. The society has lobbied for reforms in all aspects of publishing —contracts, national and international copyright, net book agreements, pensions, and the problems arising from dramatic copyright. The second volume, already drafted, will bring the narrative up to the present, concentrating on the proliferation of sources of income available to writers in the electronic era. Contracts for books now run to hundreds of clauses, not the four of the Moxon-Hunt Agreement; they specify not only paperback rights but also rights for foreign publication (pioneered by the German firm of Tauchnitz in the 1840s) and translation (reserved by Dickens as early as the mid-1850s); for adaptation, film, television, and radio production; for magazine and journal extracts; for new and collected editions; for options on future works; and they spell out authors' and publishers' commitments to publicity campaigns, to regular audits, to tax-deferred payments, and to escalating royalty percentages—the whole arsenal of "rights" exercised by publishing conglomerates. Paradoxically, the popularity that once freed authors from the shackles of publishers can now bind them faster than ever.

Bonham-Carter's book reminds us that the author's status determines the shape of his work. For one thing, control of text passed out of the author's hand quickly during the Renaissance, whereas Tennyson maintained vigilant supervision over his many editions throughout his lifetime and even after his death through the instructions given his heir Hallam. Philip Gaskell, librarian of Trinity College, Cambridge, and author of the modern successor to McKerrow, *A New Introduction to Bibliography* (1972), understands the importance of this shift to any analysis of texts. Moreover, he also knows all about the mechanics of book production and has mastered the evolution of publishing from the days of the Stationers' Company to the present. He brings to his subject, subtitled "Studies in Editorial Method," all the qualifications that conventionally trained critics lack. And he brings, too, as a result of his training, a polemical point of view, though it is fairly well suppressed until the ninth of his dozen studies of the problems editors face in preparing editions of texts as diverse as Harington's *Ariosto* and Joyce's *Ulysses*. Basically, he questions both the theory and the practice deriving from Greg's rationale of copy-text: "Greg was concerned solely with the problems of editing Renaissance texts, and his theory is an inadequate guide to editors of nineteenth- and twentieth-century works of which (as is commonly the case) the author's manuscript has survived, and in the printing and reprinting of which the author had taken an active interest" (p. 5). Examining Fredson Bowers's centenary edition of Hawthorne's *The Marble Faun,* prepared in accordance with the policies announced in the Center for Editions of American Authors' *Statement of Editorial Principles* (revised edition, 1972), Gaskell asks three questions: "These are, first, has the textual evidence been thoroughly investigated, and have the results been adequately and accurately recorded? Is the edition in fact 'definitive' in the sense that the investigation need not be repeated in the foreseeable future? Secondly, is the edited version well founded: are the principles upon which it is based generally sound, and in this particular case efficacious? And thirdly, does the editor offer a convincing treatment of the text? Are his 688 emendations of the copy-text acceptable?" (p. 189).

The answer to the first question is a qualified yes. The text and apparatus show "a very high standard of accuracy"; but there is no "record of the non-verbal variation between the manuscript copy-text and the first printed edition, for some of which the author could have been responsible. The omission of this record means that the edition is not 'definitive' in the sense intended by the CEAA. . . . This omission suppresses the evidence of the normalized punctuation, etc., of the first edition —accepted and perhaps refined by Hawthorne but not incorporated in the edited version" (p. 190).

Second, and here lies the burden of most of Gaskell's dozen examples, nineteenth- and twentieth-century texts were usually seen through the press by their authors. Thus the manuscript, or failing it the earliest in the ancestral series of printed texts, need not be, as it is for Greg, the version closest to the author's "intention." Hawthorne's printer's-copy manuscript punctuation is, on critical grounds, to be preferred to the normalized and regularized house style to which he acceded, but in many other cases—Scott, Dickens, Thackeray, Hardy—revisions in proof and after, including the incorporation of house style in accidentals, must be seen as part of the process of preparing the text for publication. In such instances, the manuscript is only a *stage*, not the final product.

Finally, Gaskell looks at the 688 editorial emendations of the manuscript copy-text, about half of which were corrections which appeared in the first British edition, printed in London, of 1860. A few appear to have derived from proof corrections made by Hawthorne. Another group that might or might not have resulted from authorial corrections has been treated in accordance with statistics on compositorial error deriving from analyses of control sections of the text. While useful as a guide to deciding doubtful cases, applied rigorously these indexes of error result in the printing of a manuscript reading almost certainly altered by Hawthorne in proof. Thus editorial principles inflexibly followed can conceal authorial intentions. A fourth group of editorial emendations regularizes copy-text "in an undesirable way." There is a real question about the need to regularize in the first place: most authors spell and punctuate inconsistently, concerned more about local effect than uniformity over several hundred pages. Surely no reader will be upset to discover both "to-day" and "today," "poney" and "pony." But the Hawthorne edition lapses into absurdities, spelling "horrour" ten times when in nine instances Hawthorne used "-or," and in the interests of regularity emending to "Emperour's" and "errour" too (p. 194). Worst of all, because more misleading, Bowers normalized the capitalizations of "nature," although Professor Freehafer has shown that Hawthorne distinguished the personification by a capital letter not otherwise employed. Gaskell gets a bit carried away in his conclusion: "The CEAA and its editors have been noble in vision, rich in good intentions as well as in funds, indefatigable in industry, and scrupulous in accuracy. These qualities, and the features of the CEAA editions that derive from them, are applauded even by the CEAA's critics. Yet the whole great enterprise seems to have gone astray. CEAA editions are not and never can be 'definitive'; their main editorial principle is unsound yet inflexibly applied; and individual editions sealed by the Center can be grossly imperfect" (p. 195).

Gaskell's book is the perfect corrective to the kind of graduate school ignorance confessed at the beginning of this essay. For each of his authors he supplies facsimiles of relevant texts (using Trinity College Cambridge materials in many cases), generates stemmata, and outlines the problems confronted in selecting or assembling a copy-text. Alert to the errors of others, he can also make mistakes himself: the final double number of a monthly serial was not ordinarily forty-eight pages long but sixty-four (just twice thirty-two), including preface, tables of contents, illustrations, and titles (half and vignette). Dickens did not preface the manuscript of each number with a plan; the plans were kept separate from the copy sent to the printers. He was seldom in mid-serial even a week or two ahead of the printers, though at the beginning he might have three or four numbers in hand, and the mid-month deadline to which Gaskell refers on page 142 got pushed back as early as *Pickwick* to the twentieth and beyond. But the issue Gaskell keeps raising is unaffected by these slips. Given this evidence of the stages of composition, he says, how would you arrive at a copy-text that is, in the word of the previous example, "efficacious"? He begins, in short, not from any notion of a Platonic form of text, fixed forever, but from a recognition of the process of communication, *From Writer to Reader*. So textual cruxes can be solved not by the indiscriminate application of inflexible theories but only by principle tempered with critical judgment.

Here, significantly, Gaskell with all his expertise differs from Harden, equally expert. For Harden has chosen the manuscript of *Henry Esmond* for his copy-text, despite the fact that Thackeray did not punctuate drafts much, that his amanuenses supplied less or more pointing than he usually did, and that the first edition, regularized and punctuated in accordance with house style, was accepted by Thackeray, read by his original audience, and used as the basis of all subsequent editions, including Tauchnitz's and Harper's (heavily altered to suit *their* house style). "Whether this is the right course to take is essentially a critical question," Gaskell concludes (p. 178); and that conclusion takes us full circle, back from a consideration of all the external forces shaping a text to our informed critical sense of its purpose and design.

Whether there will *be* any books in the future is a question raised, not quite so apocalyptically as that, by John Sutherland in his latest biannual book, *Fiction and the Fiction Industry* (1978). Sutherland has an admirable ability to generalize from the welter of facts about publication, and here he turns that talent to a study of the dire plight of publishing in England—which incidentally has only gotten worse since he completed his manuscript.[10] He picks 1973 as the crisis year, when printing costs and thus the price of books rose by 30 percent or more, the number of buyers precipitately declined, and on the reduced volume fixed expenses continued to mount. Profits fell, publishers went out of business, retail stores folded, authors produced fewer manuscripts, and even subsidiary outlets dwindled as the British film industry collapsed and the BBC cut back drastically on new productions. What in the past sustained the literary culture of England, as Sutherland demonstrated in his earlier books, was an artificially high price for books which supported heterogeneity and a multitude of minority readerships (p. xxv). The British book trade, according to Gerald Bartlett of the Booksellers' Association, presents " 'an immensity which defies efficiency, yet is in itself in the most worthwhile terms the greatest of efficiencies' " (p. xxv). All that, Sutherland argues, has been put at risk by three factors: first, the rationalization of the industry which has lessened culturally philanthropic investments (such as Oxford's long practice, discontinued a few years ago, of keeping their publications in stock for decades, instead of remaindering them);

second, the crisis in public funds that has cut deeply into university and library acquisitions budgets (and deferred the payment of an author's lending right, or royalty on books borrowed); and third, the failure of interventionist bodies like the Arts Council and the government to remedy these problems. Indeed, with the imposition of VAT on theater tickets and the draconian directives of the Thatcher government to hold down public-sector spending, the arts in Britain are even more hard-pressed today than three years ago. Another theme, growing out of his earlier work, is that the economics of book production are working against the continuation of England's long, distinguished history of fiction: "Put bluntly novels are more expensive investments for the producer, distributor and seller" (p. 229). Hence the trend toward what he calls the "American future" of the blockbuster, with all its "tie-ins," a phenomenon we've already encountered in Bonham-Carter's studies. Sutherland's book makes grim reading and should disabuse any callow graduate student of the myth of literary self-sufficiency.

Even more depressing is Siegfried Unseld's lecture on the career of the Swiss-German writer Robert Walser, whom he calls "the greatest unknown author in the German language in this century" (p. 191). Unseld, who holds a doctorate in German literature, heads one of the most distinguished publishing firms in West Germany, Suhrkamp Verlag in Frankfurt, publishers of Hesse, of the famous double edition of Brecht's *Gesammelte Werke,* of Rilke, and, posthumously, of Robert Walser. Though he writes a stilted prose sometimes crammed with undigested facts (titles of works, names of authors' friends) and though the translation seems to me to exacerbate stylistic faults (the English versions of Rilke's and Walser's poems are particularly infelicitous), Unseld comes across as a writer's ideal publisher: sympathetic, appreciative, flexible, patient, canny about markets, and above all willing to take a chance.[11] Like Sutherland, Unseld believes that good publishers are *partners* in the creation of literary works. Not for him the excuse that the public just doesn't want to buy the latest piece: "The publisher is not so intent on satisfying needs *with* his books; what he wants is to awaken new needs *for* his books. Insofar as he is interested in persuasion, education, and molding public taste, he is a kind of pedagogue. . . . He must continually keep the creative potentiality of his authors and the productive potentiality of his firm in sight, in mind, and in his heart. He must have a large heart and should always see that it receives proper sustenance" (p. 38).

Such a credo inspired the best publishers of preceding eras—the Dodsleys, Constables, Murrays, Smiths, Moxons, Blackwoods, Longmans, and Macmillans who fostered the psyches, talents, and balances of their authors. Hesse and Rilke had productive and, on the whole, successful careers, overcoming initial rejections to develop stable and beneficial relations with their publishers. But, as Unseld reminds us, "it should give us pause to realize that two great German literary figures of this century, Rilke and Kafka, were not able to live on the proceeds from their work" (p. 128). Brecht presents a more difficult case: his first three attempts to publish were total failures. Eventually he found a number of publishers for various projects, with the places of publication following his restless exile to Paris, London, Moscow, and New York: " 'His publishers didn't have an easy time with him,' " Wieland Herzfelde, publisher of Brecht's first collected edition, commented (p. 83).

But at least Brecht found an audience, even though he hampered public reception by entitling his dramas *Versuche* (attempts or experiments). Throughout his productive life Robert Walser received enthusiastic notices from Hesse: " 'If poets like Walser were among the "leading spirits," then there would be no wars. If he had a hundred thousand readers, the world would be a better place' " (p. 239). But Walser's readers numbered only in the hundreds. After nearly three decades of poverty and depression—"Every book that has been printed is after all a grave for its author, isn't it?"—Walser entered first Waldau Sanitarium near Berne, later Herisau Sanitarium, where he lived for a further twenty-three years without writing. His failure to win an audience, or a publisher who could help to find that audience, "finally succeeded in smothering what was genuine and original in him. When the world completely deprived him of his freedom and forcibly committed him to the second institution, Walser stopped writing altogether: 'It will be all over for me the moment I stop writing, and I am glad of that. Good night' " (p. 267).

Walser's aborted career is sadly cautionary. Nevertheless, it is good to be reminded, especially good to be reminded by a *publisher,* that books and authors alike are live things that flourish in nurturing conditions and can wither or die in sterile soil. No matter how original or fiercely hermetic the writer's vision, it is inevitably shaped by what he perceives to be his calling and his opportunity. Books are cultural expressions and cultural products, and writers exhibit not only the anxiety of influence but also the anxiety of affluence. To determine the text we should read, to assess the artistic achievement, to evaluate the writer's craft, to understand the values governing the expression, we must know about the manifold forces external to the writer that shape his words.

And what of the words of my title, "Slips, Sacred Commodities, and Broadway Bladder"? They are all indications of the kinds of pressures brought to bear on a literary utterance. "Slips" denotes not only the kinds of mistakes found in Thackeray, to which unsympathetic critics refer in decrying his carelessness, but also the sheets of post quarto writing paper on which Dickens composed his serials, the divisions into which the manuscript was cut up and distributed among the compositors, and the long galleys on which Dickens, Thackeray, and other authors made extensive corrections in their efforts to perfect their prose. It might also be used to describe the chopped-up holographs which Brecht would reassemble for the next version of his endlessly metamorphosing texts: "Everything needs to be revised" was his motto.

From Brecht too comes the notion of the book as a "sacred commodity," at once to be honored for its special truth and to be merchandised. "The responsibilities of the literary publisher may have changed slightly in the process of streamlining literary communication," Unseld writes, "but basically they remain the same: to be receptive to the author and the new elements in his work and to help to win him readers" (p. 44).

"Broadway Bladder" is a way of indicating resistance to that new work, the inevitable recalcitrance of a public toward the unfamiliar and the challenging. In this case, it surfaces in a letter of October 1975 to Philip Gaskell from Tom Stoppard, explaining why he has had to cut the text for the second New York production of *Travesties:*

> I have now got around to taking out the new introduction to the Dada scene. . . . Furthermore, after some paranoid 'phone calls from New York about "Broadway Bladder" [a term which possibly has no precedent in the annals of textual bibliography, and refers to the alleged need of a Broadway audience to urinate every 75 minutes] I spent the weekend trying to take 5 minutes out of the first act, and Tuesday afternoon putting the cuts in, and Tuesday evening having misgivings about the result. I have now lost sight of the line where integrity becomes pretentious sanctity of text, and where weakness becomes good sense. [p. 260] [12]

Authors continuously struggle to find the optimal compromise between textual sanctity and Broadway Bladder: Thackeray's slips and Hardy's proofs, Tennyson's revises and Brecht's *Versuche* evidence that struggle. The books reviewed here are useful reminders of the complex factors that shape achieved form, the "sacred commodity" of literature.

Notes

1. In the preface to *The Tragic Muse,* James poses a typical question: granted that books like *The Newcomes* may, in the absence of art, possess life, but "what do such large loose baggy monsters, with their queer elements of the accidental and the arbitrary, *mean*?" Responding to James, Sutherland entitles one chapter of *Thackeray at Work* "*The Newcomes:* The Well-Planned Baggy Monster."

2. Anthony Trollope, *Thackeray,* English Men of Letters (London: Macmillan, 1879), pp. 19, 137–38.

3. Dickens, "In Memoriam," *Cornhill Magazine,* 9 (February 1864), 130.

4. Sutherland, *Thackeray at Work,* p. 115. J. L. Motley once lamented: "I can conceive nothing more harassing in the literary way than his way of living from hand to mouth. I mean in regard to the way in which he furnishes food for the printer's devil. Here he is just finishing the number [*Virginians* IX] which must appear in a few days. Of course, whether ill or well, stupid or

fertile, he must produce the same amount of fun, pathos, or sentiment. His gun must be regularly loaded and discharged at command. I should think it would wear his life out" (*The Correspondence of John Lothrop Motley,* ed. G. W. Curtis, 2 vols. [London: John Murray, 1889], I, 279–80).

5. William Makepeace Thackeray, *Letters and Private Papers,* ed. Gordon N. Ray, 4 vols. (London: Oxford Univ. Press, 1945–46), IV, 223, 10 March 1861; quoted in Harden, p. 256.

6. For example, she never clears up the discrepancy among her sources as to the number of copies of the 1832 *Poems* Moxon originally printed: 450 (pp. 37, 63) or 800 (p. 52)?

7. Misstated in the text (p. 112) as £1,400.17.8., an especially embarrassing mistake since Emily Tennyson's handwritten account is reproduced on the dust jacket and as plate 2. All of us who deal with figures are liable to these trivial but humiliating slips.

8. The works of Richard Altick, James J. Barnes, John Gross, James Hepburn, and Raymond Williams will be familiar to students of English literature. Also well worth consulting are such studies as Robert Escarpit, *The Sociology of Literature* (1968), Per Gedin, *Literature in the Marketplace* (1977), Lucien Goldmann, *Towards a Sociology of the Novel* (1975), Terrence Johnson, *Professions and Power* (1972), Magali Larson, *The Rise of Professionalism* (1977), Diana Laurenson and Alan Swingewood, *The Sociology of Literature* (1971), W. J. Reader, *Professional Men* (1966), and J. W. Saunders, *The Profession of English Letters* (1964).

9. My extremely tenuous understanding of these matters owes much to the instruction of my colleagues Thomas Haskell and Martin Wiener and to the provisional formulations of our student Patrick Leary.

10. See for example the article by Peter Stothard, "Publish and Be Damned," *The Sunday Times,* 13 July 1980, p. 61, which quotes Publishers Association president Ian Chapman decrying "the worst recession in the book trade for 30 years."

11. The warmth of his appreciation of authors may have been even more evident when he delivered these essays as lectures—the introductory one on "The Responsibilities of a Literary Publisher" to the Vienna Literary Society in 1975, those on Hesse and Brecht at the Johannes Gutenberg University in Mainz, and those on Rilke and Walser at the University of Texas at Austin.

12. Micturition now affects English audiences too: Salieri announces a bladder break in Peter Shaffer's *Amadeus,* though he claims that the pause is for his sake, not the audience's. And considering how long Salieri's speeches in Act 1 are, the actor may very well need the break to rest his voice.

Pound and Around
Hugh Kenner

Michael Alexander. *The Poetic Achievement of Ezra Pound.* Berkeley and Los Angeles: University of California Press, 1979. 247 pp.

Peter Brooker. *A Student's Guide to the Selected Poems of Ezra Pound.* London: Faber and Faber, 1979. 367 pp.

Ronald Bush. *The Genesis of Ezra Pound's* Cantos. Princeton: Princeton University Press, 1976. xv, 327 pp.

Barbara Eastman. *Ezra Pound's* Cantos: *The Story of the Text.* Orono, Maine: National Poetry Foundation, 1979. xix, 141 pp.

George Kearns. *Guide to Ezra Pound's Selected* Cantos. New Brunswick, N.J.: Rutgers University Press, 1980. xiii, 306 pp.

Peter Makin. *Provence and Pound.* Berkeley and Los Angeles: University of California Press, 1978. xiv, 428 pp.

Frederick K. Sanders. *John Adams Speaking: Pound's Sources for the Adams Cantos.* Orono: University of Maine Press, 1975. xvi, 530 pp.

Richard Sieburth. *Instigations: Ezra Pound and Remy de Gourmont.* Cambridge: Harvard University Press, 1978. viii, 197 pp.

Carroll F. Terrell. *A Companion to the* Cantos *of Ezra Pound.* Volume I: Cantos 1–71. Berkeley and Los Angeles: University of California Press, 1980. xv, 362 pp.

Joyce, Yeats, Eliot, Pound were writers for what they helped create, a school of close readers. Practitioners of this skill were a long time commencing to realize that what they read closely might as likely reflect a textual vagary as an author's decision.

Estimates of the number of errors in *any* printing of *Ulysses* may run from 3,000 to 7,000 depending on how you count (if ten consecutive words have dropped out, is that scored as one error?), and when Leopold Bloom, trying hard not to think about what will happen after his wife and Boylan have sung *La ci darem,* turns his attention instead to how she sings it—"*Mi trema un poco il.* Beautiful on that *tre* her voice is: weeping tone. A thrust. A throstle. There is a word throstle that expressed that."[1]—we should be wary of admiring the Freudian "thrust" (for "thrush") until we are sure Joyce conceived it. And indeed he did not. It was the error of a 1936 Bodley Head compositor, since copied into the only editions now in print, the Random House and the Penguin.

Joyce's habit was to abandon his earlier works to their fate. Once he had gotten preoccupied with *Finnegans Wake,* the progressive textual deterioration of *Ulysses* was excluded from his field of attention. Yeats, as everyone knows, had a different attitude. He kept rewriting and revising his earlier poems, on a scale never clearly perceived until the publication of the Allt-Alspach *Variorum* in 1957. Yet the story behind the variants they recorded remains to be written, since their intricate apparatus does not distinguish (1) author's alterations; (2) the little printers' errors that come and go; (3) what can look—vide *The Wanderings of Oisin*—like decades of Yeatsian vacillation between this set of readings and that, and may actually be a record of inattention, a printer having set, say, version 7 from unrevised 5 instead of from revised 6, and the author not having noticed.

So the case of Joyce is simple: a straightforward story of textual corruption (with some subplots that pertain to his tendency to forget what he had written when he had to repair a hiatus in the proofs). That of Yeats is one stage more complicated: he made changes, still not thoroughly disengaged from normal textual entropy. The case of Ezra Pound is far more complicated. Like Yeats, he tinkered with his published texts. Like Joyce, he tended not to notice ongoing corruption. Unlike both, he tended to assume, without quite knowing it, that an author's change would be noted by readers who would somehow remember the way the text was in its earlier public state. Thus, as Ronald Bush points out in *The Genesis of Ezra Pound's* Cantos, "The gray steps lead up under the cedars" in Canto III is a vestige of a longer passage published in 1917 and later dismembered, and we still need its lost context to illuminate a lotus we encounter midway through Canto IV.

Pound used the word "Draft" on the title pages of early sets of *Cantos,* asserting his right to revise. The first "Draft," *A Draft of XVI* Cantos (Paris, 1925), contained material already many times republished and reworked, often to brilliant effect. What are now the opening lines read like this in the 1917 *Poetry:*

> And then went down to the ship, set keel to breakers
> Forth on the godly sea,
> We set up mast and sail on the swarthy ship,
> Sheep bore we aboard her, and our bodies also.

For the next printing, the April 1918 *Future,* Pound replaced "swarthy" with the inspired "swart." By about five years later his sense of the passage had changed radically, to foster the version we know:

> And then went down to the ship,
> Set keel to breakers, forth on the godly sea, and
> We set up mast and sail on that swart ship,
> Bore sheep aboard her, and our bodies also.

Lexically, this runs nearly word for word like its predecessors, though an "and" has appeared after "sea," "the swart" has become "that swart," and "Sheep bore we aboard her" is now "Bore sheep aboard her." But the major change, enforced by these verbal ones, reaches to a changed conception of the line itself.

The 1917 version had been led up to by many hendecasyllabic lines, and complies with a hendecasyllabic reading. "And then went down to the ship, set keel to breakers" is iambic pentameter with two extra unstressed syllables; omit "the" before "ship," and lo, the eleven-syllable iambic line of the *Ur-Cantos:* "I knew a man, but where 'twas is no matter:/Born on a farm, he hankered after painting." But—now a line by itself—"Ánd thén wént dówn|to the shíp"—not a fragment of pentameter but a new *kind* of line, four thudding stresses, a caesura, a Homeric dactyl. And the battle with iambics is joined. ("To break the pentameter, that was the first heave," Pound recalled in Pisa.)[2] His next stroke is a second "and," cunningly placed to prevent "Set keel to breakers, forth on the godly sea, and" from reverting to iambics (try reading it with "and" deleted). And "that swart ship," which has come a long way from "the swarthy ship," reasserts the spondaic base the way "and" asserts the thematic conjunction. *Canto I* in its final form is spondaic-dactylic, remembering Homer as well as Anglo-Saxon, and in its final form is also an "and" Canto, one event succeeding another. Its terminal "So that:"—not present till the final version—introduces causality. From "And" to "So that," one might say: the history of early thought.

I dwell on this episode in part to show how you cannot see Pound breaking the pentameter till you've seen what he was writing before he broke it; in part, too, because Ronald Bush passes the matter over with a word about "minor revisions." the excellences of Bush's book, though, are a pleasure to dwell on. His narrative of the origins of the *Cantos,* his careful glosses on the earlier versions, above all his attention to chronologies and milieux, contribute to the excellence of one of the few Pound-books worthy of its subject. Pound expected a reader's continuing collaboration, and has often received, even from the best-willed readers he has had, little more than a flaccid compliance in looking things up.

Though Bush rejects any "simple solution to the problem of what the *Cantos* are about" (p. 20), one statement about the discarded 1917 *Three Cantos* deserves citation: "Out of Pound's conflation of Dante and contemporary primitivism grew *Three Cantos,* a poem that started to describe a Dantesque journey from misdirected will toward a re-acquisition of archaic man's harmony with the vital universe. The poem was to be a ritual reawakening of ancient truths" (p. 19). Since the poem never disowned its own evolutionary strata, indeed invites us to reconstitute them, this intention persists into the ultimate text. There is wisdom too in Bush's remarks on the naiveté of attempting to ascertain "what happened to an author between time A and time B to cause him to change his mind about a version of his work. The answer nine times out of ten will only be that he reread it in a different mood" (p. 194). One target of these reflections is the late Forrest Read's influential hypothesis that what made the *Cantos* jell about 1923 was simply *Ulysses*.[3] Bush shows that it cannot have been that simple.

Canto IV, for instance, when Pound wrote it in 1919 as sequel to the now-dismembered *Three Cantos*, was already responding to Joyce's "Proteus" but also to Gourmont and James; it "records a 'seeing' of the events of *Three Cantos I* in the instant those events are being registered by an emotional reflector" (p. 203). Its use of allusion, moreover, derived from two years' close association between Pound and T. S. Eliot (1917–1919), and if Joyce provided models (Bush rightly sees "Gerontion" as a response to "Nestor") the two of them, each developing his own sense of form and method, were doing more than simply imitate Joyce. It ensued that *The Waste Land* (1921–1922) had more effect on the 1923 freeing-up of the *Cantos* than had *Ulysses*, the usable parts of which Pound had already assimilated. *The Genesis of Ezra Pound's* Cantos is intellectual history as it ought to be written. Its one major flaw is the absence of a bibliography. What (footnote, page 245) is "Read, *The Odysseans*"? The answer—and it's an article, not a book—appears nowhere save in another footnote for which we must search as far back as page 143.

The text of the *Cantos* we have, it begins to appear, is but one cross section cut through the author's intention. Visions are spherical but texts planar, an incompatibility he wrestled with all his life, and when textual minutiae escape control they compound the difficulty. The 1919 text of *Canto IV* had commenced,

> Palace in smoky light,
> Troy but a heap of smouldering boundary stones,
> ANAXIFORMINGES! Aurunculeia!
> Hear me. Cadmus of Golden Prows;
> The silver mirrors catch the bright stones and flare.

Though this "records a 'seeing'," yet as Bush notes (p. 201) we do not know in line 4 "whether the speaker is addressing Cadmus or pretending for a moment to be Cadmus. (If the latter is true, then ending line four with a semi-colon rather than a period makes sense. If the speaker had willed himself into Cadmus' mind, he might see the wonders of the choros nympharum.)"

But, a footnote reminds us, "the New Directions text slides over the punctuation with an exclamation mark": "Cadmus of Golden Prows!" Indeed it does, and so does the Faber text, and one would like to know where that mark came from. It is present as early as *Poems 1918–1921*. Is it an auctorial change? A typing error? A compositor's misreading of a blurry typescript on which ";" looked like "!"? It matters. Like many authors Pound could write with attention, then read proof with less attention, and not notice that conflicting signals had arrived on the page. And when he was his own scribe at the typewriter, his texts degenerated according to classic laws of scribal transmission; the garbled German of *Canto LI*, "Zwischen die Volkern" for "Zwischen den Völkern," was correct the first several times he typed it in draft, but once it had gone wrong he kept on recopying the error, as have all subsequent typesetters.

Typesetters, of course, do more than recopy errors, they invent them. An especially creative fellow in the employ of Nancy Cunard handset *Cantos I–XXX*, the first collected version, for the Hours Press (Paris, 1930), and his work was scrupulously copied in the first American *Draft of XXX Cantos* (Farrar & Rinehart, 1933). When Farrar & Rinehart's plates were taken over by New Directions, these errors were virtually immortalized in the American collected editions of 1948–1970. The *Draft of XXX Cantos*, published by Faber & Faber in England, also in 1933, was however not set from an Hours Press copy but from something else, conjecturally a fresh typescript. From that year commenced the long history of textual divergence between the American and British *Cantos*, a subject only partially addressed by Barbara Eastman in *Ezra Pound's* Cantos: *The Story of the Text*.

Pound and Around   31

The story of the text is unusually pertinent, since Pound's meaning is especially vulnerable to typographical errors. From 1919 on, Bush remarks, he worked by the principle "Never use a word to make the poem easier to read; add words only to particularize sense" (p. 211). This amounts to eliminating the redundancy which information theorists teach us to regard as the best safeguard against misunderstanding. The military "not repeat not" is elementary insurance against "not" being misread as "now." By a similar principle typographical errors in normal texts may pass by both unremarked and innocuous, so numerous are concinnant assurances as to what each word ought to be.

But Pound's, to his glory, are not "normal" texts; he left each word bearing, so far as might be, its individual burden of information, and woe betide us if one word has gone wrong. Thus, after two lines of Provençal—"Between the two almond trees flowering,/The viel held close by his side"—is a detail that allows us to see the troubadour as though in a manuscript illumination, holding his emblematic instrument. But from 1933 to 1971, readers of *Canto XX* could perceive this clear detail only in a Faber printing, since American texts read "The veil held close by his side." Here Pound's campaign against redundancy leaves a printer's transposition of two letters to cut us loose from all sense. (Divining no error, we grope: Who is this man? Whose veil is it?) For "viel" is the sole word that identifies him as a singer, hence as (probably) author of the Provençal lines. And once that erroneous line was in print Pound must have read it many times over, never seeing the error. He knew what he ought to see.

"Veil" got corrected to "viel" in 1971, the second printing of *Cantos I–CXVII*, by Barbara Eastman's reckoning one of 92 changes made in that printing, to be added to 138 that had been made in the first (1970). Some of these stemmed from the author, but most from other sources. The author's lists dated from several years back. By 1970 he had grown indifferent.

Earlier, he had not been. In May 1950 he wrote into my 1948 New Directions copy the following emendations to Canto IV:

32   REVIEW

> Saffron sandal so petals the narrow foot: Hymenæus Io!
> Hymen, Io Hymenæe!   Aurunculeia!
> A scarlet flower is cast on the blanch-white stone.
> And So-Gioku, saying:
> "This wind, sir, is the king's wind,
> This wind is wind of the palace,
> Shaking imperial water-jets."
> And Ran-ti, opening his collar:
> "This wind roars in the earth's bag,
> it lays the water with rushes;

The Greek characters, he said, were to indicate that the source was older than he had thought: it was Aristophanes. The other changes resolved a rhythmic perturbation effected by the Greek. A different (later?) version of these decisions got transmitted to London, and the 1954 Faber *Cantos* reads as follows:

> Saffron sandal so petals the narrow foot: Ὑμην,
> Ὑμεναιώ, Aurunculeia! Ὑμην, Ὑμεναιώ,
> The scarlet flower is cast on the blanch-white stone.
>
> So-Gioku, saying:
> 'This wind is the king's wind,
> This wind is wind of the palace,
> Shaking imperial water-jets.'
> That Ran-ti opened his collar:
> 'This wind roars in the earth's bag,
> it lays the water with rushes;

Since 1970, however, the New Directions text has read as follows:

> Saffron sandal so petals the narrow foot: Hymenæus Io!
> Hymen, Io Hymenæe! Aurunculeia!
> One scarlet flower is cast on the blanch-white stone.
>
> And Sō-Gyoku, saying:
> "This wind, sire, is the king's wind,
> This wind is wind of the palace,
> Shaking imperial water-jets."
> And Hsiang, opening his collar:
> "This wind roars in the earth's bag,
> it lays the water with rushes."

Pound and Around

We note that "Hymen, Io Hymenæe" has *not* gone into Greek, though "A scarlet flower" has become "One scarlet flower" as it didn't in the Faber text; that none of Pound's other changes have been made; but that So-Gioku has acquired a bar on his *o* and that "Ran-ti" has metamorphosed into "Hsiang," someone having discerned a Chinese, not a Japanese, source but not succeeded in getting changes made consistently. All this bears little relation to anything the poet wanted. Yes, yes, "Hsiang" was the collar-opener's authentic name, "Ran-ti" merely the Japanese form of the name of his palace (Pound's source was a Fenollosa notebook written in Tokyo, and when Fenollosa wrote "palace of Ran-ti" Pound mistook a place for a person). But, setting aside the clash of nationalities between "So-Gioku" and "Hsiang," to insert a sound like "Hsiang" into a passage whose sounds mattered so much to Pound that he tinkered to resolve a rhythm some words of Greek had disrupted—well, it is like supposing that because Shakespeare's Hamlet arose from an Irish transcription ("Amlaoibh") of "Olaf," we are entitled to require that the ghost say, "Olaf, I am thy father's spirit."[4]

Barbara Eastman duly records the American side of these matters, with speculative notes that I find implicate me in the "Hsiang" decision, and even in an aborted effort to emend "So-Gioku" to "Sung Yü." I reject this implication, even in affirming the value of her book, a line-by-line record of what happened to the American text of the *Cantos* from 1948 to 1975, with whatever authority for each change she was able to retrieve from the New Directions files. Some of the changes are necessary, some, as above, scandalous. The reader of *The Story of the Text* is hereby counseled to receive with suspicion any note containing "probably" or its synonyms.

    And even I can remember
A day when the historians left blanks in their writings,
I mean for things they didn't know,
But that time seems to be passing.
                      [*Canto XIII*]

A few more blanks would have enhanced this record.

    The reader should bear in mind also that Eastman's procedure, in its concentration on American texts, cannot convey the full story. She has collated Faber readings only when they were implicated in New Directions alterations. So Faber's extensive corrections to the Canto IV passage just discussed go unrecorded: a pity, since they have now vanished utterly from any text you can buy on the new-books market. For in 1975 the Faber text, which over the years had accumulated a number of authoritative revisions nowhere present in American texts, was scrapped forever, and what Faber customers are offered today is an offset reprint of what we get from New Directions. So it has been the evolution of this Standard International Text that Eastman has concerned herself with, and how many demonstrably authoritative readings it omits to record is a question excluded from her scope.

There's no hope by now of an "authoritative" text, or even of defining such a thing. A variorum, financed somehow (how?) and somehow published despite existing copyrights, is the only conceivable record of what has ensued from the author's and other people's urge to correct.

The urge to correct is inseparable from the fact that Pound frequently got things wrong, not seldom by trusting what he saw in print. Thus "harum" (for "haram," "pig-sty") entered *Canto XXXIX,* hence LXXIV, via a misprint in the first printing (1804) of the Clark-Ernestus Latin *Odyssey.* Achilles Fang first turned up this information in his 1958 Harvard doctoral dissertation, but Fang's work remains unpublished, and students in general have had to wait for Carroll F. Terrell's *Companion to the* Cantos *of Ezra Pound.*

Terrell's chief advantage over the editors of the old Edwards-Vasse *Annotated Index to the* Cantos *of Ezra Pound* (1957) has been two more decades of scholarship to draw on. He has also chosen a format that permits him at need to say a little more than the *Index* could. (You'll still need the *Index* if you need to be told that "père" means "father.") Thus of *Canto VII*'s "Ione" the *Index* does no more than refer us to Pound's 1914 poem "Ione, Dead the Long Year," all that could be done in 1957, whereas Terrell with the aid of Eva Hesse is able to identify "among the *New Freewoman* group a beautiful 19-year-old

French-born dancer, Jeanne Heyse, who used the name Joan Hayes and the professional name Ione de Forest. She committed suicide at her home in Chelsea, London, on August 2, 1912" (p. 31). He also reminds us that "Ione" was not Mlle Heyse's coinage, having been used by Landor and Bulwer-Lytton.

What to do with such information? For Pound doesn't divulge the girl's name and, I've read somewhere, told an inquirer that Ione's identity was "none of your damn business." Yet we have her name now, and not only was she (as we'd have guessed) a living woman, not even her pseudonym was Pound's invention. That reinforces what can't be stressed often enough, his obstinate factuality. Some *virtù*, he thought, flowed from the nonverbal world into the verbal whenever the two were in contact. No poet was ever so respectful of information, and many of his specificities say no more than that back of these words there lies something verifiable, specific.

Specificity may entail what the old-fashioned source-hunting scholars were already forgetting how to do in the thirties. One must identify where possible the exact book he used: It won't do to say "Confucius." *Canto XIII*, as Terrell rightly notes, is taken not just from the Confucian Analects but from Pauthier's French version of 1841. This is relevant because (1) Pound introduces Confucius into the poem with the first Western version he can find: not, for instance, Legge's; (2) any translation of a gnomic text interprets it, and Pound picked up Pauthier's tone and some of his diction. "La déférence fraternelle" underlies his "brotherly deference"; Legge (1892) would have supplied nothing better than "fraternal submission."

On the mysterious "noigandres" of *Canto XX* the *Companion* is less happy, though happier than the *Annotated Index*, which shed darkness by citing a line of Arnaut Daniel's in which the word doesn't occur. Here the editors of the *Index* committed the elementary error of supposing that any handy edition would do; they were using Lavaud's of 1910, the text of which had already been emended with the help of Levy's *Provenzalisches Supplement-Wörterbuch*. Pound's point, though, was that such emendations had cost intent men many hours; for fully six months Levy had been baffled, as was Pound when he visited him in 1911, by a reading in Ugo Canello's edition of 1883: "*E jois lo grans, e l'olors de noigandres.*"

Terrell correctly mentions Canello, in the midst, alas, of an obfuscatory entry which calls *noigandres* "a word of unknown meaning," the wrong foot to get off on, and after more than 100 words he is telling us that Pound "does not commit himself to any translation but in effect lets the reader devise his own" (p. 81). The entire note bespeaks stark incomprehension, notably of the fact that since the word does not exist save as a chimera of Canello's, there is no question of a translation; when it reappears in Canto XX it is dissociated, on Levy's and Lavaud's principle, into elements: *enoi,* cf. ennui; *gandir,* banish; *d'enoi gandres,* wards off sadness.

This muddle, it may be guessed, is a sign of haste. It is also an instance of the difficulties that attend annotation of what you don't yet understand, a position in which any annotator of Pound frequently finds himself. The barest information implies interpretation, since interpretation has governed the information chosen. Thus a passage in *Canto LXXIV* commences,

>   and this day the air was made open
>   for Kuanon of all delights,
>   Linus, Cletus, Clement
>   whose prayers
>   the great scarab is bowed at the altar.

Here the editors of the *Annotated Index* devoted separate entries to Linus, Cletus, and Clement, three successive first-century popes, and having looked them up the reader is no better equipped than before to see what they are doing on Pound's page. The enlightening entry would cite the Canon of the Latin Mass, where in the Commemoration of the Saints we read "... Lini, Cleti, Clementis, ... quorum meritis precibusque ...": "Linus, Cletus, Clement, [by] whose [merits and] prayers." Pound's words tell us that a priest in a scarab-shaped green chasuble is saying Mass for the Catholic prisoners, and whether Pound knew any more about Linus, Cletus and

Pound and Around

Clement than a pocket missal will tell you is not ascertainable.

One should add in extenuation of the *Index* editors that their chosen alphabetical format, by enforcing three separate entries for three names, would have misled them at times like this. Once Linus, Cletus, and Clement were dispersed through the alphabet on separate file cards, it was a natural next step for someone to seek out their identities individually. And if the editors next failed to notice that the information shed no light on the passage, well, they were in a hurry too. Jobs like the *Index* and the *Companion* are always done in a hurry, not only because patience and funding are finite and collaborators tend to disperse, but because there is much to be said for making information available to people who want it now and not ten years from now.

The *Companion*'s canto-by-canto format permits easier handling of Gestalts like Linus-Cletus-Clement (for which, and many other such Pisan clusters, readers will have to wait for Volume II); it also puts less pressure on the editor not to leave blanks for what he doesn't know. Each treatment commences with a list of sources, a bibliography of "background" references, and a checklist of available exegeses. The glosses that follow are numbered to facilitate cross reference, and cross reference is reasonably, not overwhelmingly, copious.

If less needs to be said about *John Adams Speaking*, that is because its pretensions are so modest. Frederick K. Sanders has gone through the ten-volume *Works of John Adams* (1850–1856), excerpting the passages Pound drew on for the ten Adams Cantos (LXII–LXXI) and transcribing each with enough context to leave it intelligible. Missing subjects of verbs, missing antecedents of pronouns, and other aids to comprehension excised by Pound's brisk editing are thus restored for our comfort. It is an undeniably useful book, though what Pound was about when he subjected Adams's text to such shredding will have to be a subject for someone else, Mr. Sanders having little to say on that central matter.

The best half-dozen pages yet written on the Adams Cantos are in Michael Alexander's *The Poetic Achievement of Ezra Pound*, where we may find this passage quoted:

> We then walked up Broadway
>   magnificent building, cost 20,000 pounds
>   N.Y. Currency
> Ship
> of 800 tons burden lest levelling spirit of New England
> should propagate itself in New York
>   whole charge of the Province
> between 5 and 6 thousand pounds N. York money

with this comment:

The ship is to carry N.Y. money away to England, but Pound's implication of context can make it appropriate for "Ship" to suggest to us Hampden's Ship Money, and loop us backward in time to the taxation that started the English Revolution (later linked by Adams with Magna Charta). The lines of parallel and contrast intersect, articulate and give relief to the cross-hatching of detail. The Adams Cantos offer sustained proof that collage of secondary material can transcend scrappiness and pastiche, to create significance and force. [p. 190]

It is now with some bewilderment that we turn to *John Adams Speaking* to find that the "Ship of 800 tons burden" was a Dutch East India vessel under construction in a Manhattan shipyard, noted by Adams in a diary entry of 20 August 1774, and that the words about the leveling spirit of New England come from a different entry of two days later, and that it is Pound who has fused them without so much as a mark of punctuation. (The text of these Cantos, by the way, is especially suspect, though not, I think, here.) Sanders argues persuasively in his introductory essay that Pound's transpositions and elisions of Adams's materials serve an array of themes we are meant to be following, but he doesn't confront the question of how Pound meant the sequence to exist as a verbal artifact. When disparate things are elided it is the poem that becomes responsible for their connections, yet the poem affirms that it is somehow history. All this asks for more light.

"For all their polish," writes Michael Alexander elsewhere,

> Pound's poems are unfinished; the parts are highly finished, but they require the reader to compose and complete them. The particular

instances are so stated that, when taken in conjunction with each other, they project unspoken corollaries, and it is the relation between these unspoken corollaries—in the reader's mind—that brings out the counterpoint. The contemplation of the parts is an aesthetic process; the unfolding of their implications a detective one; the result is catalytic, emotional. Thus a Pound poem is static and may be blank until it is understood, when it becomes dynamic and delivers its charge. [p. 42]

This is well put, and keeps a particular reader in mind: the contemporary Briton who can make nothing of Pound, and decides either that he was an American poseur, or that however genuine he is too difficult for any but specialists. It may benefit, too, the American whose besetting temptation is to turn the *Cantos* into a project to work on (and when the last day comes he may have experienced no poetry, but his master will see that he has been industrious).

Taking his reader through the entire verse canon, Alexander lingers with fine tact to make useful points, as when he sees "Phaselus Ille," a squib on a magazine editor, as an occasion to reflect on the power and limitation of allusion. The title points to Catullus, hence to a Mediterranean tradition of adventurous voyaging which the editor under scrutiny belies. "The conservation of a tradition by citing a single word is characteristic of Pound's own Alexandrian procedures. The accurate echo is as neo-classical as the recapitulation in 'Lycidas' of the genealogy of pastoral poetry back to its source in Orpheus, or the synthetic use of Homeric formulae in Tennyson's 'Ulysses'" (pp. 64–65).

And if the citation "is so glancingly set up that it will not be noticed by our 'generation witless and uncouth,'" we are bidden remember that "literature, for all its universal pretensions, belongs only to the literate" (p. 65). Alexander recalls an American student who thought that Christ was killed in a cavalry charge, and adduces British undergraduates as well, "uncontaminated by contact with foreign languages, classical literature or the Bible": all University students of English (p. 65).

Teaching such folk any poetry at all, particularly poetry such as Pound's, can be a weaving of ropes of sand when it is not an exercise in autohypnosis. George Kearns's *Guide to Ezra Pound's Selected* Cantos and Peter Brooker's *Student's Guide to the Selected Poems of Ezra Pound* are designed as classroom aids. Kearns's notes are leisurely, discursive, and engaging, the best of them too long for a review to quote. Brooker's are numerous and businesslike, and frequently so thorough the neophyte is apt to be bewildered. No one who needs to be told that "poignard" means "dagger" is likely to be brought closer to "Poem by the Bridge at Ten-Shin" by Brooker's specifications of how Pound has departed from the Li Po original. Michael Alexander, talking with urbane intentness about how poetry works, may be wasting his effort too, but it seems an effort more coherently conceived. The real difficulties of Pound's pages are not the allusions but the moments when the reader must undertake responsibility for an emotional fusion, and if we can't be taught how to do that we can be aided by example. "Emotion, indeed, is the origin and end of Pound's poetry," Alexander writes. "What Pound 'has to say' is 'the world is thus and thus'; but what he communicates is always emotion and attitudes charged with emotion" (p. 47). Annotation may remove impediments in the way of emotion, but of emotion itself annotation takes no notice. There are times when provision of a note, however accurate, is the worst service one can do a student.

One alludes to students not only because poetry in our time exists chiefly in classrooms but because it was a persistent Poundian theme that traditions of understanding and feeling can be lost between two generations. The name of Remy de Gourmont may serve as synecdoche for one such tradition, subtle, comprehensive, not readily summarized, and now virtually disregarded by historians of modern French culture. (A student I once tried to steer toward Pound and Gourmont was deterred by her Romance Language advisers, who counseled that a dissertation entailing Gourmont would in no wise aid her at job time.)

Gourmont's presence pervades the *Cantos* in ways that escape indexes, somewhere to one side of any of the celebrated passages that array precious details like notes of music and do not specify a principle of co-presence.

> La faillite de François Bernouard, Paris,
> or a field of larks at Allègre,
>   "es laisser cader"
> so high toward the sun and then falling,
>   "de joi ses alas"
> to set here the roads of France.
> Two mice and a moth my guides—
> To have heard the farfalla gasping
>   as toward a bridge over worlds.[5]

When the *Companion* gets that far we may count on it to translate "faillite" (bankruptcy), identify Bernouard as printer, disciple, and sometime publisher of Gourmont, relate the Provençal to Ventadorn, and apprise us of previous occurrences of many of these motifs. But in his *Instigations: Ezra Pound and Remy de Gourmont* Richard Sieburth does more. He shows us, no, not how these details fit together ("fit" is the wrong metaphor), rather of what movements of sensibility they serve as notation, a most Gourmontian principle. Bernouard's fiscal collapse in 1929 is implicated in the faltering of the *Cantos*, which in their last reprise of Ventadour's lark-song, "so high toward the sun and then falling," introduce a "full Icarian resonance": once too near the sun, hence now a humble trust in lesser guides, mice and moths, following the example of "that active, apperceptive love which Pound also discerned in Gourmont." The "two mice and a moth" are "minute psychopomps," guiding the soul ("psyche"), hence the modulation into the butterfly ("farfalla"). And in "to have heard the farfalla gasping" we may discern "Gourmontian delicacy and precision: seeing, hearing the half-alighted butterfly's breath by its wingbeats, almost as one would listen to incense" (pp. 157–58).

Seldom a "source," Gourmont was everywhere an example; Pound's indebtedness was "not so much for specific ideas . . . as for a certain manner of holding them, a certain quality of active, limpid mind" (p. 3). This is the mind of the *Cantos* when they are not busy asserting. As Pound wrote in a letter of 1928, "'Je révère plutôt le bon sens que l'originalité (soit de Remy de

G., soit de Confucius)'" (p. 1). "A certain manner"; "a certain quality": scholarship is normally wary of such elusiveness, but Sieburth has coped admirably. Gourmont's example, he persuades us, led Pound in his reading of Flaubert, in his way of "including the real, much as a cubist collage includes a metro ticket" (p. 121), in his variations on the eternal feminine, in his rapt perceptions of the natural world, "apprehended with a paradisal serenity" (p. 153). His book does justice to the most important single unexamined area of Pound's intricate heritage.

Peter Makin's *Provence and Pound* attempts something more polemical: "To present Provençal culture to those who know Pound, and Pound to those who know Provençal culture; and both, if possible, to those who know neither" (p. 4). Pound "allowed himself great economies by ignoring all detail except that which struck him, and instead sniffing for the 'breath' that animates the cultural product. He was therefore automatically a revisionist in every subject he undertook" (p. 4), and one purpose of *Provence and Pound* is to examine, with the aid of modern Provençal scholarship, the view of Provence that he arrived at. Makin concludes, much as Pound would have hoped, that "some standard critical ideas in Provençal letters should be revised in Pound's direction; that more than once the essential grasp of human situation, without any data are miscompiled, has been lacking" (pp. 4–5).

One case in point is the *translatio studii* by which, in Canto VI, Pound has Provençal culture passing from Eleanor of Aquitaine "via Sordello and Cunizza to Guido Cavalcanti and the young Dante" (p. 204). This is not simply a literary culture; "it is a kind of cultural dynasty which passes on a certain awareness by personal contact, and which refertilizes this awareness by personal energy and courage" (p. 204). It entails, too, the passing on of Troubadour songs and their consequent availability to Dante: something normally denied on philological grounds. But Makin shows us prodigies of philological analysis (e.g., Santangelo's in *Dante e i trovatori provenzali*) depending on unreal assumptions, as that Provençal poetry was normally composed and preserved in memory and transmitted viva voce, scribes arriving late on the scene and concerning themselves only with the compilation and recopying of anthologies (*chansonniers*) too expensive for the likes of Dante. He argues, though, that not only were the troubadors literate (many were educated in monasteries), they were at ease with pen-in-hand composition, using rhyme schemes so elaborate they would need to be worked out like crossword puzzles. Not costly books but innumerable single sheets of paper, now lost, would have carried texts rapidly from man to man and to Cavalcanti or Dante, and a study of textual transmission that depends on extant *chansonniers* is therefore productive of chaos (as it is) because it excludes a whole stratum of reality, the kind Ezra Pound's strong sense of the real led him to presuppose.

So intricate is the field of Makin's material that the expository problems it presents have resisted satisfactory resolution. The orderly movement presented by his ten chapters, 282 pages of text, has been achieved at the cost of relegating much substance to the 108 pages of notes, and to no detail there does the index confer access. So the book requires leisurely study, and will be longer making its mark than it should. The same, it is not inappropriate to remark, applies to the Pound it portrays.

While Pound study still expends most of its energy making smooth the way of beginning students, works such as those of Bush, Sieburth, and Makin imply a new and no longer defensive maturity, and a substantial readership too that has passed beyond the elements. Such books set standards future workers will be constrained to observe at the cost of seeming trivial, and imply that it will be no trivial matter at all to undertake what seems the next requisite, an authoritative account of the evolution and present state of the text.

Notes

1. James Joyce, *Ulysses* (New York: Random House, 1961), p. 93.

2. *The Cantos of Ezra Pound* (New York: New Directions, 1970), p. 518.

3. Forrest Read, "Pound, Joyce, and Flaubert: The Odysseans," in Eva

Hesse, ed., *New Approaches to Ezra Pound* (Berkeley and Los Angeles: Univ. of California Press, 1969), pp. 125–44.

4. Olaf>Amlaoibh>Amlethus>Hamlet. See Brendan O Hehir, *A Gaelic Lexicon for Finnegans Wake* (Berkeley and Los Angeles: Univ. of California Press, 1967), p. 367.

5. *The* Cantos, p. 802.

The Carroll Connection
Peter Heath

Morton N. Cohen with R. L. Green, eds. *The Letters of Lewis Carroll.* New York: Oxford University Press, 1979. 2 vols. xxxviii, 614 pp. and viii, [615]–1245 pp.

Denis Crutch, ed. *The Lewis Carroll Handbook.* Revised Ed. Hamden, Conn: Dawson/Archon Books, Inc., 1979. xix, 340 pp.

Anne Clark. *Lewis Carroll: A Biography.* New York: Schocken Books, 1979. 288 pp.

William Warren Bartley III, ed. *Lewis Carroll's Symbolic Logic.* New York: Clarkson Potter, 1977. xxv, 496 pp.

Few authors can have known less of the ebb and flow of literary reputation than C. L. Dodgson, alias Lewis Carroll. Though some of the early reviewers missed the bus, the two *Alice* books caught the fancy of the public at once; thirty years and 250,000 copies later, they were undisputed nursery classics; and although nothing of Carroll's subsequent writing—save only *The Hunting of the Snark*—achieved anything like comparable success, there was really no need for it. Alice, and Carroll, and Tenniel seem as nearly indestructible and universal as anything the Victorian age produced, and time has only served to widen and confirm the verdict. A year or two ago, the West German periodical *Die Zeit* empanelled a jury of literary critics to draw up a list of the world's 100 best books. The predictable chauvinism of the outcome caused an international flurry of indignation, so that literary journals in France and Italy (and very likely elsewhere) proceeded to publish their own equally chauvinistic lists. Apart from a solitary Italian vote for *Pinocchio*, no other "children's book" got so much as a mention anywhere; but *Alice* inevitably was on every list, with Carroll's name—equally inevitably—misspelt throughout.

It is therefore no exaggeration to claim that *Alice* (using the name for both works together) is the best, and best-known, children's book ever written; unmistakably it is at the very top of its class. But whether that is really the correct, or only, class for it is another question. That it should appear at all on a list of the world's great *literature* is enough to suggest that although, with new editions and translations published every year, it has fully maintained its hold on a worldwide juvenile readership, it has also in some way escaped the "children's book" category, and has succeeded in doing what no other member of that class has ever before done, namely, to establish itself as an international masterpiece on literary and even philosophical grounds as well.

Gulliver, Don Quixote and *Robinson Crusoe,* the obvious counterexamples, are no real exceptions to this statement. They are adult books later commandeered for the nursery, and although such estimable modern writers for children as A. A. Milne, Kenneth Grahame, E. Nesbit, and J. R. R. Tolkien (a marginal case) undoubtedly enjoy the continuing devotion of many adult readers, it is pretty certain that they do so more for nostalgic reasons than for any peculiarly literary quality that they possess for the reader *as an adult.* They are read, one supposes, to recapture the pleasant experiences of childhood (including that of being a child reader); but that is *not* the reason why so many persons, often of a highly academic and unsentimental bent, are to be found following Groucho Marx's advice and annually rereading their *Alice.* It is not the vicarious pleasures of childhood memory that they are after, but the actual pleasure of reencountering both an accomplished literary artist and a powerful if oddly unconventional mind, which for all its apparent playfulness has something very telling to say to the late twentieth-century consciousness. *Alice,* against all the odds, has not dated in the least; in a world increasingly dominated by Boolean algebra on the one hand and political lunatics on the other, it has steadily gained in relevance. Indeed, it would hardly be too outlandish to see it as a sort of modern *Pilgrim's*

Progress in which ordinary common sense and decency have to battle it out against a succession of arrogantly crazy or threatening authority figures, to be saved and vindicated only when the dreamer wakes, the phantoms suddenly vanish, and a long-lost sanity returns.

That (whether Carroll intended it or not) is the embedded fable that keeps the book alive for many of its modern readers, though it is not of course the only possible interpretation or the only source of its appeal. Foremost among its other attractions is a uniquely penetrating brand of humor, which, because it is grounded in logic, has ensured that the jokes do not fade or fizzle with time but remain perennially apt and fresh and quotable. Add a style so pure and economical that even the wildest episodes and characters become, in the telling, as believable, if by no means as sensible, as a dictionary, and it is really no wonder that *Alice* has survived with ease and has become a sort of universal cult book. Its initiates can trade allusions without need of a reference and can find in it, at a moment's notice, a touchstone and parallel for every folly and monstrosity that arises to confront them in the modern world. We all know an "Alice in Wonderland" situation when we see one, and there is undeniable comfort in so recognizing and labeling it, just as there is—for another sort of reader—in identifying some piece of disgraceful public nonsense as a product of the "inverted" world outlook of bourgeois capitalism, or dogmatic Marxism, for that matter, or of any other ideology that presumes grotesquely to dictate our understanding of the world. As has often been observed, Wonderland is an archetype of all such systems of social paranoia, since it is in effect the adult world of "telegrams and anger" seen, judged, and finally condemned as fraudulent and nonsensical by the innocent eye of the child.

The perception of *Alice* in this light is by no means anything new; the political satirists were already busy with her in the early years of this century. Such productions as *Clara in Blunderland, Lost in Blunderland, John Bull's Adventures in the Fiscal Wonderland,* and above all Saki's *Westminster Alice*—all for some reason directed at Balfour's Liberal administration of

1902–1905—are among the most effective of political lampoons, not only for their own wit but also because of the closeness with which they are able to stick to the inverted world of *Alice*. It need hardly be said that she has never since been neglected in this connection; for the political cartoonist she has been, since Tenniel himself, a never-failing standby. But the last twenty years, since the publication of Martin Gardner's *Annotated Alice,* have been marked additionally by a maturer interest and more scholarly insight into the depths of this extraordinary work. It was at this point in fact that the book began finally to climb out of the playpen in which earlier critics had chosen to impound it, and to take its place as an unashamedly adult contribution to world literature.

Since then, the foundation of Lewis Carroll societies in England, America, and Holland, with other less formal groupings active in France, Germany, Japan, and even (who knows?) the Soviet Union, where Gardner's book has recently been translated, has done much to focus enthusiasm and inspire coordinated research. The writing on Carroll has been not unfairly described as a "cottage industry," and though far too much of this now enormous secondary literature is admittedly lightweight, journalistic, or uselessly whimsical in character, there is no lack of serious and even ponderous critical essay-writing and bibliographical endeavor. Many of the more enduring exercises in this genre have by now been usefully gathered into such collections as Robert Phillips's *Aspects of Alice* (1971), the "student" editions of the text by Donald Rackin (1970) and Donald J. Gray (1971), the "Carroll" volume of the *Cahiers de l'Herne* (1971, edited for French readers by Henri Parisot), the files of *Jabberwocky* (the organ of the English Lewis Carroll Society), and Edward Guiliano's *Lewis Carroll Observed* (1976). The last named has produced a heroically planned comprehensive bibliography of the international literature, 1960–1977. Published too late (1980) for discussion here, it vastly augments the rather meager information hitherto available on this subject in *The Lewis Carroll Handbook*. A similar augmentation may also be hoped for, in due course, with the appearance of a full-scale checklist of the literally hundreds of "ordinary" English and American editions of *Alice,* at present in preparation by Byron Sewell. And by then, no doubt, still other such projects will be in progress, though the production of a definitive complete edition of Carroll's nonmathematical writings is something which appears, like the cooking of the White Knight's pudding, to lie as yet in a distant and perhaps forever problematical future.

The starting point for any such edition will have to be the *Handbook,* in which alone can be found an approximately complete census and description of everything that Carroll published, or that has since been rescued from oblivion. This work is of fairly ancient vintage, deriving from a *Bibliography* first published by S. H. Williams in 1924 and later expanded, with the collaboration of F. Madan, into its present format in 1931. Subsequently revised and enlarged by R. L. Green in 1962 and reprinted in 1970, it has lately been reissued for a fourth time, with further revisions by Denis Crutch. About forty new entries have been supplied, of which half relate to previously unrecorded items; and many others have been shortened, modified, or brought up to date. In short, Mr. Crutch has had plenty to do, and for most of the way his scholarship and learning can be depended on. Carroll bibliography, due to the author's fussiness, is a *very* complicated business with many small details still awaiting settlement, and only an expert can afford these days to fool with it. Crutch is an expert all right, but one's gratitude for his labors is nevertheless tempered by the feeling that a good deal more *could* have been done to flush out the fuddy-duddy antiquarianism and gossipy bookmanship that make the old compilation an agreeable maze to get lost in, but hardly, by modern standards, a very orderly or authoritative work of reference. The latest additions and excisions are not very easily distinguished from the earlier text; a new system of numbering now coexists, confusingly, with the old one; and in several respects there seems to have been least improvement made precisely where it was needed most. The old list of *Alice* translations—always hopelessly inadequate—has for no very good reason been banished entirely, with a passing reference only to Warren Weaver's *Alice in*

Many Tongues—a work that is itself outdated and in any case long out of print. The tables of English and American editions —another most amateurish feature—have been no less perfunctorily supplemented, with all the old gaps and errors left standing; the long-winded discussions of doubtful and in some cases probably nonexistent ephemera are allowed to meander on as tediously as ever; redundant and "phantom" entries have not been successfully eliminated; and virtually every misprint in the earlier versions is faithfully reproduced (with additions) in the new. Although no good Carrollian, and particularly no Carroll collector, can afford to be without the new *Handbook*, it is regrettable to say the least that with so much activity in the field, another ten years or so must now elapse before there can be any hope of remedying its more exasperating defects. It really wants rewriting altogether, on a different and more professional plan, whereby the needs of the everyday collector, who merely wishes to identify his possessions, are no longer so excessively subordinated to the minute description of trivial rarities which practically nobody is ever going to set eyes on outside an exhibition showcase or a fireproof library vault.

The extravagant prices now charged (and paid) for signed copies, scarce pamphlets, and first editions are but one indicator of the current Carroll vogue; the proliferation, at every level of cost and taste, of Alician images, objects, and by-products is another. It seems safe to say that no literary work has ever spawned such a variegated physical progeny, from T-shirts and figurines to comic strips, postage stamps (real and fictitious), stained-glass windows, and advertisements. The stream is never-ending, and in this connection at least it is of course Tenniel, rather than Carroll, who bestrides the scene. Perhaps too little attention has been paid to *his* achievement in creating so remarkable a gallery of instantly recognizable archetypes and in withstanding so easily the challenge of a multitude of successors who have seldom even escaped his influence, let alone usurped his preeminence. But then Carroll it was, with his own strong visual faculty (though without quite the necessary talent), who perceived in the first place the importance of the illustrator and the trouble needed to select and supervise him in his work. Despite the undeniable nuisance he made of himself, he was well rewarded in the end, not only by Tenniel, but also by Holiday, Frost, and Furniss, his later collaborators; and before condemning the modern excesses of commercial exploitation, it is at least worth recalling that this too was really inaugurated by Carroll himself. In the 1890s he sanctioned and promoted both an Alician biscuit-tin (though he strongly objected to advertizing the biscuits it was supposed to contain) and a self-devised "Wonderland" stamp case, which themselves are now scarce items for the miscellaneous collector. For all his personal modesty as an author and his somewhat eccentric efforts to detach the real-life Dodgson from his better-known literary persona, Carroll in fact was never in the least averse to pushing the sale of his books or extending their fame by the use of various innocent promotional devices. The unworldly mathematician of legend was actually quite a sharp businessman, though in fairness it must be added that he never tried to "cash in" unworthily on his success, was often generous in donating the proceeds to good causes, and always insisted on giving the public a well-made and worthwhile article for its money.

An author who attempts for whatever reason to conceal himself from his readers and to avoid the normal penalties of renown is always liable to produce an opposite result and to find himself the object of *more* curiosity than he would ordinarily have deserved or generated in the first place. Carroll certainly made that mistake, and the effect has been to engender in his public a seemingly limitless hunger for details about his private life and personality. Those details were in fact made quite fully available in the respectable and interesting *Life and Letters* published soon after his death by his nephew, S. Dodgson Collingwood. Few people, as it turned out, can actually have had a more outwardly uneventful life than Dodgson, who spent twenty-five years as a mathematical lecturer at Christ Church, Oxford, and continued ever afterwards, in the easy-going fashion of those times, to inhabit the college without teaching duties, though he still made himself useful for several years as Curator of the Senior Commonroom. Only once in his life did he ever leave England, on a slightly improbable clerical expedition to Russia in 1867. The rest of his time was spent on his writing and his hobbies, on brief though frequent forays to the London theaters and picture galleries, and on visiting with friends or holidaying in lodgings at Eastbourne, or at the house in Guildford where he had eventually settled the unmarried sisters of his numerous if not very exciting family. Perhaps because (on Collingwood's showing) there really was so little of note about his doings—no love affairs, no scandals, no significant incursions into public life—the attention of biographers largely lapsed for a generation thereafter, and as late as the centenary of his birth, in 1932, Edmund Wilson could complain with justice of the absence of any modern life of him or any collected edition of his writings. Soon afterwards the situation improved somewhat, notably with the publication of the ill-named but nevertheless valuable *Complete Works,* issued in one volume by the Nonesuch library (1939); but it was not until the mid-1950s, when R. L. Green produced his two-volume edition of the *Diaries* and Derek Hudson brought out the first reasonably scholarly modern *Life* (reissued, with pictorial embellishments, in 1976), that any substantial addition could be made to the raw material provided by Collingwood. More recent accounts by Green himself (1960), J. P. Wood (1966), John Pudney (1976), and Jean Gattegno (1977) have appended further commentary and interpretation, though without doing much more than recycle the existing and perfectly well-known facts. The latest to join the line, Anne Clark's *Lewis Carroll: A Biography* (1979), is also the first for some time with a claim to tell us anything much that we did not know already. The piecemeal discoveries made over the years by members of the Lewis Carroll Societies, and by some others, are here usefully incorporated. Though Miss Clark does not appear to know that Carroll gave Alice Liddell (Mrs. Hargreaves) a wedding present —it was a picture of Christ Church Quad—she has herself unearthed a fair smattering of new information, especially about the family antecedents and the undergraduate period at Oxford. The details are all competently put together and readably narrated; but the style is more clear than vivid, and although the author can be commended for her restraint in *not* indulging, as too many others have done, in sentimental hero-worship or ill-advised attempts to probe the Dodgsonian unconscious, the result is a little lacking in the third dimension of emotional penetration and insight. Carroll's life comes across, but not the man who lived it; and since the latter is actually a good deal the more interesting of the two, there is a sense that what *makes* the life interesting has not been adequately explained.

The supposed strangeness of Carroll's mind is itself something of a popular illusion, based on the fact that not so very many people are too closely acquainted with English academics in general and with mathematical logicians in particular. To anyone who does have knowledge of the breed, his alleged eccentricities will cease to be very striking. Special talents apart, and perhaps also the notorious taste for nubile small-girlhood, he is really a quite average specimen of a not unfamiliar type: mild and considerate; obsessively industrious; touchy and puritanical in some things, unexpectedly broad-minded in others; seldom quite at ease in company, though cheerful enough among friends; and busily preoccupied day in and day out with verbal and intellectual tricks, jokes, puzzles, and conundrums of every conceivable kind. Had it existed in his day, he would surely have adored the London *Times* crossword (which so regularly quotes or alludes to *Alice*); it seems a moral certainty that he would not only have solved it regularly but would also have tried his hand at setting it as well; and in that event, if he did not fail by excess of ingenuity, it seems equally certain that his clues would have been like nobody else's. The man who could concoct sorites problems about babies managing crocodiles and hedgehogs *reading* the *Times,* who suffered from what he called "quotation-hunger," who had a nocturnal mania for anagrams, and who was forever devising acrostics and word-link puzzles of one description or another was simply a natural crossword-addict born before his time, and the only real puzzle here is how he did not contrive to invent them in the first place, as he invented so many other frivolous but agreeable methods of occupying his own leisure and that of his correspondents and friends.

Carroll's interest in logic became a major preoccupation of his later years, coming in the 1880s at about the same time that his enthusiasm for photography went out. Though his work has a modest place in the history of the subject, it never attracted much of a following among logicians, partly because his symbolic methods had a look of overcomplication and partly because the *kind* of logic he cultivated, in the wake of Boole, De Morgan, Jevons, and Venn, was soon afterwards relegated to the sidelines by the more powerful and versatile techniques of Frege, Peano, and Russell. Professor W. W. Bartley's recent republication (1977) of Carroll's *Symbolic Logic* Part I, supplemented by numerous "lost" portions of its never-completed sequel, and an extensive correspondence with Cook Wilson (the only other logician in Oxford approximately capable of arguing with him), is a fine bit of technical editing (and printing), which has already begun to revive interest in Carroll's largely solitary and independent achievement. There are no really staggering revelations, but it is now very much easier than before to see, for example, the reasons for Carroll's persistent skirmishing with the "logicians" over negation, and the "existential import" of universal proposition. It is also more apparent that he and his school were engaged in another type of inquiry than that pursued by Russell and his. The difference, broadly speaking, is that whereas Russell wished to draw as many conclusions as possible from the smallest number of premises (thereby creating an axiomatic system of logic), Carroll's aim on the contrary was to extract a single, uniquely determined conclusion from the *largest* possible number of premises (or rather, to find mechanical methods for doing so). Since some of his late problems contain the incredible number of more than fifty complex premises, there is not much doubt that he had his method; though just how it enabled him to *construct* such problems in the first place is still a bit of a mystery.

That he should have expended so large a quantity of time

and effort in this esoteric region is itself something of a mystery and a matter for regret to the majority of Carroll admirers, for whom the typically humorous touches to be found in many of the examples are but small compensation for the general aridity of the whole enterprise. Even *Sylvie and Bruno,* that rambling amalgamation of fairy tale and Victorian novel of high society (based on his acquaintance with Lord Salisbury and his family), has patches of quite sprightly invention to mitigate its *longueurs* and is thus at least intermittently readable. The logic, however, is no more interesting for the general reader today than it ever was for the young to whom Carroll commended it (ahead of his time) as a "fascinating mental recreation." But in his own mind, at least, it was clearly the most important of the many enterprises that preoccupied his later years. Even the book on religious difficulties that he contemplated was something, he felt, that others could do as well as he; but the logic could be done by nobody else, and if he did not do it, it would never be done at all. His sudden abandonment of photography at this period has been something of a puzzle to his biographers, who have usually supposed it due either to alarm at a possible scandal over his increasing predilection for nude studies of his little subjects, or else to the obsolescence of the wet-plate process at which he was an expert; yet neither explanation is altogether convincing. He could, after all, have easily reformed his practice in the one direction or persisted with it in the other. A more obvious reason, under the circumstances, might well have been simply that if the logic was to get itself finished, he no longer had *time* for photography, any more than he now had for dinner parties. Carroll had never, throughout life, been troubled by serious illness, but already by his early fifties he was beginning to talk and think of himself as an "aged, aged man." In his later period he seems beset by the fear that his powers of work would soon be declining, that time was running out on him, and that if he did not give it all his attention, his most significant project, the logic, would be left an incomprehensible torso. Once the curatorship was at an end, once *Sylvie and Bruno* was out of the way—and it took him far longer than expected—the logic became his first priority, and, too late as it turned out, he therefore dropped most of his other activities in order to get it done.

Two things, however, were not given up: the lifelong habit of cultivating the society of small girls and the equally constant practice of letterwriting that went with it. The connection between them is obvious enough; it was necessary to keep in touch and it was also necessary to make all sorts of arrangements with the parents—usually the mothers—in order to "borrow" the children, one by one if possible, for purposes of photography or as companions to the theater or the London picture galleries. Carroll wrote incessantly on such matters to the dozens of families up and down the country with whom, at any time, he was on terms of active acquaintance. As the children grew up, he generally saw much less of them or dropped them altogether, though a favored few continued to enjoy his friendship and practical help until marriage, and even after. The often very amusing and typically "Carrollian" letters that he wrote to the more spirited and responsive of these Victorian maidens are on a level with some of his very best work and deserve to be much better known than they are. Collingwood published a number of course, and a selection of some two hundred or so was brought out in 1933 by one of the recipients, Evelyn M. Hatch. But the full range of this correspondence has hitherto remained terra incognita to all but the few specialists who may have bothered to track down specimens in libraries and private collections around the world. The recent publication of Morton Cohen's massive, and massively annotated, two-volume edition of *The Letters of Lewis Carroll* (with R. L. Green assisting) is really the first occasion on which Dodgson the letterwriter has made anything like a full-dress appearance in print. Not only are we thereby presented with an enormous addition to the literary corpus; we also receive from it a very large amount of detailed information, much of it not otherwise available, as to what he was doing at any time and how he was related to the circle of friends that surrounded him.

One calls it a "circle," but apart from his colleagues in Oxford, who are naturally not much in evidence as correspon-

The Carroll Connection

dents, it was not really an interconnected group at all. The majority of its members probably had little or no knowledge of one another, since they were simply a random selection of middle-class families whom Carroll had come to know through chance encounters with their children, on trains or park benches, in the streets of Oxford, or on the beach at Eastbourne. He obviously anticipated and prepared for these occasions by always traveling with a supply of games and puzzles to inveigle the young ladies into conversation, or with safety pins to assist them in their efforts at paddling in the sea. Once the ice was broken, it seldom took him long to ingratiate himself with the parents and to become—for a few years, at least—the welcome friend, photographer, and correspondent of the whole family. But since the only reason for these associations was his interest in the children, their foundations inevitably tended to be somewhat frail and temporary; the child-friends grew up, the interest generally waned, and the original warmth gave way to an amiable politeness as new associations of exactly the same sort arose to replace them. The pattern is constantly repeated, and the only real change to be seen is the increasing success with which Carroll, in his later maturity, was able to persuade the more amenable parents to let their offspring stay with him alone, for a week or two, at his seaside lodgings, or (in rare cases) be photographed in the nude at his improvised studio in Christ Church. Once into his sixties, he is even to be found entertaining quite full-grown young ladies, with parental permission, to intimate little dinners in his Oxford rooms. With increasing age, in other words, he was able to embark on ventures that would not have been allowed him earlier, and could also afford to treat "Mrs. Grundy" with ever-diminishing respect. For all that, it is plain from the letters that these modest indulgences, though patiently angled for, were utilized with extreme discretion and a scrupulous care for the susceptibilities of all concerned. The popular idea of the Reverend Mr. Dodgson as a salacious old gentleman with a taste for nymphets will not withstand serious examination of the evidence; the taste was certainly there, but it was more aesthetic and Platonic than overtly sexual, and though a number of the mothers may have had their doubts about him, and refused his solicitations accordingly, there is nothing to suggest that those who granted them were afterwards led to repent of their good nature. Dodgson was in every respect a gentleman, and the unusual privileges accorded him were never, it seems, abused.

For all the speculation that has surrounded it, the interest of this aspect of Carroll's character is not particularly great, and the mere perusal of a mass of such lightweight letters, all essentially on the same set of topics, would soon become monotonous. Fortunately, in Professor Cohen's selection, they are interspersed with many others to adult correspondents on everything from the mail-collection arrangements at Christ Church to the affairs of the inhabitants of Tristan da Cunha, where one of Carroll's brothers spent a harrassing few years as the local clergyman. There are letters to the various illustrators (other than Tenniel) of his later works, to Savile Clarke, who made fairly successful adaptations of *Alice* for the London stage, to Lord Salisbury, the prime minister, who seems to have tolerated Carroll's periodic badgerings with sense and kindness, though he seldom did anything about them, to Ellen Terry, whose response was much the same, to Tennyson, with whom he subsequently quarreled, and to a number of other literary figures—the Rossetti family, George MacDonald, Charlotte Yonge, et al.—whom he frequented or photographed or had dealings with. But even here, though there is much of passing interest to the Carrollian and though the letters, in this respect, are certainly far richer in content than the drily factual diaries (which cover a good deal of the same ground), we look in vain for any profound originality of general reflection or intimate revelation of the inner self. Carroll on this evidence knew a great many people, and some of them fairly well; but he had no regular confidant, as Edward Lear did for example in Emily Tennyson or Chichester Fortescue, and so he never gets to tell anyone at length about himself or to engage on level terms in an extended epistolary friendship. Shy as he was, he would probably have shrunk from this in any case. He really had too *many* correspondents, and when not merely concerned with factual inquiries or practical arrangements, he preferred to remain with them on the level of sociable small talk, autobiographical reportage, and the giving or receiving of the well-meant and often useful advice.

Only in the letters to children, therefore, is he really quite unreservedly himself; but the revelation there, though open enough and never condescending, is almost invariably playful teasing and make-believe, and the self-portrait a comically exaggerated caricature. Here he is writing on 10 December 1877 to Agnes Hull:

At last I've succeeded in forgetting you! It's been a very hard job, but I took 6 "lessons-in-forgetting", at half-a-crown a lesson. After three lessons I forgot my own name, and I forgot to go for the next lesson. So the Professor said I was getting on very well: "but I hope", he added, "you won't forget to pay for the lessons!" I said *that* would depend on whether the other lessons were good or not: and do you know? the last of the 6 lessons was so good that I forgot *everything*! I forgot who I was: I forgot to eat my dinner: and, so far, I've quite forgotten to pay the man. [I, 291]

Carroll always paid close attention to the style in which his young correspondents chose to address him; a "yours sincerely" invariably struck him as a sign of coldness and lost affection. When Agnes, four years later, must have made some demur at this literalness, she was rewarded as follows (30 April 1881):

Hateful spider,
    (You are quite right. It *doesn't* matter a bit how one begins a letter, nor, for the matter of that, how one goes on with it, or even how one ends it—and it comes awfully easy, after a bit, to write coldly—easier, if possible, than to write warmly. For instance, I have been writing to the Dean, on college business, and began the letter, "Obscure Animalcule," and he is foolish enough to pretend to be angry about it, and to say it wasn't a proper style, and that he will propose to the Vice-Chancellor to expel me from the University: and it is all your fault!) [I, 424]

Mild reproofs of this sort, with an associated joke or leg-pull, are a common feature of Carroll's treatment of his young friends (just as they are in *Alice*); they can hardly have known, in some cases, whether they were supposed to take him seriously or not. Here is a final example, addressed to the sisters Julia and Ethel Arnold in March 1874:

What remarkably wicked children you are! I don't think you would find in all history, even if you go back to the times of Nero and Heliogabalus, any instance of children so heartless and so entirely reckless about returning story-books. Now I think of it, neither Nero nor Heliogabalus ever failed to return any story-book they borrowed. That is certain, because they never borrowed any, and that again is certain, because there were none printed in those days. [I, 209]

The occasional nugget of this kind is worth a good deal of panning through more run-of-the-mine material. What holds it all together and makes it pleasurably readable is the consistent easy lightness of Carroll's style, which prevents him from ever being merely dull in the way that most people would naturally be at times, and above all the splendid erudition of Professor Cohen's footnotes, whereby every obscure reference is explained, every parallel with the diaries noted, every gap in the narrative accounted for, and virtually every name in the text provided with dates and an identity and a brief summary of whom they married and what afterwards became of them. In this way we are furnished with a remarkably complete picture of almost the whole of Carroll's social life, and it becomes possible to see, as it scarcely was before, what a very large part the child-friendships actually played in it.

It is true, of course, that the 1,400 or so letters printed, out of the 7,000 gathered together by the editors, are still only a minute fraction of the nearly 100,000 recorded, over a fifty-year writing lifetime, in Carroll's own elaborate register. (His method of keeping this record is described in his little booklet "8 or 9 Wise Words about Letter-Writing," which Professor Cohen usefully reprints as an appendix.) When one comes to think of it, the sheer quantity of pen-work involved, in that clear-handed purple ink, in order to reach such a total, is absolutely staggering; six letters a *day* on average must have gone out over the years from the Christ Church mailbox; Professor Cohen himself has enough for another eight large volumes, and if everything were still available, more than 100

The Carroll Connection

more would be needed and a couple of dozen Professor Cohens to edit it all. It is no wonder that Carroll was always behind time, that he took, on occasion, up to five years in replying, and that he generally had 70 or 80 on his waiting-list. The marvel is rather that he ever had time for anything else; the "wheelbarrows full, almost" of which he complains to one correspondent was for once no exaggeration whatever.

A good deal of this burden was of course entirely of Carroll's own making. A compulsive fusspot, he could not resist harrassing his publisher and hounding his illustrators almost to distraction with constant petty criticisms and suggestions or minutely worded instructions or anxious inquiries as to how things were getting on. Professor Cohen's volumes include many characteristic specimens of such missives, but the bulk of them are said to be reserved for separate publication. The correspondence with Tenniel in particular and with the ever-patient Macmillan brothers should be well worth having. Whether we are losing very much by the disappearance or nonpublication of the still immense remainder may perhaps legitimately be doubted. The letters to Alice Liddell, destroyed by the stupidity of her mother, are obviously the biggest loss, and we are still pretty much in the dark as to how or even when *Through the Looking-Glass* was created and prepared for the press; but beyond that it seems reasonable to suppose that the present selection is a fair one and that further publication would simply give us more of the same, with fewer specks of gold among the dross of unimportant communications about college and commonroom business, or equally trivial epistles to Mrs. Dyer—the seaside landlady—the Oxford tradespeople, the postal and railway authorities, the photographic suppliers, and so on. Thanks to Professor Cohen and Mr. Green, we know our Lewis Carroll pretty well by now, and quite as well as we have any need or right to. The pattern of his life-style is fully established, and it would be most surprising to learn that the unrecorded portions of it differ in any way from those that are here so comprehensively displayed. A few of the little girl-friends may still indeed be unaccounted for, and there may well be other caches of correspondence in private hands that have yet to see the light. But Cohen's recent publication, through Argosy Press, of a handsomely produced but really rather dull little series of such letters to Xie Kitchin and her mother, which had somehow escaped his dragnet, is warning enough that we are near the bottom of the barrel (or wheelbarrow), and that to ask for more would be to court disappointment and tedium. Nor, in all probability, will there be many more such curios as the canceled "Wasp in a Wig" episode from *Through the Looking-Glass*, which surfaced a few years ago and aroused at least as much interest as its merits deserved.

The fact is that we should all like to see unearthed a few more fragments of genuinely "Carrollian" material, whereas only a modest proportion of his huge miscellaneous output is actually up to that level. With an author of Carroll's compulsive writing and printing habits, it is always possible that something unlooked-for may turn up; but chances of its measuring up to expectation are not very great. The lost script of "Morning Clouds"—his only attempt at a play—could well prove an utter disaster to his reputation if it were ever to be recovered, which is not to say that a large number of people would not be anxious to read it; the vanished volumes of the diaries are more likely to be of interest, if only because they cover the years that saw the gestation of the inadvertent masterpiece that is chiefly responsible for his fame; but if the other volumes are anything to go by, they will add not a whit to his purely literary renown, and it is only biographers and critics who will have much to gain from them. A few more verses may yet be identified in forgotten magazines; a few more juvenile efforts from the early home-made periodicals may yet—like the recently published *Rectory Magazine*—be released to assuage the curiosity of the public. The new biography that Professor Cohen is now rumored to have in hand will certainly be a most valuable distillation of his long, unconscionable labors, and can only be awaited with impatience. Till then, the best that the good Carrollian can do is to recognize that, to all expectation, "the tale is done"; to thread his way happily through these magnificently edited *Letters;* and, if nothing else will do, to remember Groucho, and once more get out his *Alice*.

The Kenneth Burke Problem
William E. Cain

Kenneth Burke. *The Philosophy of Literary Form.* California Library Reprint Series: No. 45. Berkeley and Los Angeles: University of California Press, 1974. xxvi, 462 pp.

Many would agree with Wayne C. Booth's statement that Kenneth Burke is "without question the most important living critic."[1] But there are dissenters, notably Grant Webster, who declares in his massive study of "postwar literary opinion" that Burke, "largely ignored or rejected," is best regarded "as an old-time American crank inventor who might have been Edison except that his work lacks any relation to reality outside his own mind."[2] Burke's critics have often differed in their judgments, but here the disagreement is especially sharp. Booth sees Burke as a verbal wizard, the designer of a great verbal system, while Webster describes him as a solipsist, adding that "Burke's system is explicable only in its own terms, but no reason is given for adopting them, over, say 'Jabberwocky.'"

There is, I believe, a Burke "problem" that accounts for these opposite evaluations. Burke's career is one of the curiosities of modern literature; and though he has been written about often, he has not been written about well, in the right tone and with the proper critical leverage. He is either accepted wholeheartedly—by, for example, Stanley Edgar Hyman and Howard Nemerov; or else he is dismissed out-of-hand, as when Marius Bewley accuses him of being trapped in a rarefied vocabulary and engaged in producing books that we read "with something of the fascination with which one studies the combination of aimlessness and purpose that characterizes life in an ant hill."[3] But while there are reasons for the "problem" that Burke poses for his critics, there are not easy or satisfactory ways of resolving it. Burke's writings both stimulate and frustrate us; he is and will remain a problematical figure, difficult to approach and evaluate.

Burke is hard to pin down as a critic, in part because he works in so many fields, including literature, sociology, economics, psychology, and political science. His range is intimidating, and he strikes us at times, as Armin Paul Frank remarks, as a "veritable one-man department," moving forward with his labors unmindful of what his friends and foes say about him.[4] Having created his own subject matter—Burkology is the best name for it—Burke appears not to need the contributing presence of other critics. His system, laid out in his *Grammar* and *Rhetoric of Motives*, is so intricate that only he knows how to use it, and he alone can speculate about new areas into which it might be projected.

The more Burke writes, the more imposing and isolated he becomes: His "dramatistic" system almost seems to be controlling him, rather than the other way around. As Timothy C. Murray has pointed out, Burke's texts possess their own momentum, and his many prefaces, forewords, introductions, expansive footnotes, and interviews signify his effort to maintain control over his swirling system.[5] Perhaps, however, it is misleading to depict Burke as a prisoner caught, like the hero of one of Chaplin's films, in the gears of his own machinery. He may now seem a lonely if heroic figure, victimized by his terms, and no longer in touch with his readers. But then Burke's critical identity and relation to his audience have been troubled and uncertain since the beginning of his career. One question in particular, as Merle E. Brown observes, presses on us as we read Burke: "To whom could he possibly be writing?" "His audience," Brown adds, "is never included actively in his writing; it is never specified with precision."[6]

Brown's question is tough to answer because Burke is equal parts virtuoso and poseur. More successfully than most critics, he manages to keep his reader off-balance and unable to anticipate the course of his critical explorations. To borrow Richard Poirier's well-known phrase about Mailer, Frost, and other of our most interesting writers, Burke is very much a

The Kenneth Burke Problem

"performing self," "dramatically" present in his texts, acting out roles, exuberantly trying on and testing attitudes. So interested in "dramatism" himself, Burke is intensely dramatic in style, as he strives to entertain, cajole, and baffle his reader's attempts to keep pace with him.

Burke's thought is always in motion, if not always in progress or slanting in a direction that we can chart. It spirals with suggestions, alternately dazzling and disappointing us. There is considerable unevenness in Burke's work, and his reader must be patient. Sometimes our investment of time and energy is unprofitable: We can read Burke for many pages yet not feel we have gotten anywhere. But then we will catch him in an inspired moment, and he will delight us with the pointed aside or startling conjunction of terms (his "perspectives by incongruity"). When Burke is read for the systematic argument he is straining to present, he can be tedious, even interminable. But when he is read and valued for his marvelous intuitions about texts, and appreciated for his "dance" (one of his favorite words) of mixed solemnity and whimsy, seriousness and jocularity, he can provide us with an experience that is unique in criticism.[7]

But the Burke "problem" is even more vexed than my description has so far suggested. Despite his productive career and despite having generated much commentary and reaction, Burke has not had much influence. He is one of a kind, and this highlights his limitation as well as his distinction. Though harsh in its directness, Fredric R. Jameson's recent assessment is difficult to quarrel with: "This immense critical corpus, to which lip service is customarily extended in passing, has—read by virtually everybody—been utterly without influence in its fundamental lessons, has had no following, save perhaps among the social scientists, and is customarily saluted as a monument of personal inventiveness and ingenuity . . . rather than as an interpretative model to be studied and a method to be emulated."[8] As Jameson suggests, there is plenty of nodding in Burke's direction. Particularly during the 1970s, we heard a good deal of vague talk about Burke having "anticipated" French structuralism and poststructuralism. Some right-minded readers want to give credit where it is felt to be due. Others, however, seem impelled by the curious belief that structuralism and its offshoots will be made less menacing, less disruptive of our critical habits, if their insights about "language" and "system" are located in the American critic Burke. If this questionable motivation leads to a rereading of Burke, it is perhaps worth encouraging, but not if it is simply another effort to tame and domesticate the new modes of continental criticism. This is unfair to Burke and will likely issue only in more calls for his rediscovery and gestures towards him as the great (and still unread) forerunner of avant-garde criticism. Many insist that we need to rediscover Burke and see the relevance of his work, but no one has yet tackled the assignment and shown how and why Burke bears on criticism today.

Burke's *Philosophy of Literary Form* is the best place to begin such a revaluation. Originally published in 1941, it contains what the inveterate punster Burke describes as "thirty-minded" pieces. Most are essays and reviews, but there are also two forewords, an "Instead of a Foreword," letters to the editor, a "Dialectician's Hymn," and the long (137 pages) title-essay, first printed in its entirety in this book. The *Philosophy* is typically Burkean in that it both absorbs and irritates the reader. It is often bracing in its suggestiveness, as when Burke tosses off comments about sacrifice, scapegoating, and ritual. But the *Philosophy* has many dull stretches where Burke deals at length with books that have been forgotten or seem negligible—for example, Neurath's *Modern Man in the Making*, Ludovici's *Secret of Laughter*, Chevalier's *Ironic Temper: Anatole France and His Times*. When Burke rehearses and analyzes the argument of these books, we feel little obligation to follow him. The *Philosophy* also falters when Burke focuses on texts—such as the exchange between Malcolm Cowley and Archibald Macleish on "art" and "propaganda"—that are mildly interesting but finally too limited for us by their historical situation. Sometimes the dated quality of the book is slightly disturbing, if also rather quaint, as when Burke refers to "the soundings that the Japs are said to be taking of our Western coast line" (p. 151).

The dated parts of the *Philosophy* are a problem today, but they do not explain Burke's failure to influence his contemporaries in the 1940s. The start of Burke's career coincided with the rise of the New Criticism, but he was never a member of this or any other movement. Many of his principles in fact go against the grain of the New Criticism and help to clarify the reasons for his marginal status. In a foreword, for example, Burke explains that he prefers not to deal with "the internalities of a work's structure." This, he contends, is too much like what a "reporter" does, and he is instead concerned with the "general problems" of structure and the "function" of characters and scenes. Unlike Cleanth Brooks, for instance, Burke focuses primarily on general, theoretical issues; he does not limit himself to the single text and indeed he warns us that if we are looking for "the specific criticism of books" we might be disappointed. But by aiming to provide a "theory of criticism of books," Burke locates himself outside the boundaries of the New Criticism. And this both separated him from the critical orthodoxy of his time and ensured that his work would not much affect pedagogy. Brooks, Robert Penn Warren, Robert Heilman, and the other New Critics make analytical tools available to their fellow critics and teachers. Their methods can be taught readily and learned easily, whereas Burke's schemes are difficult to master and harder still to apply. Burke builds a system, embracing science whenever it seems profitable to do so. The New Critics, on the other hand, rely upon the trained sensibility and power of individual judgment, standing opposed to science, system, and interpretative machines that violate the organic unity of the text. As Jameson points out, "Virtually *everybody*," including the New Critics, reads (and continues to read) Burke. But his writings have been conspicuously without influence on practical criticism and classroom teaching, where critical methods win legitimacy, privilege, and continuity.

Burke, of course, does not entirely forego the specific reading of texts. In the *Philosophy*, for example, he offers shrewd analyses of *Julius Caesar* and *Twelfth Night*. But both essays are less valuable for what they say about the plays than for what they indicate about Shakespeare's keen awareness of the audience's expectations and his means of "persuasion." Neither of these essays is intended as a complete reading; both, rather, are meant to "illustrate" (Burke's word) theoretical concerns and problems in method. Both of the essays are also quirkily conducted, as Burke—performer extraordinaire—assumes the roles of Antony in *Julius Caesar* and the Duke in *Twelfth Night*, transforming these characters into "critical commentators" on Shakespeare's rhetoric and "processes of appeal." Burke's procedure, then, is not only theoretical but also buoyant and eccentric. He flaunts our sense of critical decorum and refuses to adopt the New Critics' patient methods of explication. While Burke's freedom, playfulness, and brisk approaches to the text may be attractive to us, they doubtless made his New Critical readers uneasy and unsure about what he was up to, and hence made Burke all the more a critic to be admired but not imitated. His tones and attitudes, however stimulating, come across as not serious enough—not serious, that is, in the New Critical manner. He does not appear deeply enough engaged in the critic's labor of disciplined textual analysis, and is not willing to subordinate his own verbal flights to the authority of "the words on the page."

Many of the readings in the *Philosophy*, especially in the title-essay, are devoted to Coleridge's writings. But to say this is somewhat misleading, since Burke's comments on specific Coleridge texts are scattered and undeveloped. Again moving outside the field selected by the New Criticism, Burke explores "Coleridge himself" rather than his texts. Though Burke stresses that he bows to no reader in admiring the "structure" of these texts, he wants to "commune" with the writer, to get "inside his mind" and discover what the poems "do" for the poet. Referring at one point to "The Ancient Mariner," Burke observes that

> to grasp the full nature of the symbolic enactment going on in the poem, we must study the interrelationships disclosable by a study of Coleridge's mind itself. If a critic prefers to so restrict the rules of critical analysis that these private elements are excluded, that is his right. I see no formal or categorical objection to criticism so conceived. But if his interest happens to be in the structure of the poetic

The Kenneth Burke Problem

act, he will use everything that is available—and would even consider it a kind of vandalism to exclude certain material that Coleridge has left, basing such exclusion upon some conventions as to the ideal of criticism. The main ideal of criticism, as I conceive it, is to use all that there is to use. [p. 23]

Eminently sensible as an ideal, Burke's statement here cuts against New Critics' emphasis on the text itself. Again he stamps himself as an outsider, opening up the text to biography and everything else "there is to use," while Brooks and the other New Critics see extratextual references as distracting us from our steady concentration on the verbal object before us.

For Burke, understanding the "psychology of the poetic act" calls for knowing about and deploying biography, social background, historical context. And many of Burke's own remarks about Coleridge "use" the poet's drug and marital problems to gloss the poetry. But Burke does not often succeed in enriching the poems through this line of analysis, and he frequently simplifies the texts and badly reduces the complexity of the poet's mind. In dealing with "The Ancient Mariner," for instance, Burke crudely aligns details from Coleridge's life with scenes in the poem. "Do we not find good cause to line up," he explains,

as one strand in the symbolic action of the poem a sequence from marriage problem, through the murder of the Albatross as a synecdochic representative of Sarah, to the "blessing of the snakes" that synecdochically represented the drug and the impulsive premarital aesthetic (belonging in a contrary cluster), to an explicit statement of preference for church, prayer, and companionship over marriage (with the mariner returning to shore under the aegis of the praying Hermit, and the poem itself ending on the prayerful, moralizing note that has annoyed many readers as a change in quality)? [p. 72]

This seems to me little more than a verbal logjam. Burke is drawing one-to-one correspondences between "The Ancient Mariner" and Coleridge's life, and he disfigures both the poet and his poem in the process. Severely limiting his range of responsiveness, Burke divides the text into "levels," which are then placed in a slick relation with one another. His performance is impressive after a fashion, but for what it reveals about his own ingenuity and addiction to terms, not for anything that it enables us to perceive in the poem or discover about Coleridge. As so often happens when Burke interprets a text, he is crippled by what Benjamin DeMott has aptly called his "iron inattention to tone."[9]

Burke's interpretative practice is disappointing. And this brings us, I believe, close to the center of the Burke "problem." His ideals and aims are compelling in their exploratory breadth and open-mindedness, and when set down in order, they read like a primer in how to move beyond the limits of the New Criticism:

1. In all our inquiries, we ask "leading questions," and hence "structure" the field that we investigate. "Every question," Burke asserts, "selects a field of battle, and in this selection it forms the nature of the answers" (p. 67). We do not, that is, make objective reports about the text in and of itself, but rather introduce interpretative contexts that create the shape and structure of the text.

2. Literary texts share in the same kinds of concerns that "motivate" other texts. We adopt labels—literature, history, economics, and so on—for purposes of classification, but finally there are just "texts," all of which can be treated as "strategies."

3. Criticism is practiced on all texts, not merely on the special group we call "literature." "The analysis of aesthetic phenomena," Burke claims, "can be extended or projected into the analysis of social and political phenomena in general" (p. 309).

4. We make "symbolic acts" in our lives as well as in texts. Literature is by no means divorced from life, but is involved in, bound to, and fundamentally "like" life. "The question of the relationship between art and society," Burke stoutly adds, "is momentous" (p. 235).

5. A true critical method gives "definite insight into the organization of literary works," but it also "automatically breaks down the barriers erected about literature as a specialized pursuit" (p. 302). To essentialize and privilege literature is, Burke warns, ultimately to trivialize it, to cut it off from everything with which it shares forms and values. And valoriz-

The Kenneth Burke Problem

ing "the literary" is, in addition, the surest way to transform a rich area for study into just another "academic" pursuit.

But Burke does not proceed from these fine principles to an authoritative, concrete analysis of texts. He has an acute sense of linguistic strategies, but no feeling for tone. He can assemble complex verbal machines, but, given to applying hammer-blows to the texts that he interprets, he seems unable to respond to subtlety and delicacy in language. Burke's range of interests is broad, and his aims make many readers sympathetic to his general critical project. But then one confronts the actual analyses of "structure" and sees poems buried by the layers of terms and categories. Burke's goals are invigorating, but his practice as a critic is too often bruisingly heavy-handed, subverting the potential richness of those goals.

The *Philosophy* fails to give us really illuminating, powerful interpretations. And it is this failing that sets Burke a notch below the other great, independent-minded critics of this century, F. R. Leavis and William Empson. Their work is uneven, sometimes coarse and objectionable, but their engagements with texts are dynamic and incisive. We accept their limitations as critics and go on reading them because they confirm their authority, time after time, in their interpretative work.

Much of Burke's best critical writing in the *Philosophy* and his other books, especially his *Language as Symbolic Action,* deals with Shakespeare. But it is one measure of his shortcomings that none of these essays commands the repeated serious attention we devote, for example, to Leavis's writing on *Othello* and *Measure for Measure* or to Empson's probing studies of *King Lear, Othello, Hamlet, Measure for Measure,* and other plays. To be fair to Burke, he does insist that he desires a theory about the criticism of books, as opposed to the detailed reading of specific texts. And to make my own bias clear, perhaps I am too dogmatic in expecting Burke's method to validate itself in textual interpretation, thereby earning and renewing its authority in both practical and pedagogical forms. But Burke does claim that his method provides "definite insight" about literary works. And to focus more on his theory than on his practice simply exposes the limitations of the theory—its crudity, reductiveness, mazes of terms, and rhetorical figures. Burke has been constructing his theoretical engine for half a century; but the more he complicates and tinkers with it, the more he removes it from our understanding and sympathy. The final volume in Burke's trilogy, the *Symbolic of Motives,* has been promised for almost three decades. And one cannot help but wonder if Burke's theory has led him to a final dead-end, where elaborations and adjustments might be made, but not any progress, and not any hook-up with the world outside the system.

So the Burke "problem" persists. He is truly one of a kind—ingenious and inventive, a performer with a flair for the dramatically surprising insight. But he probably will not influence contemporary criticism in a profound way. He will continue to be read by "virtually everybody," yet always remain on the verge of being rediscovered. His productiveness, his resistance to the New Critical orthodoxy, his arguments for relating literature and the other disciplines, and for tying literature to life—all this makes him an important and admirable figure. But Burke's system is too grandiose and unwieldy, and his interpretative practice swerves too often into reductiveness. Reading Burke can be a marvelous experience, but he is likely to stay a marginal critic.

Notes

1. Booth, "Kenneth Burke's Way of Knowing," *Critical Inquiry,* 1 (September 1974), 1.

2. Webster, *The Republic of Letters: A History of Postwar Literary Opinion* (Baltimore: Johns Hopkins Univ. Press, 1979), p. 175.

3. Marius Bewley, *The Complex Fate: Hawthorne, Henry James and Some Other American Writers* (London: Chatto and Windus, 1952), p. 222. For a full account and examples of criticism on Burke, see *Critical Responses to Kenneth Burke, 1924–1966,* ed. William H. Rueckert (Minneapolis: Univ. of Minnesota Press, 1969). This volume includes an excellent bibliography of writings by and about Burke. Useful introductions to Burke's work include Stanley Edgar Hyman's *The Armed Vision: A Study in the Methods of Modern Literary Criticism* (1947; rev. ed. New York: Vintage Books, 1955), pp. 327–85, and René

The Kenneth Burke Problem

Wellek's "Kenneth Burke and Literary Criticism," *Sewanee Review*, 79 (Spring 1971), 171–88. More detailed studies are George Knox's *Kenneth Burke's Categories and Critiques* (Seattle: Univ. of Washington Press, 1957), and William H. Rueckert's *Kenneth Burke and the Drama of Human Relations* (Minneapolis: Univ. of Minnesota Press, 1963). Both books are informative, but they are too deeply inside Burke's system to be satisfactory. Neither achieves a critical perspective on its subject. Burke himself has discussed his work and career in interviews in *Michigan Quarterly Review*, 11 (Winter 1972), 9–27, and *Sewanee Review*, 85 (Fall 1977), 704–18.

4. Frank, *Kenneth Burke* (New York: Twayne, 1969), p. 11.

5. Murray, "Kenneth Burke's Logology: A Mock Logomachy," *Glyph 2* (Baltimore: Johns Hopkins Univ. Press, 1977), p. 151.

6. Brown, *Kenneth Burke* (Minneapolis: Univ. of Minnesota Press, 1969), p. 14.

7. Burke's own words about William Empson are apt: "Empson is still, unfortunately, inclined to self-indulgence, as he permits himself wide vagaries. But presumably that is his method—so the reader, eager to get good things where he can, will not stickle at it. He will permit Empson his latitude, particularly since it seems to be a necessary condition for his writing" *(The Philosophy of Literary Form,* p. 422).

8. Jameson, "The Symbolic Inference; or Kenneth Burke and Ideological Analysis," *Critical Inquiry*, 4 (Spring 1978), 509.

9. DeMott, "The Little Red Discount House," *Hudson Review*, 15 (1962–63), 551–64; reprinted in *Critical Responses,* p. 362. In his *Philosophy,* Burke refers on several occasions to a forthcoming monograph on Coleridge. This publication has never appeared, and Burke's inability or unwillingness to integrate his thoughts about that difficult poet has kept him from having much effect on Coleridge studies. In the important books by J. R. de J. Jackson (1969), Owen Barfield (1971), Paul Magnuson (1974), Lawrence S. Lockridge (1977), Katharine Cooke (1979), and Edward Kessler (1979), he is not even cited. An exception to the rule is Reeve Parker's *Coleridge's Meditative Art* (Ithaca and London: Cornell Univ. Press, 1975), where Burke is praised as "a critic of signal importance for understanding Coleridge" (p. 79).

Tom Sawyer Once and for All

Robert C. Bray

Paul Baender, Terry Firkins, and John C. Gerber, eds. The Adventures of Tom Sawyer, Tom Sawyer Abroad, *and "Tom Sawyer, Detective."* Vol. IV of *The Works of Mark Twain,* Iowa-California Edition. Berkeley: University of California Press, 1980. xvii, 717 pp.

Mark Twain, like the other canonical writers of nineteenth-century American literature, is being done up once and for all: a complete and definitive edition of his works, each volume with scrupulously established texts, judicious introductions, explanatory notes, and all textual apparatus fully revealed at the back of the book. Moreover, everything is beautifully printed on opaque, acid-free paper and sewn into a red-orange library-buckram binding that is serviceable, if unattractive, and clearly designed to survive as much use as it is likely to get. And as further evidence that this is truly fine bookmaking, each volume includes a colophon.[1] These are the most obvious features of the volume at hand from the Iowa-California Edition of *The Works of Mark Twain,* volume four of a projected twenty-two that are intended at last to put him on the library shelves in precisely the words he wanted.[2]

Even within the imposing world of corporate editing that is the Center for Editions of American Authors (CEAA), the Iowa-California Edition is one of the largest projects, and it is both ironic and appropriate that Mark Twain be the author so distinguished. For he was, in his own phrase, the imposter in his profession, the single "demotic" writer among the nineteenth-century group, and the only one over the years who has not required regular academic subsidies in the classroom to assure survival in the culture at large.[3] Indeed, so mythic a presence is

Twain's in our midst that a major concern of modern Mark Twain scholarship has been to *de*mythologize his life and work in the face of an entrenched popular acceptance of the legend.[4] Yet separating the person from the persona has proved unusually difficult, given the persistent masking of the subject, Samuel Clemens–Mark Twain, who made a career of literary iconoclasm while at the same time cherishing the fame, fortune, and respectability of the traditional man of letters. Twain's popularity, consummate though it seemed in his lifetime, is as strong as ever today, if one may judge by the titles in print, the white-suited impersonations of the stage shows, and the television specials, and—not insignificantly—the bustling shrines at Hannibal, Missouri. This confabulation is the people's Mark Twain, and their essential book is *Tom Sawyer:* not the academically preferred *Huckleberry Finn,* nor still less the gamut of darker writings from the later years, but *Tom Sawyer,* a novel whose incidents seem wholly to have passed into the popular imagination, until we think of it more as having "happened" than as having been written. No other American text or author has this authority. Mark Twain, for better or worse, is as close as we come to a national hero of letters, and *Tom Sawyer* is a masterpiece by acclamation. Hence what better challenge, what higher responsibility, than to give both book and author a kind of final monumentality?

Yet in the realization this laudable goal has turned out to be problematic. Those who have followed the progress of the Iowa-California Edition know that this *Tom Sawyer* has been in preparation for more than ten years, and is the result of a corporate endeavor by members of what Edmund Wilson back in 1968 called "the Mark Twain industry." In a memorable indictment of the entire CEAA enterprise, "The Fruits of the MLA," Wilson charged that all this textual editing was so much make-work and that a kind of *"trahison des clercs"* was being committed on the one American writer who belonged not to the academy but to everybody. Astoundingly, Wilson's attack was supported by a letter from one of the editorial workers at the Iowa Center for Textual Studies, admitting that the Mark Twain project was a "boondoggle" on which he and his fellows spent their time "reading *Tom Sawyer,* word by word, backward, in order to ascertain, without being diverted from this drudgery by attention to the story or the style, how many times 'Aunt Polly' is printed as 'aunt Polly,' and how many times 'ssst!' is printed 'sssst!' "[5] Well, after all, those were the Sixties and something like this was bound to occur; nonetheless, one assumes that such subversion at Iowa was quickly rooted out! This sort of publicity was, and is, devastating to textual critics and criticism, a breed and a field apart, seldom understood and almost never appreciated by the rest of us. Wilson was in due course answered, though whether effectively is doubtful.[6] But one of his questions remains troublesome long after the controversy has died down: Is the production of CEAA editions like the Iowa-California Twain really practicable? The embattled Paul Baender was still working on his *Tom Sawyer* a full decade after Wilson's ambush, so apparently the cumbersome machinery of corporate copy-text editing requires this much time to produce a volume which ostensibly presented nothing formidable in the way of textual problems. Is the CEAA-approved *Tom Sawyer* worth the long wait? The answer, as will appear, is at best a qualified yes.

While gathering the three Tom Sawyer narratives into a single volume is a logical editorial arrangement, the place of the two later stories alongside their grand progenitor is highly invidious. But where else could the vagrant *Tom Sawyer Abroad* (1894) and "Tom Sawyer, Detective" (1896) have appeared in the complete works? And there is something to be learned through reading all three books right through in chronological order: a reminder of Twain's appalling decline as a writer in the last decade and a half of his life, and a new sense of how rare and fine a book the original *Tom Sawyer* (1876) is in his canon—a well-made novel.

John C. Gerber, who provides the historical introductions for all three narratives, is at his best with the best book. One of the goals of such introductions ought to be to help us read a classic with fresh eyes, though the constraints put on the exercising of critical judgment by the CEAA often result in essays emphasizing sources and the history of composition, publication, and reputation at the expense of saying just what it is about a given work that has made it last.[7] Gerber handles the historical background of *Tom Sawyer* in exemplary fashion. He quickly scotches the notion that the novel was ever intended *for* boys, though obviously *about* them, and countenances Walter Blair's earlier view that *Tom Sawyer* was conceived and structured as a satire on the jejune boys' books that Twain had grown up with in the 1840s and '50s and which continued to be published throughout the century.[8] *Tom Sawyer,* though Twain remembered it as "a hymn, put into prose to give it a worldly air," was in its own time a revisionist attack on the "moral boy" formula as represented by Little Rollo and Ragged Dick, whose ethical universes demanded and extracted the strictest poetic justice.[9] Twain, on this view, deliberately attempted to characterize boys more as they were to be found in life, and, according to Twain's good friend and arbiter absolute of literary realism, William Dean Howells, he succeeded: *Tom Sawyer* was done "with a fidelity to circumstances which loses no charm by being realistic in the highest degree."[10] This from Howells's enthusiastic review in the *Atlantic;* but earlier, and in private correspondence after he had edited the manuscript for Twain, Howells was advising him "to treat it explicitly *as* a boy's story.... If you should put it forth as a study of boy character from the grown-up point of view, you'd give the wrong key to it."[11] At this point the book was written and most of the revising done. Yet to Howells's recommendation, says Gerber, Twain "readily agreed" (p. 16). So we must conclude either that Twain was consenting to publicize *Tom Sawyer* as something it was not—a book for boys—or that Gerber's previous contention that the novel was intended for adults "from the outset" is in error (p. 8).

Such inconsistencies arise from, among other things, trying to infer literary intention and structure from historical evidence. Not surprisingly, the documentation surrounding *Tom Sawyer* is far from unequivocal. Twain vacillated notoriously in his attitudes toward his books, from the anxious insecurity of the intuitive artist, to a crassly commercial stance of "do what it takes to sell the thing," to outright lassitude and uninterest in his efforts once completed. Gerber's treatment of the history of *Tom Sawyer*'s composition, while it establishes that Twain took considerable pains in writing and revision, actually obscures the question of the kind of book he finally wrote. Only a single footnote tells us that there has been an interpretive controversy concerning *Tom Sawyer*'s structure nearly coeval with the life of the novel. In our own time the debate has focused on the crucial issue of Tom's "maturation." Walter Blair, in "On the Structure of *Tom Sawyer*," argued that Tom does indeed grow up in the course of the novel, a point of view later seconded by Hamlin Hill's scrutiny of the original manuscript's annotations and marginalia, which seem to imply Twain's intention to have Tom mature.[12] Other critics, however, have not been convinced, discovering in the novel neither maturation nor much real structure at all beyond Twain's usual episodic formulation.[13]

Ordinarily, Gerber's reticence on the question of structure could pass as good scholarly deportment when dealing with a classic: Let readers induce the structure for themselves. But two of *Tom Sawyer*'s most remarkable qualities—its tight organization and its obvious *finish*—are unusual in Twain's work and ought therefore to compel discussion. For the problem of *Tom Sawyer*'s structure might ultimately turn not so much on the debate over maturation as on the palpable finesse Twain shows with a classically comic mode, a narrative of several story strands snugly woven into a fabric that both pleases in overall design and ends in a manner altogether more satisfying than the perplexing irresolution of *Huckleberry Finn* or the egregious trickery of *Tom Sawyer Abroad*.

Tom Sawyer succeeds because its "hymn to boyhood" is strictly controlled by the comic form, a form which here is both conventional and conventionally handled, which provides a clean, well-lighted place sufficient to repress the hyenas of burlesque, and which keeps the good fun always pointed toward the realization of the narrative's poetic power, be this in Tom's passage from boy to man, or, less seriously, in his situational change from lost to found, poor to rich, and scorned to loved. In all of this, for once, the "matter of Hannibal" is well served by its formal vehicle.

Some of the best of this matter of Hannibal is not to be found in the well-known "genre scenes," but is rather tucked away between them. Consider as an example the church-service scene in Chapter 5, flanked as it is by the more famous "Sunday-school Bible-recitation" and the subsequent "Monday-morning tooth-pulling." Tom's fidgeting and suffering through the seemingly interminable service, his fascination with the beetle, and the disruption caused by the bitten dog—these are the familiar elements of comic genre. But what stays in the mind is the picture of Tom's involvement with the sermon:

The minister gave out his text and droned along monotonously through an argument that was so prosy that many a head by and by began to nod—and yet it was an argument that dealt in limitless fire and brimstone and thinned the predestined elect down to a company so small as to be hardly worth the saving. Tom counted the pages of the sermon; after church he always knew how many pages there had been, but he seldom knew anything else about the discourse. However, this time he was really interested for a little while. The minister made a grand and moving picture of the assembling together of the whole world's hosts at the millennium when the lion and the lamb should lie down together and a little child should lead them. But the pathos, the lesson, the moral of the great spectacle were lost upon the boy; he only thought of the conspicuousness of the principal character before the onlooking nations; his face lit with the thought, and he said to himself that he wished he could be that child, if it was a tame lion. [p. 68]

Stylistically, this is a fine passage, subtler in rhetoric and thought than its counterparts in *Huckleberry Finn* (Huck's report on the "preforeordestination" sermon at the Grangerford's church, and the "funeral orgies" for Peter Wilkes in Chapter 27), if only because of the third-person point of view. The paragraph deftly integrates the unexpected motive of the apocalypse with the moral status of the boy Tom, whose penchant for exhibitionism is a problem that, under the "maturation" hypothesis, must sooner or later be overcome.

The apocalyptic is introduced several times in the novel, most notably in the dramatic thunderstorm on Jackson's Island (pp. 135–37, a splendid passage, too long to quote), and in the other thunderstorm that speaks to Tom personally at the end of Chapter 22:

And that night there came on a terrific storm, with driving rain, awful claps of thunder and blinding sheets of lightning. He covered his head with the bedclothes and waited in a horror of suspense for his doom; for he had not the shadow of a doubt that all this hubbub was about him. He believed he had taxed the forbearance of the powers above to the extremity of endurance and that this was the result. It might have seemed to him a waste of pomp and ammunition to kill a bug with a battery of artillery, but there seemed nothing incongruous about the getting up such an expensive thunderstorm as this to knock the turf from under an insect like himself. [p. 166][14]

This is the sublime obverse to the beautiful millennial vision of an earlier Sunday, as it also stands in contrast to the landscape idyls that recur from time to time in the novel. Tom and Huck in their respective books get a very similar moral catechism, including the romantic perception of death in the landscape which is an important part of the initiatory knowledge of both.[15] The difference between them, however, might be that the moral lessons never "take" on the wily Tom Sawyer.

At all events these serious passages and others are centrally relevant to the "maturation" view of *Tom Sawyer,* which must show how they are organized to foster and test the boy's moral growth. Otherwise the interpretation will remain doubtful. Moreover, these materials need to be studied in the same context as the more familiar "genre scenes"—the whitewashing, the grave robbing, the Sunday school, etc.—before the complete ethical universe of the novel can be said to be known. And all of this would be a necessary preparation for determining *Tom Sawyer*'s place in Twain's total work. Only then could we confidently accept Gerber's invitation to consensus: *"Tom Sawyer,* we would all have to agree, has neither the art nor the profundity of *Huckleberry Finn,* but as an 'idyll of boyhood' it has no peer, anywhere" (p. 30). A final judgment in a final text would have been nice, but it is premature. The best that we can say now is provisional: If in *Huckleberry Finn,* as is almost universally acknowledged, Mark Twain found his idiom, then the discovery was made easier by the good luck that in *Tom Sawyer,* a decade earlier, he had already found his subject.

At this point it is fair to ask whether a discussion of the serious themes of *Tom Sawyer* is germane to the evaluation of a definitive edition. I hope that the problem of the novel's structure in relation to Gerber's historical introduction has suggested that it is, and I would maintain that the relevance extends further: into the province of the explanatory notes, if not right to the established text itself. When Gerber calls *Tom Sawyer* "first of all a reminiscence" (p. 3), he is falling in with a longstanding preoccupation of Mark Twain scholars, the relationship between autobiography and fiction. An often tacit assumption of such scholarship has been that works like *Tom Sawyer* and *Huckleberry Finn* are essentially autobiographical. Hence Dixon Wecter, coming at the question from the direction of the biographer in *Sam Clemens of Hannibal* (1952), finds through assiduous digging any number of connections between the boy in Hannibal and the boy in St. Petersburg. But what is important to the biographer may be distracting to the reader and the critic of fiction. Wecter's book remains the richest "source of sources" for Twain's early life and work, and is frequently referred to in the notes to the present edition, though not always with the proper care in distinguishing life from art that we have a right to expect. For the connections between them are never simple, and in Twain's case they are quite complex, as Mark Twain scholars above all should know. Twain had a memory that was at times phenomenally accurate, as in the sketch "Villagers of 1840–43," written late in life, but at others wholly unreliable. Perhaps the best way to describe it is *eidetic:* and there is a clue to his transforming genius in the whimsical remark in the *Autobiography* that when he was younger he "could remember anything, whether it had happened or not," but in old age he could remember only what didn't happen.[16] Even a brief experience with Mark Twain is enough to warn off those who fondly believe in a reflexive equation between autobiography and fiction; those who persevere must cultivate skepticism if they are to avoid being taken in by the plausibility of Mark Twain and his Hannibal sources.

John Gerber, of course, has persevered. He is, after Walter Blair, the dean of Mark Twain scholars. But in his explanatory notes for *Tom Sawyer* he has to some extent nevertheless been taken in. The great danger in writing annotations is a keenness to uncover things that can slip into pedantry. The urge to locate some passing allusion in historical reality, or even to assert that something *is* an allusion, can blind the inquirer to the rules of logic and evidence. Let me hasten to say that much of what is elucidated in Gerber's notes is good to know and authoritatively set down. The notes on Missouri folklore and superstition are particularly welcome: One finally learns what is behind the folk beliefs that shooting a cannon over the water or floating a quicksilver-filled loaf of bread would cause the rising of drowned bodies. And the identifications of popular sources for Tom's romantic adventures—pirating and playing Robin Hood—serve as another piece of evidence that Twain was, throughout his life, better acquainted with American popular culture than most of his peers.

Yet *Tom Sawyer* is on the whole too much annotated. The edition is encumbered with superfluous notes which do not elaborate or clarify anything necessary to the story, which posit some autobiographical connection where none is implied, or which are otherwise misconceived. When Twain writes of Tom's Aunt Polly that, in the matter of home remedies for family illnesses, she was "armed with death . . . on her pale horse, metaphorically speaking, with 'hell following after' " (p. 109), do we really need to be told that the allusion is to Revelations and that Mark Twain showed his familiarity with the image in other contexts? What reader is *not* familiar with "death on a pale horse"? The passage in question is wholly comic, the allusion itself is casual, and a twelve-line note is clearly too much about too little (p. 484). Even more dubious is the gloss on a Jackson's Island passage (the coming thunderstorm, p. 136) where the boys feel "The Spirit of the Night" passing by just before the terrific storm breaks. Gerber notes: "Shelley began his poem 'To Night:' 'Swiftly walk o're the western wave,

Spirit of Night' " (p. 486). One honestly does not know what to make of this. Is Shelley's poem being asserted as the source for Twain's phrase? If so, on what grounds? Given the rich context of superstition in the novel, a source in folklore would seem more likely, but the direction of the note is left entirely to the bemused and annoyed reader.

Matters are worse with the notes on Hannibal people and places. *Tom Sawyer,* for all its "genre scenes," does not develop the sense of place to a notable degree. Twain was, as always, interested in character and social custom, in what went on *inside* the church and *inside* the hearts of the people within it. Chapter 5, containing the church service discussed above, opens with the words "About half past ten the cracked bell of the church began to ring" (p. 66). There is not a sentence further that attempts to describe or place the church. Nonetheless, Gerber chooses to append a note: "The bell in the steeple of the Presbyterian church in Hannibal came from the wrecked steamer *Chester*" (p. 476). Now this has all the blank irrelevance of a direct non sequitur. All Twain tells us of the bell is that it was cracked. Is this supposed to be the same bell? Is this even intended to be the Presbyterian church?[17] And what does it matter anyway, since the narrative attaches no importance whatever to the church as a particular building or place? Similarly, Tom Sawyer's schoolhouse, though accorded only three words of description ("the little isolated frame schoolhouse" [p. 77]), is treated to a long note speculating on which of the two schools Clemens attended is here being referred to, concluding, with a logic that annihilates the need for the note, that it is impossible to tell from such a sketchy description (p. 479)! The compulsion to find some biography in everything here reaches the ridiculous, offering us nothing concrete at all about Clemens, Twain, Hannibal, or *Tom Sawyer,* because (as any reader knows) the author did not intend any particular schoolhouse in the first place.

These are among the most extreme examples, but they do point to a general problem with the autobiographical approach to annotating a fictive text: the details of person, place, and incident drawn "from life" are rarely such as to enrich the reading of a kind of literature that has already transformed them to a new and higher use. And in the case of *Tom Sawyer* it must be said that the particulars of Hannibal people and places are not so important as they are made to seem in Gerber's annotations; in fact some of the asserted relationships between Hannibal and *Tom Sawyer* turn out to be incredible. Without intent, the result tends to mislead. The CEAA advises explanatory notes where these are "desirable or practicable."[18] Printing only those that fit in this category would eliminate a considerable fraction of the notes to *Tom Sawyer* and, as we shall see, almost all the glosses on the other two texts. As it is, however, there is one consolation for the reader: All volumes of the Iowa-California Edition are "clear-texts," relegating all notes to the back, amidst the textual apparatus, where they may easily be ignored.

Turning to the established text of *Tom Sawyer,* one soon discovers from Paul Baender's textual introduction that the work has been time-consuming but not especially difficult (the copy-texts for all three of the Tom Sawyer narratives are based on manuscripts, necessitating tabulations of all alterations in them; this is the practice for all volumes of the Iowa-California Edition, and goes beyond what the CEAA requires).[19] Because the only version of the book known to have been revised by Mark Twain himself is the original manuscript (MS1), the choice of copy-text is straightforward. The editorial process thus centers on collations against the copy-text manuscript and a series of emendations to it, duly listed and occasionally argued for. The editing was further facilitated by Twain's own revisions to MS1, which consisted, Baender tells us, "primarily of minor verbal changes and the deletion or insertion of brief passages which hardly affected the narrative sequence" (p. 505). Another way of putting this is to point out that accidentals (paragraphing, punctuation, and word forms) far outnumber substantives (words and word order) in the revisions. To this extent Edmund Wilson's sarcasm in the "Aunt Polly–aunt Polly" matter is justified: Accidentals are in fact what Paul Baender and his editorial assistants spent most of their time on. And so while the new copy-text edition of *Tom Sawyer* is much needed and appreciated, the seemingly endless tabulations in the apparatus—over two hundred pages worth—are harder to justify, though perfectly consistent with Iowa-California practice.

The text itself appears to have been admirably established. Random collations against other editions with potential copy-text authority (the first American edition of 1876 and the Author's National Edition of 1899–1917, for example) show variations accounted for and most of the important cruxes discussed in the textual notes (I have not, however, myself examined the original manuscript, which is in the Georgetown University Library). There are only fifty-four emendations of substantives in the copy-text, nearly all of them minor, and again the most important of these are—with one notable exception—explained in the textual notes. (For an example of an emendation that was *not* made, though in my opinion was indicated, see note 14 of this review.)

The exception happens to be a substantive emendation that bears directly on interpretation. At the beginning of the "whitewashing" chapter (Chapter 2) Twain writes a landscape evocation: Hannibal and the distant Cardiff Hill are as lovely that summer morning as "the Delectable Land." This is immediately followed by Tom's appearance on the scene and his dismay at the prospect of hard work ahead (p. 46). The copy-text (MS1), the other manuscript (MS2), and the first English edition (E1) all read "the gladness went out of nature and a deep melancholy settled down upon his spirit" (p. 533). Baender inferentially emends to "all gladness left him," as in the first American edition (A1) and subsequent American printings; this he presumably does on the grounds that such a comparatively major change was Twain's intention as expressed in the galley proofs (which no longer exist). Yet in the absence of direct evidence—and without a textual note to rationalize the decision to emend—one can argue that the change weakens the initial iteration of an important theme in *Tom Sawyer*: the romantic relationship between the landscape (nature) and the character and temperament of the boy. As we have seen, Tom both reads the book of nature and prints his own moods in it.

The substitution of a flatter, thematically neutral reading for "the gladness went out of nature" might subtly influence interpretation, though the irony is that the MS1 language has not been generally known in America until now, when we get a quick look at it in the table of emendations as a rejected reading. And while the meaning of *Tom Sawyer* will obviously never rest on this single emendation, it is a case such as theoretically minded textual critics are fond of pointing out, even though the tendency this time seems to be away from manifest intention and toward the implicative—something of a departure from customary copy-text editorial practice.

Terry Firkins, the editor for *Tom Sawyer Abroad* and "Tom Sawyer, Detective," has a more interesting story to tell about his copy-text labors, more interesting really than the novellas themselves. *Tom Sawyer Abroad* was bowdlerized in its serial publication in *St. Nicholas Magazine* (November–April, 1893–1894), the red-penciling being done by the magazine's editor, Mary Mapes Dodge. The textual problem thus created for the modern editor is compounded by the fact that much of her expurgation somehow got carried over into the book publication by Charles L. Webster & Company in the spring of 1894, though, even more curiously, the first English edition was set from authoritative copy (pp. 238–39). As with *Tom Sawyer*, the surviving holograph manuscript becomes the copy-text, but the difference is that Firkins has the responsibility of restoring the text of the novella and presenting it to the American reading public for the first time.

But let me pose a question that, on its face, seems ridiculous. Is what Mark Twain wrote in this case what he "intended" to appear in print? After all, he did *Tom Sawyer Abroad* for money. He wanted to make money on the serialization and on the book. He was delighted to get $4,000 from *St. Nicholas* (a children's magazine). And he even wrote to Fred J. Hall, the manager of Webster & Company, to say that in preparing the piece for a children's magazine he had "tried to leave the improprieties all out; if I didn't Mrs. Dodge can scissor them out" (p. 247). Are these the words of an author seriously concerned with his manuscript? Or, to put it more radically, might not this be seen as giving Mrs. Dodge carte blanche to make *Tom Sawyer Abroad* into whatever she felt was appropriate for her audience? The consequent bowdlerization certainly weakened Twain's already feeble tale, as readers can discover by comparing the present edition's reading of Jim's long argument proving that the Sahara Desert was not created by the Lord (Chapter 9, pp. 310–11) with the denatured version from the magazine (and therefore from all previous American editions). Such restorations are long overdue and very welcome. But it is less than completely honest on the editor's part to make much of the bowdlerization without sufficiently making clear Twain's less than devoted attitude toward *Tom Sawyer Abroad*. Does Twain's letter to Hall, and through him to *St. Nicholas*, amount to a statement of intent? Apparently this bothered Firkins, too, for in his textual introduction he quotes only the first part of the relevant passage from the letter to Hall: "I have tried to leave the improprieties all out" (p. 622). Gerber does quote the full passage (as above), but also thinks that Twain would have shown himself upset with Mrs. Dodge's freedoms had he favored posterity with a written irruption on the subject (p. 248). But he did not. Thus we are left with a restored book, about the original violation of which Mark Twain did not care enough to get mad.

"Tom Sawyer, Detective" completes the volume and is an even slighter effort than *Tom Sawyer Abroad*. In the decade following its publication the story achieved a measure of notoriety because of its source. Twain, perhaps without realizing what he was doing, had borrowed the plot from an earlier novel by the Danish writer Steen Steenson Blicher, and the fact was noticed by Valdmar Thorensen, who first queried Twain about the resemblance and then published his discovery in a journal article of 1909 (pp. 348–49 and note). Twain's readiness to appropriate someone else's plot for his potboiler is sad enough, but the saddest aspect of "Tom Sawyer, Detective" is the manner in which Mark Twain plagiarizes himself. Here his obsession with mysteries reduces Tom and Huck (especially Huck, who has the telling) to the one-dimensional level of show-off detective and obtuse sidekick. So little does the once precocious Huck have to say that he is forced to repeat verbatim a few of his lines from the glory days of *Huckleberry Finn*.[20] And Tom seems to say "Huck, ain't it bully!" every other page or so, as Huck slavishly follows him through the uninteresting murder investigation. Tom's antics make us forget the "maturing" boy of *Tom Sawyer*, recalling instead the way in which *Huckleberry Finn* was nearly destroyed by the burlesque of its ending. Perhaps giving "Tom Sawyer, Detective" parity is not such a good idea, for after reading this wretched story one is ready to call for a *selected* edition of Mark Twain.

But of course "Tom Sawyer, Detective" gets the same objective editorial treatment as the other two narratives, as it should. One final word about the explanatory notes: they exhibit the same problems, a fortiori, found in *Tom Sawyer*. But if in the earlier instance there was at least an allusive context of people, places, and superstitions for annotation, necessary or not, with the latter works it is obviously a case of desperately searching their literary deserts for something, anything, to gloss. Gerber is reduced to explaining Mark Twain's already transparent jokes (p. 494, note 257.33) or discussing the cost of postage in the first half of the nineteenth century (pp. 493–94, note 256.24). As for the rest, there is nothing in either set of notes that could not be omitted, and the space saved.

All in all, the scholarly matter in this *Tom Sawyer* edition comes to about half of the 717 pages. Is this too much? The editorial policy for the Iowa-California edition says no, that every bit of the apparatus needs to be printed, so that Paul Baender, Terry Firkins, and John C. Gerber may be plainly vindicated in their efforts. To the extent that the choice of the copy-text needs to be rationalized and the emendations noted, one can agree. Likewise important are the historical and textual introductions. But the rest of the space might better be filled with the original illustrations from the three Tom Sawyer narratives, or the book simply shortened and its price thereby lowered. Thirty dollars, forty dollars or even more for a single volume of the Iowa-California edition? One can still buy used copies of the entire Author's National Edition for this much money, and now the new edition is, ironically, being sold by subscription to academic libraries—the only institutions obliged to buy it—the way Twain peddled his early books at the premium price of two dollars per volume. Yet in spite of the inflated prices and the consequent straitening of the market to the point that not even Mark Twain scholars will be buying the edition, the Iowa-California people remain committed to their format. It is futile to expect any change.

And so the Tom Sawyer narratives, three-in-one, take their place on the five-foot library shelf that someday will be filled with the orange-bound complete works of Mark Twain: *Tom Sawyer* in clear-text, intended for the general reader, who will probably never read it between these covers but in other printings of the established text from other publishers, should that particular dream of the CEAA ever come true. The textual apparatus at the back will now and then be consulted by such scholars as are concerned to speak to each other about editorial theory and practice. And in this sense *Tom Sawyer* will become timeless, as befits a true classic. Yet in another, more melancholy sense—in Edmund Wilson's sense—this *Tom Sawyer,* indeed the entire Mark Twain Edition, risks becoming timeless through being ignored—a white elephant analogous to Twain's baneful Paige Typesetter: something that takes too long to produce, costs too much, and finally does not work because it is not practicable. If *Tom Sawyer* in this or any other edition cannot be familiarly read, it will never be exactly Mark Twain's book, however exact the words.

Notes

1. As handsome as this book is, it must be said that the review copy has frequent smudgings of the ink in the printed textual apparatus; checks of two other library copies, however, revealed all clean pages.

2. The University of California Press is also publishing the Mark Twain Papers in eighteen volumes, ten of which have appeared; the texts of the Mark Twain Papers are likewise approved by the Center for Editions of American Authors.

3. A glance at the latest *Books in Print* reveals more than two dozen popular editions of *The Adventures of Huckleberry Finn,* and fifteen of *Tom*

Sawyer. By contrast, William Dean Howells's best known novels, *The Rise of Silas Lapham* and *A Hazard of New Fortunes*, are represented in only two editions each.

4. The classic and still controversial beginning of the "revision of Mark Twain" was Van Wyck Brooks's *The Ordeal of Mark Twain* (1920), which spoke of some "deep malady of the soul" in Mark Twain and of his "arrested development" as a writer. Bernard DeVoto challenged Brooks's interpretation in two books, *Mark Twain's America* (1932) and *Mark Twain at Work* (1942), the latter study based on DeVoto's extensive work with Mark Twain's papers and manuscripts. DeVoto hoped to show that Mark Twain rescued himself from human and artistic oblivion—the products of financial disasters and personal tragedies—in his last two decades as a writer. Hence the Brooks-DeVoto controversy, as it has come to be called, became both a critical and a biographical argument about the subject—and so it has continued to this day. For a useful review of the question, see Louis Leary's casebook *Mark Twain's Wound* (New York: Crowell, 1962). Then in 1973 Hamlin Hill published his revealing biography of Twain's last decade, *God's Fool* (New York: Harper & Row, 1973), which quickly blew the embers of Brooks-DeVoto into full flame through its unflinching narrative of Mark Twain's disintegration *both* as a man and as a writer during the period 1900–1910. Hill has become the chief spokesman for the demythologizers, who by no means form a majority among Mark Twain scholars. In an overview of Twain scholarship written in 1974, Hill criticized the stolidity of much of the work being done and insisted that "the most urgent need today in Mark Twain scholarship is for a thorough psychological study of the man himself beneath the palimpsest of the comic legend—his rages, his gaucheries, his obsequiousness before great wealth, all his various monstrosities" (Hamlin Hill, "Who Killed Mark Twain?" *American Literary Realism*, 7 [Spring 1974], 119–24). But Hill's work, and especially *God's Fool*, has not gone unchallenged, nor has it dislodged the "legend" or the myth: William R. Macnaughton has recently published a new book, *Mark Twain's Last Years as a Writer* (Columbia: Univ. of Missouri Press, 1979), which purports, once again, to find artistic strength and integrity among the final writings.

5. Edmund Wilson, "The Fruits of the MLA," in *The Devils and Canon Barham* (New York: Farrar, 1973), p. 162. Wilson's essay originally appeared in two parts in the *New York Review of Books* for 26 September and 10 October 1968.

6. Paul Baender, for example, rejoined—in a letter printed in the *New York Review* for 19 December 1968—that it had not been *Tom Sawyer* that the people at Iowa were reading backward, but *Huckleberry Finn*. And they had abandoned the practice, anyhow, after discovering it was no more accurate than the ordinary way! Baender also claimed in his letter that the Iowa-California Edition of Mark Twain "has received no money whatever from the

MLA, and it began before the Center for Editions of American Authors was organized" (p. 38). Yet the verso to the title page of this volume—and all others which so far have appeared in the Iowa-California Edition—bears the following note: "Editorial expenses were in part supported by grants from the National Endowment for the Humanities of the National Foundation on the Arts and Humanities administered through the Center for Editions of American Authors of the Modern Language Association."

7. The MLA's *Statement of Editorial Principles and Procedures*, rev. ed. (New York: Modern Language Association of America, 1972), which is the official handbook for CEAA editors, stipulates that "though the writer of [the historical essay] cannot wholly avoid critical judgments . . . his primary responsibility is to present an account of the genesis and growth, the publication, and the reception and reputation of his text" (p. 11).

8. Walter Blair, "On the Structure of *Tom Sawyer*," *Modern Philology*, 37 (August 1939), 75–76.

9. Blair, "On the Structure of *Tom Sawyer*," p. 77.

10. Howells and Twain had connived to have the *Atlantic* review coincide with the appearance of the first American edition of *Tom Sawyer* (from the subscription house of Elisha Bliss: American Publishing Company), but publishing delays resulted in a fine review too early for the book it touted: Howells's notice appeared in the *Atlantic Monthly* for May of 1876, but *Tom Sawyer* did not appear until December of that year (p. 28 and note).

11. Frederick Anderson, ed., *Selected Mark Twain–Howells Letters* (Cambridge: Harvard Univ. Press, 1967), p. 61.

12. Hamlin Hill, "The Composition and the Structure of *Tom Sawyer*," *American Literature*, 32 (January 1961), 379–92.

13. See especially Alexander Cowie, *The Rise of the American Novel* (New York: American Book Company, 1951), p. 609; and, more recently, Judith Fetterley, "The Sanctioned Rebel," *Studies in the Novel*, 3 (Fall 1971), 293–303.

14. Here is an occasion on which the copy-text might well have been emended: "about the getting up of such an expensive thunderstorm," as in the second manuscript of *Tom Sawyer* (MS2), in the first English edition (E1), and the "Autograph Edition" (Ya) is clearly more idiomatic than the copy-text's reading. It seems likely that Twain might have meant either "getting up such an expensive thunderstorm," or "the getting up of. . . ." But probably not "the getting up such . . ." as in the copy-text. Baender offers no textual note on this crux.

15. For Huck it occurs in the opening paragraph of Chapter 32; for Tom in the opening paragraph of Chapter 8 (p. 87 in the present edition).

16. Albert Bigelow Paine, ed., *Mark Twain's Autobiography* (New York: Harper & Brothers, 1924), I, 96.

17. Gerber cites Wecter (*Sam Clemens of Hannibal,* p. 86), though Wecter gives no information concerning why Twain chose to make the churchbell cracked, nor whether the Presbyterian church of Hannibal is the one being recreated in this scene from *Tom Sawyer.*

18. *Statement of Editorial Principles and Procedures,* p. 10.

19. The CEAA insists on a textual essay, a report of all changes and emendations in the copy-text, a report of policy on the matter of compounds hyphenated at the end of the line, and a historical collation of post-copy-text editions in the author's lifetime (*Statement of Editorial Principles and Practices,* pp. 8–9).

20. For example, compare this opening from "Tom Sawyer, Detective": "and everything's so solemn it seems like everybody you've loved is dead and gone and you most wish you was dead and gone too, and done with it all" (p. 357), with its source at the beginning of Chapter 32 of *Huckleberry Finn.*

Constructing and Deconstructing Autobiography

Jerome H. Buckley

George P. Landow, ed. *Approaches to Victorian Autobiography.* Athens: Ohio University Press, 1979. xlvi, 359 pp.

In his recent monograph *The Forms of Autobiography,* William C. Spengemann demonstrates how elusive the genre has become. The term that once denoted an author's self-history now frequently has no such meaning at all, for it is widely invoked to cover any attempt at self-definition and by the structuralists freely applied to texts in which the "death" of the author is to be assumed and from which all "referentiality" beyond the self-subsistent verbal artifact must be excluded. The ideal autobiography, as Spengemann imagines it, may now be quite unhistorical, that is, far removed from the facts of experience and all real events in time, a pure fiction creating a self never to be identified in actual life.[1]

Introducing the essays he has assembled as *Approaches to Victorian Autobiography,* George P. Landow seems aware that such extension of the term to every sort of "self-representation" will end only in destroying all sense of a distinct literary genre. "Autobiography," he suggests, must have a sharper denotation: "To qualify as autobiography a work must not only present a version, myth, or metaphor of the self, but it must also be retrospective and hence it must self-consciously contrast two selves, the writing 'I' and the one located (or created) in the past" (p. xliii); and if the work does not meet these requirements, it might better be considered an example of "autobiographicality." I should accept Landow's working definition but add that the retrospect should be sustained at some length so as to review a whole phase of development or at least a considerable portion of the writer's lifetime, and I should prefer to speak of the alternative as "subjectivity" rather than "autobiographicality." At any rate, some of the essays in the Landow volume concern books readily recognizable as more or less formal autobiographies, and others deal with manifestations of the subjective impulse—or whatever it was that led a number of nineteenth-century authors to reveal or conceal personal matter in other forms—the lyric, the novel, the critical essay.

Convinced that the poets conducted the boldest and most innovative experiments in Victorian autobiography, Elizabeth K. Helsinger writes persuasively of *In Memoriam,* which should "qualify" without much question, but less cogently of "The Scholar Gypsy" and "The Buried Life," in which the subjective note is surely strong, and only with obvious strain of Browning's "Childe Roland," which is scarcely "autobiographical" in any standard sense of the word. Frederick Kirchhoff is happier in coining the term "anti-autobiography" to describe William Morris's curiously impersonal *Icelandic Journals,* where Morris is seen attempting to identify with the bleak heroic setting as a symbol of stoic endurance and so "a natural correlative to private aspirations" (p. 302). And David J. DeLaura is perceptive in analyzing the subjective component in the prose masters, the way "De Quincey, Carlyle, Newman, Ruskin, Arnold, and even Pater spend their lives defining and redefining their own vocations, shaping and reshaping their past experience for present purposes, while ostensibly talking about something else: society, literature, or religion" (p. 351)—though, I should insist, the something else to all of these, except perhaps De Quincey, is usually of real rather than merely ostensible concern.

Apart from his attempt at a more precise definition of terms, Landow devotes most of his wide-ranging introduction to a discussion of the prevalence of autobiography in the nineteenth century and the general sanctions for an increased subjectivity. Both in his view are symptomatic of cultural crisis, the breakup of a tradition, which forces reliance on personal rather than communal values. The Victorians, he claims, were essentially modern in their appeal to myth, their use of persona, their wasteland images of an atomistic society, but at the same time as autobiographers they were oddly innocent by twentieth-century standards, pre-Freudian, able to present psychological experience which the typical post-Freudian would quickly suspect, self-consciously label, and tend to embody "in more explicitly fictional modes" (p. xv). Moreover, despite their temptation to withdraw into a world of private impressions, they were much aware of their audience and of their own responsibility for "public discourse." If they were less assertive than Rousseau of unique individuality, they were also less convinced that the quest for selfhood would mean rewarding discovery rather than simply further alienation. They were generally far more respectful of fact than the Romantics, and more distrustful of personal recollection as a guide to absolute truth. Herbert Spencer indeed, as Landow reminds us, repeatedly corrected his falsifying memory of the past by resort to old letters and diaries; and others, though less skeptically, sought similar documentation for their life histories. The Victorians, in short, had a new and rather unsettling sense of the difficulties and dangers of self-scrutiny.

Most of Landow's contributors touch at some point on the problems of design and truth in autobiography, which Roy Pascal lucidly expounded some twenty years ago.[2] How have the disparate details of a varied life, both private and public, been selected and arranged? What unity or continuity has the writer found in his remembered experience, or imposed upon it? How is the finished record to make its claim upon our attention as a work of literary art of distinct appeal in itself and not entirely or even primarily as a gloss upon a career, like Mill's or Newman's, for example, in which we may have considerable outside interest? Phyllis Grosskurth maintains that we have "a right to demand factual accuracy—and certainly emotional sincerity—from an autobiography" (p. 36) but also a reasonable expectation to obtain something of the illusion we receive from reading a good novel; and by this measure she finds the *Memoirs* of John Addington Symonds lacking in the power to animate scenes and characters or to imagine any living forces beyond his own painful introspection. Linda H. Peterson sees Mrs. Oliphant, on the other hand, as having discovered or invented a pattern for her *Autobiography* in a recurrent emphasis on the tension between her two roles, the dedicated mother and the hard-working popular novelist who is reduced by her maternal duties to the status of a second-rate artist. George Bornstein detects an "antinomial structure" in John Butler Yeats's *Early Memories,* reflecting such a need to think in dichotomies as that which helped shape the greater vision of the painter's son. And Sarah C. Frerichs describes Elizabeth Sewell's *Autobiography* as the half-conscious conflict between self-expression and self-denial, the need for assertion and the conditioned feeling that achievement was "unfeminine." She suggests that the reader is held by the challenge "to determine where concealment ends and revelation begins" (p. 198).

In a stimulating essay of broader social impact Luann Walther explores what she calls "the invention of childhood." A good many of the Victorian autobiographers, she concludes, followed the dictate of a literary convention to present a double image of their early years, to show childhood struggle, suffering, and deprivation, and yet to convey the sense of childhood beatitude through glimpses of a lost Eden and an angelic mother. Howard Helsinger, stressing the writer's relation to his supposed reader, examines another sort of design, the strategy adopted to enhance credibility. Thus Trollope emerges as the clubby gentleman telling with genial candor only what it is seemly to record; Darwin and Mill evince their commitment to fact and objectivity by avoiding introspection; Newman takes the role of "the autobiographer accused," whose self-defense against charges of duplicity convinces by his meticulously honest analysis of motives; and Gosse becomes the artist eager to "fashion" his own personality, even at the cost of evasive lies, and ultimately to see the self as simply "the creation of its language" (p. 62). In the second of her two papers, one of the best in the volume, Elizabeth Helsinger discovers a pattern in the materials rather than in the stance of the writer. Ruskin's *Praeterita,* she concedes, may seem amorphous and discontinuous, insofar as the narrative reaches not one climactic revelation but presents at least seven separate conversions. The method, however, she goes on to show, is spatial rather than temporal; the self does not so much grow in time as respond to the spirit of place; and physical settings, intensely realized —especially the magical cities, Rouen, Geneva, and Pisa—come to represent phases of an extraordinary sensibility.

Where Elizabeth Helsinger writes informatively of structure, two other essayists less adroitly exploit the techniques of structuralism and inevitably lapse into its customary jargon. Both emulate Jeffrey Mehlman's effort to isolate a hidden level of text that will question, contradict, and so invalidate the autobiographer's declared or apparent intention.[3] Claudette Kemper Columbus, writing—sometimes impenetrably—of *Praeterita* as "thanatography," seeks to demonstrate the "hollowness" of Ruskin's assured rhetoric, the meaning of his "wordlessness," the falsity of the articulate "*moi*" (she is borrowing here from Jacques Lacan) and the eventual denial of a positive self-image by "the destructive dynamic of the silent and negating *moi*" (p. 110).[4] Her effort yields an elaborately strained and quite unconvincing reading of the title *Praeterita* and proceeds to a search, in unlikely contexts (some drawn from other books), for sexual innuendo and impotent pun, which, we are to believe, the repressed silent Ruskinian *moi* might unconsciously have intended.

If such criticism leaves nothing positive of Ruskin, Michael Ryan's probing of the "grammatology" of the *Apologia pro Vita Sua* leaves scarcely more to admire in Newman. Arguing that the apologist's logic is specious and his language imprecise, Ryan moves through a semantic play with terms to a larger repudiation of the genre itself. He deconstructs what he regards as already a deconstruction, since "all autobiography inevitably deconstructs its own presuppositions" (p. 153—that is, its initial assumption that there is any self to be known and written about), or, again, "We might say that this deconstruction of the category of the self is carried out in all autobiography" (p. 155). Both Ryan and Columbus reflect the structuralists' essential distrust of literature and the verbal medium, an impatience with what the latter calls "the incipiently robotic nature of language" (p. 110). Their bias belittles not just two monumental Victorians but ultimately the whole humanistic enterprise.

Other contributors with more positive intent point to hidden autobiographical patterns, though their readings sometimes seem more ingenious than definitive. In a second essay Linda Peterson declares biblical typology the key to Browning's self-portraits as well as to *Sartor Resartus* and to Mill's mental history. Most of Browning's typological allusions, it seems to me, are clearly demonstrable, but it is less certain, I should think, that the central dialectic of *Sartor,* apart from some incidental wasteland imagery, reflects the expulsion of the Israelites from Egypt, and it is hardly likely that "Mill's *Autobiography,* which makes no explicit use of types, derives its basic pattern of bondage-crisis-confusion-redemption from the Exodus" (p. 241). Avrom Fleishman finds a more plausible source of Mill's underlying design in the recurrence of the idea and image of progress until the "myth" is embodied in the idealized Harriet Taylor. But his suggestion that the symbol of the sun establishes the secret unity of Butler's autobiographical *Way of All Flesh* is not persuasive. Old John Pontifex does indeed stare into the sunset shortly before his death, and his grandson Ernest years later laughs into the sunshine from a railway carriage window, but two rather dissimilar salutes to the sun in the course of a long novel scarcely constitute a pattern or prove, as Fleishman alleges, that Butler himself was a secret sun worshipper.

Finally, two essays in the last section of the volume concern a theme broached in many of the earlier contributions, the relations between autobiography and fiction. Mutlu Konuk Blasing, insofar as I can follow the involutions of his prose, argues that Henry James virtually devised a new novel, "a literary creation," when in the prefaces to the New York edition he imagined his own past, invented connections for a life and work without "relatedness," and so made of himself and his true subjective existence a satisfying aesthetic object. With less reliance on paradox Robert L. Patten examines the way in which Charles Dickens by a series of reversals, beginning with his own initials, translated his autobiography into the autobiography of David Copperfield and thus through fully realized fiction confronted "apocalypse" with fortitude and imposed upon the chaotic truth of life an inspiriting design. To discover and affirm such continuity in actual experience was, we may assume, for all Victorian autobiographers the devoutly desired but often unattainable ideal.

In a volume illustrating modern "approaches" to criticism as well as Victorian "approaches" to a genre, it is hardly reassuring to find so many careless mistakes and lapses in scholarship. Numerous errors no doubt are typographical and more or less routine, but there is no excuse after page proof for a badly scrambled long quotation, and some of the many misspellings seem more than printer's slips: e.g., *principle* for *principal*, *lightening* for *lightning*, *spector* for *spectre*, *vinyard* for *vineyard*. If a Joycean pun were intended, it would be amusing to see a monk described as Ruskin's *altar ego* (p. 113), but two other errors within the preceding twelve lines suggest that the writer was not deliberately so facetious. Incorrect titles appear in both text and notes: Tennyson wrote "Supposed Confessions," not "The Supposed Confession"; Proust was author of *A la Recherche du Temps perdu* rather than *En Recherche* . . . ; the Kintner edition of a familiar correspondence properly carries the name *Elizabeth Barrett Barrett*, not *Elizabeth Barrett Browning*. Tennyson's wife, after his elevation to the peerage, is not correctly to be called Mrs. Tennyson, and John Henry Newman was not "Cardinal" when he wrote his *Apologia*. Though some of the essays are written with clarity and care, others aspire gracelessly to a modish opacity. Sometimes the grammar stumbles, and some of the constructions (e.g., *cannot help but*) fall short of general acceptance. Taken one by one, these may seem trivial matters. In the aggregate, however, they do not inspire confidence, and their appearance may prove more destructive than the most dedicated deconstructionist could wish.

Notes

1. Spengemann, *The Forms of Autobiography: Episodes in the History of a Literary Genre* (New Haven: Yale Univ. Press, 1980). See esp. the introduction and the

detailed bibliographical study of current research on autobiography, pp. 170–245.

2. Pascal, *Design and Truth in Autobiography* (Cambridge, Mass.: Harvard Univ. Press, 1960).

3. Mehlman, *A Structural Study of Autobiography: Proust, Leiris, Sartre, Levi-Strauss* (Ithaca, N.Y.: Cornell Univ. Press, 1974). Landow in his introduction (p. xlii) quotes Mehlman's declaration that he has tried "to reach that level of analysis at which a persistent textual organization is revealed, whose coherence throws into jeopardy the apparent intentions of the author."

4. Columbus in her notes acknowledges indebtedness to Mehlman, Derrida, and Lacan, but her present essay achieves its own degree of portentousness: e.g., "The repeated 'silent' dyings of the *moi* paradoxically pronounce its ontological *difference* from the hyper-verbal, eloquent, positive pen" (120).

Buns and Butter: A Taste of the Afro-American Cultural Canon

John Oliver Perry

Michael S. Harper and Robert B. Stepto, eds., *Chant of Saints: A Gathering of Afro-American Literature, Art, and Scholarship*. Urbana: University of Illinois Press, 1979. 490 pp.

Thick in size and cultural complexity, this anthology includes at least one representative, often substantially more, from a wider than usual range of cultural categories. Here is a fine array of current fiction, seven writers from Ellison to James McPherson to Gayl Jones (and interviews with four of them), and of poetry (big selections from Robert Hayden, Derek Walcott, Michael Harper, and Jay Wright with several others making appearances), and four prose pieces on jazz and blues (African roots, New Orleans, Duke Ellington, and Coltrane, a continuing presence especially in Harper's poems). But there are also speeches, memoirs, other interviews, personal and cultural history, ethnology, literary, music and art criticism, and plates to show sculpture, painting, and photography. As with any anthology of current work, no matter how broad its aims or how culturally definable the group it represents, the selection makes its patterns, allusions, interconnections, by virtue of limitations and omissions. Editor Stepto invites us to see how "the varying genres and disciplines . . . speak to one another" in this "Chant of Saints," but also, despite the absence of "a few major voices"—Varaka and Baldwin, for example—he wants this selection to begin to define "the Afro-American canon in our time." We can question these ambitions, yet gladly accept the invitation to enjoy a congenial cultural gathering.

John Hope Franklin, in his brief foreword, cautiously comments on "the air of security, if not solidarity and self-esteem, if not chauvinism, that permeates this work." And he goes on to describe the social world of black American intellectuals and professional artists who achieve group recognition here: "They teach their art and craft at an impressive array of American colleges and universities"—of the editors, Harper directs the writing program at Brown, Stepto the graduate Afro-American program at Yale—"or they write, paint, or photograph full time, or their daily preoccupations are in activities very germane to [their] creative efforts." After a delay in general appreciation, Robert Hayden became a consultant at the Library of Congress (nevertheless, his recent death has not been widely eulogized by the white literary establishment). The younger novelist Toni Morrison was working as an editor and part-time teacher, at least while writing *Song of Solomon* in 1976. Such are the relatively secure niches these black writers have achieved for themselves; they are not self-exiled from the American scene. There are no folk poets here or angry street and prison writings from Malcolm X, Eldredge Cleaver, Claude Brown, Don L. Lee, Etheridge Knight. A wide range of fairly simple and direct black women poets, often connected with southern, historically or predominantly black colleges, is inadequately represented here. We do have Sherley A. Williams's complex multiple perspective poem around Bessie Smith, but Lucille Clifton and Alice Walker appear only in criticism. The chauvinism is of a special social class in a quiet decade, with the securities and self-esteem earned by many decades of struggle to arrive at solid middle-class status in America.

The editors of this collection make much of the analogy with Dr. Alain Locke's ground-breaking Harlem Renaissance anthology, *The New Negro,* which began as a 1925 issue of *Survey Graphic.* Yet despite its evident connections with the upper levels of the white cultural establishment, so far *Chant of Saints* has not been heard outside its own circle, and no major reviews have yet appeared. So we ask, must black writing, like early jazz, appear to be a "new force," appealing to the dominant cultural appetite for the avant garde and the outre, in order to be listened to? Although much here is experimental in technique —Harper's poems, Leon Forrest's fiction, Alice Walker's personal and Stepto's poststructuralist criticism—apparently the taste has not developed generally. But can the voice of black writers, with its continuing or potential echo of a shameful and cruel history, ever be heard by the dominant majority?

One alternative that black writers and activists found in the sixties was to separate forcibly from the mainstream and to express their outrage in a language and style calculated to shock and offend. *Black Fire, an Anthology of Afro-American Writing,* edited in 1968 by LeRoi Jones (soon to become Amiri Baraka) and Larry Neal, often used violent street language, extreme chauvinism, and obscenity. It took dead aim at white oppression inside and out of what other black anthologists still tried to call the consciousness of "Our Darker Brothers." For a few years historical circumstances—the Vietnam war, economic and cultural expansion—seemed to support a black separatist rebellion within a weakening capitalist-imperialist system. The establishment, however, easily co-opted the diffuse cultural revolution initiated by blacks; the Nixon coalition repressed the leaders and organizations, biracial or black, that were most active for radical change; and the Vietnam war slowly collapsed as too expensive and intractable.

The Baraka group of hell-raisers is almost totally ignored in *Chant of Saints*. The present group of professionals and professors feels relatively comfortable within an American black cultural tradition and is not seeking to separate it from the dominant Western modernist schools. What is "revolutionary" about the last stage Melvin Dixon traces in "Toward a World Black Literature" is merely the hero's going "beyond the immediate African tradition . . . or European colonization" to "universal concerns"; he seeks "a new synthesis—a spiritual harmony in the New World which is essential to sustaining the African-American way of life." Black culture "redeems" itself by becoming "a conscious contributor to world culture," which, Dixon optimistically assumes, will accept the gift of enrichment and liberation. In the last selection Robert Hayden employs his optimistic, universalist, or cosmic perspective and ends a planetary alien's report on America:

> confess i am curiously drawn unmentionable to
> the americans doubt i could exist among them for
> long however psychic demands far too severe
> much violence much that repels i am attracted
> none the less their variousness their ingenuity
> their elan vital and that some thing essence
> quiddity i cannot penetrate or name

Gone is Baraka's sense of amerik-k-ka, gone any effort to eradicate oppressive white cultural values within an aroused black consciousness. The search for African roots goes on in anthropological and historical terms, not political or religious ideologies; and the general American context, including centuries of slavery and racism, is considered the vital fluid in which those alien roots were modified and thus flourished. There is a sense of triumph here, if not complacency. Blacks have done more than heroically endure in America. They have created works of art, and not for themselves alone, but supposedly for all Americans. So the elitism feels different from white middle-class intellectual cliquishness and self-esteem, for what we sense here is not haughty exclusion and bristling wit, but rather a simple pride in the attainment of community respect. These writers display southern courtesy and the Christian ideals of giving and forgiving in a consciously magnanimous if not downright saintly way.

Feeling secure in their basic role as broad cultural contributors, these artists and intellectuals go on to identify with very advanced aesthetic, professional, and artistic goals which are technically highly developed. The complex American experience of race that they share is perhaps more gentle than that of less educated, lower-class blacks. It can thus be freely exploited in their modernist style as part of a natural social process, like an ordinary childhood tragedy or a big family's rich language of private allusions. In his very different political art and practice, the once rabidly revolutionary and now widely mistrusted Amiri Baraka (also presently secure as a professor at SUNY-Stony Brook) still identifies with the Third World and the majority of black Americans, the 75 percent who live on below-average incomes. While presenting scenes of racial discrimination and deprivation, the cultural workers in *Chant* identify more with the 25 percent who have lately made impressive economic and social gains in America, and they seem generally complacent about the growing class disparity between blacks and whites. In an essay by Chinua Achebe, we get the only direct attack on colonial racism exposed in Conrad's *Heart of Darkness*. Presumably for Achebe this is a continuing problem mainly in the insensitive ignorance of academic critics. Derek Walcott's sense of his Caribbean colonial heritage is nostalgic, scarcely critical at all.

The Joyce-Eliot-Pound modernist aesthetic has long been thoroughly assimilated to black American experiences by the older artistic leaders of this group, Ellison and Hayden. The younger writers take their place, therefore, in a rather specialized Afro-American canon, one that makes room uneasily for the self-alienated (if not black- and self-hating) exile Richard Wright. Their adjustment to America gains from the comparison, for in two essays here Wright is taken back into the community, seen as after all a positive black voice, just as Joyce is an Irish one. Both are conceived as once lost souls, now redeemed in their people's judgments by their supreme dedication to artistic truth. With powerful drives toward personal and cultural integration, these writers attempt to join in their mind and work the best of what they know and have experienced in Western civilization. They do so with acknowledged difficulty, but Ellison, for example, warns here explicitly against letting "the anachronistic social imbalance ... dominate ... as a major theme and focus" for black art (or life), and he speaks resignedly of the "apparent invincibility to change" of this "social imbalance." As potentially active political persons, these artists see their social function in developing sensibilities and forms, the living power of the Word, and they trade in generally competing professional ideas and ideals. They are not concerned, for the most part, with developing nations or with organizing social forces to seek common ground for political action.

The contrast with Baraka is irresistible. Also working with avant-garde concepts as well as black folk traditions, Baraka helped evolve a black aesthetic in which poems *became* political action: "We want poems/like fists beating niggers out of Jocks/ or dagger poems in the slimy bellies/of the owner-jews. Black poems to/smear on girldemamma mulatto bitches/whose brains are red jelly stuck/between 'lizabeth taylor's toes. Stinking/ Whores! We want 'poems that kill!' " But however much they revolt our sensitivities, Baraka's strategy of retaliatory violence and racism, his indulgence in every street crudity including vulgar antisemitism and unmitigated sexism, did *not* poetically "kill" or "clean out the world for virtue and love." Avant garde as it was in many of its activist theories, this black aesthetic of rage did not inspire educated, poetry-reading blacks to turn from rebellion to revolution. Furthermore, it effectively alienated the separatist black movement from all but the most dogged, and presumably the only reliable, white liberals and radicals. Apparently Baraka has recognized these limitations, and his present political-artistic strategy has shifted to participatory street theater cum mixed-media action-propaganda with a racially mixed group and audience.

Proponents of postmodernism may question this use of art and its effectiveness, but last fall, after a black high school football player was shot, Howard Fast's *Freedom Road,* starring Mohammed Ali, was canceled on Boston television for fear —shared by some blacks—of arousing black youth in a "racially tense time"; so perhaps the establishment itself acknowledges the potentially revolutionary power of even a commercially exploited popular culture medium. The question then remains, particularly in the presence of this anthology: What is the social and political responsibility of intellectuals and artists who share unavoidably at least some of the pain or fascism, if not the poverty? Indeed we all personally suffer, but some blacks and most whites have ready intellectual and emotional defenses. We deny how racism operates, as Dick Gregory says, to make us all niggers in a power and status hierarchy without widespread social authority as well as widely acknowledged moral or spiritual ideals. To avoid superficial agitprop, the crux of a genuinely human and artistic response to racism in America lies in creating and catching a committed, personally engaged tone.

What, then, of the bemused, almost nostalgic way Sterling A. Brown recounts his student experience with racism at Williams? In his remarkably sustained book-opening ramble on "A Son's Return," he uses delicate irony and understatement at the limits of communication with all but his own black students and friends. They are expected to smile knowingly and wink, for they too have undergone similar trials as token Negroes; with the help of a few mostly confused whites, they too managed to wrest a narrow place and a usable education from a racially "imbalanced" system. Speaking for a good many others, no doubt, Brown reveals with confident humor his once carefully obscured depths of feeling for the small body of supportive friends—almost all black and struggling like himself. After Williams and Harvard and the Harlem Renaissance gave him certain tools for survival, Brown says he had to go south to learn "the strength of my people . . . the fortitude . . . the humor . . . the tragedy . . . folk tales." And now he has outworn T. S. Eliot and Pound and Anglicanism and pursues "folkstuff." About this he complains: "You get a lot of nonsense [from critics] about the spirituals talking about the good ole days. . . . I want [one such critic] to ask his mamma where he heard that the Negro did not contemplate his low condition. . . . The whole picture of the Negro I saw was flagrantly ridiculous. Sometimes the motive was not ignorance, but evil, and that I have fought and am continuing to fight."

These are moving and honorable words of courage from the seventy-two-year-old dedicatee for this anthology, and we can believe that at Howard for decades Sterling Brown has fought and has taught others to fight racism with the tools of critical realism, close reading, and hard thinking. But the limits of these tools, which so many of us intellectuals espouse, become, to use Hayden's word, "unmentionable" in Brown's conclusion. There he joins forces with the conservatism of Robert Frost and only agrees "somewhat" with his "liberal friends" whether "it matters who runs the game." His stoic "I'm going to play my hand out with the cards that come," is indeed "a strong statement of a man's belief in America and in himself." But the apolitical cultural stance which pervades *Chant* leaves unconsidered what vision of a better society, what principles for political organization, what kinds of leadership for collective action, what alliances and strategies, and, yes, what humane, supportive, ennobling arts can build the new social relationships and the new consciousness all Americans must have if the game is to continue at all?

The last essay in *Chant of Saints* is Robert Stepto's consideration of these fundamental questions but under the guise of contemporary black artists asking what strategy now, "After Modernism, after Hibernation"? The answer is sought in recent poems by Michael Harper, Robert Hayden, and Jay Wright. Hibernation, defined by Ralph Ellison as "a covert preparation for a more overt action," becomes for Stepto "artistic apprenticeship," and posthibernation the initiated aesthete's state of mind. Instead of seeing or seeking new social ideas and forms for collective and personal liberation, he describes an isolated literary strategy of self-discovery, purification, and Orphic sacrifice to achieve a paradoxical "postapprenticeship" transcendence of and immanence in "the posthibernation terrain." Thus the modernist quietist fathers—Yeats, Eliot, Stevens—are overcome in what seems only another self-contained flowering of Yale's fantastic Bloom. One is at least puzzled how the Yale graduate program in Afro-American studies finds a powerful direction from such vapid instructions as these:

What must be understood [in Jay Wright's poems] is the fundamental incongruence between the idea of nation and that of historical field (and, hence, the distinction between static and perpetually evolving centers of spirit) which informs the dyeli's ["another namer of names" . . . a tribal African "professional archivist"] song of self-discovery much as it influences the Harper and Hayden poems. *Invisible Man* calls for certain very particular universal, as opposed to national, images . . . which live and enliven the living principally because they are not constrained by national or generic boundaries. Harper's emblem of the apple tree (blossom *and* root) and Hayden's portrait of kin (in death *and* dance) are such images; they are evolving centers of spirit.

But how does this carry us beyond Yeats into postmodernism, out of the tower onto the posthibernation terrain? Harper's major, though least accessible poem, "uplift from a Dark Tower," preserves, in fact, the whole traditional modernist perspective, is a shadowy, ironic, historical, allusive vision from Yaddo. Rejection of direct combat by black or white artists on the given American terrain one can well understand, but surely "national or generic boundaries" need not be seen or created simply as constraints, as destructive segregations, nor are they merely the means to "the poet's final destination"—a universal image like Harper's appletree or even, as Stepto surmises for the obscure Jay Wright, a cyclical posthibernation return to hibernation! Ethnicity and cultural alliances surely are humanity's principal means for socially coalescing, for politically cooperating and moving each other and each other's understandings. "To enliven the living in the historical field" requires a struggle to understand and change interpersonal and group relationships surely more pointed that Stepto's suggestions. He expects Afro-American writers to probe the paradoxical mysteries of an aesthetic, cosmic, or intrapersonal "X created by the travels of speech and rite along and across geographies of circumference [that] becomes a '*'—a star . . . the light by which one's form is finally seen."

In "Elegies for Paradise Valley," Hayden recalls childhood memories of the Detroit ghetto. Here an acute sense of historical social interaction fuses with great generosity of spirit and is intensely evocative of personal and community strengths. The fifth elegy, calling of the roll of dead street people, evokes not only Villon's ballade, "Ou sont la neige de longtemps," but Dunbar's "Timor mortis conturbat me," and takes an honored place among traditional laments for poets. However, in "American Journal" Hayden concludes by calling "america as much a problem in metaphysics/as it is a nation earthly entity." There may be truth in those saintly words, but for most of humanity, certainly for the majority of Afro-

Americans, America precisely as an earthly nation is very much *the* problem. And it is a political problem concerning choices and change more than a moral or metaphysical, aesthetic, or epistemological one.

For the fiction writers too the most common posthibernation strategy seems largely to play an isolated waiting game. Individualized characters make their existential nay-saying witness before a tight, unresponsive community, as in James McPherson's trial scene, "A Sense of Story"; preempting the jury's decision, the oppressed black man "assigned himself . . . his doom" for killing his white boss—an option the Miami rioters protesting white justice are not likely to consider. As in Richard Wright's work, blacks here show scarcely more potential for supporting group action than does the white bourgeoisie. In John Stewart's "Shadows in the Moonlight" set in Yankee-haunted Trinidad, a black prostitute muses on her grim past and her daughter's similar fate. In Ernest Gaines's story an intensely isolated former prison inmate, Robert X, is last seen standing in the rain in front of the black minister's house; this challenge to the little southern town's civil rights leader is offered without expectation of effective organized action —either in 1968 or, apparently, now.

To the extent that this anthology weaves a thick texture of distinctly black (or, if it matters whose game it is, Afro-*American*) cultural experience, it does provide an expanding universe of meanings and thus multiplies the resources for productive lives for us all. Even as an alien among the special rituals, genres, allusions, and histories of this "nation," one need not be constrained by the differences felt. Responding to these offerings, one marvels and is puzzled, struggles to comprehend and joins now and then joyously in the social and shared meanings—the only kind there are. Still the limitations are those of a very special, privileged, professional class of artists and intellectual workers. There are moments when one feels not only ignorant or inexperienced in their special cultural ways—the more reason to read and reread so that individual difference does not demand social deference—but feels also and unfortunately cut out. And sometimes that inevitable limitation is made good by a general tone of well-being and largeness of group feeling. Only rarely does complacency, avowed elitism, obscurantism—the adoption of dominating one-upsman strategies of art or criticism—destroy the sense of our participating in a beautifully cooked, pleasantly intimate, yet suggestively varied family meal. The need is urgent to solidify more effectively and sharpen the social program of that cohesive but still relatively powerless black American minority that can vote 92 percent for Jimmy Carter and get almost nothing for its pains. Still a well-prepared meal is a delight, and this one achieves not only high professional standards but also lovingly bountiful proportions. It is a great American blessing that most of this particular group of black artists and intellectuals can still appreciate such large, familiar, human-family images. It is to the less contented black Americans, however, that we must turn for the expression of cultural forms and feelings available for political action.

Expatriate Lives: First Biographies of Maugham and Auden

Stanley Weintraub

Ted Morgan. *Maugham: A Biography.* New York: Simon and Schuster, 1980. xxi, 711 pp.

Charles Osborne. *W. H. Auden: The Life of a Poet.* New York: Harcourt Brace Jovanovich, 1979. 336 pp.

Describing a famous English writer's enseamed visage, a contemporary once referred to its "extraordinary patina of age. I have never seen so old a young face; it might have been overhanging a medieval cathedral during centuries of frost and sun."[1] In Ted Morgan's *Maugham* a photographer asks the novelist if he wants the lines of his face retouched. "Certainly not," he objects, "it's taken me 80 years to get those lines. Why should I allow you to remove them in two minutes?" (p. 556). The same writer? Storm Jameson, rather, had been talking about W. H. Auden, who once said of himself, "My face looks like a wedding-cake left out in the rain" (p. 320).

Since Maugham and Auden had more in common than their well-remembered facial furrows (despite the generation gap they died only eight years apart, in 1965 and 1973), it may be useful to look at their personalities, if not at their writings, together. For example, both William Somerset Maugham and Wystan Hugh Auden (like George Orwell and T. S. Eliot) left futile testamentary injunctions against biographies as well as against the publication of their letters. Nevertheless, several memoirs of Maugham appeared almost before the earth on his grave had settled, one of them by his writer-nephew Robin. Now a ruthlessly candid biography, authorized (but not censored) by his executor, is in print. Maugham would have liked none of these books. Yet in his lifetime he yearned for recognition as a major writer.

Charles Osborne's biography of Auden, the first of what surely will be many, also had the cooperation of his executors. An unauthorized three-volume biography of Orwell is now two-thirds in print, with a counterbiography authorized by his widow commissioned and in progress. And because Eliot has been the subject of several controversial memoirs, his widow is now editing his letters and seeking a pliant biographer.

Once beyond the grave there is little a writer can do to stifle the curiosity about him which his life and work have whetted. Only men of action, Auden insisted, were worth biographies —not writers, who lived more inwardly. "Biographies of writers . . . are in bad taste. . . . To be sure, some, in a sense all, of his works are transmutations of his personal experiences, but no knowledge of the raw ingredients will explain the peculiar flavour of the verbal dishes he invites the public to taste: his private life is, or should be, of no concern to anybody except himself, his family and his friends."[2] Even autobiography was taboo. "Literary confessors," Auden declared, "are contemptible, like beggars who exhibit their sores for money, but [they are] not so contemptible as the public that buys their books."[3]

Auden's will itself, according to his literary executor Edward Mendelson, is silent on the subject of biography, although elsewhere Auden said that he hoped "to make a biography impossible" (*TLS*, 4 April 1980). Further, Mendelson notes, Auden qualified his opposition to biographies of writers with an exception in the case of Anthony Trollope, because Trollope had written an autobiography which "leaves out a great deal," because he was also an employee of the Post Office and thus a man of "action," because he was a world traveler, and because he was "a very eccentric character." All of these reasons, Mendelson observes, also apply to Auden—even the stint at the Post Office, where Auden in the 1930s worked for its films unit. Although Mendelson adds, "I doubt there is much moral or legal justification for preventing a book from being written about a dead man," the fact remains that Auden was opposed to biographies of writers, presumably including himself, and asked recipients of his letters to destroy them. His intent was clear, but whether a writer puts a legal or moral embargo upon his private papers—or even destroys those in his own possession—his life remains literally an open book. "Burn this letter!" as an injunction has for centuries prompted the recipient to treasure the document; and given the monetary value of a manuscript (once the author is recognized), one can predict that few friends or other owners of literary or historical paper will indulge a writer's pyromaniacal whims. A single sheet of a contemporary letter—given the attractiveness of the author—can bring more than a thousand dollars in the auction rooms, and few people deliberately destroy dollar notes, let alone thousand-dollar ones. (One thoughtful and revealing letter from Maugham quoted at great length by his biographer concludes with the futile line, "Perhaps when you have read it you will oblige me by tearing it up" [p. 346]).

Whatever the private motives of Eliot and Orwell, it seems clear that Maugham and Auden, who both managed to live into the first years of their century when a public avowal of homosexuality was not public death, may have felt that the closet would be kinder to their reputations. And both spent much time abroad because their sexual lives could be better accommodated by other venues than London, where the Sexual Offenses Act of 1967 (already seen as inevitable in Maugham's last years) finally erased the 1885 clause which helped do in Oscar Wilde.

While Maugham lived abroad (mostly on the Riviera) after the 1914–1918 war because his first male secretary-companion, the American Gerald Haxton, was persona non grata in England, Auden alternated between New York and the Austrian village of Kirchstetten, where he shared homes with his sometime collaborator, the American poet Chester Kallman. Curiously, both Maugham and Auden married women they did not love, one living his life largely apart from her, the other residing entirely apart (but for brief friendly visits). In Auden's case marriage was an authentic good deed—a legal way to get Thomas Mann's daughter Erika out of Nazi Germany and under the protection of British citizenship. Maugham, on the other hand, had been flattered by the attentions of the estranged wife of a wealthy businessman, Syrie Wellcome, had a daughter by her, and married her partly out of guilt and partly because he thought the arrangement was a splendid facade. When Syrie wanted more than a facade, however, the marriage disintegrated into bitterness and recrimination.

Their biographers further document for each writer a single passionate heterosexual attachment. Maugham, at thirty, began an eight-year affair with Ethelwyn ("Sue") Jones, the beautiful but sexually promiscuous actress-daughter of one of the leading turn-of-the-century playwrights, Henry Arthur Jones. Although she would not marry him, she lives on as "Rosie Driffield," Maugham's most attractive female character, the first wife of the grand old man of English letters (patterned on Thomas Hardy) in the underrated *Cakes and Ale*. "You say," Maugham wrote to an American student, "that my women are unpleasant. That is a reproach I have often heard. I suppose it's justified. On the other hand let me say this: I have great difficulty in recalling in fiction or the drama the figure of what is generally meant by a good and noble woman who is alive and human; it must be a very difficult thing to create. Do not talk to me about the Shakespearean heroines; Beatrice and Rosalind are the only ones who are not fools or prigs. And then there is this: I belong to a generation in which women were in a state of transition. . . . The average woman of my generation . . . had neither the merits of her mother nor of her daughter. She was a serf set free who did not understand the circumstances of her freedom" (p. 346).

Auden's affair, at thirty-nine, was with a young and attractive New York woman, Rhoda Jaffe, who had been doing secretarial work for him. She even divorced her husband, probably in hopes that Auden would marry her. The two-year relationship nonetheless ended, without rancor but without marriage. "I enclose an impersonal (honest) love poem," he once wrote her, "which I defy you to say is obviously written by a queer. Lots and lots of love, darling. You are *so* good" (p. 223). One would like to think that there is some ember of the memory in

Auden's "Lay your sleeping head, my love,/Human on my faithless arm," but subsequent ambiguities suggest a boy. More elegiac about a broken idyll are the lines from "The More Loving One":

> How should we like it were stars to burn
> With a passion for us we could not return?
> If equal affection cannot be,
> Let the more loving one be me.

Critics will be looking into Auden's poetry of 1946–1947, and beyond, for evidences of Rhoda.

Paradoxically, Maugham was a far more complicated, yet more predictable, human being. Almost certainly the lesser writer, his writings may prove to hold up better than Auden's, an irony he would have appreciated, having grown accustomed to hearing himself referred to as one of the leading second-rate writers. (It was an assessment in which he reluctantly concurred.) Auden's finest lyrics reach a level Maugham never achieved in prose, but Maugham's best plays, short stories, and novels are likely to keep reaching more readers. In their lifetimes, however, Maugham's reputation gradually receded as Auden's escalated, and more than the quality and range of their writings was responsible. The writer, Maugham contended, "sees character through his own personality and so must betray himself in every line he writes. To my mind, in the end his work is interesting if his personality is interesting" (p. 346). Still, Maugham attempted all his life to conceal much of his personality from his work, exposing only a sour and world-weary irony which the public took to be sheer cynicism.

By far the warmer personality was Auden's. He cultivated audiences and readers through a quirky charm. "Sincerity," he said, "always hits me something like sleep. I mean, if you try to get it too hard, you won't" (p. 329). And he professed no great illusions about his writing. "In the end," he claimed, "art is small beer. The really serious things in life are earning one's living so as not to be a parasite, and loving one's neighbour" (p. 332). Maugham set his financial and social sights higher, but the stammer which afflicted him all his life and which reinforced his cultivation of privacy (the handicap was transmuted into Philip Carey's clubfoot in *Of Human Bondage*) inhibited public contacts. In any case, he preferred snobbery. Auden, however, practically invented the postwar traveling circuit of poets who read for pay at American colleges and universities, and for many his genial, ravaged face above a lectern and his gin-lubricated anecdotal readings became the reality of poetry.

While Auden thrived in bohemian fashion, the generation-older Maugham was sinking into a querulous and well-publicized senility, his body—but not his brain—periodically rejuvenated by the lamb-fetus injections administered by Paul Niehans, a fashionable and expensive Swiss "youth doctor." Maugham's years of paranoid decline are so harrowingly related by Morgan, and at such length, that one wonders whether the senile stages of a creative life deserve that many pages (sixty-four, plus copious endnotes) in an already long literary biography. Commercially, at least, the answer must be in the affirmative, for it is the period most discussed in the early reviews of the book, and their shock waves probably generated sales.

For the aficionado of literary gossip, no part of Ted Morgan's book is likely to be too long. Maugham published his first novel, *Liza of Lambeth,* in the year of Victoria's Diamond Jubilee and published his last in the tenth year of the reign of Elizabeth II. A lot of literary talk and a lot of literary tales are accommodated in that span, although Morgan also adds to the length of the book by pausing almost every time a new character is introduced to furnish a potted biography and an irrelevant story or two—often juicy. The result, while infuriatingly inartistic, can't be all bad, since the book was named a Book-of-the-Month Club main selection, a guarantee of the publisher's investment.

Commercial considerations aside, *Maugham* has the distinction of being the first full biography of its subject, and it is full indeed. The extent of its documentation is prodigious, although the biographer is far less sure of the factual background in which he overambitiously places Maugham. That failure damages Morgan's credibility. *The Yellow Book,* for example, was neither Wildean nor decadent (p. 49), and Fisher

Unwin's "Pseudonym Library" was not paperbound (p. 54). Wells and Shaw are cited as World War I slackers (p. 186), while Maugham goes off "to do his bit," although Morgan fails to note that by 1916 Wells was fifty and Shaw sixty. Writers from Thomas Hardy to John Updike are labeled as Maugham contemporaries entirely because he lived from one's generation into another's (p. 397); and the rebelled-against legal government of Spain in 1936 is curiously labeled the "anti-Franco side" (p. 493). Queens of Rumania and Spain are referred to at times when there were no such monarchs (p. 513), and "a new painter everyone [in New York] was raving about called Magritte" in 1949 (p. 522) happens to be an artist past fifty who had staged his first Manhattan one-man show in 1936. Such examples abound, the price of a zealousness in establishing ambience which is abetted by a failure in copy editing. A failure in editing at a higher level is visible in the book's prolixity, and in its violation of basic canons of biography. The biographer should have solid evidence before he indulges in mind reading, for example (pp. 478–79), and he should be permitted just so many trivial tales (as about the hairs in his subject's nose, p. 512) per yard of prose and even fewer repetitions of his thesis statements about "bondage" and bitterness which Maugham felt at the disproportion between his commercial success and the "second-rate" tag critics persisted in affixing to his writing. There are more restatements of theme than in a Tschaikowsky symphony.

Since Maugham wanted to be a writer even before he entered medical school, his decision not to practice was only dependent upon his edging into the literary trade before his medical training had to be counted upon for income. *Liza* made the break possible, but a string of unsuccessful novels and plays kept him living largely on a small inheritance until 1907, when *Lady Frederick* made it big on the strength of a daring scene in an otherwise Pinerotic play in which the older woman appears to the young lover (whom she wants to shake off) uncoiffed and *sans* makeup. The real daring was that of actress Ethel Irving. Other leading ladies had timidly returned the script.

Before *Lady Frederick,* Maugham was preparing to dip into his capital for a refresher course at St. Thomas's Hospital, so that he could apply for a post as ship's surgeon. After its success he could dip into his drawer for plays rejected earlier, and he soon had four running at once. Larded with epigrams just a bit more cynical than Wilde's, and exposing an English morality closer to Edward VII's private life than his public one, Maugham's plays made money and gave him the leisure to travel to exotic places he could now afford, to hobnob with the titled and the famous, and to write short stories based, like his plays, on accurate reportage and an ear for witty dialogue. He could even afford the time to take *The Artistic Temperament of Stephen Carey* out of the bottom drawer and turn it into his autobiographical masterpiece.

After *Of Human Bondage*, Maugham's problems paradoxically became more serious. As Auden once put it, in a line not quoted by Morgan, "The criticism that can be made of Maugham, as it must [be] of all but the greatest masters, is that, having succeeded in becoming himself, he [was], as a writer, . . . content to remain so."[4] Contentment may have had little to do with it. The artistic success of *Of Human Bondage* was one he could not repeat. (One goes through growing up only once.) He was rich and famous and had to live up to his billing, despite the need to mask the potential scandal of his private life and the obstinate stammer which constricted his public life. Becoming even richer and more famous was a torment Morgan recounts straightforwardly and chillingly.

The commercial colossus of Maugham's later years, *The Razor's Edge* (1944), would anticipate the lives of several of the next generation of English writers who emigrated to America at the time that W. H. Auden settled in New York. The novel charts the spiritual odyssey of a young man who, like those in the Christopher Isherwood–Gerald Heard–Aldous Huxley circle, found attractions in Eastern nonattachment. While it made multiple millions for the opulent-living Maugham (*Rain* had only earned a million), Auden—minus the stimulus of the Spender-Day-Lewis-MacNeice group which had helped make him the central poetic voice of the English 1930s—had given up the comfortable semisqualor of his New York flat to teach through the war years at Swarthmore College, where he lived in equally disorderly fashion on the first floor of an old frame house.

A distinguished poet—he had become famous in 1930 at the age of twenty-four—he nevertheless had to earn a living. In the late 1940s, back in New York, this required literary journalism, college lecturing, and the occasional published poem or slim volume. He looked, he confessed, like "an unmade bed," and lived a disheveled life (when not on the move) of morning writing and afternoon indolence which in no way, as recounted in Charles Osborne's biography, illuminates the writer's life or work. We accept the idea that the life of a commercial writer, as Maugham surely was most of the time, is likely to be crass. Yet in Auden's presumably more sensitive life, especially in the post-London years, we learn little of the tensions and the passions which generated the writings, good and bad. Rather we have chronicled Auden's tedious homosexual milieu in New York, interrupted intermittently by anecdotes about his opera libretti work with Stravinsky, most of them extracted from Robert Craft's books. Osborne's research (fortunately or unfortunately he knew Auden for twenty years) is based upon so limited a number of biographical sources that without Craft/Stravinsky the later chapters would be thin indeed. Typical is the quotation ending an Auden letter to Stephen Spender: "O, by the way, *Time* is doing a cover-story on me. I'm terrified" (p. 273). We never learn why Auden claimed to be terrified, what the story related—or if it actually appeared.

More so than Morgan, Osborne supplies the texture of the life without its meaning and without its drama. We learn, for example, that Pearl Harbor is attacked by the Japanese in December 1941, plunging the United States into the war (and presumably the West Coast in particular into hysteria). The next line tells us, "Auden spent a few days in California during the Christmas holidays, and visited the Mann family at Pacific Palisades, a suburb of Los Angeles. 'Auden was here to lunch with us, while Erika was at home. He was boyish and nice as always,' Thomas Mann wrote to a friend" (p. 210). We have all the facts—but the account is one-dimensional, all life having escaped. For a biography to have a context in which its subject develops, one needs more than unrelated facts.

Auden's "conversion" in 1940 from Marxist skepticism to the Anglican faith of his fathers is another case in point. Reacting from his disillusion with the Left, Auden, who "had been an extremely eccentric Marxist, . . . now became an equally eccentric Christian, one in whom the Audenish outweighed the Christian elements. He was able to accept Christian dogma more easily than Marxist dogma, or to at least pay more lip service to it, because it is, as dogma, less dangerous. . . . He had always, like most liberal humanists, accepted the moral tenets of Christianity. Now he was prepared to swallow its supernatural aspects as well for the sake, one might say, of a quiet life. Whether a quiet life produces better poetry than a turbulent life is debatable" (p. 203). The entire reconstruction of Auden's pilgrimage to Canterbury (which Auden never permitted to interfere with his private life) suggests a superficiality which is belied by much of his writing yet sustained by some of it. Osborne never comes to grips with the duality in Auden which was both artistic strength and artistic weakness, and remains for a future biographer to probe.

Osborne's Auden is a charming "character," but his *W. H. Auden: The Life of a Poet* is the surface account of the progress of a career, not the development of an artist; and rather than the dissection of his inner creative and emotional life it is a listing of its episodes. Even the fertile 1930s are without excitement, although the many published memoirs of the participants communicate an intensity of commitment they seem to have shared. The closest one comes to that is in each lump of quotation from Auden himself—and Auden penned enough reminiscences, often interjected into reviews and other occasional pieces, that an autobiography could be stitched together from them—and from the self-revelatory verse.

One of the more unlikely Auden lines to be self-revelatory, said the poet in his sixties, was one "which, had I intended it to be a caption for a Thurber cartoon, I should today be very proud of; alas, I did not, so that I now blush when I recall it: 'And Isobel who with her leaping breasts pursued me through a summer'" (pp. 56–57). Very likely, Osborne concludes, it was expunged from Auden's first book of poems, which was unsuccessfully submitted to T. S. Eliot at Faber and Faber in 1927 and represented the "frivolous" years at Oxford. Auden's verse seems to have become highly accomplished in short order after that, but the metamorphosis is only explained away in the poet's Berlin period by a sentence which is clever rather than useful: "Something in the much lauded Berlin air seemed to be conducive to both a mental alertness and a moral laxity" (p. 58). Why the Audenesque style and message spoke to its age as other post-Eliot attempts did not is never made more than a mystery. Many of the readers of the often obscure *The Orators* (1932), we are told, "found it moving and significant, among them a number who were to distinguish themselves in literature and the arts in later years" (p. 92). We never learn who they are (or were) or why they found it "moving and significant." Only Stephen Spender is quoted, calling *The Orators* "one of Auden's most vital, but also his most cynical, gangish and brutal work" (p. 93). The description chosen by Osborne is even more ambiguous than the work itself.

Spender, it must be noted, is thanked for sharing his memories of Auden with the biographer and for permitting access to his letters. Apparently one nonmemory is that Auden "entice[d] the virgin Stephen into his bed," an allegation Spender has since declared (*TLS*, 14 March 1980) "he neither obtained from me nor checked with me, and about which I alone today am in a position to give evidence." Deservedly, Osborne retaliated (*TLS*, 26 March 1980) by quoting Spender's letter to him which followed receipt of the American edition. In it Maugham's old crony thanked the biographer for "this scrupulous and well put-together book," which he found "extremely informative" and had read "with pleasure and instruction." Which Spender was more factual—the December one or the March one? And which Osborne?

Edward Mendelson is also thanked for reading the typescript, suggesting "useful leads" and correcting some errors, "despite the fact that this is not an 'authorized biography'" (p. 9). Yet Mendelson—who, according to the copyright page, gave permission for all quotations from Auden's published and unpublished work—has also weighed in with a *TLS* disclaimer (directly beneath Spender's) accusing Osborne of "amusing fictions in his new biography of Auden. Scholars and critics would be wise . . . to show caution in their use of the book." But it appears that Mendelson, too, had read the book in first draft, offering "about fifty" comments and corrections which were incorporated into the text. "About acknowledgments: do forgive me for sounding prissy and tiresome . . . but I'm trying to avoid making unnecessary explanations afterwards," Osborne quotes him as writing (*TLS*, 28 March 1980). "Could you possibly just thank me for reading the MS, correcting minor errors and one or two leads? . . . Could you also have a phrase about 'although this book is not an "authorised biography"' or some such form? It's all to make my life easier later." Is *W. H. Auden*, then, less "authorized" a biography than *Maugham*? And what facts are facts? As Osborne has discovered, biographers must take the heat for their facts as well as their nonfacts, and for the no-man's-land between them. And as Ted Morgan has learned, it is far safer to relate scandal about the relationships of one's subject with others if both principals are thoroughly dead.

There is yet another posthumous parallel. In his final years Maugham continued to punish Syrie (although she had died) by becoming paranoid about what he was leaving to their daughter Liza. Even though the villa on Cap Farrat was in her name (for tax purposes), as were many of his paintings, Maugham had the canvases taken from the walls and sold at Sotheby's, giving Liza only a fraction of the takings. Gerald Haxton's pallid successor, Alan Searle (addicted, like Auden's housemate, to cruising after rough trade), abetted the meanness, worrying about how he would maintain his style after his master died. Maugham did everything he could to satisfy Searle, even attempting to adopt him as a son and disinherit Liza on the grounds that she had been born before he married her mother. The courts threw out the adoption as well as the disavowal of paternity, but after Maugham died at ninety-one and was interred at the foot of the Maugham Library wall at the school he had excoriated in *Of Human Bondage* (King's in Canterbury), Searle sold everything movable in the mansion, from documents to doorknobs, before relinquishing it to its legal owner.

Auden's estate was also to be settled at law, but too late to make Osborne's book. Although Auden had left everything to his companion of thirty years, Chester Kallman, the harddrinking Kallman did not survive his friend very long. Then the Auden papers—the most valuable part of his property —went to the New York Public Library, as Kallman had told friends he wanted; but his father, a retired dentist of Maugham-like years, contended that there was no documentary evidence of gift and that he had inherited, in absence of a will, whatever had belonged to his son. In 1980 the Library won. Via the courts, Auden had paid his debt to New York for the happiest, if not the most creative, years of his life.

Auden, one might add, genuinely liked Maugham's work, however different it was from his own. Reviewing Maugham's valedictory *A Writer's Notebook* on the front page of the *New York Times Book Review*, Auden wrote, "We shall miss you. Of course we shall find new writers to read, but art, like friendship, is personal, that is, unique, and no writer is replaceable by or even comparable with another. Thank you for having given us so much pleasure for so long, [and] for having never been tedious."[5] Because one might say the same of Wystan Hugh Auden, we have only seen the beginnings of biographies of both men. The ice is broken.

Notes

1. Storm Jameson, *Journey from the North* (New York: Harcourt Brace Jovanovich, 1970), pp. 306–7.

2. W. H. Auden, foreword to *A Certain World*, as quoted in John Fuller, "The Private Face of Auden," *TLS*, 7 March 1980, p. 253.

3. W. H. Auden, "*Hic et Ille*," in *The Dyer's Hand* (London: Faber and Faber, 1963), p. 99.

4. W. H. Auden, "Notebooks of Somerset Maugham," *The New York Times Book Review*, 23 October 1949, p. 1.

5. "Notebooks of Somerset Maugham," p. 22.

For Mark Schorer with Combative Love: The *Sons and Lovers* Manuscript

Mark Spilka

D. H. Lawrence, Sons and Lovers: *A Facsimile of the Manuscript,* ed. Mark Schorer (Berkeley and Los Angeles: University of California Press, 1977), 624 pp.

A hefty volume, this facsimile manuscript of *Sons and Lovers* weighs about eight pounds; the handsome red cloth binding stretches 14¼ by 10¾ inches to accommodate king-size British pages; the spine is two inches thick to accommodate their glossy bulk. The volume can be read cumbersomely on desks or tables, but only heroically in beds or armchairs. Its price ($75) is also hefty and may stagger even heroic Lawrence scholars; but library purchases will hopefully ease that burden. It may help to know that my wife—who may be more impressed by conspicuous scholarly consumption than by armchair heroism—is proud to be married to a man who owns such a beautiful book. Certainly there aren't many coffee tables around with one like this on them.

The editorial apparatus seems slight for so grand a volume: a brief introduction by Mark Schorer and a supplement listing textual variants in the British edition of the novel; and even that list is confined to alterations, deletions, and additions affecting style and clarity. Lacking British editions, foregoing mechanical changes, American scholars can still follow the list with the Viking Compass edition, which runs a page or two behind British paginations—e.g., Compass 148 or 147 for British 149.

The contents consist of six handwritten fragments from the first four chapters of the penultimate version of the novel, then called *Paul Morel,* and the complete handwritten manuscript of the final version from which Duckworth's printers worked. The fragments—erratically numbered—total only fifty-eight pages; on page 3 of the introduction Schorer lists their page relations to the full manuscript in a footnote. The complete version —also erratically numbered—runs to some 540 pages. Lawrence's handwriting is happily quite legible throughout; as Schorer notes, even the excised passages can be deciphered. By his late twenties Lawrence had apparently much improved on his "execrable" scribble at sixteen, when like Paul Morel he clerked in a Nottingham factory.

The editing of this volume was Mark Schorer's last scholarly task before his death on 11 August 1977. As his final remark in the introduction suggests—"I have a journey, sir, shortly to go" (p. 9)—he had a strong sense of the fitness of this ending. In the famous essay "Technique as Discovery," with which he launched his own critical career in 1948, Schorer had condemned *Sons and Lovers* as a modern example of technical ineptitude. Lawrence had failed to use technique, he argued, "to discover the full meaning of his subject."[1] His well-known "impatience with technical resources," together with his use of fiction as personal therapy, had led to confusion rather than mastery of his themes. In this fictional exploration of his own early "sickness" as his mother's son and lover, he had become too personally involved with his material and had often contradicted his own intention to show "the crippling effects" of oedipal love.[2]

In this early application of New Critical formalism to fiction, Schorer himself contradicts two formal principles: He prefers Lawrence's stated intentions in his letter about the novel to his editor, Edward Garnett, to his actual intentions as the novel itself reveals them; and he takes Jessie Chambers's complaints against the novel in her memoir, *D. H. Lawrence: A Personal Record* (1935), at face value:

The handling of the girl, Miriam, if viewed closely, is pathetic in what it signifies for Lawrence, both as man and artist. For Miriam is made the mother's scapegoat, and in a different way from the way that she was in life. The central section of the novel is shot through with alternate statements as to the source of the difficulty: Paul is unable to love Miriam wholly, and Miriam can only love his spirit. These contradictions appear sometimes within single paragraphs, and the point of view is never adequately objectified and sustained to tell us which is true.[3]

Of course, both statements are true; they are co-existing conditions, and Lawrence even devotes specific chapters to their alternating predominance. In "The Defeat of Miriam" the mother's hold on Paul predominates and pulls him away from the girl; but in a subsequent chapter, "The Test on Miriam," where Paul finally breaks his mother's hold sufficiently to go to Miriam for passionate love, the girl defeats herself through her own deficiencies—on which her prototype, Jessie Chambers, might well be the last person to comment fairly.

Lawrence's intentions were far richer than Schorer realized, and in this early novel he had begun to discover the techniques needed to explore them. As Schorer rightly insists, "point of view" was not one of them, and without that Jamesian control Lawrence did sometimes yield to his prejudices. But he was more complex in his attitudes and in his own non-Jamesian techniques than Schorer at this point could allow. By 1951, however, Schorer had begun a radical shift in his own critical attitudes. In his introduction to the Harper's Modern Classics edition of *Sons and Lovers,* Schorer again traced the novel's many formal flaws to Lawrence's personal failure to confront his own split nature: but now he saw that self-betrayal as the first important sign of a lifelong "struggle for self-responsibility" and integrated being by which Lawrence would challenge the assumptions of his age and would become one of its "few truly affirmative writers." Within the space of three years, then, the "personal weakness" which so damaged the novel had become the source of Lawrence's future "literary strength"! It was a strength defined, moreover, by life-affirming motives, not by technical control; and within that context some of the novel's merits now began to surface—its "superb characterizations," the "intense purity" of its natural descriptions, the "shimmer" of "inside reality" even in its human lives and loves. What had caused so great a change of mind and heart? Apparently, for Schorer as for most of Lawrence's recent admirers, it was *Women in Love*. In 1953, writing on *"Women in Love* and Death," he came out strongly for the prophetic value of a novel which, however nauseating it seemed on first reading, was "so tremendous" in its intentions, "so central to our lives," that readers must for their own sakes "make an effort to tolerate it."[4]

In this brilliant essay the newly tolerant Schorer succeeds in isolating "the realm of psychic drama" as Lawrence's peculiar forte. Such drama poses problems for a genre defined by social context, he argues, which Lawrence doesn't altogether solve; but Schorer applauds his attempt to go beyond generic limits, and though still concerned with them himself, he seems profoundly moved by the novel's extraordinary power in exploring psycho-social conflicts through fluid, dancelike movements and visionary scenes. "No novelist speaks more directly to us than Lawrence, and if we can't hear him, we are, I quite believe, lost," he says eloquently toward the end. Then he commends to our unregenerate hearing "the real Russian bang" in the last fifty pages—"the death of Gerald in the snow, and Birkin's grievous pathos without him."[5]

Three years later, in his introduction to Harry T. Moore's *Poste Restante: A Lawrence Travel Calendar* (1956), Schorer suspends his formal reservations and celebrates unquestioningly the Lawrencian impulse to move beyond corrupting social contexts into healing landscapes.[6] In that essay too, as he defines the polar opposition of mines and fields, an unmixed view of *Sons and Lovers* emerges. Lawrence's ability to convey "the unique quality of physical experience," "the physical essences of things outside the personality," now accounts for "his power of communicating the spirit of places" in this novel, and becomes the basis too for his developing "sense of individual integrity and human relationships." Soon Lawrence would show how "deeply interdependent" men and places are, how "the corruptions of places and the corruptions of men are a single process," and how—to escape that deadly process—men must look for wilder landscapes, uncorrupted places where the "vital connections with life outside themselves" can still be kept intact.[7]

Schorer's newfound sympathy for Lawrencian quests was shown in other ways. In another essay of 1953, on the Florentine villas of Sinclair Lewis and Lawrence, he records how Lawrence had schooled himself in loneliness in the Florentine woods and had written *Lady Chatterley's Lover* there, backing "almost entirely out of society in order to give us this measure of it";[8] and in his essay of 1957 on *Lady Chatterley*, which became the introduction to the unexpurgated Grove Press edition in 1959, he connects that Florentine setting with *Sons and Lovers* country—the Haggs Farm and its environs which Lawrence still called " 'the country of my heart' "—and shows how the polarities of place in *Chatterley* derive from that abandoned but still beloved farm, where life values were first affirmed for Lawrence and the encroaching mechanizations of human nature first resisted.[9]

Thus Lawrence, slowly dying, beginning to build his ship of death, had come full circle in this novel—as would Schorer himself, some twenty years later, in his own return to the world of *Sons and Lovers*. It seems fair to say that his facsimile edition makes ample amends for early critical misdemeanors—though in fact he never quite foregoes them. He is still partial, for instance, to Jessie Chambers's account of Lawrence's self-betrayal as a man and artist. He presents it now, however, without comment as that stage in the manuscript's progress when Jessie, having moved Lawrence to retell the story of his early life "as it really happened" (p. 2), had been disappointed by the courting chapters, where he gives his mother the supremacy that Jessie thought was hers. In a similar vein, Schorer still has hidden qualms about Lawrence's early artistry; but he transposes them now to Duckworth's "brilliant editor," Edward Garnett, whose "drastic trimming" of ten to fifteen thousand words from the final manuscript implies that Lawrence—if not artistically confused—did in fact need heroic help in getting his novel into formal shape (pp. 4, 8–9). Schorer is so impressed by Garnett that—perhaps with Maxwell Perkins and Thomas Wolfe in mind—he concludes his introduction with twenty-four lines of praise for his editing to nine for Lawrence's manuscript revisions—the analysis of which he leaves, "reluctantly . . . yet happily," to younger scholars (pp. 8–9). Meanwhile he spends four of his nine pages tracing the manuscript's peregrinations from its completion in 1913 to its California purchase in 1963. His account of that purchase recalls the legend of his own lost book on Lawrence—in a steamer trunk that somehow disappeared—for which *this* retrieval may have seemed like partial compensation. Certainly he has retrieved for us this lost documentation of emerging stylistic power and its editorial redemption—now happily available for unreluctant study.

What the redeemed document reveals, however, is that Garnett was as much attuned to Lawrence's gifts as to his deficiencies. Heinemann, to whom Lawrence had first submitted the novel, had turned it down in July 1912 on the grounds that it lacked unity, that it was likely to be banned for want of reticence, and that none of its characters—not even Paul —commanded the reader's sympathy. Even a friendly advisor, Walter de la Mare, had felt that the novel needed pulling together and was "not of a piece," its real theme delayed "till half way through."[10] So Lawrence had again revised the manuscript—his fifth version!—and by November 1912 had sent it on to Garnett, who saw that it still needed the "drastic trimming" Schorer rightly praises, but who also saw its essential unity and commanding power, and—as we shall see—was not much troubled by its "want of reticence." Thus Garnett at once accepted the novel for Duckworth, and as Schorer acknowledges, confirmed his trimmings to irrelevant or repetitious passages, tonal lapses, minor matters of taste and consistency. If Lawrence was deficient in these formal amenities and still impatient with them, the essentially unified thrust of his novel was now quite evident. Unlike Perkins with Wolfe, Garnett did not create unity out of chaos; he removed whatever impeded it.

Lawrence himself was grateful for that sharp-eyed service. Though he had initially defended the manuscript for its patiently wrought form and its lifelike development (or "slow like growth"), when the proofs came in he praised Garnett for the jolly pruning, felt himself deep in his debt, and even dedicated the novel to him. Indeed, he hoped Garnett would "live a long long time" so as "to barber up" all his novels for him before they were published.[11] But such barbering became less and less necessary over the next few years. From the struggle with *Sons and Lovers* Lawrence had learned how to keep his own slow growth going without falling into irrelevancies; he became surer of his aims, more confident of the tone and manner needed to convey them; and as he moved further into the realm of psychic drama his creative intelligence burgeoned: he became his own best editor. The *Sons and Lovers* manuscript is likely to be studied less on its own merits, then, than as the initial phase of that development, when Lawrence first discovered the possibilities of slow organic growth and learned to proceed through successive versions of the same essential story. Unlike Joyce, whose static laminations Schorer so admired in 1948, Lawrence was a developer of kinetic forms; he moved through changing versions of his stories as he moved through changing landscapes.

The fact that he could "trim and garnish" when he had to may be incidental to that larger process. What Schorer makes of it, in his brief remarks, is accordingly worth challenging:

As for Lawrence's manuscript revisions, they provide us with a most astonishing laboratory for stylistic studies. Anyone interested in the operations of the literary intelligence at a high level can only exclaim with delight as he examines these changes. It is more than merely exciting to observe how Lawrence activates prose, his own, that was at first rather inert, makes specific the more abstract, censures his own youthful impulse to write purple prose and to overwrite in general, changes passive authorial descriptions into dramatic character participations, sharpens throughout and deepens his character delineation. These are only some of the kinds of changes that his manuscript reveals. His alterations require and will certainly have much closer examination than this and infinitely more detailed analysis. [p. 9]

Perhaps they do and will. But Schorer's five stylistic observations, while readily documented, do not take us very far into the operations of high literary intelligence; they merely show

Lawrence in the process of overcoming fairly obvious literary deficiencies. Here is an example of inert, relatively unspecific prose and shallow characterization from Chapter 2:

> Then he went upstairs to his wife.
> "How are ter feelin' lass?" he said.
> "I'm all right," she replied. "Why do you bother?"
> "Dunna thee ma'e th' beds, I'll do it."
> "All right—There's apples simmering in the middle drawer. Did you sniff them out?"
> "I didna," he said heartily, pleased.
> "It's a wonder, for you're like a mouse after cheese."
> "Ay, an' I s'll be glad on 'em," he said, with awkward thanks. [p. 42]

And here is the revised passage, written over the above crossed-out lines:

> Then he went upstairs to his wife, with a cup of tea because she was ill, and because it occurred to him.
> "I've brought thee a cup o' tea, lass," he said.
> "Well you needn't, for you know I don't like it," she replied.
> "Drink it up, it'll pop thee off to sleep again."
> She accepted the tea. He loved to see her take it and sip it.
> "I'll back my life there's no sugar in," she said.
> "Yi'—there's one big un," he replied, injured.
> "It's a wonder," she said, sipping again.
> She had a winsome face when her hair was loose. He loved her to grumble at him like this, teasing.

Lawrence was unsure of the last word, "teasing," which replaces "warmly and friendly" in his revision. In the proofs he would replace the final phrase, "like this, teasing," with the noncommittal "in this manner" (Compass, p. 28). But for me the word "teasing" captures more precisely the mildly peevish concession at stake in this exchange. In the first version, when Morel tries to please his wife she does him one better; her shift from peevishness to playfulness, his slightly fatuous gratitude, is merely flavorful reporting of familiar traits. In the second version we learn that she is ill, and Morel's verbal concern is deepened into a thoughtful action that catches and disarms her guarded hostility, converts it into friendly grumbling with a hostile edge; if she injures him now, he has also won for the moment her grudging and winsome acceptance of his gift. Our sympathies at this point are with him, and since he has just shut her out in the garden in the previous chapter, in his drunken anger, we glimpse an unexpectedly tender side of his makeup and of their relationship. A rather lifeless passage has been vitalized and made to serve the novel's deeper purposes. But aside from those marvelously terse adverbial observations —"injured," "teasing"—which speak so directly to feelings and relations, we gain little stylistic knowledge from our close examination.

It seems to me more crucial that this improved passage comes after several paragraphs devoted to Morel's solitary pleasure in preparing his own breakfast. Lawrence's detailed delineation of his morning habits is part of the novel's documentary function —what Doris Lessing would later deprecate as journalistic reportage on "the existence of an area of society, a type of person, not yet admitted to the general literate consciousness."[12] Here Lawrence exploits his inside knowledge of life in a mining community and in a miner's family. He describes, for instance, how Morel prefers to eat his bread and bacon with a clasp-knife rather than that "modern introduction," a fork, "which has still scarcely reached common people"; he tells us too that the pit-singlet Morel puts on is "a vest of thick flannel cut low round the neck, and with short sleeves like a chemise" (Compass, p. 27). But his effort to convey through such documentary details the typicality of a miner's morning is more than mere reportage. For the first time in his longer fiction Lawrence is getting into the conditional quality of the emotional life he knew best; he is getting into emotional rhythms, daily cycles; and the fact that he moves from those daily rhythms into an improved revelation of actual intimacies, dramatic instances of typical relations, seems to me instructive. Here we see the beginnings of those timeless effects Roger Sale long ago analyzed in *The Rainbow:* those paragraphs of conditional and subjunctive activity—how Brangwen *would* behave and feel in certain typical circumstances—followed by a dramatic exchange which animates those feelings for us.[13] Lawrence's immersion in the details of his own family life, before and after his birth, his attempt to document its typicality, and the enforced revisions by which he learned to animate the feelings appropriate to that life, prepared him for his later movement into the realm of psychic drama that best engaged his talents.

That seems to me one lesson we may learn from this "astonishing laboratory for stylistic studies": how in *Sons and Lovers* he began to work up those timeless moments that give what I elsewhere call a "religious dimension" to his fiction. His more conscious attempts to create such moments are evident in the floral scenes throughout the novel, on which Dorothy Van Ghent and I first commented in the 1950s.[14] Contrasting attitudes toward flowers in this novel—Paul's, Miriam's, Clara's, Mrs. Morel's—are for the first time in his fiction construed as relations *with* nature as well as with the self and others. One of the passages deleted by Garnett confirms the deliberateness of this pattern. In Chapter 10, shortly after Paul gets a job for Clara at Jordan's factory, he begins to bait her for her apparent aloofness from the other factory girls and from himself. In the excised passage he has avoided seeing her for several days after being impudent with her (see Compass, p. 266); then he goes down to discuss an order with her, his wrath hidden under a cheerful mask:

> "You are wearing a flower," he said. "I thought that was against your rule."
> "I have no *rule*," she said, raising the head of a rather bruised red rose.
> "No, of course, only a preference. But you don't as a rule, I believe, *choose* to wear the languishing heads of decapitated flowers, on your bosom."
> She let fall the rose with a sharp movement.
> "This," she said, "is a flower I found in the street."
> "Jetsam of lost ladies," he said. "I'd hold a conversation with it, if I were you—'The Rose and the Tomb'! Know that poem?"
> [pp. 373–74]

When she says she does not, he begins to mock her, then loses his head, saying they must act the poem out: he'll ventriloquise the rose, she the tomb, which she can do well enough since—as everyone feels—there's a skeleton in her vault.

Garnett cuts this passage because a similar argument falls hard upon it—one of many cuts where Lawrence gives more instances than he needs of the same emotional impasse. But this floral argument goes back to the scene in Chapter 9 where Paul scatters flowers over Clara's head as she kneels in the grass, in response to her belief that flowers "want to be left" unpicked, that picked flowers are corpses. "I thought you wanted a funeral," says Paul after his strange response to her forlorn beauty (Compass, pp. 238–39). Clara's bruised red rose in Chapter 10 is a sign, then, that she has moved emotionally closer to Paul, has begun to rue her unpicked state, and will eventually be ready for the smashing of the red carnations he gives her when they first make love in Clifton Woods. It is a relational sign, moreover, of a kind Lawrence would develop with greater depth and power in later fiction. In this novel it confirms his conscious movement in that direction.

Still other deletions in this facsimile volume will have confirming value for Lawrence scholars. There is, for example, Schorer's prize specimen: the moment in Chapter 12 when Paul, alone in his "pyjamas" in Clara's bedroom, waiting for her mother to fall asleep in a nearby room, pulls on a pair of Clara's stockings and decides that he must have her, then sits on the bed with his feet doubled up beneath him, listening for his chance (p. 472). Given the woolly warmth of women's stockings in bygone days and the coldness of British bedrooms, Paul may have done the sensible thing. But more probably the incident tells us something about his sexual confusions, his "ambiguous state of mind about 'sex' and 'soul,'" as Schorer notes (p. 5). And in fact Paul does identify himself physically with Clara in the previous scene in the theater, when, desiring her, "He was Clara's white heavy arms, her throat, her moving bosom. That seemed to be himself. Then away somewhere the play went on, and he was identified with that also. There was no himself" (p. 466; Compass, p. 331). Whatever the case, the stocking incident, which Garnett allowed to stand uncut in manuscript, was removed in proofs by a senior editor—possibly Duckworth himself—who seems to have censored several other scenes which Garnett allowed and which Lawrence himself toned down, involving nakedness and the kissing of cupped breasts (pp. 473–74, 491).

Obviously Lawrence's difficulties with censorship had begun even before the banning of *The Rainbow* in 1915. But the unusual point here is his early depiction of perverse behavior, comparable to the scene in the second version of *Lady Chatterley*, recently published as *John Thomas and Lady Jane,* where the embarrassed gamekeeper tells of being frightened as a boy of his future wife's pubic hair, which she had impudently exposed to him then, and of being unable to make love to her when they marry until she has him shave it off.[15] These odd sexual fetishes, now retrieved for public scrutiny, show that Lawrence felt closer to the Freudian outlook than he cared to admit. They are fair game, certainly, for Freudian and feminist critics, who have already made much of his homosexual and misogynistic leanings.

But Lawrence was so openly engaged in psychological self-exposures, and so willing to include Freudian insights within his larger and more creative purview, as to elude finally such reductive views. It seems more useful now to approach him through more inclusive problems, like the taboo on tenderness which he shares with many modern writers, and which he was able to resolve, and then only partially, in the late novel—*Lady Chatterley's Lover*—that he once wanted to call *Tenderness*. The *Paul Morel* fragments contain some interesting clues on the origin of that taboo in his early family life. Paul's father, for instance, is identified in several passages as being grossly sentimental in ways that offend his wife and children; whereas Paul's mother is characterized as unsentimental and straightforward. Morel's "sentimental play-acting" (p. 53) and "sentimental cravings" (p. 69) are given full sway in Fragment 5 when his friend Jerry Purdy comes to visit him while he convalesces, and he deliberately exaggerates his illness, adopting "a strewn, pitiful attitude on the pillows," and putting on "a worn expression" (p. 72). The dialectic as he plays up to Jerry's sympathy while his wife tries to cut through his feigning, and as he accepts two swigs of smuggled whiskey when she leaves the room, is that rare thing for Lawrence—an effective comic sequence; and Mrs. Morel's amusement at the "fondling, lavish affection" between the two men helps to define its indulgent tone. The scene is dropped from the final version, where Morel's self-pity and his wife's bluffness are more flatly exposed; but it helps here to set off a crucial difference between emotional honesty and emotional feigning from which certain startling conclusions can be drawn. Miriam's cloying spirituality and Clara's stifling possessiveness with Paul, for instance, come closer to his father's than to his mother's ways; and Paul's harshness with these women, and his inability to sustain his own affections, may stem as much from his father's poor example as from his mother's binding love. The absence of any doctrine of male tenderness in this novel, like that in *Lady Chatterley,* may not be Morel's fault. He tries often to be gentle with his son, and sometimes with his wife, but since his gentleness often dissolves into maudlin feigning or gives way to brutal rages, he sets a poor example to his son. Which may explain why the sexual doctrine which does emerge in this novel and which Paul openly derives from his father's early passion with his mother —the "baptism of fire in passion" that "almost seems to fertilise your soul and make it that you can go on and mature" (Compass, pp. 317–18)—doesn't seem to work for Morel, no more than it works for Paul's baptismal partner, Clara Dawes, who like Morel is sensually vital but emotionally suspect. Only Paul and his mother, unsentimental and emotionally honest, seem to qualify for maturity—perhaps because of their genuine affection for each other.

A fellow Lawrencian, Martin Green, once said to me that Paul Morel doesn't really have an Oedipus complex. At the time that seemed far-fetched, though I had myself emphasized the essential health of Paul's relations with his mother before his brother's death, *after* which he became her favored son and lover, and the genuineness even then of their affections. But I have since come to believe that Paul suffers, more importantly, from a male identity problem which owes as much to his father's emotional default as to his mother's ultimately absorbing and possessive love.[16] Immersion in the *Paul Morel* fragments and in the *Sons and Lovers* deletions helps me at least to clarify that problem. I think now that Paul Morel might well be able to share and sustain his affections with a tough-minded woman like his mother, a woman strong enough to give him a rough time and plenty of leeway while he works out his male identity problem for himself—a woman, that is, like Frieda von Richthofen Weekley. For Paul too is tough-minded, like his mother, and sensually vital, like his father; but when he goes to other women, he is afraid of blundering through their "feminine sanctities," as his father did before him (Compass, p. 279), and has only his mother's bluffness and his father's feigning to guide him. He favors the former, at some expense to genuinely affectionate relations; but with a tough-minded sensualist like himself, he might eventually arrive at the creaturely tenderness he senses in his father—and perhaps in Baxter Dawes—and make that his emotional credo, as Lawrence did in *Lady Chatterley's Lover*.

Immersion in this facsimile edition may have similarly clarifying effects for other Lawrence scholars. Those interested in the religious Lawrence, for instance, may want to look at some of the "lost" precisions of the original manuscript, as when Lawrence compares Morel and his wife on religious grounds:

He had no religion, she said bitterly to herself. What he felt just at the minute, that was all to him. He would sacrifice his own pleasure never, unless on an impulse, for he had plenty of impulsive charity. But of the deep charity, which will make a man sacrifice one of his appetites, not merely one of his transitory desires, he was quite unaware. He was strictly irreligious. There was nothing to live for, except to live pleasurably. She was deeply religious. She felt that God had sent her on an errand, that she must choose for God from her sense of right and wrong. So she kept undaunted, her sense of duty and responsibility bearing her onward. [pp. 20–21]

Lawrence crosses out most of this passage in the manuscript and revises it as follows: "He had no grit, she said bitterly to herself. What he felt just at the minute, that was all to him. He could not abide by anything. There was nothing at the back of all his show" (Compass, p. 14).[17]

Lawrence's reasons for making this revision become clearer in the next crossed-out passage in the manuscript, where Mrs. Morel is depicted as the sheep dog in charge of Morel's soul, who must bark in front of him and turn his own "petty meannesses back into himself," to keep him from straying, but who drives him mad instead with "moral suffering." The unhappy sheep dog image, the abstract comparison before it, and the desire to do better by Morel—to balance the terms of conflict—must have moved Lawrence to focus on essentials in both passages. Thus "religion" becomes "grit" and, in the next passage, shiftless impulse is more fairly and deeply founded in sensuality: "His nature was purely sensuous, and she strove to make him moral, religious. . . . He could not endure it" (Compass, p. 14). But as the sacrifice of moral ideas to emotional dynamics implies, Lawrence was shifting religious grounds as he revised his way deeper into parental conflict. Ultimately he would choose Morel's impulsive ways while on his own errand for God—the God of Isness rather than Oughtness—thus fusing something of his mother's religious "grit" with his father's sensuous spontaneity.

Still other signs of his religious heritage may be found in these pages. In the *Paul Morel* fragments we learn, surprisingly, that Mrs. Morel not only befriends a clergyman, here called Mr. Revell, but also composes his sermons for him. Clumsy in his speech, scoffed at by the miners and tradespeople, he turns to her for translations of his ideas into terms and circumstances which will appeal to his congregation (Fragment 3, pp. 47–52). In the completed version, moreover, we get a sample of one such sermon, deleted by Garnett, on the Wedding at Cana. The minister, here called Mr. Heaton, has just interpreted the changing of water into wine as a symbol of the transformation into spirit of "the ordinary life, even the blood, of the married husband and wife, which had before been uninspired, . . . because when love enters, the whole spiritual constitution of a man changes, is filled with the Holy Ghost" (Compass, p. 33). Mrs. Morel, who thinks to herself that the poor man, his young wife dead, has made his love into the Holy Ghost, then says aloud:

"No, . . . don't make things into symbols. Say: 'it was a wedding, and the wine ran out. Then the father-in-law was put about, because there was nothing to offer the guests, except water—there was no tea, no coffee, in those days, only wine. And how would he like to see all the people sitting with glasses of water in front of them. The host and his wife were ashamed, the bride was miserable, and the bridegroom was disagreeable. And Jesus saw them whispering together, and looking worried. And He knew they were poor. They were only, perhaps, farm-labouring people. So He thought to himself 'What a shame! All the wedding spoiled.' And so He made wine, as quickly as he could. You can say, wine isn't beer, not so intoxicating—and people in the East never get drunk. It's getting drunk makes beer so bad."

The poor man looked at her. He wanted badly to say how human love is the presence of the Holy Ghost, making the lovers divine and immortal. Mrs. Morel insisted on his making the bible real to the people, and on his having only bits of his own stuff in between. They were both very excited, and very happy. [p. 54]

At this point her son William enters and Mrs. Morel, beginning to make tea, hopes that her husband won't intrude upon her happiness. Garnett cut the passage, apparently, because it fails to advance that intrusion. But it adds a dimension to Mrs. Morel's life and character as a gifted woman who can only reach others by "bullying her clergyman over his sermons" (p. 54); and, beyond the novel itself, it gives us an example of how Lawrence's mother must have influenced his own later penchant for literary sermons. In *The Man Who Died* (1928) Lawrence would himself attempt to make a bible story more real to people of his own post-Christian persuasion; and in earlier works, like *The Rainbow* (1915) and *Women in Love* (1920), he would restore the Holy Ghost to his own earthy version of mystic marriage, whereby blood (rather than love) enters the spiritual constitution of his characters and brings the Holy Ghost to life. He was like his spirited mother, then, in trying to bring "quaint and fantastic" religious ideas "judiciously to earth" (Compass, p. 33); and like his mother's minister in his spirited view of sensual relations.

In a later passage deleted by Garnett, Paul discusses a Good Friday sermon with the Leivers family. They listen avidly as he tries—"earnest and wrathful"—to show them how the minister spoiled the bible chapter chosen as his text. "It was thus Miriam loved him," writes Lawrence, and he then indicates that it was the Disciple in Paul, the presence of the Messiah, that Miriam loved, and not the man (pp. 314–15). The passage repeats things we already know about Paul and Miriam; but it also helps to explain why his mother's religious grit appeals more to Paul than Miriam's religious adoration; and if we extend our view to Ursula's earthy scorn, in *Women in Love*, which appeals more to Birkin than the love of spiritual brides like Hermione, we begin to understand why Lawrence himself preferred Frieda's combative love to that of adoring disciples like Dorothy Brett, who also confused the preacher in him, or even the poet, with the man who contained them. It took grit, scorn, and battle, apparently, to rouse that inclusive but elusive fellow into godly being, and he liked ladies who would do that for him.

It may have been in recognition of such distinctions that Mark Schorer concludes his remarks in the supplement on textual variants with a fitting coincidence: "I am delivering the editorial apparatus for this publication to the people at the University of California Press on, as only I now see, the anniversary of Lawrence's birth, September 11, 1885. Can one image him alive today, in *this* world, at ninety-one? Where? In Taos? A shaky Dorothy Brett, still there, supporting his shaky frame? Impossible!" (p. 610).

Of course, Brett is dead now; so too is Schorer; and if I compliment him on coming closer to the rousable Lawrence in his supplement than in his introduction, it is not from any lack of gratitude for his labors. I agree, for the most part, with his heroic view of Garnett's editing. Nonetheless, as I have been laboring to show myself, it is that emerging hero Lawrence, with the gallant Frieda at his back, who provides us all with rich fare for literary redemption.

I have not touched on all that resurrected fare: the library scene in which Paul eagerly waits for Miriam; the alley scene in which the weird religious cries of the "Barm-O" man counterpoint an irate neighbor's attack on William's conduct; the several passages in which Paul's attitudes toward the new feminism seem more sympathetic than the printed novel conveys; the nice psychological touches like William's sibling rivalry with Paul and the common hatred of Paul and Baxter Dawes for Clara; the magnificent death scenes and others like them where the pen seldom falters; the improvements on the *Paul Morel* fragments in the final version; and still other scenes and possibilities which will bemuse Lawrence scholars for some time to come. My intent instead has been to show—as Schorer never does—that many deletions reveal ideas and preoccupations which helped Lawrence to become the man whose prophetic art-speech still commands our hearing; that some of those deletions might have been retained; and—to complete my own Lawrencian circle—that Schorer's inordinate satisfaction with them betrays his original misgivings about this novel, which, though now subdued, are still substantially intact.[18] But finally he comes to his task as a dying man who, like Lawrence before him, wants to build his ship of death out of vital literary strivings, and whose own vital effort is to deliver the recorded traces of those strivings trimly and efficiently into living hands. He performs this dying task, I think, with admirable success; but in *this* world, where all too many shaky disciples support our shaky frames, I think also that he would prefer a combative reception of his views, if not his labors, to an adoring one. To my departed namesake, then—much combative love, much thorny thanks for your last Lawrencian errand, much heartfelt praise for your own brave and godly going. *Poste Restante*.

Notes

1. Mark Schorer, "Technique as Discovery," in *The World We Imagine* (New York: Farrar, Straus and Giroux, 1968), pp. 3–23.

2. Ibid., pp. 11–12.

3. Ibid., pp. 13–14.

4. Ibid., pp. 107–21.

5. Ibid., pp. 120–21.

6. Ibid., pp. 147–61.

7. Ibid., pp. 152–53.

The *Sons and Lovers* Manuscript

8. Ibid., pp. 195–218; see especially p. 217.

9. Ibid., pp. 122–46; see especially pp. 123, 125, 130. It seems worth noting here that *Lady Chatterley* is Schorer's favorite in the Lawrence canon, the only novel that satisfies his formal and generic requirements while still appealing to his acquired taste for prophetic psychodrama. He believes that the novel concludes a history of Lawrencian forms (p. 132) and that it successfully combines social and psychic reality through its own richly symbolic form.

10. *The Letters of D. H. Lawrence*, ed. James T. Boulton (Cambridge: Cambridge Univ. Press, 1979), I, 421–24.

11. Ibid., pp. 476–77, 496, 501, 517.

12. Doris Lessing, *The Golden Notebook* (New York: Ballantine, 1962), pp. 60–61.

13. Roger Sale, "The Narrative Technique of *The Rainbow*," *Modern Fiction Studies*, 5 (Spring 1959), 29–38.

14. Dorothy Van Ghent, "On *Sons and Lovers*," in *The English Novel: Form and Function* (New York: Harper, 1961), pp. 245–61; see especially pp. 256–57; Mark Spilka, "How to Pick Flowers," in *The Love Ethic of D. H. Lawrence* (Bloomington: Indiana Univ. Press, 1955), pp. 39–59.

15. Lawrence, *John Thomas and Lady Jane* (New York: Viking, 1972), pp. 225–26.

16. For further discussion of the male identity problem, see my essays "Lawrence's Quarrel with Tenderness," *Critical Quarterly*, 9 (Winter 1967), 363–77, and "On Lawrence's Hostility to Willful Women: The Chatterley Solution," in *Lawrence and Women*, ed. Anne Smith (London: Vision, 1978), pp. 189–211.

17. Within these crossed-out lines the phrase "to live pleasurably" has also been crossed out and replaced by "the pleasant sensation of living" (p. 21).

18. Schorer's view of Garnett's infallibility should be cited here: "Every deletion that Garnett made seems to me to have been to the novel's advantage. Nothing important is lost, ineptitudes disappear, and the novel emerges as tighter and more smoothly paced than it would otherwise have been" (p. 9).

American Serials

Martin Roth

Bruce Granger, *American Essay Serials from Franklin to Irving.* Knoxville: University of Tennessee Press, 1978. ix, 277 pp.

This is the first published study of the American literary serials, sequences of framed essays that appeared regularly in American newspapers and magazines during the period 1722–1811. Their generic uniformity was not exaggerated by Rufus Griswold in 1849, when he wrote that "an era in essay writing was commenced by Steele and Addison, in their periodical papers suggested by the follies of contemporary society. . . . This era closed with the productions in America of the Salmagundi of Irving and Paulding, the Old Bachelor of Wirt and his associates, and the Lay Preacher of Dennie." With the exception of *Salmagundi*, the range of structure, subject matter, tone, and rhetoric over the span of a century and through the urban cultures of England and America is remarkably narrow.

Professor Granger's study is a thoroughly serviceable work. It is sufficiently inclusive, sufficiently selective, and sufficiently summary for all purposes of contextual and background study to which these essays can be apparently put. It is (again, and throughout, with the exception of *Salmagundi*) as good a book as the essays deserve, since it can efficiently take the place, in our critical record, of the original material. To rest satisfied with the information and the extracts that this study contains would result in little if any loss of knowledge or pleasure.

There is only one further study of this material that I would like to see, a critical study addressing itself to the question of why these essays have so little to give us in themselves and why they seem so obstinately irrelevant to that other body of American literature that we prize, teach, and study—written by some of the same authors. What we have here is ninety years of continuous American literary production, often by the best available local talent—however limited that may have been—covering stretches of our literary history when there was no other interesting work being done. What we have here is work by Benjamin Franklin, Tom Paine, Philip Freneau, John Trumbull, and Francis Hopkinson brought together to discover an unilluminating sameness. The study I suggest would be something like those scientific experiments that are worth doing because they show no positive results. It would be a study in literary conservatism, a study in the literary armoring that hides behind the mantle of influence. There is something intractable at work here to go so far and last so long. It has something to do with the journal context and the essay format but more, I believe, with the civilizational stance of the originators—Joseph Addison, Richard Steele, and Samuel Johnson. (In the original serials, Addison, Steele, Pope, Swift, and Johnson submit themselves to a uniformity and interchangeability of voice, manner, and subject.)

What I have said and intend to say about the American serials treated by Professor Granger in his book is an overstatement, to be sure, and it is no more damning than similar generalizations addressed to the drama and fiction of this period in American literature. As there are exceptions to the former generalizations, so there are to the latter: Franklin's essay on *"Kitelic* poetry," early numbers of *The Prattler,* the sixth number of *The Old Bachelor,* and scattered parts of Freneau's serials. But a negative estimate is, I believe, implicit in Professor Granger's book as well, and it controls his strategies of commentary.

The American essay serials are, to use Emerson's phrase, sepulchres built to the fathers. They are manifestly expressive of extreme cultural inhibition, literary bondage. They were written by disparate talents who allowed themselves to become individually and regionally homogenized by the earlier voices of Addison, Steele, and Johnson. The influence of these three writers here is nothing less than scriptural. The American writers, for the most part, seem to be working under the influence of a power so hypnotic that they are content to reproduce structures and topics for no other reason than that they were *their* structures, *their* topics. And the commentary becomes correspondingly microscopic: "The members of Proteus Echo's club are not as sharply differentiated professionally as those of the Spectator. While both clubs include a country gentleman, merchant, dilettante, and clergyman, the Templar and Captain Sentry have been replaced by an astrologer and a Bostonian of unspecified profession" (p. 29). The casual rhetorical, substantial, and even referential appeal of these American essays is by and large to the moment of English origination. The intact reverence for Augustan moments present even at the end of this literary period is eerie: In 1794 Joseph Dennie writes that "the Public. . . . have allowed me the praise of reviving in some degree the Goldsmith vivacity in thought & the Addisonian sweetness in expression" (p. 146); and in 1811 William Wirt writes: "Is it not strange that such a work [*The Spectator*] should have ever lost an inch of ground? . . . What person, of any age, sex, temper, calling, or pursuit, can possibly converse with the Spectator, without being conscious of immediate improvement? [I regret] that such a book should be thrown by, and almost entirely forgotten, while the gilded blasphemies of infidels . . . are hailed with rapture, and echoed round the world" (p. 189).

The parameters of Professor Granger's work are the familiar "journeys" from didacticism to whimsy, essay to the novel, Addison and Steele to Lamb. But I hear rather a staying in place and a commentator who becomes increasingly grateful for a touch of whimsy (or the statement of a whimsical intention), the hint of a familiar voice, and a novelistic (or rather a concrete) moment of place and character.

If the content of the serials is the conservative impulse itself, that would account for their few energetic themes: the attack on American education and the literary criticism, a concern for purity of genre, tone, and style. Above all, what these serials express, and even express well, is a fierce misogyny, controlled by the Augustan serialists and Pope, turned inward in the Romantic period, but in the latter half of the eighteenth century often perilously close to rant, as in the early books of *Tom Jones*. What stands out as the central appeal of the Augustan serials is their criticism of female fashions and manners. Both in England and America, groups of men chose to write about women, about women's culture, however unfairly they portrayed it: of women together at tea, women gossipping, women putting on airs, applying cosmetics, entering into love intrigues, brutalizing their husbands. What stands out most clearly is their treatment of clothes and female nakedness; they chose to write about women choosing to display themselves, and it engaged deep anger: "Where the semblance of *modesty* is wanting, there is strong ground to presume the absence of the virtue itself. . . . Is there worth in the female, who tramples upon what she has herself been educated to revere as good decorum, at the capricious instance of an idle fashion-monger? . . . A despicable courtezan, who commands the gallantries of a vitiated capital, is often known to lead one half the female world by her fantastic whimsies" (p. 157). Franklin chose to be a woman, Silence Dogood; others chose to be connotatively womanish—the Prattler, the Meddler, the Busy-Body, the Trifler—or unwomanish—the Old Bachelor, the Pilgrim, the Hermit, the Philosopher of the Forest.

A "dream," like the following from *The Prattler*, is not uncommon in the serials, where the editor finds himself arraigned before a tribunal of hags and sluts and accused of sexual libel:

"At the upper end of the table, raised a few steps above the rest, a matron was seated, toothless, wan and meagre, to whom, contrary to the common rule, age had not given even the appearance of wisdom." On her left hand was "a sour-faced, thick-lip'd young wench" serving as clerk. "On her right sat a pert-looking hussey who seemed conscious of her superior rank and qualities. Her face was well nigh eclipsed by a huge deep *Frizet*, or kind of wig, that covered her head; and she seemed to be a very leading person in the *Convention*. . . ." The other members were a motley group: "Some wore aprons, and some carried baskets, and some greasy bags, the ensigns of their various callings; for some of all callings made a part of this august body—*Orange Maids, Poulterers, Pastry-Women, Leather-dressers,* and God *knows how many more.*" Silence being commanded, the matron charged me with being "the writer and promoter of many *infamous Lampoons*" against her sex. [pp. 58–59]

By all accounts, the American serials, even from the pens of such firebrands as Tom Paine and Philip Freneau, are conservative and a force for politeness, but that can be largely construed as a generic intention to monitor change in America and to retard or prevent any cultural or artistic development. If their purpose was to civilize America, and if that purpose was implicitly defined as holding to an Augustan line, a literary line primarily manifest in the early serials, then one can understand the pathos of a sequence of literature which endlessly repeats the format, voice, and themes of the early serials themselves. One can see a similar sterile drama at work in *Modern Chivalry*, but that work is engaging because the formal elements of Augustan culture are identified with emptiness and totally alienated from the substance and energy of the American continent—a step toward the formula of Emerson and Whitman who would tend to identify Europe as form without content and America as energy without form. I believe that this may help to explain the attraction of Sterne, who offered the serialists a way of dropping out of the dilemma without facing it.

Our later, more significant writers touch the serials in various ways. Melville's first production was a short serial, "The Authentic Anecdotes of 'Old Zack,'" which he devoted to heterosexual erotics. Hawthorne may very well have been sensitive to the notion of the author as voyeur, a close looker at females and female clothing, a posture that appears in his most serial-like sketch, "Sights from a Steeple," and in *The Blithedale Romance*. We have long needed a comprehensive study of the American serials, partly because of their influence on writers such as Hawthorne and Melville. Now, at last, a book is available which introduces us admirably to this body of material. However one regards the material itself, it was worth studying as literature, and Professor Granger's book is an excellent example of scholarly summary.

Pope: "Practical Poetry" and Practicing Poetry

John Dixon Hunt

Morris R. Brownell. *Alexander Pope and the Arts of Georgian England.* Oxford: Clarendon Press, 1978. xxvi, 401 pp.

Dustin H. Griffin, *Alexander Pope: The Poet in the Poems.* Princeton: Princeton University Press, 1978. xvii, 285 pp.

Miriam Leranbaum. *Alexander Pope's "Opus Magnum," 1729–1744.* Oxford: Clarendon Press, 1977. xii, 187 pp.

Howard Erskine-Hill and Anne Smith, eds. *The Art of Alexander Pope.* Totowa, N.J.: Barnes and Noble, 1979. 235 pp.

Pope himself authorized those critics who try to see him whole. The *Epistle to Dr. Arbuthnot* suggests a mythic pattern in Pope's life—"That not in Fancy's maze he wandered long,/But stooped to Truth and moralized his song"—and commentators, in their turn, have tried to view his career as a coherent whole. Ronald Paulson's "Satire, and Poetry, and Pope," for instance, convincingly demonstrated "some elements of a continuum between his earliest and latest works"; Frederick M. Keener's *An Essay on Pope* tried "to read his works and his life together"; Thomas R. Edwards, Jr., scanned the whole canon with persuasive skill in *This Dark Estate.*[1] And, though Maynard Mack insisted in *The Garden and the City* that *"l'esprit de système* was foreign to his temperament," that very book offered a fine example of relating parts to whole by showing exactly how Pope's activities as a gardener at Twickenham functioned in at least the satiric works of the 1730s and 1740s.

Of the books under review, Morris R. Brownell's inevitably faces the issue of the gardening squarely. Indeed, the subject occupies by far the largest part (206 pages) of his work with sections on painting, sculpture, and nongarden architecture given much less scope (this, of course, seems perfectly proportionate to Pope's spread of interests). Brownell's approach in all cases is expository, leisurely, encyclopedic. He marshalls all possible references inside and outside Pope's writings to each of the arts discussed. The section on sculpture is perhaps the one to benefit most from his thorough gathering of material: This reviewer at least had never quite appreciated the extent of Pope's interest and active participation in the design and erection of items in the Poets' Corner, Westminster Abbey. His role as "overseer" there and as advisor on style and inscriptions and his membership on the Shakespeare monument committee are all clearly narrated, the relevant secondary sources used and noted. Pope's scorn for the misquotation of Prospero's lines on the monument's scroll ("that Specimen of an Edition is put on the Scroll, which indeed Shakespeare hath great reason to point at") nicely rounds off the section.

Where Brownell does not much venture is back into the writings from which he has so carefully prised every useful item. I was struck by comparing his painstaking narrative with Dustin Griffin's early pages on Pope's penchant for leaving behind him a fit memorial—whether in paint, in reputation, or in a "deathbed edition." In 1740 Pope wrote of his hopes "to erect such a *Particular* & so *Minute* a Monument of his & my Friendship, as shall put to shame any of those Casual & cold Memorandums we see given by most ancient & Modern Authors." He was, in fact, speaking of his correspondence, but as Griffin points out (p. 11) the deaths of Gay, of old Mrs. Pope, the impending death of Arbuthnot, and the speaker's own extreme fatigue ("say I'm sick, I'm dead") all contribute to the memorial, even lapidary tone of the *Epistle to Dr. Arbuthnot*. The two approaches by Brownell and Griffin to Pope's absorption in funerary sculpture, on the one hand, and memorial structures outside sculpture, on the other, complement and augment each other: it seems a slight shame that each could not have reckoned with the other's concerns.

Similarly, Brownell's exposition of Pope's architectural taste and practice is vastly more useful because more comprehensive than Howard Erskine-Hill's essay, "Heirs of Vitruvius: Pope and the Idea of Architecture" in *The Art of Alexander Pope*. But whereas Erskine-Hill attempts to re-view the poetry in the light of Pope's architectural ideas, Brownell is concerned only with setting out the details of those ideas and their translation into structural form. The fact that Erskine-Hill proposes that we should discover Pope's "temple-building in verse" (p. 151) and then offers a strained and implausible analogy between Palladian style and proportion and the *Moral Essays* does not affect my point that Brownell is essentially uninterested in seeing the poetic consequences of the other arts in which Pope involved himself.

That is a fair demand, I think, from literary historians and critics. Judged, however, as an account of one man's role in four eighteenth-century arts, an account of connoisseurship, patronage, and practice, Brownell's handsome and well-illustrated volume cannot be challenged. The first section of the book discusses Pope's interests in painting; and here Brownell does extend his analysis into the poetic consequences of those interests. Pope was an enthusiastic amateur artist, a frequent sitter to the other painters for his portraits, and a connoisseur.[2] Brownell rehearses all these aspects, including Pope's friendships with artists like Charles Jervas, Godfrey Kneller, and Jonathan Richardson, Sr. He then takes up the theme of *ut pictura poesis*, in particular answering Lessing's attack on Pope's literary pictorialism in *Laokoön* of 1766. The analysis is judicious and sensible, both in making clear when Pope simply invoked, say, sketching to illustrate a point about the "carelessness of 'talking on paper' " (p. 28) and in revealing how Pope was less concerned to force identity between the arts than to illustrate "the imaginative effect of figurative language" (p. 45). In discussing the frequent invocations of painting in his Homer commentary, Brownell makes clear that Pope, unlike Lessing, did not confuse painting with sculpture; in this, as elsewhere in his study, Brownell emphasizes the continuities between Pope and the High Renaissance, where painting was admired for its energy and action. So, in this first section at any rate, we are given some discussion of the relevance for a reading of Pope's poetry of his visual interests. Brownell rarely ventures beyond the sensible and obvious, as in the analysis of ideas of portrait painting in the *Moral Essays:* paraphrase of the *Epistle on the Characters of Women* does not, to my mind, adequately penetrate the theme at which Pope's poem directs its attention—how the slippery, volatile human personality can ever be captured except in a series of portraits. Brownell glosses the lines "Come then, the colours and the ground prepare!" as Pope advocating "mere sketches" (p. 62), which he says connoisseurs "prized above finished paintings." Neither do Pope's lines suggest sketching, nor is it surely true to make such sweeping claims for connoisseurs' priorities in taste.

But the important point about Brownell's opening section on Pope's involvement in and fascination with painting is that it determines the whole thesis of the larger landscape gardening section that follows. Within the first few pages of the book we are told that Pope's competence in painting and drawing was of considerable consequence later to his landscape design and architecture (pp. 4, 9, and 13). Now that is undeniable, though the absence of many finished examples of Pope's landscape drawings makes it still something of a surmise. But Brownell's thesis about Pope's gardening career is that it was fully and determinedly "picturesque," and much of the impetus for this idea comes from his discussion of Pope's painterly interests. It must be said at once that I think Brownell's emphasis upon the picturesque nature of Pope's landscape gardening quite absurdly exaggerated; but my objections are also partly based upon his conduct of the argument.

The thoroughness of Brownell's treatment of the subject is not in doubt. He surveys Pope's sensibility to landscape, as it is revealed in his poetry, his concepts of design, his influence on Twickenham neighbors, his collaboration with others, especially professional, landscape architects, his various attitudes toward different kinds of landscape—that of the great house, the villa, the *ferme ornée*—and his design of garden buildings. Much of this is scrupulous re-presentation and systematization of

Pope's Art 159

material already known, as well as some new discoveries and suggestions. (An appendix, listing views of Pope's villa, has in fact already been superseded by Morris Brownell's own catalogue for the exhibition organized in the summer of 1980 at Marble Hill House; this excellent publication with all the views of Pope's villa, grotto, and garden illustrated, including the Jonathan Richardson portrait of the poet in his garden with the obelisk in his mother's memory in the far distance, thought lost by Brownell in his book but now happily at the Yale Centre for British Art, is an important and essential supplement to the book under review.)[3] Among the more important of Brownell's new offerings is the suggestion that Joseph Spence's description of the gardens of Horatio in Part II of *An Essay on Pope's* Odyssey (1727) is "a unique and substantially accurate account of Pope's garden at Twickenham during its first decade of existence" (p. 125). We certainly lack good accounts of the gardens during Pope's lifetime, as Brownell laments.[4] Especially in his discussions of the villas of Pope's neighbors and the country seats Pope saw on his various annual journeys Brownell brings a solid foundation of information from county histories and contemporary guidebooks.

What is in question is the writing of garden history. Brownell shares with many other writers a teleological concept of the English landscape garden. He invests its early stages with the "myth of prolepsis," whereby what will eventually be realized is read back into beginnings; final outcomes are diagnosed in preliminary maneuvers.[5] Horace Walpole was among the first offenders in "The History of the Modern Taste in Gardening," and his version of landscape history has largely defined subsequent narratives. Brownell invokes Walpole (p. 146), who cited Pope's garden at Twickenham for its importance in the development of the picturesque style; but Walpole was writing long after Pope's death (probably in the 1760s) and in the midst of new concepts of gardening which included notions of the picturesque for which he sought antecedents from the times of his "hero," William Kent. When we are told that Pope had a "prophetic . . . eye for picturesque landscape" (Brownell, p.

101), we are being told about his successors, not about his own ideas, for he could have known nothing, obviously, of later picturesque landscape theory and practice.

The picturesque taste of the later eighteenth century was certainly nourished by a tendentious reading of congenial predecessors. It is certain, as Brownell rightly argues on several occasions, that Pope's Twickenham was "an important influence on the development of the picturesque garden" (p. 137). One had only to review last summer the paintings, drawings, and engravings that Brownell gathered at Marble Hill House to realize that during the later eighteenth and the nineteenth centuries a picturesque color was retrospectively applied to Pope's domaine. But that is an entirely different point from establishing how Pope himself viewed these same "scenes." Part of the problem, I believe, stems from Brownell's not distinguishing sufficiently the thoroughgoing aesthetic and taste that had established itself by the 1780s and Pope's undoubted pictorial enthusiasms, which were, however, not crazily applied to everything.

Pope undoubtedly valued paintings as forms which, training his eye to contemplate the real world, he then discovered in nature itself. It is also undeniable that Spence's *Anecdotes* records his invocation of painting techniques and structures to explain what he wanted in the relatively new art of gardening: "All gardening is landscape-painting" (Brownell, p. 133). And others spoke similarly of Pope's landscape designs: "Mr Pope and Kent were the first that practiced painting in gardening. But Lord Petre carried it farther than either of them" (Southcote, quoted in Brownell, p. 172). My queries concern whether such scattered remarks constitute as complete an aesthetic as Brownell constructs for Pope and whether we can read a picturesque taste from them into everything Pope saw or did.

Writing about Pope's visit to Sherborne castle, Brownell quotes his proposal to erect a tower on a neighboring hill in order to terminate the view from the "Deep Scene" by the cascade. From there the temple would appear, Pope wrote, "as in the clouds, between the tops of some very lofty Trees that form an Arch before it, with a great Slope downward to the end of the said river." Brownell then comments: "Pope's idea is a striking expression of the picturesque sensibility in gardening, a taste for the prospect of a classical temple through trees 'decay d' in clouds, as in the paintings of Claude. The description as a whole reveals at this early date Pope's 'prophetic eye of taste' for the picturesque" (pp. 116–17). For Brownell all prospects that Pope views are picturesque, all picturesque viewing is translated into garden forms; to clinch matters there is often a quotation that sums it all up. In this case it is from Walpole (never mind the date at which he was writing). Time and time again views that Pope contemplates are described as picturesque (e.g., pp. 114, 116, 132, 161), when there is little evidence in the texts cited to suggest that anyone before Gilpin would have eyed them in that way. Such sleights of hand are too frequent to ignore, and of course they build up for the unwary reader an almost irrefutable case for a picturesque Pope far ahead of his time. One particularly slippery example occurs when Brownell talks of the engraving by Nathaniel Buck (1733) of Netley Abbey, which is neat and topographical, and says that it shows how Pope's taste was far closer than Buck's to that of William Bellers's view of 1774. The discussion of Pope's visit to Sherborne is similarly glossed by an engraving of 1883.

The relentless application of his thesis inevitably pushes aside other versions of garden history, of which Brownell is nonetheless aware. He touches briefly and interestingly on Pope's habit of seeing scenery in terms of theatrical designs. At Hotwells, near Bristol, Pope looked down the Avon Gorge where "Rocks & River fill the Eye, and terminate the View, much like the broken Scenes behind one another in a Playhouse" (quoted, p. 90). In both pastorals and the *Odyssey* translation Brownell also points to theatrical implications in Pope's organization of imagined space. There is also the suggestiveness of "scenes" as a word frequently applied to gardens, including Pope's own. Now the close connections between garden and theater from the Renaissance onwards are an ineluctable element in early English landscape garden design; we have as yet little evidence available, but it was a theme—especially given Pope's own remarks—that deserved more examination.[6]

Similarly, whenever Pope may have invoked painting, it would generally have been classicized landscapes by Claude, Dughet, or their northern imitators. This aspect of his taste for pictures needs connecting with his (and his contemporaries') fascination with the classical past, including the classical past of villa and garden. Maynard Mack has argued that inspiration for the Twickenham garden was classical. Horace, Martial, and Pliny all provided accounts of Roman gardens. The difficulty was that few if any examples actually survived, and their forms had to be extrapolated, often tendentiously, from literary sources: Brownell quotes one commentator of 1740 to the effect that Horace in his Sabine villa "had that taste for wild natural gardening which has obtained so much among us of late" (p. 123). Robert Castell's *The Villas of the Ancients Illustrated* was a similar attempt to reconstruct Pliny's gardens, and surely it reflects the garden taste of the Burlington circle as much as accurate scholarship. But, further, antique gardens were often thought to be recreated, reinvented in Renaissance Italy; though Pope never traveled there, he had ample opportunity to talk with those who did and see relevant engravings. Some larger assessment of his gardening concepts as part of his ambition to make Rome of use, to make Horace and Homer speak good English, would have helped the balance of Brownell's discussion. He admits himself that the "idea of the grotto Pope describes [in 1725] is altogether classical" (p. 257); he is less convincing about its metamorphosis in the 1740s into "the architectural equivalent of the picturesque garden" (p. 270). Its continuities with Roman and Renaissance nymphaeums and grottoes—those, for instance, that William Kent so admired at Pratolino—are just as important.

Now Brownell is alert to these possibilities, but simply not eager to follow them up or to argue very effectively against them. Pope's "principles of naturalistic design" (p. 118)—an awkward, even misleading phrase—cannot accommodate the garden traditions which he did know and, eclectically, drew upon, even if it allows him comradeship with "Capability" Brown. When Pope looked through the Roman triumphal arch of the Oxford Physick Garden and remarked that "all gardening is landscape-painting. Just like a landscape hung up," was he not perhaps aware of the fact that this particular garden was one of several established by the Danvers brothers in the previous century and considered by John Aubrey to be among the first examples of Italianate gardening in England? At Rousham, too, the Roman-Italianate resonances are very strong indeed—in matters of design, iconographical echoes, even the naming of architectural features; I cannot help feeling that those associations and themes were every bit as important to Pope as his picturesque analogies. At Sherborne, Pope told Martha Blount that the gardens were "Irregular," which Brownell at first finds "surprising," since they contained many "formal features" (p. 114); but he argues that the irregular disposition of such elements jibed perfectly with "his own sense of the picturesque." Perhaps what we have here—and Brownell is surely right to make so much of this visit to Sherborne—is Pope's very unprogrammatic response to *variety* in gardens. It is perhaps less crucial that variety was a prerequisite of painted views than a strong personal need of Pope's (as Griffin's book demonstrates). It matches his own undoctrinaire taste for various architectural styles, which Brownell himself sets out; above all, I suggest, it matches the early practice of landscape gardening in the first fifty years of the eighteenth century, where we must recognize far more eclectic, atavistic attitudes than are usually allowed. Brownell even provides some intriguing evidence of Pope's taste for the "gardenesque" (pp. 116, 153), which is beginning to be considered just as vital a device in the landscape garden as the picturesque.[7]

In all, *Alexander Pope and the Arts of Georgian England* is a spacious, well-documented, and thorough study. Its partiality for its subject at times exceeds the evidence, as when "it can be convincingly demonstrated" that Twickenham was a major influence on Hagley (p. 219) or the Leasowes (p. 235) only to dwindle a few pages later into "circumstances suggest" (p. 221) or "the possibility" (p. 237). Pope did not, perhaps, play as central a role in gardening history as Brownell would like to admit; perhaps if he had known of William Brogden's work on Stephen Switzer he would have been able to right the balance.[8]

And fondness for one's subject is no bad thing: a small appendix challenges the myth of Pope's indifference to music and uses one of Spence's *Anecdotes* to suggest a rebuttal of the late eighteenth-century story of hostility to Handel.

Pope's gardening is of consequence, not just because it was, so to speak, there, but because he himself saw its connections with his writing. The "Practical Poetry" of gardening is rarely separated from his other concerns: as Swift inquired of Bolingbroke in 1730, "Pray my Lord how are the gardens? have you taken down the mount, and removed the yew hedges? have you not bad weather for the spring-corn? has Mr Pope gone farther in his Ethic Poems?" And it was in connection with his ambitious project to write a series of ethical poems that Pope made the famous remark to Spence in 1730 that "there in particular some of ye Gardening Poem will be of Service." The reference is to the "Epistle to Burlington," the first to be published of the *Moral Essays,* though eventually accorded fourth place in their sequence. It is a remark that has always intrigued me, and I once tried to argue what service a poem about gardening could have provided.[9] As Brownell's work does not concern itself much with relating Pope's interest in other arts to his career as a writer, I looked to Miriam Leranbaum's study of Pope's "Opus Magnum" in the hope that some light might be shed on this matter.

Her aims are clearly stated in the preface and admirably carried through in the pages that follow. She proposes to bring together and evaluate all the available evidence for Pope's ambitious plan between 1729 and the poet's death in 1744. This involves some intriguing detective work, making what she can of hints and suggestions in Pope's correspondence, conversations, and such published materials as the withdrawn Index of the 1734 folio *Essay,* the footnotes in the octavo *Works* of July 1735, and the rare "Advertisement" of the 1744 edition of *Epistles to Several Persons.* There is no prolepsis here, and each clue is scrupulously examined without any sense of needing to place it in some *a priori* critical order. Of one aspect of her topic she is fully confident: "Certainly persuasive, however, is the sheer amount of evidence, however fragmentary, amorphous, and confusing, attesting to Pope's wholehearted concern with the scheme, beginning in 1729 and continuing through the planning and composition of the epistles he collected and published together in 1735 as Books I and II of the Ethic Epistles" (p. 129). Leranbaum's second aim is to examine the four epistles of *An Essay on Man* and the four *Moral Essays* "as inter-related parts of the larger scheme in order to suggest some possible ways in which our understanding and appreciation of them can be enriched by seeing them in this perspective" (p. vii). In practice, this part proves less ambitious than it sounds; though there are local insights, the full philosophical scheme of the *opus magnum* is not involved and her inquiry is maintained along lines which largely attend to compositional matters.

The book's detailed arguments are far too meticulous to be paraphrased adequately here. Through the continuing uncertainties and unsettled structure of the great work she follows what trails she can. In particular, she makes much of the two manuscript versions of the *Essay* in the Pierpont Morgan and Houghton libraries, using fragments not recorded in the Twickenham Edition; there is also a quite extensive comparison of Lucretius' *De Rerum Natura* and Pope's *Essay*. She suggests most convincingly from internal and external clues that the Latin served as "a formative prototype" for Pope's work (an important claim for a poet so acutely conscious of genre); the *Essay*'s ordering of subjects and the focus of each of its epistles corresponding to each pair in Lucretius seems well argued; yet, as always with this long-term project, Pope's dependence upon *De Rerum Natura* grew less as his own sense of the *opus magnum* grew clearer (p. 58). Nothing in its "uneasy patchwork growth" (p. 89) is easy to pin down; the *Epistle to a Lady* seems not to have been conceived as part of the larger plan until (Leranbaum surmises) Pope realized that by linking it to *An Essay on Man* II, via the *Epistle to Cobham*, it would serve. As she admits, this examination of Pope's long endeavor is hampered by his own vacillation between *système* and empirical disorder, between *thèse* and flux or variety of idea, between long-term project and immediate publishing or writing needs. Pope may not have liked "loose ends" (p. 3), and this tendency was confirmed by his later collaboration with Warburton, whom F. W. Bateson described as characterized by "a certain officious tidiness" (quoted by Leranbaum, p. 179). But in a poem which Leranbaum admits grew securely out of the *opus* project Pope contrariwise admits that "Life's stream for Observation will not stay,/It hurries all too fast to mark their way." On the one hand, Pope connects the two epistles on the use of riches to the second epistle of the *Essay,* which suggests his determination to shape a whole; on the other hand, the withdrawal of the Index in 1734 suggests a contrary uncertainty about his plans. Obviously not a poet to waste good material, the *Fourth Dunciad* is shown to have absorbed sections on education designed for the *opus magnum;* yet similar attempts to write of political education in the *Brutus* epic of Pope's final years, which Leranbaum treats lengthily in its relationship with the *opus,* came to nought.

My main disappointment with the book is that it does not make more use of Pope's poetic themes and poetic texture. The handling of the *Epistle to Burlington* may illuminate this, for nothing much is made of its "gardening" motif in assessing why and how it should take its place in the larger ethical scheme. Leranbaum talks rather generally of what she calls "basic themes" (p. 133), and her paraphrases of, say, the Timon passage (p. 113ff.) do not have the specificity of scrutiny that Pope's lines require. "Gardening" is apparently one of the "fashionable 'hobbies' " (p. 109) to which the *Epistle to Burlington* attends; but Pope himself hardly saw the art in those terms; nor would he have connected it exclusively with "prodigality" (p. 128). At the very least, as Leranbaum admits (p. 124), he saw landscape gardening as the expression of public responsibilities. Yet it was, he frequently acknowledged, *his* ruling passion and its prime quality of "variety" answered many of the complexities he was writing about elsewhere in his ethical epistles. Perhaps therein lay its opportunities for "service" to the *opus magnum;* but we are not told.

What is often at play even in Pope's ethical writings is some calculated image of himself—as contriver of ethical masterpiece, as sage surveyor of "all this scene of man" (a buried theatrical metaphor?), or alternatively as the local scrutineer of moss or minds. This was an aspect which, in the retrospect of Dustin Griffin's book, was missing from Leranbaum's. She quotes in her discussion of Lucretius the letter which Pope and Bolingbroke wrote to Swift on 15 September 1734: "The design of concealing myself was good, and had its full effect; I was thought a divine, a philosopher, and what not? and my doctrine had a sanction I could not have given to it. Whether I can proceed in the same grave march like Lucretius, or must descend to the gayeties of Horace, I know not, or whether I can do either?" Griffin acknowledges Leranbaum's discussion when he brings his thesis to bear upon the *Essay*. Here he discovers two voices, "his chastiser's and his Horatian voice" (p. 151). Further, he diagnoses two personal relationships at work in the epistles (and not coextensive with the two voices by any means), one between Pope and his reader, the other between Pope and Bolingbroke. And so he shows the *care* with which Pope manipulates his poetic selves to balance two divergent ways of looking at man without favoring either (p. 164); this is in addition to the more familiar dichotomy of the *Essay on Man*'s seeing both "cosmic setting" and the folly and pain of "human littleness."[10]

That is a fair enough example of Griffin's method. His *Poet in the Poems,* to use its more illuminating subtitle, has a fascinating thesis, set out with ease, skill, and some of Pope's own sprightliness; yet it does not yield as rich returns as one feels it should, especially when the materials it is tried upon are as resistant as *An Essay on Man.* It is a book that could have usefully received some pruning, for over texts where his thesis can offer scant return he proceeds in a rather expository way, as if the book were the outline both of his pursuit of a fruitful idea and of the need to provide running commentary on the poems in the mode of undergraduate lecturing. (That is *not* a sneer—Griffin writes lucidly, clearly, and with a persistent eye for what we need to notice about a poetic text as we read it; but not all of it by any means is apt and relevant to the book's main thrust.)

Griffin sees Pope learning throughout his career to use various poetic selves which have a complex and changing relationship to his "real" person. Pope was "plainly one of his own favourite subjects" (p. 3), and his career "may be described as his gradual discovery that he was his own best subject" (p. 100). Pope did nothing without calculation—Johnson said that "he hardly drank tea without a stratagem"—and his self-revelations in letters or poems are always carefully designed. Griffin seeks to clarify those designs. He invokes twentieth-century role-playing theories and notices that though "a role may be derived from the public world . . . it can be redefined and embraced in accordance with the needs of the psyche so as to become an integral part of one's 'nature' " (p. 22). This, of course, refreshingly complicates the conventional anxieties about the discrepancies between Pope's statements and his actions, about which Griffin's preliminary chapters are illuminating.

Pope's self or selves parallel his ambitions or frustrations with the *opus magnum*. Sometimes he entertains the notion that a self may be shaped and "harmonized" (p. 31); sometimes he has to view himself as a bundle of incongruities (p. 53); Griffin sees him making poetry out of each of these rival perspectives. But it is in the actual discussion of the early attempts to do so that I felt disappointments. There are some suggestive remarks about Pope's early roles—but for a thorough analysis of some of his Restoration selves (rake, lover) James A. Winn's essay "Pope Plays the Rake: His Letters to Ladies and the Making of the *Eloisa*," in *The Art of Alexander Pope*, is more to be recommended. There are chapters devoted to the works before and included in the 1717 volume, to the familiar epistles Pope grouped together in the initial 1735 quarto (before the four *Moral Essays* were segregated), and to *An Essay on Man*. Griffin is quick to admit the thinness of his case on occasions (p. 103) or its prima facie weakness (p. 127). But he works hard to shape from the materials a repertoire of selves. Insights tend to be isolated, but sharp: he develops the view put forward by Ripley Hotch that *An Essay on Criticism* is more about a young poet than criticism itself.[11] Pope's question "In Tasks so bold, can Little Men engage?" allows new complicities to emerge between the poet of *The Rape of the Lock* and its dramatis personae; there is some tough interrogation of the 1717 Preface to suggest that Pope manipulates selves both to protect himself from hostile criticism and to claim single-handed triumphs; the essence of *An Essay on Man,* as we have already partly seen, is argued as being constituted by Pope's "very self-consciousness as rhetorician and philosopher" (p. 129). But sometimes it is less Popean selves which he displays for our attention than simply "recurrent concerns of Pope's imagination" (p. 131).

In his final two chapters, devoted to the *Horatian Imitations* and to *The Dunciad,* Griffin moves onto more fertile ground. Pope set about presenting "my Self to my Self for Argument and Subject," just like Montaigne, in the 1730s, and in the case notably of the Horatian poetry Griffin of course finds that the territory is heavily colonized already; but he clears his own patch occasionally. He searches for "poetic autobiography" (p. 166) in satires that he calls "self-centered or egocentric" (p. 215); he says little about the Adversarius that is unexpected. Where he is, perhaps, liable to surprise is in his arguments that Atticus and Sporus are not simply antitheses of a self Pope wishes to celebrate, but contain, respectively, qualities he himself shares with Addison while wishing to stress the differences and "a grotesque version of himself" (p. 182). Griffin demonstrates that "a major 'source' " for the Sporus portrait seems to be attacks on Pope and that these personal hostilities are included in order to be confronted and, finally, repudiated.

On *The Dunciad* in its various manifestations Griffin's ingenuity is less conspicuous and more profitable, though to my mind he plays down the adventurousness of recent commentary and stays close to those recent critics, like Emrys Jones, of whom he does approve.[12] He suggests that the poem sprang in part from Pope's own need to distance himself from what he considered dunciadic labors in the 1720s. The "autobiographical document" that results, including apparatus and notes, displays Pope's real powers (p. 217): "as man and poet in the critical apparatus, as shadow-hero to Cibber, as narrator, as presenter and master of the show, as creative imaginer and transformer, as keeper of a mighty prison or monument" (p. 269). Above all, and here Griffin is at his best, Pope invokes theater imagery in order to display his own creative showmanship. Pope gives "Stage and Town" interchangeable status in *The Dunciad*, while the last chapter of *Peri Bathous* ironically anticipates the whole city becoming one vast theater; Pope views such raging theatricality with mixed feelings. But Griffin argues not only that Pope reactivates the old metaphor of *theatrum mundi* but goes so far as to imitate the pantomime impressario John Rich and revel in his show of dunciadic spectacle, upon which as producer he orders the curtain to fall.

Many of Griffin's themes and passing ideas get caught up in the essays collected into *The Art of Alexander Pope*. Pope's interest in freaks and monsters is the subject of Clive T. Probyn's "Pope's Bestiary: The Iconography of Deviance," a wide-ranging examination of how Pope's imagery links him with late seventeenth-century notions of man as animal (Hobbes's, Rochester's). The exuberant creativity of Griffin's version of *The Dunciad* is taken up by Philip Brockbank's "The Book of Genesis and the Genesis of Books," in which the presence of Milton, Newton, Descartes, and Leibnitz is kept alive through the reading of a poetic text which everywhere yields to its agile commentator the excitements of the natural world and of the poetic wisdom that attends to it. And, to give a final example, Griffin's references to the metamorphosis of public and private in Pope's texts are taken up variously and with skill by Frank Stack's examination of the *Epistle to Bolingbroke*, by I. D. MacKillop's "The Satirist in His Own Person," and Simon Verey's "Rhetoric and *An Essay on Man*."

This collection of essays, above all, returns us to a Pope fully active in an eighteenth-century context; yet his aptness for our own concerns is equally clear. It is a particular pleasure to find the poetry read so consistently well by all contributors, more dedicated to its richnesses and difficulties than to their own points of view (short essays do tend to eliminate the numbing effects of sustaining a thesis through a whole book). The tone, approach and standard are clearly and remarkably set by the first piece in the miscellany, David B. Morris's "Civilized Reading: The Act of Judgement in *An Essay on Criticism*." I confess it was by no means the first essay that I turned to in the volume, but that was my mistake: it is truly original and very important.

Morris takes issue directly with critics, like Griffiths and Hotch, who find Pope's ideas on criticism less interesting than his parade of being a poet. He offers, instead, the proposal that *An Essay on Criticism* "is an original and significant document in the history of critical theory" (p. 15). Basically, Pope creates a middle way between the two critical traditions available to him, that of Authority and that of Taste; neither will serve him as *principles* of literary criticism, and he offers to sketch the alternative, "a criticism of judgement" (p. 18). Yet judgment acts in a post-Edenic world of flux (altering customs, lapsing creeds, decaying languages), and it is for Pope the same gift as Locke's "probable reasoning," God's compensation to man for "want of certain knowledge." Its exercise must be attended by generosity (not the attribute of "coffeehouse witling" or "ill-tempered crank") and by due sense of propriety: this last involves obtaining and maintaining a sense of poetic wholeness, of variety (Pope's gardening concerns are aptly registered here), and of that sympathetic imagination by which we approach any author. Morris claims (rightly) that Pope attempts to place "literary analysis on the foundation of a coherent theory": he recovers for us, excitingly, an eighteenth-century Pope, yet, intriguingly, it is a Pope we need today as never before.

Miscellanies stand a better chance, one suspects, of not letting (in Pope's words) "The Author of the Whole escape." *The Art of Alexander Pope* achieves a more than average success. Pat Rogers meditates upon the "chemistry" of time and space in *Windsor Forest*, a powerful plea for the poem's integrity; Robin Grove follows, through Pope's reworkings of *The Rape of the Lock*, his increasing conviction that "amongst the things we value lastingly is mutability itself"; Felicity Rosslyn, considering Pope's translation of *The Iliad* XXII–XXIV, focuses upon his strong sympathies for old age, yet another insight upon the public and private poet. Prefacing all these eleven essays, Erskine-Hill's editorial introduction seemed, at first, surprisingly defensive. With contributors like his, who needs apology?

But then I detected larger and yet more local concerns. When I was taught Pope at school and university in the 1950s, he was still largely an Arnoldian creation; since then Pope criticism has decisively revised such nineteenth-century notions, and the books under review here all continue to do so. But perhaps it is Erskine-Hill's experience occasionally, as it is mine, that students still resist a poetry and a poet made anew in the last thirty years in ways which they should appreciate but still find it hard to do so.

Notes

1. Paulson, "Satire, and Poetry, and Pope," in *English Satire* (Los Angeles: William Clark Memorial Library, 1972); Keener, *An Essay on Pope* (New York: Columbia Univ. Press, 1974); Edwards, *This Dark Estate: A Reading of Pope* (Berkeley: Univ. of California Press, 1968).

2. The standard work here, upon which of course Brownell draws fully, is W. K. Wimsatt, *The Portraits of Pope* (New Haven: Yale Univ. Press, 1965).

3. *Alexander Pope's Villa, Views of Pope's Villa, Grotto and Garden: A Microcosm of English Landscape*, Greater London Council publication (SBN 7 168 1155 3).

4. A fragment of another account has recently been published; Malcolm Andrews transcribes this passage, from a manuscript tour journal of the 1740s, in *Journal of Garden History*, 1 (1981).

5. I borrow my phrase and my argument from Quentin Skinner, "Meaning and Understanding in the History of Ideas," *History and Theory*, 8 (1969), 24. It should be noted that Brownell expresses his own skepticism with Walpole's "History" on p. 172; but this concerns the evaluation of Kent at the expense of Pope in the early promotion of the English Landscape Garden.

6. I have surveyed the topic in rather broad terms in my "Theatres, Gardens, and Garden-Theatres," *Essays and Studies 1980*, ed. Inga-Stina Ewbank (London: John Murray, 1980), pp. 95–118.

7. See, for example, John Harris's essay, "Some Imperfect Ideas on the Genesis of the Loudonesque Flower Garden," forthcoming in the next Dumbarton Oaks Symposium of papers on J. C. Loudon.

8. Brownell seems to have missed William Brogden's Ph.D. thesis, "Stephen Switzer and Garden Design in Britain in the Early Eighteenth Century" (Edinburgh, 1973), and his essay, "Stephen Switzer. 'La Grand Manier,'" *Furor Hortensis*, ed. Peter Willis (Edinburgh: Elysium Press, 1974), pp. 21–30.

9. "Gardening, and Poetry, and Pope," *Art Quarterly*, 37 (1974), 1–30, which

reappeared, somewhat revised, as the second chapter of *The Figure in the Landscape, Poetry, Painting and Gardening during the Eighteenth Century* (Baltimore: Johns Hopkins Univ. Press, 1976).

10. The terms are Reuben Brower's in *Alexander Pope: The Poetry of Allusion* (Oxford: Oxford Univ. Press, 1959), p. 237.

11. "Pope Surveys His Kingdom: *An Essay on Criticism,*" *Studies in English Literature,* 13 (1973), 474–87.

12. Jones, "Pope and Dulness," *Proceedings of the British Academy, 1968* (London: British Academy, 1969), pp. 231–63.

Dreiser in the Making

Thomas P. Riggio

Yoshinobu Hakutani. *Young Dreiser: A Critical Study.* Cranbury, N.J.: Associated University Presses, 1980.

F. Scott Fitzgerald said somewhere that a writer's childhood is his capital. That Theodore Dreiser collected sizable dividends from this source is by now a commonplace. So it is surprising to come across a book that sets out to prove that "his fictional efforts and the history of his early life were inseparably intertwined" (p. 9). The argument in itself is not objectionable; in fact it is welcome, given the tendency in Dreiser studies to separate biographical and critical matters. Our knowledge of the relation between Dreiser's life and his fiction is fragmentary, mainly because no critical biography exists. Unfortunately, Yoshinobu Hakutani's book, despite the promise of its title, tells us nothing new about the young Dreiser. What Hakutani says about the novelist's life before *Sister Carrie* he derives from an uncritical reading of *Dawn* and *Newspaper Days,* and consequently *Young Dreiser* contains neither original biography nor fresh critical insights.

The question *Young Dreiser* poses is the oldest in the Dreiser camp, namely, "whether he is really a literary naturalist" (p. 189). Hakutani thinks not, believing that the roots of Dreiser's philosophical and aesthetic ideals are to be found in the experience of his adolescence and young manhood, not in naturalistic theory. Though this reasoning is familiar enough, it gains some authority by way of Hakutani's industry and the sincerity of his interest in Dreiser. He argues his point tenaciously for eight chapters. There is an essay on American literary naturalism and one on its French counterpart; a chapter on each of Dreiser's two bulky autobiographies; a chapter each on his editorial work and his free-lance writing in the 1890s; an analysis of the four short stories he wrote before 1899; and a final essay on *Sister Carrie*.

The *Sister Carrie* section highlights the strengths and the flaws of the book as a whole. Hakutani is best when he is synthesizing already known ideas, and the beginning student would find here a capable introductory reading of the novel that brings together the known facts of the book's history. His thesis, however, forces the reader into a debate that was news in Stuart Sherman's day. Hakutani does indeed quote Sherman and Philip Rahv on Dreiser's naturalism; and the thrust of his argument is to prove them wrong. The old straw men of Dreiser criticism—his use of "chemisms," his inconsistent determinism, the influence of scientists like Elmer Gates—are rolled out and defended to show that Dreiser was more than a half-baked mechanist when he wrote his first novel. Hakutani says nothing here that H. L. Mencken, Eliseo Vivas, and Ellen Moers did not say years ago. Moreover, his critical commentary often misses Dreiser's meaning. Of Hurstwood's decline he says, "Such elements as environment and heredity are not to blame for his downfall; he himself is to blame" (p. 188). If nothing else, this simplifies Dreiser's story, which tried to do away with blame by demonstrating how environment—and other physical factors, if not heredity—affected personal choice. On Carrie's appeal for Hurstwood he writes, "Why Carrie captivates such a titan as Hurstwood in the presence of his wife is not cogently explained" (p. 182). Hurstwood a titan? Was Carrie ever in the same room with Mrs. Hurstwood? Because Hakutani has trouble expressing himself clearly at times, it is difficult to know whether such statements stem from faulty thinking or fuzzy prose.

One must also wonder what the *Carrie* chapter, ostensibly the culmination of the study, has to do with the subjects of the previous chapters. There is no clear answer, since the book is more a collection of discrete essays than a unified exposition of a central theme. As I have suggested, Hakutani has a tendency to revive moribund topics, and the result is that each chapter appears to exist in a critical time warp. The pages on American literary naturalism, for example, bring together the points of view found in the work of Charles Walcutt, Donald Pizer, Edwin Cady, and Lars Åhnebrank; the section on French naturalists, much of which Hakutani published in article form in 1964, is dated in the same way. Hakutani's bibliography, in fact, does not list a single book or article written about Dreiser in the last decade. This fact helps explain why the central point of *Young Dreiser,* that Dreiser's fiction was shaped by "his American experience," is limited by the outdated notion that he is a literary anomaly, an instinctual writer who had no cultural predecessors. "Few American writers really interested Dreiser" (p. 32), Hakutani says—seemingly unaware that recent scholarship, recognizing that Dreiser too "must have had a long foreground somewhere, for such a start," has established his place in an American tradition that includes the transcendentalists, Poe, Whitman, Twain, Crane, and the late nineteenth-century urban realists.

As a result of such blind spots, what is valuable in Hakutani's approach—his insistence that Dreiser's biography be used to clarify his fiction, that even the journalistic hackwork is important as an index to his thought—leads only in a circle. That is, after determining that Dreiser is not a French naturalist, he relies on Dreiser's writing (*Dawn* and *Newspaper Days*) to prove that Dreiser's writing (the fiction) came directly from experience. The fallacy is too obvious to belabor, but it does open up the question of the connections between autobiography and other forms of creative writing.

Anyone trying to explain how fiction and autobiography complement each other might start with Henry Miller's dictum: "Autobiography is the purest romance. Fiction is always closer to reality than fact."[1] Miller means that the truth of autobiography lies more in the writer's conception of the forces that shaped his end than in the biographical accuracies over which scholars later grapple. The concealments, half truths, and fabrications at the center of classical autobiography, from Augustine and Rousseau to Thoreau and Henry Adams, point to the ways writers struggle to understand and articulate their private sense of emerging ego. In Dreiser's case, for example, what he had to say in *Dawn* about his mother's possible lovers probably would have no value in a biography of Mrs. Dreiser. But as a facet of Dreiser's psychological makeup, it reveals his persistent need to identify his own hungers with the people he loved. If, in this aspect, autobiography is an apologia for one's life, in the case of the writer it is also an apology for his art.

By the nineteen-teens and twenties, when Dreiser was writing his memoirs, he naturally patterned the account of his life in the 1880s and 1890s to meet the demands of his later literary biases. The meaning he imposed upon the past had a logic that grew out of his conception of himself as a writer. Henry James addressed himself to this process when he cautioned that art often creates "life," not vice versa. The unconscious revelations built into the metaphors, symbols, and characterizations of fiction are found as well in a writer's history of himself. Dreiser gave form to his own story in a manner consistent with the complex sensibility that went into the making of his fiction. In the case of autobiography, the job of critical inquiry is to ascertain the reality behind the expression, so as better to understand the mind behind the art. The naive assumption that there is a one-to-one relation between the personal narrative and the life leads Hakutani, as it did W. A. Swanberg before him, to read Dreiser's autobiographies as if they were exact transcripts of times past. In doing so, Hakutani overlooks the crucial fact that many of the theoretical positions Dreiser espoused ran counter to what circumstances had taught him. The major deterministic posture of his fiction, for instance, came under severe strain in his autobiographies, which plot a story of spiritual success achieved under conditions that make most of his fictional people look privileged. Those who speak of figures as diverse as Carrie and Cowperwood and Clyde Griffiths *being* Dreiser ignore how selective he was forced to be in creating character out of his own experience.

There is, of course, a sense in which the young Dreiser of the autobiographies illuminates his first novel. Both his story and the story of Carrie Meeber recount how individuals are cut off from the freedoms implicit in the beliefs of nineteenth-century philosophical idealism. This was not a popular story to tell then, and Dreiser was not the only one telling it. When he wrote *Sister Carrie*, Mark Twain, Henry Adams, Frank Norris, Stephen Crane—to name only a few Americans—had come to the same general conclusion; so had the European writers Dreiser most admired—Balzac, Spencer, Hardy, and Tolstoy. From these he learned how to look at his sister's life, and eventually his own, and make a narrative out of it that was important and moving because of the way he had of imagining action and character in fictional form. What distinguishes Dreiser from others on this side of the Atlantic is the completeness with which he broke from the prototypical American impulse toward unfettered freedom. His characters can no longer imagine a perfect freedom away from society, either in nature or a lost childhood. Instead they strive for a personal identity within a society where they do not understand the rules; a society that often strangles their natural impulses and shapes their pained consciences. But they show little inclination to transcend the social order, unless that term could be applied to their desire to conquer it. As Dreiser makes clear in the case of Carrie, there is only the illusion of freedom. Even if one avoids the fate of Hurstwood, even if one succeeds, there remains the sense of unfulfillment that an earlier moral realist called "the hunger of imagination." In such configurations of meaning and values Dreiser's history of himself has most in common with his fiction.

Though Hakutani chooses a less than productive mode of inquiry, there are a number of reasons to thank him for his work. First, he provides the reader with a precise outline of *Dawn* and *Newspaper Days*, which are out of print and rarely discussed in detail; and he has read the manuscripts, which differ significantly from the published texts. Also he has interesting chapters on Dreiser's editorial work and his freelance writing, and unlike most commentators he takes this early journalism seriously, arguing that it prefigures the concerns of *Sister Carrie*. Hakutani does not uncover unknown writing or deal with the textual problems confronting the student of Dreiser's pre-1900 period. This sort of original research is being done in several quarters, however. T. D. Nostwich's forthcoming edition of Dreiser's unpublished newspaper articles (Iowa State University Press) contains previously unidentified material directly related to the early short stories and to *Sister Carrie*. The new edition of *Sister Carrie* (University of Pennsylvania Press) presents for the first time a text based on Dreiser's complete manuscript, and the volumes of memoirs and diaries in preparation at the University of Pennsylvania all will add to our understanding of Dreiser's career. This kind of work needs to be done before a clearer picture can be had of the young Dreiser.

Note

1. Henry Miller, *The Books in My Life* (New York: New Directions, 1952), p. 37.

Eliot upon the Rood of the Times
Ronald Schuchard

Keith Alldritt. *Eliot's* Four Quartets: *Poetry as Chamber Music.* London: Woburn Press, 1978. 141 pp.

George Bornstein. *Transformations of Romanticism in Yeats, Eliot, and Stevens.* Chicago: University of Chicago Press, 1976. xiii, 263 pp.

Ann P. Brady. *Lyricism in the Poetry of T. S. Eliot.* Port Washington, N. Y.: Kennikat Press, 1978. 120 pp.

Lyndall Gordon. *Eliot's Early Years.* Oxford: Oxford University Press, 1977. xii, 174 pp.

Nancy Duvall Hargrove. *Landscape as Symbol in the Poetry of T. S. Eliot.* Jackson: University Press of Mississippi, 1978. xiv, 234 pp.

James E. Miller, Jr. *T. S. Eliot's Personal Waste Land: Exorcism of the Demons.* University Park: Pennsylvania State University Press, 1977. xi, 176 pp.

A. D. Moody. *Thomas Stearns Eliot: Poet.* Cambridge: Cambridge University Press, 1979. xv, 365 pp.

David Newton–De Molina, ed. *The Literary Criticism of T. S. Eliot: New Essays.* University of London: Athlone Press, 1977. vi, 217 pp.

A. C. Partridge. *The Language of Modern Poetry: Yeats, Eliot, Auden.* London: Andre Deutsch, 1976. 351 pp.

Balachandra Rajan. *The Overwhelming Question: A Study of the Poetry of T. S. Eliot.* Toronto: University of Toronto Press, 1976. viii, 153 pp.

M. L. Rosenthal. *Sailing into the Unknown: Yeats, Pound, and Eliot.* New York: Oxford University Press, 1978. viii, 224 pp.

Stephen Spender. *T. S. Eliot.* New York: Penguin Books, 1976. xv, 269 pp.

Stanley Sultan. Ulysses, The Waste Land, *and Modernism: A Jubilee Study.* Port Washington, N. Y.: Kennikat Press, 1977. xii, 92 pp.

Derek Traversi. *T. S. Eliot: The Longer Poems.* New York: Harcourt, Brace, Jovanovich, 1976. 238 pp.

At the time of T. S. Eliot's death in 1965 the criticism of his work had been policed and contained for three decades by fallacy-minding New Critics whose textual tenets were the guardians of the poet's private life. Every schoolboy had been catechized in the institutional view of his impersonal and discontinuous career. The skeptical poet expressed the spiritual aridity of the modern sensibility in *The Waste Land,* but after his sudden conversion in 1927 he turned his aesthetic interests toward moral, religious, and social concerns to become the pope of modern letters. Eliot scholarship, in the absence of challenging biographical matter, at least enjoyed interpretive consistency within this seemingly invulnerable schema, but critical studies had become exhausted at the hands of impersonality. Several critics already had begun to argue that Eliot was, after all, "interested" in personality, and some intriguing rumors had begun to accrue. But who would have believed that the seventies were at hand?

The fiftieth anniversary of *The Waste Land* in 1972 did not in itself save Eliot's reputation from eclipse: the rescue was effected by the discovery and publication in 1971 of the original drafts, which showed that the poem was indeed a personal document, and by the simultaneous anniversary of *Ulysses,* which focused attention on the two works as artifacts of modernism. Such activities also signaled the need for essays in revaluation, though *Eliot in Perspective* (1971) and *Eliot in His Time* (1973) were more appreciative and interpretive than revaluative. Eliot's uninvited detractors remained politely behind the scenes, musing over the astonishing information that

Eliot said his celebrated poem "was only the relief of a personal and wholly insignificant grouse against life," a clear invitation to pry into origins. During the festivities T. S. Matthews's incendiary biography, *Great Tom* (1974), finally blew the seal off Eliot's privacy. What began as a jubilee ended three years later as the critical extravaganza of the century. Over forty full-length studies and over a thousand essays lay at the base of *The Waste Land,* too late to shore up the ruins of impersonality.[1] During the confusion the biographical and psychological "fallacies" were relicensed to unmask the poet in or through his work. The sudden appearance of psychobiographical and psychopathological essays, subjecting to analysis Eliot's "fear and hatred" of women and sex, opened the door for looking at Eliot's poetry and criticism as the exorcism of neurosis.

The inevitable shift of interest to "personality" was a widespread phenomenon that grew partially out of a demand to rethink the relation between criticism and biography. In response, as the books presently under review began to appear, the Modern Language Association held in 1977 a special forum called "The Uses and Misuses of Biographical Perspectives on Late-Nineteenth and Early-Twentieth-Century English Literature," a hugely attended session that revealed the mixed enthusiasm, alarm, and uncertainty of panel and audience alike. In light of the work that has followed upon the breakaway studies, a theoretical and practical resolution seems distant.

This review examines a comprehensive selection of books from the last half of the 1970s which reflect the nature of the pressing critical problems of interiority and represent the ongoing concerns of Eliot studies. It begins with *The Literary Criticism of T. S. Eliot,* whose essayists sound many of the problems and attitudes that permeate the longer studies. The most truly revaluative volume of the decade, it reveals yet another impulse of the postcelebration period: the appearance of Eliot's less friendly critics to let the would-be martyr, whether self-imaged as Saint Narcissus or as Saint Sebastian, have his burning arrows.

David Newton–De Molina charged his distinguished assemblage to address "the question of T. S. Eliot's all-pervasive recent *influence* in literary criticism in English, and the question of his true or distinctive *greatness* as a literary critic." While the essayists obliquely or obligingly allude to these qualities, their common aim is to probe the authenticity of the work and to deflate the myths that encompass it. This is not a new development; vexed critics have regularly shouted out in periods of Eliot overpraise, notably Kathleen Nott in *The Emperor's Clothes* (1949) and Rossell Hope Robbins in *The T. S. Eliot Myth* (1951). What most characterizes these new essays is their collective cataloguing of Eliot's failures as a critic. While it is important to the present stage of Eliot studies that his recognizable failures be justly stated, as some are, his critics too often fail to bring a more just understanding to the familiar areas of prejudice and antagonism that continue to provoke them.

The late Professor F. W. Bateson's essay represents the traditional view of several modern critics who were early followers of Eliot, only to have him become, like Wordsworth to Browning, their "lost leader" after his conversion. Taking off from his earlier 1971 perspective of Eliot's "pseudo-learning" as an outgrowth of his Americanism, Bateson again asserts the inferiority of the poetry and criticism after Eliot's breakdown in September 1921. To Bateson, a "serious and profound" skepticism characterizes the pre-1920 quatrain poems, and the early criticism, which he believes anticipates the poetry, propagates "a sceptical social philosophy . . . that might have seemed to herald a new Voltaire" (p. 18). As for the emotional origins of the early poetry, he holds that it is "reasonable" to connect them with the death of Eliot's French friend, Jean Verdenal, and his marriage to Vivienne Haigh-Wood, though in the absence of sufficient evidence he leaves the matter to "literary detectives," such as James E. Miller, Jr., who makes Eliot's relation to Verdenal and Vivienne his special province in *T. S. Eliot's Personal Waste Land*. To a younger Bateson and other assiduous followers of the skeptical poet, *The Waste Land* came as a great disappointment: "It was, indeed it still is, chaotic and pretentious" (p. 8). Arguing that the poetry develops independently of the criticism after Eliot's breakdown, Bateson underscores Eliot's poetic admission that the twenty years between the wars "*were* 'largely wasted'" (p. 13). In the vacuum the early essays were left to become "unfortunately the ancestral gods of the non-political I. A. Richards and the dead-end critics of American 'explication'" (p. 18). Predictably, the later inferiority of Eliot's work is said to be accompanied by the displacement of the early skeptical voice by a "conformist successor" (p. 14) and by a "moral advance" that is more aptly seen as a "general social surrender" that led to "a return to complete respectability" (p. 3). Lyndall Gordon's *Eliot's Early Years* does much to correct Bateson's view of Eliot's skepticism, but from his own perspective Bateson catalogues Eliot's subsequent betrayals —the untimely conversion, the royalism, the "unsavory class-consciousness," and the "sheer snobbery" behind the criticism (pp. 14, 15). These querulous passages indicate one of the barriers to revaluation in the decade after Eliot's death: an inability to achieve the necessary distance from the man and his life.

Graham Hough's more balanced essay "The Poet as Critic" places the early criticism among the circumstances of composition to show that "Eliot was a critic in the old sense, like Johnson or Hazlitt. His criticism had to make its way in the ordinary literary traffic of the time" (p. 46). Hough also finds new strength in the later essays, which do much to resolve "an inconsistency between his formulated programme and the actual nature of his poetry" (p. 62). Giving new currency to C. K. Stead's earlier delineation of the dichotomy between "classical authority" and "the dark embryo" in Eliot's work, Hough cuts through the apparent discrepancies of tone to show the "uneasy union" of the critical and poetic voices, the formal critic creating, of necessity, a favorable milieu for the poet's "obscure creative embryo." The criticism that maintains its vitality is that which is closest to the poet's concern for the creative process, language, technique, and tradition. It is when the critic oversteps these concerns into social and religious problems that he becomes "deeply uninspiring" (p. 63). Hough's chiseled judgment of Eliot's extraliterary criticism is matched only by Stephen Spender's wry perspective: "On the whole, Eliot's social-religious activities make one reflect on how extraordinarily ineffective the Church of England has been in bringing Christian principles to bear on political life" (p. 241).

Denis Donoghue, in pointing to the failure of the *Criterion* to reunify the mind of Europe with a lost sense of Classicism, also explores the "friction" in Eliot's mind between his literary and social voices. As an editor, Eliot was his most valuable self when he put his intelligence to bear upon literature and critical ideas. But on the larger social and political scale his temperament was given to defining principles, not to applying them to particulars, so that in facing the acts that threatened the collapse of Europe, the insecure editorial mind was continually strained. To Professor Donoghue, "the whole effort was somehow artificial, a function of his will at odds with his talent" (p. 40). Again, Stephen Spender has his own inimitable way of passing similar judgment: "The *Criterion* resembles thick slices of bread with a little nutritious butter very thinly spread over it. There is much editorial conscience but remarkably little passion. . . . Current politics are discussed on the level of theory by theoreticians without influence or realism and there is practically no sense of the tyrannies, revolution, murders, tortures, and concentration camps going on in the world outside. Nor is there very much sense of the extraordinary vitality of literature in Europe and America during the 1920s and 1930s" (p. 236).

Other critics identify similar frictions and paradoxes in adjacent areas. William Righter's methodical probing of the supposed philosophical basis of Eliot's criticism shows the presence not of a directing philosophy but of a conflict between the general critical concerns of the synthesizing philosopher and the particular concerns of the individuating poet-critic who suffers a "philosophical refusal" when the critical act endangers the "aesthetic mystique" of the work. "It is," Righter concludes, "as if the 'philosophical critic' underwent some kind of imaginative failure. . . . The fragments of philosophical language add up to little more than a distant evocation of what they might have meant" (p. 137). Similarly, R. Peacock's absorbing study of Eliot's contribution to the poetics of drama reveals that his partial failure as a drama critic results from his refusal to shift the focus of his criticism from Elizabethan–Jacobean drama to reputable contemporary work. And W. W. Robson, in laying bare "the neo-classical trappings" of *The Use of Poetry*, asserts that "nowhere is the relation in Eliot between the innovating poet and the literary traditionalist more uneasy" than in this volume (p. 150). While the poet in the critic directed attention away from the personality to the poetry, the "attitudinizing" Eliot, Robson holds, could so condemn a personality that he single-handedly made Shelley "the least known of the major English poets" (p. 153). C. K. Stead argues more plausibly that because Eliot's most influential criticism failed to look at the Romantic poets squarely, "the Modernist movement perhaps lost the proper sense of its own inheritance" (p. 206). But nowhere are the psychological origins and effects of Eliot's antiromantic criticism examined as closely or as impatiently as in George Bornstein's *Transformations of Romanticism in Yeats, Eliot, and Stevens*, discussed below, where "in attacking romanticism Eliot combated not a historical force but a projection of his own problems," and "in denouncing Shelley he sought to keep down his own hysterica passio" (pp. 116, 125).

In most of these essays the degree of sympathy that the authors hold for the problems of Eliot the critic may be measured by their implicit respect for Eliot the poet. But there is little sympathy behind Samuel Hynes's long smouldering belief that "Eliot failed as a Christian critic" (p. 87). Professor Hynes covers much the same ground as others who have found Eliot's statements on poetry and belief, heresy and orthodoxy, and Semitism to be incomprehensible. The study brings much rhetorical questioning and suppositional answering but no new perspective to this troubled area of Eliot studies, the very area in which critics most often fail to bring a just understanding to their study. Spender sees Eliot's alleged anti-Semitism as an outgrowth of "twentieth-century political wickedness" (p. 230), and Bornstein's point of view should be quoted at length:

For Eliot, Jews aroused persistently negative responses. Additionally, he thought that introduction of Jewish names was somehow funny and could be used to show Western degeneration ("She entertains Sir Ferdinand/Klein"). . . . Just as the romantics symbolized deviation from the Latin tradition, so did Jews represent refusal of Christian orthodoxy. A man anxious to deny forces within himself has an insatiable need of scapegoats, and Eliot maintained one of the most plentifully stocked demonologies of modern times. Given Eliot's occasional denials of anti-Semitism, partly on grounds that such prejudice constituted sin in the eyes of the Church, one wonders what he thought anti-Semitism was. [p. 150]

Critics attacking an apparent weakness or inconsistency in one of Eliot's intellectual positions invariably seek support from his notorious statement in *After Strange Gods* (London: Faber, 1933) that in a healthy culture "any large number of free-thinking Jews" is undesirable (p. 20). Since this remark was made during the time of Hitler's rise to power, it is used to impute an indulgent racial prejudice to Eliot. How frequently will these repetitive accusations and emotional attitudes appear until a dispassionate critic reconstructs the historical social situation in which Eliot made his comments? In an age of growing secular liberalism, Eliot as a Christian did not think that a large number of free-thinking Gentiles was any more desirable for the preservation of religion as a basis for culture. The growth of religious deracination among large numbers of Jews, not orthodox Judaism, was Eliot's cultural concern. "It seems to me highly desirable," Eliot wrote in *Notes towards the Definition of Culture,* new ed. (London: Faber, 1962), "that there should be close culture-contact between devout and practising Christians and devout and practising Jews. Much culture-contact in the past has been within those neutral zones of culture in which religion can be ignored, and between Jews and Gentiles both more or less emancipated from their religious traditions" (p. 70). Eliot may have failed as a Christian critic, but not because he was anti-Semitic.

During the seventies there was an important critical turn toward establishing the lost continuities of Modern with Victorian and Romantic literature. George Bornstein sets out to show how romanticism is central to modernism, particularly how Yeats and Stevens gradually and creatively transformed the "Greater Romantic Lyric" into a modern poetic mode. His chapters on Yeats and Stevens, showing their altering responses to romanticism at various stages in their careers, are probing and provocative. The nature of Eliot's engagement, however, necessitates "special explanation" at the outset: "I see the underlying tension of his work as the conflict between the fear and fostering of explosive powers within the psyche often associated with imagination. In prose he externalized such daemonic forces and projected them most often upon the romantics, while in poetry he sought to snare the eruptions in a framework of order" (p. xii). In arriving at his view of Eliot's psychic life, Professor Bornstein apparently drew upon the biographical revelations of the early seventies, and while he admits that "suppression of biographical information hinders full understanding," he nonetheless assumes full reader acceptance of his psychological premise and boldly constructs a critical argument upon it. The unearned ascription of a psychic profile to an author's life, and the interpretation of his work on the assumed truth of that profile, seems to me one of the misuses of psychobiographical criticism.

Though Professor Bornstein declares that his aim is "not to devalue but to revalue Eliot," his revisionist study is often mean-spirited in its execution and tone and delights in turning Eliot's "warped" criticism of the Romantics back upon him: "One of the deepest perversions in modern critical adoption of Eliot's own contrast between Eliotic maturity and Shelleyan adolescence is its neat reversal of the truth" (p. 143). Bornstein's admirably researched narrative traces in Eliot's writings the stages of his "tempestuous" relation to the Romantics—from his early "psychic possession," to his subsequent "fear and distrust," to his partial reconciliation in *Four Quartets*. But the scholarship becomes facile and misdirected when Bornstein repeatedly attributes the cause of Eliot's antiromanticism to a terror of psychic disorders and holds that for Eliot romanticism was "a convenient brown demon upon which to project fears of personal and cultural deviation" (p. 97). The spiritual terror that pervades Eliot's poetry is greater than any psychological fear of the unconscious, and the failure to perceive the former understandably leads to a belief in Eliot's fear of the latter. Thus Graham Hough also observes that the early Eliot has been "excessively willing to stop short of any traffic with the unconscious," and he too shows that for the later Eliot "it is in this inarticulate region that the poet's conscious activity begins" (pp. 61–62). Where Bornstein loses his proper perspective, I think, is not only in a reductive psychological view of Eliot's emotional conflicts, one that neglects the presence of any guiding intellectual stance, but in having to devalue the poetry and its modernist techniques in arguing their imaginative inferiority to the Greater Romantic Lyric.

As a poet, Eliot is made out to be inferior to the Romantics, a poet of "fancy," mechanical "association," and failed vision rather than of imaginative "mental action." As a critic, he is said to write in fear of the Romantics, terrified by the violent subterranean forces which they readily accepted and guided toward vision. In his poetry Eliot channels these dark forces "into a restraining framework and even embodies them in disciplined form, but he does not integrate them into a developing mental process. Eliot's radical contribution to the tradition of the ecstatic moment is fear, resulting in defense" (p. 139). Professor Bornstein argues that the suffering in Eliot's early poetry is passive, that by *The Waste Land* "Eliot had not yet found the active conception of suffering that Christianity later opened to him, and absence of such dynamism constitutes the true antiromanticism of the poem" (p. 146). Bornstein's view clashes with that of A. D. Moody, who argues in his *Thomas Stearns Eliot: Poet* that in *The Waste Land* Eliot "put an end to English romanticism by taking absolutely seriously the feelings it had soothed . . . and his anti-romanticism consisted in putting romantic feelings into practice" (p. 109). To Professor Bornstein, only in *Four Quartets,* particularly in "East Coker," does Eliot salvage his covert romanticism through the creation of a Greater Romantic Lyric, defined by its pattern of description-vision-evaluation, which the author uses throughout to measure the failures of imaginative vision in Eliot's poetry. He rightly concludes that Eliot was "romantic against the grain," an apt phrase, but in arguing that Eliot was afraid to be a Romantic, in presenting him as a demoniac writing defensively in fear of imagination and nature, he misses the opportunity to probe the darker horror and the genuine romantic vein that run beneath the classical surfaces of Eliot's work.

M. L. Rosenthal's tripartite study comes closer, I think, to showing the structural continuities between nineteenth- and twentieth-century lyric poets and to delineating characteristically modern transformations. The main artistic contribution of Yeats, Pound, and Eliot "is the modulation toward a poetry of open process, largely presentative, which tends toward a balancing of volatile emotional states" (p. 205). For all its unique qualities, *The Waste Land* is seen as a characteristic achievement in open structure, ending in the readiness to move out into new states of awareness. Rosenthal, like Bornstein, also looks at their poetry in relation to the Greater Romantic Lyric, but instead of decrying *The Waste Land* as an "abortive psychodrama," as Bornstein labels it for its "anatomy rather than transformation of fallen consciousness," Rosenthal portrays it as "an extended lyric structure in sequence form," opening into transcendence. He associates the "depressive" movement of the poem with Stevens's "Sunday Morning" ("Downward to darkness, on extended wings") and with Yeats's hermits in "Meru," all of them showing the movement of the "open sensibility" in modern lyric poetry: "The movement, in other words, is from a state of depressive awareness to one of depressive transcendence.... The total flux of aroused awareness is a condition of the whole poem—a set of possibilities, not purposeful fiction or argument. Within this flux the depressive state inseparable from a sufficiently open sensibility is countered by momentary holdings against the chaos threatening the speaker from both without and within. A lyric poem is, in this way of seeing it, a sensibility in motion" (p. 168).

Stanley Sultan similarly maintains that *The Waste Land* and *Ulysses* have in common not only an open form but also "the impulse to autobiography normally associated with Romanticism, the great parent which Modernism, the offspring as dialectical antithesis, opposed and eventually supplanted—but inescapably resembled" (p. 75). Professor Sultan does not explore the romantic-modern synthesis in any detail; he attributes most of the numerous similarities between the two works not to direct influence but to the presence of a "profound modernist confluence." But from the uncertain order of *The Waste Land* drafts he pieces together a likely sequence to demonstrate one significant influence of *Ulysses*. In his plausible reconstruction of the poem's composition, he argues that Eliot's thematic inspiration and crystallization came late in the process, evidenced in part by the rapid and largely unaltered writing of "What the Thunder Said" and the subsequent revisions of earlier sections. To Professor Sultan, the primary theme of "potential salvation" and the motifs of sterility and despair came in a sudden burst of creativity, and in his eyes this creativity was dramatically catalyzed by the pattern of myth and allusion in *Ulysses*. Lyndall Gordon, in her brief appendix on the two works, holds that Eliot was not profoundly influenced by Joyce, but her close physical examination, in another appendix, of the paper and typewriters used for the drafts does not disprove Professor Sultan's conjectural and plausible hypothesis. In presenting alternative and equally plausible chronologies, Gordon concludes that there is not yet sufficient evidence to resolve the problem of sequence.

These circumstantial reconstructions of poetic composition are intriguing, as are most other archeological story lines, but the common interest is directed less toward a greater understanding of the creative process than to the discovery of Eliot's original *intention* in the poem. Hugh Kenner argued in *Eliot in His Time* that Eliot set out to write a neo-Augustan urban satire, and while Lyndall Gordon argues that at first Eliot made "the dream of sainthood" an unmistakable priority, James E. Miller, Jr., claims that the driving emotional preoccupation was the poet's loss of his Paris friend, Jean Verdenal. The deep-running curiosity over Eliot's intention may point to the further unraveling of the New Critical fabric in the seventies, but if in the sixties *The Waste Land* was dessicated by critical restraint and consistency, it is now swamped by conjecture and diversity.

The most overwhelming of the new psychobiographical approaches is that of James E. Miller, Jr., in his *T. S. Eliot's Personal Waste Land*. There is not space here to probe the ingenious associational logic and the artful critical methods with which he presents a homosexual interpretation of *The Waste Land* and other poems, particularly "Ode" and "Little Gidding," but I will attempt to recount the main line of the argument's conception, execution, and completion. When Eliot wrote in "In Memoriam" (1936) that Tennyson's lyric on Hallam gave him a "shudder that I fail to get from anything in *Maud*," his "extravagant response" to that lyric suggests to Miller "his own deep identification with it—and inspires wonder as to whether there is not a similar structure of circumstances in Eliot's own life" (p. 3). To Miller, Eliot seems to be inviting a future critic to deal with similar levels of unconscious life in *The Waste Land*, and he accepts the invitation.

Miller begins with the resurrection of an essay by John Peter, published in some issues of *Essays in Criticism* (July 1952, pp. 242–66) before Eliot successfully suppressed it in others. Without naming names, Peter offered a "new interpretation" of *The Waste Land* on the premise that "at some previous time the speaker has fallen completely—perhaps the right word is 'irretrievably'—in love. The object of this love was a young man who soon afterwards met his death, it would seem by drowning" (p. 245). Peter's account of the suppression appeared in *Essays in Criticism* for April 1969. Subsequently, Miller holds, scholars have, to say the least, treated Peter's premise "gingerly"; in effect they have created a conspiracy of silence around it. Miller now dares to collect all the available biographical information to enlarge upon Peter's original thesis. He roundly criticizes previous critics for failing to mention Jean Verdenal, but nowhere will those critics find a mention of Emily Hale in *T. S. Eliot's Personal Waste Land*.

Little is known about the French medical student whom Eliot befriended in Paris while he was at the Sorbonne. After Verdenal's battlefront death in the Dardenelles in 1915, Eliot remembered him in the dedication of *Prufrock and Other Observations* (1917), followed by a Dantean inscription that begins "Now you are able to comprehend the quantity of love that warms me toward you." Miller gives evidential weight to the separation of the dedication and the inscription until 1925, but, printing history aside, the Berg Collection manuscripts show them together at the outset. In synopsis, Eliot and Verdenal had a period of what the author calls "abbreviated fulfillment" in 1910, and Verdenal's death on 2 May 1915, news of which supposedly reached Eliot immediately, "may well have impelled him into a hasty marriage on 26 June that was largely meaningless except as an irrational response to his loss" (p. 24). Out of his hatred of female physicality, Eliot soon "thrust in apparent offering" Vivienne at Bertrand Russell, who "helped" Eliot with his difficult wife and his sexual failure, "(though, of course, psychoanalysis would no doubt trace origins of his sexual paralysis to his childhood)" (p. 94). In the next few years Eliot prepared himself to bring about an "imaginative transfiguration" of his feelings for Verdenal in *The Waste Land,* thereby exorcising his pain and grief.

To Miller, Eliot's critical writings, which often contain personal revelations, or which suggest that what he says of another can be said of himself, provide further evidence for interpretation. In a 1934 "Commentary" in the *Criterion,* Eliot recalled his student days in Paris with the image of Verdenal coming across the Luxembourg Gardens with a branch of lilac, thus suggesting to Miller the likely association of lilac with Verdenal in the poetry. In "The Burial of the Dead," for instance, both Eliot's emphasis on "girl" rather than "hyacinth," in " 'They called me the hyacinth *girl,*' " and his placing the lines in quotation indicates his intention for the reader to make an ironic masculine association: " 'They called me the hyacinth *girl*'! The meaning thus becomes clearly possible, and is not far removed from Eliot's memory of Jean Verdenal carrying the branch of lilac across Luxembourg Gardens in the Paris of his youth" (p. 71). Proceeding, as he describes it, "in a kind of cryptanalytic way," Miller attempts to clear up the interpretive problems of the poem by reference to Eliot's haunting memory of and desire for Verdenal. No pertinent allusion, not even "the Dog far hence," escapes analysis: "Whatever else the Dog may be (and explicators have proposed every conceivable mythic possibility), he is surely the Dog within, the lust of memory that will not let the past lie buried but digs it up for a psychic confrontation that may be terrifying, paralyzing, even castrating, rendering one impotent as a fisher-king in a waste land. Memory and desire, memory and desire. 'Hypocrite reader!—my double, —my brother!' Thus Eliot . . . makes psychic accomplices of us all" (p. 77). Verdenal is Phlebas, and he is an accomplice in the "awful daring of a moment's surrender," a moment which was consummated in the original drafts of the "Damyata" section, which is allegedly addressed to Verdenal: "your heart responded/Gaily, when invited, beating responsive/To controlling hands" (p. 130). Suppositions build upon suppositions, until the reader is finally asked to see Verdenal as the primary figure of the "familiar compound ghost" in "Little Gidding," Eliot's final valediction for his friend.

Some would believe the critic. Others would not. But in the absence of an authorized biography this interpretation of the man and his work cannot be disproved, only objected to. Miller anticipates objection in his preface, where he says his "only interest in the life is the light it might shed on the poetry" (p. ix), and again in an afterword, where he claims that "we have not been reductive with the biographical data, diminishing them to the grossest possible terms to exploit their potential for sensationalism" (p. 163). To this reader, no number of prepared disclaimers can reverse the sensational tone of the early chapters or the knowing manipulation of casual biographical documents and textual material. As a conjectural edifice, the study serves neither the life nor the work. And the author's final apology, that the poetry can be read in this way even if the Verdenal conjectures prove groundless, that "Eliot's imagination could have transformed the meager facts beyond recognition" (p. 59), that Verdenal could be invented, does not serve criticism.

Eliot's Early Years is also "an attempt to elicit the autobiographical element in Eliot's poetry by measuring the poetry against the life" (p. 2), but it employs greater primary materials to reach radically different readings and conclusions. Lyndall Gordon synthesizes many new biographical fragments to illuminate factually the years leading up to *The Waste Land*, providing significant information on the influence of Eliot's mother, Charlotte Champe Eliot; his first love, Emily Hale, who exchanged over two thousand letters with Eliot over the course of her life; and other figures who influenced his intellectual development. This resourceful spiritual biography also makes extensive use of the unpublished poems and notebooks in the Berg Collection to reveal the confessional and meditative voices that were subsequently muted in the depersonalized surfaces of his published work. Though it is unfortunate that her use of the poems is restricted to title and paraphrase, except for those fragments published in Valerie Eliot's facsimile edition of *The Waste Land,* the limitations hardly hinder the compelling account of Eliot's subterranean religious quest as "a slow incubation and maturing of motives" (p. 23). Gordon succeeds in probing the "obscure creative embryo" that has intrigued but evaded other critics, and in the process she delineates a revolutionary new chronology of Eliot's poetic and spiritual development.

Gordon locates the beginning of Eliot's spiritual journey in 1910, when an intersection of personal problems and fears resulted in the "defining experience" of his life, a vision of peace, as embodied in a poem entitled "Silence." By 1914 the once-aspiring philosopher had become a would-be saint, a preoccupation that gave rise to a group of intense religious poems, including "After the turning . . . ," "I am the Resurrection . . . ," "So through the evening . . . ," "The Burnt Dancer," "The Love Song of Saint Sebastian," and "The Death of Saint Narcissus." The discussion of the poems is preceded by a thesis that some readers, long married to the apparent discontinuity between Eliot's preconversion and postconversion poetry and criticism, will find startling and unsettling: "The turning-point in Eliot's life came not at the time of his baptism in 1927, but in 1914 when he was circling, in moments of agitation, on the edge of conversion" (p. 58). Others will find it to be the assertion and confirmation of what they have long suspected (though they will be disappointed that the author fails to confront the recurring allegations that Eliot seriously considered Buddhism).

In the "period of sterility" from 1914 to 1919 Eliot wrote clusters of visionary fragments, most of which were subsequently transformed into *The Waste Land*. Though Eliot was also writing his satiric poems, Gordon contends that the unpublished fragments make them seem "a digression from his poetic career" (p. 91). And in examining these fragments she shows both the circumstances and the psychology of Eliot's suppression of "the dream of sainthood" in the poem, which "originated in the purely personal record of a man who saw himself as a potential candidate for the religious life but was constrained by his own nature and distracted by domestic claims" (p. 118). The final chapter, "Conversion," traces the series of personal crises in the twenties that gave increased impetus to Eliot's arduous spiritual journey. "The difficulty in studying Eliot's life," Gordon concludes, "lies not in his religious search, which seems quite straightforward, but in isolating what was innovative and original in his vision of the world from what was idiosyncratic and sometimes distorted" (p. 136). Isolating the idiosyncratic at the expense of vision is one of the present problems of much psychobiographical criticism, and this is one of the few books to find a proper balance.

The line of resistance to reading the poems through biography and earlier drafts is led by Derek Traversi, who appears to have been drawn into Eliot studies by his belief that the poetry must be read *qua* poetry, not as autobiography or philosophy. The result of the latter tendency "has been to divide a remarkably continuous and coherent body of work . . . into parts, which the critics then proceed to exalt or to decry in accordance with their own prejudice" (p. 7). In upholding the integrity of the text, Traversi, A. D. Moody, and Balachandra Rajan are no less interested in the poet in the poem, but such interest, says Moody, "is no invitation to probe his private life" (p. 79). One of the seldom recognized paradoxes of Eliot's criticism is that while it insisted on a theory of depersonalization for the poet, it urged a theory of repersonalization for the critic. Through what Eliot called "intelligent saturation" in the poet's work as a whole, the critic can perceive the personal pattern that runs beneath the objective surface. These three critics adhere to Eliot's belief that within the poetry itself the poet will "give the pattern, or we may say the undertone, or the personal emotion, the personal drama and struggle, which no biography, however full and intimate, could give us."[2]

Each of these three approaches Eliot's poetry with a belief in its "remarkable continuity" and "power of wholeness." Rajan's opening chapter, "The Overwhelming Question," originally published in 1966, was aimed at those adherents of the New Criticism for whom continuity was an alien concept, and some readers may have forgotten the necessity and revolutionary context of his assertion that Eliot's poetry "is not simply a series of individual excellences but a totality fully experienced and lived through" (p. 18). To other readers the case for continuity may seem late in coming, but it takes time to shift the interest of criticism from the cultural to the personal pattern where evidence of continuity lies. Overarching this general critical problem was the stronger belief in the thematic discontinuity of Eliot's earlier and later works, and it is this specific issue that these three critics, along with Lyndall Gordon, address.

Traversi and Rajan follow the same working thesis, that each new poem, as Traversi puts it, "derives from those which preceded it and looks forward to what was to follow" (p. 7). Though he examines only *The Waste Land, Ash Wednesday,* and *Four Quartets,* the discussion takes place within a larger context. *The Waste Land,* for instance, "stands in a close relationship to both his earlier and his later verse, summing up the positions reached in the 1917 and 1920 volumes and anticipating —though not entering upon—the aim of the later work, which is the creation of poetry at once fully contemporary and genuinely 'religious'" (pp. 53–54). Rajan places the major poems in a symbolic continuum to characterize the trajectory of the oeuvre: "the spiral of process and the circle of design," "Gerontion" building upon the position defined in "Prufrock," each poem in succession representing a spiraling advance into knowledge, each poetic reenactment validating the quest, each poem circling back to its beginning in the unending search for reality. And likewise for Moody, each major poem is a new stage in the poet's ongoing search for self-transcendence.

The strength and value of these three studies come not from the freshness of explication but from the critical power, or "intelligent saturation," with which the authors delineate significant interpenetrations among the poems. The readings of the poems are exceptionally close, synthesizing much previous explication, and were it not for the pursuit of a consistent poetic personality, each study would read as a periphrastic study in a worn-out critical fashion. Though Moody's avowed interest is in Eliot the poet, he is at his best when he brings the criticism to bear on the poetry, and in the most original chapter of the book he follows the poet into his plays to observe the playwright revising the poet's vision. One provocative observation springs from a return to the Greek and Shakespearean plays from which Eliot departs, where Moody attempts to come to terms with the neurosis of Eliot's art. While the neurosis has personal origins that remain in darkness, it is the modern form of an ancient neurosis that is endemic in western culture, "the alienation of man from that to which he properly, of his nature, belongs—his being cut off from the vital universe, from others, from much in himself" (p. 290). Eliot's poetry, Moody concludes, "articulates the woe that is in the marriage of alienated neurotic egos; the atrophy and perversions of spirit in the crowd that flows over London Bridge; the pitifulness of its recreations, and the depressed resignation of humble people who expect nothing; the waste of living and partly living, of loving and partly loving; the sense of life turning to dust and ashes in the mouth; the anxiety, and fear, and sick loathing; the conscious impotence of rage at human folly, and the consequent self-contempt; and the death-wish" (p. 298). This is far from the last word on neurosis in Eliot's poetry, but for the moment it is, if the most traditional, the most balanced.

For all the current interest in biography, continuity, neurosis, and the romantic-to-modern line, it is surprising how many of these critical studies skip over or give only nodding, even offhanded, recognition to "Prufrock," a poem seemingly regarded as critically formulated and pinned on the wall. In *The Language of Modern Poetry: Yeats, Eliot, Auden*, A. C. Partridge remarks that Prufrock, "meditating upon the fatuity of existence, is recognized as a self-conscious misfit of middle-age, about to pop the 'overwhelming question' to a lady with whom he probably had little affinity" (p. 146). To Miller it is "a poem in a basic sense about a man who cannot love women" (p. 66). To Bornstein Eliot creates "an artificial dreamworld to satisfy Prufrock's frustrated erotic desires," a charge ironically leveled by Eliot against romantic poetry, and the poem "shows in practice what Eliot's prose shows in theory—that the real impetus of the charge was need to domesticate his own imagination" (p. 133). Rajan focuses on the "comic ambience" that he sees pervading Prufrock's "slumming tour" through illusion towards an ultimate evasion of reality, but he too glosses Prufrock's "visions" and the ways in which Lazarus and John the Baptist, "the proper ambassadors of reality in the poem," point through the comic gestures to the horrible substrata of terror and paralysis that drive Prufrock's unarticulated spiritual dilemma toward "some overwhelming question." To leave Prufrock in a "comic failure," to see his struggle as a defiance that collapses into "mere sartorial rebellion," is to drop a thread early in the pattern of Eliot's work. Surely Prufrock is not merely an aging, self-mocking Lothario paralyzed by indecisiveness. To some he is a man of dark visions and darker revisions, and Eliot seems to be looking back to Prufrock in his essay on "Cyril Tourneur" (1930): "But occasionally the intensity of the vision of its own ecstasies or horrors . . . may give to a juvenile work a universality which is beyond the author's knowledge of life to give, and to which mature men and women can respond."[3] The Prufrock responded to in most of these studies would hardly be capable of either ecstasy or horror. Too much attention is paid to his "personality," and to the patterns and gestures of his external life—too little to his mind in extremis.

Stephen Spender, in *The Destructive Element* (Boston: Houghton Mifflin, 1936), was among the first to examine the "purely isolated sensibility" of the poet in his poetry. It is instructive to return to that influential study, where Spender declares that in *The Waste Land* "what Eliot most certainly has done is to immerse himself in the destructive element" (p.144). Spender perceived very early Eliot's "haunted world" and the spiritual terror underlying his poetic quest for salvation, and in his recent *T. S. Eliot* he continues to see that Eliot had "a haunted imagination—haunted by real fears and fantasies, the starkness of which has become fogged over in the mass of exegesis gathered round his work" (pp. 13–14). But in his discussion of *The Waste Land* he turns traditionally to the "central theme" of the poem, the breakdown of civilization, rather than to the mind immersed in the destructive element. There seem to be two critical voices at work, that of the critic on the poet dominating that of the poet on the poet.

Spender met Eliot in 1928, and in periodic meetings Eliot often confided his feelings about art and criticism. Many of Eliot's informal remarks are recorded in the text, giving it a personal, even intimate quality. But there, I think, the intimacy stops, for in Spender's discussion of the work it does not seem that he really reveals in his public critical voice what he privately perceives and feels. It seems that the critic holds back from the expectant reader, generally pointing to the horror and the boredom and the glory, but leaving his intimate and profound understanding of Eliot understated. The study suffers from its comprehensiveness, likely dictated by the Modern Masters format. It is good to have Spender's book on Eliot, but it reminds us that too many of the best critics are writing for the growing number of commercial series. The greater need is to understand more deeply the nature of Eliot's poetic experience than to make the general contours of his work more widely known.

Several new studies focus on specific aspects of Eliot's poetry —the language, the lyricism, the landscapes, and the voices in *Four Quartets*. A. C. Partridge's comprehensive study of the poems offers mainly a descriptive analysis of Eliot's style and rhetorical devices. Partridge is more interested in the workings of language and form than in the "plain sense" of the poems, which he tends to paraphrase or summarize as he moves along. He examines the ritualistic and incantatory use of language in *The Waste Land*, and though the poem has some technical greatness, he finds it "not the most satisfying" of Eliot's poems, and leaves it to a future critical generation: "The evocative processes and fortuitous shape are puzzling, and the impression gains ground that this is a private poem, to which the reader is denied access, if not by the theory of impersonality, then by a negative biography, hinted at in lines 111–23. Only time can reveal the answer" (p. 171).

Nancy Duvall Hargrove sees Eliot's poetry as the record of a continuous search for redemption, but this interest is secondary to the ways in which the landscapes of the poems symbolically reflect the condition of culture, the modern sensibility, and inner mental states. *Landscape as Symbol in the Poetry of T. S. Eliot* departs from Marshall McLuhan's earlier observations on the influence of Tennyson and Baudelaire on Eliot's landscapes, and as Hargrove makes her way through Eliot's urban and rural settings a pantheon of critical authorities offers support and guidance. While the narrative progresses in a rather formulaic academic style, what gives it an engaging personal quality is the fact that Hargrove has personally visited, photographed, and researched the landscapes of Eliot's poetry. Her first-hand descriptions of places are accompanied by suggestive information about the historical background and local and traditional associations. The most interesting and original chapter examines the rarely discussed "Landscapes" poems of the 1930s—"New Hampshire," "Virginia," "Usk," "Ranoch, by Glencoe," and "Cape Ann," which together she shows to be experiments in preparation for *Four Quartets*. Rising above the analysis of symbolic value is the valuable portrayal of Eliot as a landscape poet drawing upon nineteenth-century landscape traditions, and the real contribution of the book lies in its illustration, with the help of forty photographs, of how rich is the sense of place in Eliot's poetry.

Ann P. Brady argues in her *Lyricism in the Poetry of T. S. Eliot* that Eliot consciously mines and extends the ancient lyric tradition throughout his poetry; but her short study turns out to be more appreciative and apologetic than scholarly. She portrays Eliot, "no mean poet," as a calculating lyric craftsman, but she is rather casual in describing the effects of Eliot's lyric methods: "Without hitting the reader over the head, [*The Waste Land*] does lead to, or at least points to, a resolution" (pp. 42–43). And later the reader is told that "there is no doubt about the hollow men. They are lost and hopeless. This poem is rock bottom in the Eliot scale" (p. 45). Though some of the early poems may not be characteristically lyrical, they often allude to lyrical moments and situations. The discussion thus strains to reach its primary objective, the fourth section of each quartet, where each section "distills the essence of the quartet in which it occurs" (p. 94). Because of metrical and musical irregularities she finds it "less problematic" to discuss them in the order of "East Coker," described as a "passion lyric," "Little Gidding," itself a "purgation lyric," "Burnt Norton," with a less evident pattern, and "The Dry Salvages," a Marian lyric. Telescopically, the lyrics "compress the salvation history of the individual and of humankind" (p. 103). After a somewhat pedestrian description of stylistic elements and lyrical techniques, the author concludes unabashedly that the four lyrics are "among the most functionally original in twentieth-century poetry, and are of an artistic quality not surpassed" (p. 103).

One of the rewards of undertaking this omnibus review was the discovery of Keith Alldritt's replaying of *Four Quartets*. *Eliot's* Four Quartets: *Poetry as Chamber Music* is one of the most readable, original, and provocative studies of Eliot's poem to appear in the decade. Thankfully missing are the belabored explications, the convoluted academese, the unground critical axes, and the self-presenting ingenuity that so often upstages the author and the work at hand. While the study recognizes the presence of intense personal experiences, it does not present the poem as an autobiographical or psychological document. And though Alldritt recognizes but does not accept the Christian ideology of the poem, he refuses thereby to aesthetically underread the verbal quality of a poem that is primarily "about the layers of verbal consciousness" (p. 109). He discusses *Four Quartets* as a symbolist poem in the continuing symbolist tradition that extends from Gautier and Mallarmé through Pound and Eliot to MacDiarmid's *Briggflatts*. In drawing upon the symbolist use of musical analogies he further characterizes the tradition itself and presents an illuminating and unforced discussion of the poem's integral relation to its musical metaphor.

Alldritt shows that while the poet's personal voice is present in the poem, it is but the "poor player" to four other voices, all different versions of the self. As in a classical quartet form, the separate voices allow for contrast, tension, debate, and discussion: "The four verbal roles which we hear may be described as those of the lecturer, the prophet, the conversationalist and the conjuror. The rapid and complex interaction of these four voices and the unmistakable inference that there is a distinction to be made between the poet and his four verbal instruments account for that unremitting intricacy of tone which constitutes much of the meaning and achievement of the poem" (p. 39). Alldritt examines each of the quartets, convincingly pointing to the shift from one voice to another, comparing the range and capacity of each, and showing how at the end of "Little Gidding" the four "sound together in their own best and most educated terms in that unity towards which the quartet form characteristically aspires" (p. 64). Once pointed out, the changes of voice and tone are almost as noticeable as they are in *The Waste Land*. Moody also perceives four "instrumentalities of the mind" in the poem, which he characterizes as "the voices of natural experience, of thought which moves into meditation, of meditation which moves into prayer, and of prayer which would culminate in vision" (p. 199). Although he does not extend his own thesis, Moody would, I think, agree with Alldritt's analysis of the interacting voices: "The author of the work is not just one voice, nor does he apprehend reality in one way, nor does he talk about it in one verbal style. He is a set of different, sometimes insufficient, sometimes contradictory perceptions and his modes of language vary. The poem may be defined as a process of investigation, of exploration into the nature of the self. And the initial, formal assumption is that the self is a plurality" (p. 51).

Alldritt examines the sonata pattern to show how it is the chief unifying principle of the various experiences of the poem. One of the most significant of these experiences is the poet's recurring sense that language has a limited power to voice his ontological quest. One such instance, pertinent to observations in this review, comes in the last section of "The

Dry Salvages," where the poet writes that to "dissect/The recurrent image into pre-conscious terrors—/To explore the womb, or tomb, or dreams: all these are usual/Pastimes and drugs, and features of the press." Alldritt astutely observes, in commenting on the psychoanalytical notion of consciousness which these lines address, that *"Four Quartets* assumes the language of psychology to be easier and less revealing of human realities than the language of ontology" (p. 117).

The symbolists regarded being as something musical, hence the recurring musical analogies, and the struggle of the arts in their various mediums, such as language, is a struggle to transcend the medium, to aspire, in Pater's words, to the condition and power of music. In the last lines of "The Dry Salvages" the poet speaks of "music heard so deeply/That it is not heard at all, but you are the music/While the music lasts." Full consciousness is thereby defined as a musical condition. As the poet strives for the unheard music, the four voices of his plural self continue their verbal struggle, leading him to speak in "Little Gidding" of "Knowing myself yet being someone other." Says Alldritt, in a penetrating observation of a modern transformation of romanticism: "Such consciousness is very familiar, even particular to the major literature of this century. The antithesis is as central to Yeats's later poems and to *Ulysses* as it is to *Four Quartets* and can be seen to result from a stage in civilisation in which rapid accretions in definitions of consciousness threaten to obscure and deny its deeper origins" (p. 122). This fine book will regenerate the discussion of consciousness and form in *Four Quartets.*

Eliot must have greatly envied Shakespeare the enduring privacy of his life, still elusive of intense biographical curiosity and psychological probing. And yet Eliot brooded upon Shakespeare's secret mind during the whole of his career. Prufrock's horrific visions drive him to confront, like Hamlet, an "overwhelming question" that he cannot formulate. And in his essay on Hamlet, Eliot was more preoccupied with Shakespeare's obscure private motive than with the fact of artistic failure: "Under compulsion of what experience he attempted to express the inexpressibly horrible, we cannot ever know."[4] The epigraphs from and allusions to Shakespeare's works in Eliot's early poems point to moments of internal extremity, and in 1925 he turned again to the consciousness beneath the work: "It is not only the external history of Shakespeare's life that is deficient. It is that internal history, which may have much or may have little relation to the external facts, that internal crisis over which our imagination is tempted to brood too long—it is this that we shall never know."[5] Eliot longed to perceive and even empathize with the intense personal moments that haunt the surface of Shakespeare's work, and the relation between personal horror and impersonal art remained one of his foremost preoccupations as a poet and as a critic. He said of Baudelaire, as he said of numerous authors, that Baudelaire was "a man with a profound attitude toward life, for the study of which we need every scrap of his writing."[6] Problems of consciousness, sensibility, neurosis, wholeness, and continuity were not unfamiliar to Eliot. It might be said that he was himself a not so coarse critic of interiority.

There is no richer grid than Eliot's oeuvre for working out the relation of criticism and interiority, and for that undertaking—the critical challenge of the eighties—every scrap of his writing is needed. There can, however, be but slow progress in Eliot studies until the Eliot estate begins to commission the construction of a scholarly base, beginning with an authorized critical biography. Further, all serious critics need the unpublished poems that support Gordon's study, the 1926 Clark Lectures on metaphysical poetry that inform Moody's book, and the Eliot–Verdenal letters that are missing from Miller's study. One hopes that Valerie Eliot's edition of the first volume of letters will appear early in the decade. Volumes of uncollected prose must someday come, as well as a critical edition of the poems (especially of the deleted drafts of "Prufrock") to accompany those of *The Waste Land* and *Four Quartets*.[7] But the long-term problem of materials is perhaps less immediate than the plurality of analytical languages that vie for adoption. Eliot critics must soon define what it is they want from the life, and they must know that the language of psychology too easily describes it.

Notes

1. See Audrey T. Rogers's omnibus review of Eliot research from 1970–1975, "Eliot in the 70's: A Mosaic of Criticism," *T. S. Eliot Review*, 2 (Spring 1975), 10–15.

2. Eliot, *Selected Essays*, new ed. (New York: Harcourt, 1964), p. 180.

3. Ibid., p. 166.

4. Ibid., p. 126.

5. Eliot, "Shakespeare and Montaigne," *Times Literary Supplement*, 24 Dec. 1925, p. 895.

6. Eliot, "Poet and Saint . . . ," *The Dial*, 82 (May 1927), 424.

7. Helen Gardner's important study, *The Composition of* Four Quartets (New York: Oxford Univ. Press, 1978), is reviewed extensively by A. Walton Litz in Vol. 2 of *Review* and was not included in this essay at the editors' request.

The Literary Scholar Faces the Computer

Philip H. Smith, Jr.

Robert L. Oakman. *Computer Methods for Literary Research.* Columbia: University of South Carolina Press, 1980. xi, 235 pp.

Survey reports of computer applications in the humanities usually succumb to one of two opposite perils: either they are brief and anecdotal and tell too little to be informative; or they give too much detail, fill pages with the kind of coding unavoidable in literary data processing, and end by confusing the reader. Robert Oakman's *Computer Methods for Literary Research* avoids the rocks on both sides of the channel and provides a survey and an introduction to a subject that for many literary scholars is still far too arcane. The author's intent, as set forth in the preface, is that the literary scholar gain "a clearer perspective about the machine as a research tool." Oakman has done an admirable job of fulfilling that intention.

The principal audience for Oakman's book (aside from those of us active in the field who will appreciate its summing up of scattered materials) will be those literary scholars and humanists who sense the power of the computer and suspect that it can be harnessed to some of their research tasks. They will be simultaneously instructed and disillusioned: they will acquire the fundamental ideas of computing, and they will be disabused of some of the more euphoric hopes they may have.

The book is organized into two major parts, one on fundamentals of literary computing and the other on selected applications in the field. Each of the eight chapters ends with a brief list "For Further Reading," while a thirty-three-page selected bibliography follows the last chapter. This bibliography is in turn divided into ten different subject sections (Textual Criticism and Editing, Content Analysis, etc., not exactly matching the chapter divisions) which I found difficult to manage: the search for a particular reference may take the reader through several sections before he is successful.

Part I of Oakman's book makes an excellent introductory tutorial for the literary scholar who is not already familiar with computing. Chapter 1, "Computers for Information Processing," tells the uninitiated what a computer is, describes the binary system of notation and arithmetic, and illustrates the operation of a computer with examples wisely chosen to be appreciated by the humanist. There are as many metaphors to describe a computer as there are people who think about the machinery; I find Oakman's view of a computer clear, useful, and helpful, telling neither too much nor too little.

Chapter 2 deals with "Getting Literary Materials in and out of the Machine," while Chapter 3 is entitled "Flowcharting and Programming for Literary Analysis." Chapter 2 surveys the most tedious aspect of literary data processing, while Chapter 3 introduces the literary scholar to the kinds of intellectual discipline the programmer must apply to computing problems.

The background provided by Part I is a necessary foundation for Part II, which provides a clear overview of several specific areas of literary computing. It begins, appropriately, where literary data processing began: with the machine production of text concordances. The first chapter (Chapter 4) presents the history of this endeavor and describes several of the concordances that have been made by computer in the last two decades. Chapter 5 surveys "Information Retrieval: Historical Dictionaries and Scholarly Bibliographies," and includes flow diagrams and a sample computer bibliography entry.

"Textual Editing with a Computer," by which is meant the production of collations and critical editions, is the topic of Chapter 6, while Chapter 7 is devoted to "Stylistic Analysis." This last area is the most difficult of all in that it is the least straightforward, the least susceptible of unambiguous mechanical treatment.

I know of no survey of literary data processing which comes

close to Oakman's in coverage and quality. Carefully written, pleasing in style, and attractive in physical appearance, the book is a far cry from some of the computing manuals through which Oakman himself must have suffered. The twenty-seven figures include numerous flowcharts and pictures of particular types of machinery. It is unfortunate, however, that the latest information in this excellent book, bearing a 1980 copyright, dates from the summer of 1977. In all likelihood computerized typesetting would have done little to shorten the publication time, despite the hopes for that medium. As for the figures, the actual computer printouts are poorly reproduced and hard to read, a fact which mars the book's general attractiveness.

The last chapter of the book, "Further Considerations: Archives, Packages, and Future Prospects," ends on a cautionary note, as Oakman reviews some of the wilder prognostications made for literary data processing. Unquestionably the computer can be useful in literary research, as it is in other branches of scholarship, in science, and in business. But there are dangers in the use of the computer—not the chance of radiation or smoke in the skies, but the possibility that the computer will be used where it is simply inappropriate. Oakman, for instance, deals at length and very fairly with the Reverend Andrew Q. Morton's studies of the authorship of St. Paul's epistles in the New Testament.[1] The public, including the scholarly public, cannot be too wary of what "the computer tells us." Not only can the computer be used to manipulate the wrong data—or at any rate data which do not necessarily answer the question we think we asked—but the machinery can also be dragged into an act where it is not even useful. Morton's work provides a case in point. One can reasonably doubt whether it was necessary to use a computer to count the occurrences of *kai* in Greek New Testament texts, and then to divide by the number of sentences. Although Michael Levison, Morton's collaborator on the computing side of the work, makes the point that people just can't count accurately, using the computer here seems like killing flies with a sledge hammer. Perhaps more serious in its final consequences is the conviction which a computer-aided project may engender in those who read about it: that since the computer drew the conclusion it must be true. An egregious example of such misuse may be observed in *The Limits to Growth* by D. H. Meadows, et al. (New York: Universe Books, 1972). Here we read how a computer, plied with large numbers of hypotheses about pollution, the depletion of natural resources, and the possible effect on the world economy, yielded all-too-specific predictions about the future of mankind. The published reviews of *The Limits to Growth* generally assumed that what the computer had said must be truth. "GIGO" is a computing acronym which stands for "Garbage In, Garbage Out"; it is a blunt way of saying that if data are insecure, no amount of massaging them is going to produce answers of any value. If a computer-based study concludes that Bacon did indeed write Shakespeare's plays, one still must examine the hypotheses which the computer juggled. And if the frequency of *kai* per sentence is a valid measure of who wrote St. Paul's letters, it is valid whether or not a computer was used to calculate it.

Even when the computer is used with restraint, it is seldom used with ease. Despite rapid progress, computing is today, at least from the user's point of view, at the stage of the automobile in 1910. Each new computer that is manufactured, each new software system that is developed to ease the human interface, is different from the last. This year's model has a completely different gear-shift pattern from last year's, and the steering wheel has been moved to the right and is now a tiller. A command "L" in one computer editor is "T" in the next, and so on. What one computer knows as a "file" of data its nearest relative calls a "dataset," with "file" referring to the device on which the data is filed (the disk drive, the tape drive—in short, the filing cabinet).

Not only have conventions not settled down, but the sheer volume of detail, of what one colleague calls "pseudoknowledge," is daunting. And whereas I can imagine that one day the command "LIST" will have a meaning throughout computing as standard as is the meaning of the word "record" when used in reference to a tape or disk file, I cannot imagine how the job

Literary Scholarship and the Computer

of mastering a computing system can be made "simple" in the way that most consumer products are simple to operate.

Even widely used computing packages such as the SCRIPT formatting program require considerable knowledge, skill, and cleverness if they are to render more than minimally useful results. While mastering such a system is not a lifelong chore, as is, for example, attaining fluency in a foreign language, neither is it as simple as learning to drive a car. Routine tasks can be dispatched with relative ease, but the new and the untried continue to demand support from knowledgeable consultants. Thus it is that even "well-documented" program packages —which do fairly straightforward things like making concordances—remain almost unfathomable to many humanists. And I fear this is a natural situation. It is not that the humanists are slow-witted, or even that the programs are poorly documented; it is that the amount of information—the number of choices, the results of each choice, and the interaction of the choices—is so great that even the fullest documentation leaves a great deal unsaid. And it is a rare humanist who wants to read and master volume upon volume of technical writing.

If one is presented with a broad menu of tasks which a machine can do, one must learn how to order from that menu. The modern automobile offers very little choice: it either moves forward or backward or not at all, and it steers either to right or to left. A computer which offered so few choices would be no computer at all, or at any rate would not allow the user to do the interesting things surveyed in Oakman's book. It is precisely the wealth of opportunity presented by computing machinery that makes choosing among alternatives a science, or at least a body of knowledge, in itself. This same richness of choice makes one skeptical about the future of computing for the masses. Much is being said these days, and much being written in the Sunday supplements, about the wonders of the microprocessor and of the microcomputer which everyone is going to own in a few years. Along with the computer-in-the-home comes, we are told, interactive television; one will be able to ask his TV set (or rather the data base behind it) for airline timetables, this week's grocery prices at the Safeway, and the sum of knowledge in the world's libraries. In view of the number of North Americans who do not know how to use a telephone correctly, or where to look up the current population of Philadelphia, one may reasonably doubt that large numbers of people are going to master the complexities of exploiting anything like the full wealth of the systems we are being promised. This may be as good a moment as any to predict that the proposed interactive TV of the next decade will find its overwhelming market in games, a billion-dollar Pong system.

In the early 1970s our group at the University of Waterloo developed a collating scheme not unlike the COLLATE program, which Oakman describes in some detail beginning on page 129. Our assumption, based on a consideration of the problems faced by Petty and Gibson in their Henry James collation, was that the computer would easily get lost when the texts under comparison diverged.[2] Our program, which we called CURSOR, integrated the human operator even more closely than does COLLATE, precisely because we were acutely conscious of the limitations of machine "intelligence." Indeed it was the scholar himself, and not a typist, who was supposed to operate the CURSOR, our belief being that only the scholar would know what comments he wanted to make on the discrepancies among the collated texts. While the program worked —the CURSOR developed into a neat little language with a tidy set of (apparently) reasonable commands for noting differences, for realigning the machine on the two or more texts after a discrepancy had been found, and for handling certain anomalous situations—the project was a failure. We found that the temperament which was happy to learn a set of commands to be issued to a computer terminal did not reside in the same scholars as did the temperament to collate texts. Our local literary scholars (for whom the system was designed) were simply not comfortable working with a computer, however friendly we tried to make the man-machine conversation.

The very existence of the numerous excellent collation

Literary Scholarship and the Computer 215

projects which Oakman describes indicates that our disappointment is not universal. There is, however, a lesson to be learned from the experience at Waterloo, and that is, quite simply, that literary data processing is not for everyone. The temptation to harness a computer to the tedious chores of literary research is strong and widely distributed. But successful exploitation of the machinery for scholarly goals requires a discipline of its own and a turn of mind that is not necessarily found in every scholar who covets the power of the computer.

From literary scholars who are not temperamentally prepared to work with a computer, the spectrum stretches to scholars who are all too ready to compute, and to write programs, and eventually to devote their lives to tending machinery. For literary data processing *is* a profession in itself. Though to some degree they appear merely a bag of tricks, the skills required for literary data processing are difficult, require long training and experience, and are not simply "picked up" in the standard two-week FORTRAN course given at the computing center. Those literary scholars who have managed to carry out research projects on the computer and still go on being literary scholars are a small minority. Theirs is a rare combination of interests and skills.

Oakman's section "Getting Literary Materials in and out of the Machine" provides an excellent introduction to what remains the most onerous and time-consuming part of literary data processing. To type into a computer (even using the most modern cathode-ray-tube terminals connected to sophisticated computer editing systems) all of the novels of, say, Virginia Woolf, would be enormously time-consuming and therefore very expensive. Add to this cost the difficulty of weeding out the human typographical errors and one most earnestly wishes for a machine to do the work. Unfortunately there seems no promise of such a device, not even beyond the horizon. There are numerous clever machines which will, with very high accuracy, read a printed page *provided* it is printed in some type font which is known to the machine. And, as Oakman notes, one can buy a special typeball for an IBM typewriter, type out the novel using that typeball, and have the typed pages read by machine. What is lacking, and will probably be lacking for a very long time, is a machine which does not impose some special limitation on the typing it can read: a machine, in other words, to which one could give a paperback edition of a novel and from which one would then receive, in short order, a magnetic tape with the novel inputted with machine accuracy. Such machines are frequently announced, and just as frequently they are found not to live up to their promises. There was a time when the *Thesaurus Linguae Graecae* was planning to input its treasury of Greek literary text via an optical print reader; this, too, had to give way to the "keyboarding" of ninety million words.

Optical character reading has failed, to date, for the same reasons mechanical translation of languages has failed, and the computerized study of theme as an aspect of literary style has produced such meager results: there really is a difference between the human mind and the "electronic brain" of the computer.

Oakman touches on this limitation in the chapter he devotes to stylistic analysis. There was a time when it was thought and said that "a computer can do anything a human brain can do." Indeed, a computer does a great deal that a human brain simply cannot do, at least not within a reasonable length of time. Computers are capable of performing mathematical tasks which astound laymen and impress even mathematicians; and it seems logical to assume that if a computer can do math which I can't begin to do, it must be a lot smarter than I am and therefore quite easily able to do the tasks that I do with ease. Like translating languages or finding literary themes or even reading newspapers. Alas, this is not the case.

The reading of printed material appears to be the simplest of the category of tasks that a computer does poorly and a child does well. Where the universe of possibility is small—as in the case of a document written with a special IBM typeball—the computer is very clever indeed at reading letters correctly. It is when the universe is very large—as it is in an ordinary evening paper, with its dozens of type fonts, type sizes, and typographical errors—that the computer stumbles. It is not the number of fonts alone that staggers the machine, but rather the possibilities of broken letters, slightly skewed letters, and other exceptions to the quite rigorous and rigid rules by which it deciphers the printed word. What the human being seems to do is to make wise judgments about unorthodox-shaped letters, judgments based on the content of the sentence or article he is reading. The ability to focus on a topic the whole of life's experience is what distinguishes the human mind from the "electronic brain," and this is nowhere so dramatically demonstrated as in the more intuitive, less codified areas of natural-language manipulation, including the production of sentences and the criticism of literature. Oakman's doubts and his warnings on the topic, in his discussion of literary analysis, are very much to the point.

Despite the negative comments above, literary data processing remains a promising adjunct of humanistic research. Quite possibly in another generation the conventions of computing will have been standardized, and scholars will have been routinely trained to make the computer ease their burdens. If this happy day dawns, it will owe much to *Computer Methods for Literary Research*.

Notes

1. Morton's own writings, such as *Christianity and the Computer*, with James McLeman (London: Hodder and Stoughton, 1964), leave out most of the details, while discussing at length the implications of his findings for Christian theology. Of Morton's numerous publications (cited by Oakman) I find the most illuminating to be "Literary Uses of the Computer," *New Scientist*, 39 (15 Aug. 1968), 340–42.

2. George R. Petty, Jr., and William M. Gibson, *Project OCCULT: The Ordered Computer Collation of Unprepared Literary Text* (New York: New York Univ. Press, 1970).

Chaucer Manuscripts and Texts

N. F. Blake

The Canterbury Tales: *A Facsimile and Transcription of the Hengwrt Manuscript, with Variants from the Ellesmere Manuscript,* edited by P. G. Ruggiers. Norman: University of Oklahoma Press; Folkestone: William Dawson, 1979. liii, 1024 pp.

Troilus and Criseyde, *Geoffrey Chaucer: Facsimile of Corpus Christi College Cambridge MS 61,* with introduction by M. B. Parkes and Elizabeth Salter. Cambridge: D. S. Brewer, 1978. 23, 151 pp.

The study of Chaucer has been making important advances of late, particularly in relation to our knowledge of the manuscripts in which his poems are extant. Two English scholars, A. I. Doyle and M. B. Parkes, have made major contributions here. They have written an important essay, "The Production of Copies of the *Canterbury Tales* and the *Confessio Amantis* in the Early Fifteenth Century" for the recent Ker festschrift;[1] they are responsible for the paleographical description of the Hengwrt manuscript (Hg) in the new facsimile; and Parkes has written the paleographical section in the facsimile of the Corpus manuscript. In addition, the Variorum Chaucer project under the general editorship of Paul Ruggiers of Oklahoma progresses; the facsimile of Hg reviewed here is issued as part of that project, since it will form the base text of the *Canterbury Tales* in the Variorum edition. And although the *Canterbury Tales* has received most attention recently, a new edition of *Troilus and Criseyde,* inaugurated by Derek Brewer and now edited by B. Windeatt, is nearing completion in Cambridge.

The work of Doyle and Parkes should lead to a fundamental shift in attitudes and texts in Chaucer studies and will thus open up a new and exciting era of Chaucerian scholarship.

They show that entrepreneurial activity in Chaucer poems and other vernacular texts flourished at the beginning of the fifteenth century and that this activity affected every aspect of a manuscript's production. However, these new discoveries have been grafted on to accepted editorial assumptions about the poems, whereas they ought to generate a reexamination of the textual tradition and editorial methodology of all Chaucer's poems. That reexamination should no longer consider the poems in isolation. It is on these points that I particularly wish to focus in this essay.

The new Hg facsimile is remarkably cheap, and the standard of photographic reproduction is decidedly poor, as is the quality of paper. The book is bulky, however, because each page of Hg has a facing page with a diplomatic transcript together with all the variants in vocabulary, spelling, and punctuation in Ellesmere (El). Although Doyle and Parkes in their article in the Ker festschrift note that, of the four earliest manuscripts of the *Canterbury Tales* (Hg, El, Harley 7334, and Oxford Corpus Christi Coll. 198), none has special authority in its presentation and organization (p. 194), the editors of the facsimile have presented Hg against the evidence of El. Hg is not allowed to stand by itself; it is presented as a reflection of El as though El were the superior manuscript. The diplomatic text is lineated according to the standard lineation based on El so that Hg's text is made to appear nonstandard and hence deviant. This attitude is also fostered by the retention of El's tale grouping as part of the numbering, even though that grouping has little relevance to Hg, and by observations at the bottoms of certain pages about the incorrectness of Hg's order (e.g., p. 510). Such claims are merely stated, not proved. Surely a facsimile should present the manuscript evidence in as uncontentious a way as possible by means of a plain text so that the reader can approach it with a fresh eye. Even the paleographical introduction is not without fault in this respect since its authors incorporate their explanations of the state of the manuscript with their description. It is sometimes difficult to separate fact about the manuscript from hypothesis about its genesis. It is also regrettable that the facsimile uses black-and-white photography, since the variations in the color of the ink in Hg form such important evidence about the copying of the manuscript.[2]

As the Hg facsimile is presented against the normal standard text of El, one may well be surprised that the Variorum editors claim they will use it as their "base text" (p. xvii). They do not explain their meaning. They do not accept Hg's order, they think it has omissions, they assume its editor has occasionally altered the words of his exemplar, and they use a lineation based on a different manuscript. Presumably by "base text" they mean that Hg's words are usually preferable to those of other manuscripts for those parts of the poem it contains, though it is for them incomplete. Hg is a very odd base text if that is the case, and it is certainly not what most scholars would understand a base text to be. How can the manuscript which has the best text and which, apart from a few missing folios at the end, appears to be complete, leave out pieces of the poem which the editors feel are genuine and also have an order which is not considered authentic? Previous *Canterbury Tales* scholarship suggests that this problem could be solved in two ways, though each carries with it implications that have not been squarely faced.

One solution is to develop the views of earlier scholars like Skeat, who accepted different authorial versions of the poem as reflected in the states of the various manuscripts.[3] This is an inescapable solution if one is to believe that El preserves the correct order of the poem at Chaucer's death, as the editors of the Hg facsimile appear to do (p. 510), even though many scholars like Skeat in the past and Parkes more recently believe that El is an edited text.[4] If there are different authorial recensions, we would have to accept that there were A, B, and C (or more) versions of the poem, each of which would exist as separate entities in the Chaucer canon. Hence, Hg might be the base text of its own recension, but could hardly exist as the base text of the recension represented by El's tale order. Each recension would have its own base text. However, the theory of separate authorial recensions is doubtful. The poem is fragmentary. Why should Chaucer issue different recensions of an incomplete poem, particularly as the parts of the poem (unlike, say *Piers Plowman*) were not written in the order in which they were to occur in the poem? Are we to assume that Chaucer arranged provisional versions of an incomplete poem for publication even though he was still working on it? Furthermore, it is often claimed that the geographical references in the links should be arranged in the order in which the places would occur on a journey from London to Canterbury. If so, Chaucer must have planned the links and the order of the tales early on in the poem's composition—a fact which would seem to preclude provisional versions with different orders. The theory of different authorial recensions is fraught with so many difficulties that it is better discarded.

The other solution is that Chaucer issued the parts of the poem separately as they became available and that the parts were only gathered together after his death. This is the currently favored solution and, though they do not say so, seems to lie behind the explanations to the problems of Hg offered by Doyle and Parkes in their paleographical introduction of the facsimile. This theory was popularised by Manly and Rickert in their monumental edition of the *Canterbury Tales*. If we accept this theory we must surely admit that there was no Chaucerian order to the poem because Chaucer never issued a recension of the fragments in his preferred order. Had he done so, the theory of independently circulating fragments would be unnecessary. Consequently, to prefer El's order to Hg's, as the editors of the facsimile do, is merely to prefer one fifteenth-century editor's order to another's; the orders have nothing to do with Chaucer. If fragments of the *Canterbury Tales* were circulating independently before Chaucer's death, it will be difficult to decide what parts were written by Chaucer rather than by imitators. In such a situation it is inevitable that others would imitate him and write new tales or adapt existing ones, since that was the medieval way with texts. The fact that early manuscripts include certain fragments as part of the *Canterbury Tales* would be no guarantee that they were all by Chaucer, any more than omission in such manuscripts would be a sign of spuriousness. The genuineness of each tale and link would have to be proved, and that is likely to be an impossible task. Furthermore, we would also have to abandon the reliance on one manuscript as the base text of the poem. If the tales or groups were circulating independently in multiple copies, it is extremely unlikely that one scribe would have been fortunate enough to acquire the best copy of each tale or group and then to write a manuscript which could act as our base text for the whole poem. Manly and Rickert realized this and so never declared that Hg was their base text, although in practice they relied upon Hg where it was available.[5] Their actions underline why the theory which they helped to propagate is unsatisfactory. If Hg contains the best text, the theory of independently circulating fragments becomes an unnecessary encumbrance. Finally, one may wonder why Chaucer would wish to issue parts of a poem he was working on independently and how he decided when a group of tales was sufficiently complete to be issued in this way. We are today so accustomed to the groups into which the poem is divided that we accord them special status as though Chaucer always imagined them to exist in this way. But the tales which exist within the present groups no doubt started life as independent tales before they were linked with others to form those groups; and in the same way these existing groups were intended to be linked with other groups to form larger units until all groups were linked together to form one group—the completed *Canterbury Tales*. We are foolish to grant the groups we know a privileged status, for they merely reflect the state of the poem when Chaucer died. The groups have become fossilised, but Chaucer did not intend them to have this status. Any other solution implies that he had already finished his poem, that it was complete. Such a notion is absurd.

Since Chaucer has been studied in the twentieth century more than any other medieval writer, one might suppose that we are now able to read his poem in reliable editions. This is not the case, for the arguments used to support all editions we read today are faulty. All editors conflate the manuscripts in an arbitrary way and choose those bits from different manuscripts for which they have a particular affection. The evidence of the manuscripts has never been interpreted rigorously, for editors rely on their own "feel" for what Chaucer must have written. It may be that the fragmentary nature of the *Canterbury Tales* and the literary eminence of its author have made Chaucer a poet who seems to be sui generis and hence one to whom the canons of normal editorial procedure do not apply. It is time that his texts were treated in the same way as other medieval texts. In this the work of Doyle and Parkes should prove significant.

Their article in the Ker festchrift tells us that in the first quarter of the fifteenth century a group of scribes was responsible for producing many manuscripts of vernacular texts, principally by Chaucer and Gower. From the makeup of these manuscripts it appears that the scribes were working in the London/Westminster area independently of one another. They copied manuscripts or parts of manuscripts on a piecework basis for an individual or a committee with access to the exemplars of the texts. This committee was acting in an entrepreneurial manner by financing the production of manuscripts, either to order or as a speculation, and hired the scribes to copy the exemplars as necessary. That the production was speculative is suggested by the fact that the customers could have employed the scribes themselves, unless the committee had access to texts which were not generally available.

The first thing to note is that four early manuscripts (perhaps the four earliest extant) of the *Canterbury Tales* were written by scribes working for this committee. This suggests that the committee had access to an exemplar of the poem from which early copies were produced. This was not the view of Manly and Rickert who thought there were two distinct types of manuscript production of the poem, commercial and private, and it was in part to support this view that they developed the theory of independently circulating fragments.[6] Doyle and Parkes have proved that in the early fifteenth century there were no organized scriptoria for vernacular manuscripts and that there was only one type of vernacular manuscript production. The Manly and Rickert view of the production of the poem's manuscripts is thus made untenable, and the raison d'être for the theory of independently circulating fragments disappears.

However, the way in which some *Confessio Amantis* manuscripts were produced differs from that used for *Canterbury Tales* manuscripts. The latter were all written essentially by one scribe throughout with only headings and marginalia added in a different hand. Some manuscripts of *Confessio Amantis* were copied by several scribes who worked in isolation and probably simultaneously. The committee was evidently able to break up *Confessio Amantis* into sections which could be copied by different people so that the different stints, when assembled, would form a complete manuscript without a break. Each scribe had to work to a fixed format in copying his quota. Although the authors do not comment upon this feature, it is clear that the text of *Confessio Amantis* was sufficiently established for it to be divided into pieces of equal length which, if copied uniformly by different scribes, would make up a manuscript without any gaps or deficiencies.

The *Canterbury Tales* was not in this position, although one might have thought it would be if the organizing committee owned an exemplar which they issued to various scribes. Textually all four of the early copies of the poem differ among themselves, even though two were copies by one scribe and the other two by a second. We have the unusual problem of four manuscripts, written by only two scribes probably for the same entrepreneurial committee, with considerable differences in order, language, and presentation. It is a situation which seems to support the theory that the committee had access to more than one exemplar, though, as we have already seen, there are difficulties about accepting different authorial versions or independently circulating fragments. If the committee had one exemplar, why should it abandon it in whole or in part as other copies came to hand? Furthermore, if the exemplars were complete, they would be available for dismemberment and simultaneous copying by different scribes in the same way as the manuscripts of *Confessio Amantis* were copied. How can this state of affairs be explained?

The answer may lie in the fragmentary nature of the *Canterbury Tales*. If the exemplar owned by the committee consisted of unrelated fragments, it would need ordering, and this may have encouraged the committee to add missing links, tidy up the language, and spruce up the presentation of the text. This could mean that they had only one exemplar consisting of separate fragments which the committee was continually reordering and revising. If the additions and omissions were noted in the exemplar, it would be changing so much that it would be impossible to consider that exemplar an established text which could be divided up into sections for different scribes to copy simultaneously. A theory along these lines enables us to understand why an improving order is associated with a deteriorating text.

Hg is important because it is probably the earliest extant manuscript of the *Canterbury Tales*; it "reproduces with remarkable fidelity sources better than those used by most other copies and subjected to less adaptation and amendment" (p. xix). In fact Doyle and Parkes are unwilling to state that Hg is earlier than El, and it is possible that the relative datings of these two manuscripts cannot be resolved paleographically. Even in ordering and presentation they are not prepared to accept that Hg is earlier, no doubt partly because of Parkes's own work on the *ordinatio* and *compilatio* of manuscripts.[7] These represent two different ways of arranging textual material in manuscripts, and it could thus be argued that the more sophisticated arrangement in El need not prove a later date if the editor of Hg was trying to arrange the material in accordance with different principles. Since Doyle and Parkes have themselves shown that Hg and El were written by the same scribe (probably working for the same committee), it seems unlikely that the two orders were produced in isolation from each other. Indeed, other scholars have pointed out the dependence of El's order on Hg's.[8] As it happens, Doyle and Parkes are persuaded that the Hg scribe got the various fragments of the poem he was to copy in a piecemeal fashion, and if they are correct in that belief it is difficult to see how El can be earlier than Hg unless the scribe got the constituent parts of El in a piecemeal way as well. For if El is earlier than Hg we should have to explain why a committee used fragments in a piecemeal way after it had already commissioned one manuscript and so would have at least one complete copy available. Even *ordinatio* and *compilatio* are insufficient reasons to account for such a state of affairs. In any case, Doyle and Parkes point out that El is written in a way which suggests careful planning and deliberation—a factor which seems to preclude piecemeal acquisition of its fragments. It would indeed be strange if a scribe used a complete exemplar for his first copy and a fragmented, piecemeal exemplar for his second. Hence there would seem no reason to deny that El was copied after Hg, since that assumption best explains their differences in order and falls in line with what textual critics increasingly feel about the relative importance of Hg and El.

Nevertheless, the question whether even the editor of Hg got his material piecemeal needs further discussion. It is likely that Hg is experimental in its makeup since there are irregularities in its compilation. But it need not follow that these discontinuities "can be explained most intelligibly by interruptions in the availability of exemplars of consecutive portions of the series of tales and links and by attempts to take advantage of what was available while it was so, with a minimum of adaption, if unavoidable, and some anticipation of the possibility of future insertions" (p. xxvi), since other explanations are available. Two views as to the makeup of Hg seem possible: either it was caused by the interruption in the availability of the exemplars, as Doyle and Parkes claim, or it arose through indecision on the part of the editor about how to arrange for the first time disparate fragments so as to produce a complete poem. If the interruption of exemplars is accepted, one needs to determine which pieces arrived in what order and why—and this Doyle and Parkes fail to do. They accept the principle of interruption of exemplars without working out the details, perhaps because the details would be so contentious. The discontinuities which they use to support this view consist of the abnormality of some quires, the presence of blank pages, and changes in ink—none of which can be discussed in detail here. What may be stated is that some of these discontinuities cannot be explained by the interruption in the supply of exemplars. The quires of the Miller's Tale are irregular, but no one would suggest that these parts came to the scribe at irregular intervals as though the tale were circulating in parts. Similarly, the quires of the Franklin's Tale are irregular, though Doyle and Parkes provide an explanation which need have nothing to do with the supply of exemplars. The scribe was going to follow the Franklin's Tale with the Nun's Tale (as it is called in Hg), but decided to hold back the copying of the Nun's Tale until a later time. As he left the exact number of folios blank to accommodate this tale —which was subsequently entered into the appropriate space— it cannot have been any interruption in the supply of his exemplars that caused the irregularity of quiring in the Franklin's Tale. The scribe must have had access to the Nun's Tale if he knew exactly how many pages to leave blank in order to accommodate it.

If some of the irregularities in quiring can be explained by reasons which have nothing to do with the supply of the exemplars, then it may well be that all irregularities can be explained without recourse to that particular theory. The problem is that Doyle and Parkes have accepted current editorial attitudes about the text and its order; they accept that there is an "authentic order" (p. xxix) and that certain pieces are genuine even though they are not in Hg. They have therefore to explain Hg against the background of this normal text, a circumstance which has forced them to make assumptions about the composition of Hg that occasionally conflict with their own evidence. It would have been better if they had approached Hg without any preconceived attitudes. The manuscript would then have been allowed to reveal what it can about the state of the text when the committee told the scribe of Hg to start copying. Like the editors of the facsimile, Doyle and Parkes would have been better advised to approach Hg by itself without constantly relating it to other manuscripts and putative authentic orders. If Hg is examined in its own right, it is possible to see that there is an order in its composition, and such an order necessarily implies that the editor had all the pieces before he started work. Why should he leave a gap for the Nun's Tale unless he had such an order in mind? It may be better to assume that the discontinuities in the manuscript were the result of technical factors (as in the Franklin's Tale), changes of plan, and uncertainty how to bridge the gaps in the poem which were revealed when the pieces were put in an order. But that sort of uncertainty is best explained as arising from a first attempt at arrangement; the theory of piecemeal acquisition is unnecessary and should be discarded.

The new facsimile of Corpus Christi Coll Cambridge 61 (Cp) of *Troilus and Criseyde* differs from that of Hg in several ways. It contains no diplomatic transcription, and the text in the manuscript is therefore allowed to stand on its own. It is printed in color so that variations in ink are visible. The general quality of the photographic reproduction and of the paper in this facsimile is far superior to that of the Hg facsimile. Cp is a different kind of manuscript from Hg for it is written in a display script, it contains the famous frontpiece of Chaucer reading his work to the court, and it has gaps throughout the poem which suggest that up to ninety further illuminations were planned. Cp was a deluxe manuscript, even though it was not completed as planned. Hence the introduction to the facsimile consists not only of a paleographical section by Parkes but also of an art historical section by Elizabeth Salter.

The textual tradition of *Troilus* has received less attention recently than that of the *Canterbury Tales,* perhaps because Root's work on the manuscripts and his edition are considered definitive.[9] He thought the manuscripts were divided into three groups, α, β, and γ. γ is considered the latest and most authentic of these recensions; to it belong both Cp and the Campsall manuscript in the Pierpont Morgan Library, which have formed the base texts of most modern editions. Nevertheless no modern edition is based on one base text exclusively, for all manuscripts omit passages which the editors accept as genuine and so include in their editions. Hence modern editions of *Troilus,* as of the *Canterbury Tales,* are composite. No editor has justified his editorial procedure, though the efforts of the various editors have produced what Parkes refers to as "the received text" (p. 1). The editors of *Troilus* imitate those of the *Canterbury Tales* by choosing a base text and then altering or supplementing it in a quite arbitrary way. If there are three recensions of *Troilus,* there should be three base manuscripts; it is not in order to use material from one recension to supplement that of another. If Chaucer revised his poem, we must remember that revision can involve deletion as well as addition. All modern editions of *Troilus* contain a version of the poem found in no single manuscript and thus cannot represent Chaucer's intentions for the poem.

Quite apart from that fact, Root's work on the manuscript tradition needs revising. Doyle and Parkes in the Hg facsimile show that a fragment of *Troilus* which is apparently of the γ recension was written by the scribe of Hg. So it is likely that the committee was preparing this poem, as well as the *Canterbury Tales,* for publication. However, as the scribe of Hg was writing early in the fifteenth century, γ manuscripts must have appeared early in that century, for even Cp and the Campsall manuscript may have been written in its first decade. This means that α, β, and γ manuscripts may have been copied at the same time, and therefore it may be difficult to substantiate Root's chronological progression of the text from an α to a β and then a γ version. But if manuscripts of *Troilus* were being produced simultaneously by an entrepreneurial committee in the London/Westminster area, the developments in the poem and variations among the manuscripts may be attributable to this committee rather than to Chaucer himself, as is the case with the *Canterbury Tales*. This matter needs further investigation.

As a deluxe manuscript, Cp is not the earliest manuscript of the poem to be written, for the version was carefully planned and then copied from another text. So Parkes does not face with Cp the same sort of problems he and Doyle faced with Hg. Hence he confines his introduction to a straight paleographical description, and he rarely ventures into literary or textual problems. Although he follows modern editions in accepting a received text, this hardly interferes with the presentation of paleographical evidence, and his introduction is much clearer and easier to follow than that in the Hg facsimile. Salter, however, is more influenced by the claim that Cp has pure text. She uses this claim to complement the evidence of the frontpiece illumination which exhibits a pictorial "vocabulary to express matter newly and traditionally relevant to the poem" (p. 22). The excellence of the text thus seems to support the veracity of the illumination, which in its turn confirms the excellence of the text. Neither link in this circular argument is well-founded. The frontpiece is part of the *ordinatio* of the poem, the means used by the editor to make his text presentable to a patron or potential customer. Since the poem is courtly, it was desirable to make the poet courtly too; hence the traditional motif of the preacher/author reading his works, so ably documented by Salter, is exploited. The frontpiece was introduced to make the manuscript more attractive; in modern terms it was the packaging which made the wares marketable. The illumination may have little or nothing to do with the poem or poet. Similarly the purity of the text in Cp may owe more to the editor than to Chaucer, for the editor may have wanted to make the text more courtly and acceptable. The text of the *Canterbury Tales* as found in Hg was modified by later editors to make it smoother, less alliterative, and generally more courtly. The same thing could easily have happened with *Troilus*. We may have been misled by these fifteenth-century editors to expect certain attributes in a Chaucer poem and so to prefer some manuscripts above others. The evidence of Hg suggests that Chaucer's language and style were somewhat rougher than the standard we have come to expect. Since the editor of Cp took such care with the presentation of his text in its *ordinatio*, he may also have smoothed and purified the language and meter.

Notes

1. *Medieval Scribes, Manuscripts and Libraries: Essays Presented to N. R. Ker*, ed. M. B. Parkes and Andrew G. Watson (London: Scolar, 1978), pp. 163–210.

2. J. M. Manly and E. Rickert, *The Text of the* Canterbury Tales, 8 vols. (Chicago: Univ. of Chicago Press, 1940), II, 475–79, identified three inks; Doyle and Parkes in the new facsimile trace other shades of ink which have importance in such matters as the inclusion of the Nun's Tale. Also see G. Dempster, "On the Significance of Hengwrt's Change of Ink in the Merchant's Tale," *Modern Language Notes*, 36 (1948), 325–30.

3. W. W. Skeat, *The Evolution of the* Canterbury Tales (London: Chaucer Society, 2d ser. 38, 1907).

4. Skeat, p. 20; Doyle and Parkes, in *Medieval Scribes,* p. 186.

5. G. Dempster, "Manly's Conception of the Early History of *The Canterbury Tales,*" *PMLA,* 61 (1946), 379–415, particularly pp. 394–95.

6. Ibid., pp. 403–8.

7. Parkes, "The Influence of the Concepts of *Ordinatio* and *Compilatio* in the Development of the Book," in *Medieval Learning and Literature: Essays Presented to R. W. Hunt,* ed., J. J. G. Alexander and M. T. Gibson (Oxford: Clarendon, 1976), pp. 115–41.

8. N. F. Blake, "The Relationship between the Hengwrt and Ellesmere Manuscripts of the *Canterbury Tales,*" *Essays and Studies,* NS 32 (1979), 1–18 and references there.

9. R. K. Root, *The Manuscripts of Chaucer's* Troilus (London: Chaucer Society, 1st ser. 98, 1914), and *The Book of* Troilus and Criseyde *by Geoffrey Chaucer* (Princeton: Princeton Univ. Press, 1926).

Bishop Bibliographed: The New Descriptive Bibliography?

Craig S. Abbott

Candace W. MacMahon. *Elizabeth Bishop: A Bibliography, 1927–1979*. Charlottesville: University Press of Virginia for the Bibliographical Society of the University of Virginia, 1980. xx, 227 pp.

In 1967 Fredson Bowers predicted as imminent "a revolution . . . in the bibliographical description of nineteenth- and twentieth-century books." This revolution would result, he said, from a growing awareness of the amount and kind of detail required to describe modern books adequately, detail that in part could be discovered through close comparison of copies of an edition by machine collation: "I do not see how any future definitive bibliography of modern books can be issued that has not made extensive use of this machine-collation."[1] That same year, Warner Barnes's bibliography of Elizabeth Barrett Browning appeared. The revolution was underway. Barnes used machine collation extensively, discovering a variant state or concealed impression within every edition examined and revealing a welter of typographical variation previously unsuspected.[2] In the following year, Edwin Bowden's bibliography of Thurber, employing machine collation and other methods, provided a model for bibliographers attempting to analyze the multiple impressions from multiple plates typical of twentieth-century publishing.[3] While acknowledging that "the value of the Hinman machine" had been "amply demonstrated" and that thus "we cannot now do without it," G. Thomas Tanselle expressed a fear that bibliographies might present a mass of irrelevant detail that would obscure their function as histories of the published forms of a body of work. And he asked: "If machine collation of multiple copies is necessary for dependable bibliographies, can we realistically expect such bibliographies to be produced in the future except in conjunction with the research for editions?"[4]

Whether or not they have borne out his fears, the past few years have, it seems, answered Tanselle's question and have continued the revolution that Bowers predicted. Machine collation and refined methods of description are seen, for example, in the Pittsburgh Series in Bibliography, under the general editorship of Matthew J. Bruccoli, as well as in other recent bibliographies. And among further developments in the bibliographic description of modern books are the detailed (and often entertaining) attention to dust jackets in Bowden's Thurber, the systematic organization and numbering of entries in Bruccoli's Fitzgerald, the use of photographs of title and copyright pages in the Pittsburgh Series, and the use of plating to organize impressions in James L. W. West III's Styron.[5] Also during this time have appeared articles reviewing and recommending methods of describing type, paper, bindings, dust jackets, and colors, and articles on bibliographical taxonomy and tolerances.[6] The revolution is not over, of course. It suffers from a corresponding lack of development in the analytical bibliography of twentieth-century books. We are better at describing them than at relating their physical features to the processes that produced them. Nor has the influence of the revolution been universal. Some recent bibliographies seem relatively untouched by it—and for that matter by Fredson Bowers's 1949 *Principles of Bibliographical Description,* which included three chapters on the description of nineteenth- and twentieth-century books and which remains the standard work, most recent developments merely refining or supplementing it.[7]

Because of these developments and because of her acknowledgment of Bowers "for his careful attention to the text and for the time he spent in making helpful suggestions concerning changes and revisions" (p. xi), Candace W. MacMahon's bibliography of Elizabeth Bishop will have the attention of bibliographers. The series in which it appears, as a Linton R. Massey Descriptive Bibliography, has reflected some of the developments in descriptive method. In its second edition, B. C. Bloomfield and Edward Mendelson's Auden bibliography added dust jacket descriptions, and it made limited use of machine collation (for first and last impressions of Auden's earlier books) and of the centroid color charts. More recently, Joe Maynard and Barry Miles's bibliography of William Burroughs took a bibliographical step backwards. It did not use bibliographical taxonomy to show relationships between the items described (an item being described and called an "edition" whenever there was revision or a change of publisher or binding), and it did not describe typography (despite Maynard's preface that talks about seeing the "psychedelic" page that "baffles you for the moment, but suddenly you see what the artist saw, and you're out, gone, ZAPPED!").[8] In preparing her bibliography, MacMahon had a smaller body of work to contend with than Bloomfield and Mendelson and fewer fugitive items than Maynard and Miles had. Like them, though, she had the cooperation of the author whose works are the subject of the bibliography. (Bishop died on 6 October 1979, when the bibliography had reached galleys.) MacMahon's bibliography makes more use of machine collation than the others in the series. It pays more attention to textual variants, describes dust jackets at greater length, and adopts some advances in descriptive method. Like the Auden and the Burroughs, it should prove invaluable, even if it is not without shortcomings and flaws.

If, as Tanselle says, a descriptive bibliography is "a history of the forms in which a given group of books was presented to the public,"[9] MacMahon chooses to offer a partial history. In her introduction she explains that in Section A are described "first printings, cloth and paper, of all trade editions, American and English, of Elizabeth Bishop's separate publications" (p. xiv). Thus for *North & South* (A1) she describes the first impression but not the second or third. Despite her statement, she describes the first American impression of *Brazil* (A5) but not the

English edition (or is it an impression?). For *Poems: North & South—A Cold Spring* (A2), she describes the first impression, does not describe the second, and does describe the third because it is a new "trade edition," that is, the paperback "edition." When, in one of the letters quoted by MacMahon, Bishop expresses her hope that Houghton Mifflin will use for *Poems* (A2) "the same shape and size of page as the *first* printing of *N&S*" and "the same type" (p. 15), one wonders just what the second and third printings, or impressions, look like. MacMahon does not say. Nor can one tell whether MacMahon has been able to examine the undescribed impressions. She lists them and gives the number of copies in each but does not cite points that would differentiate them from other printings and does not give repository locations for them. And although she has employed machine collation, one cannot determine its extent, that is, whether it includes the undescribed impressions. She reports the variants discovered, for example, by collating the fifth with the first impression of *The Diary of "Helena Morley"* (A4), and she evidently collated the third with the first, discovering no variants. It cannot be determined, though, whether she collated the second impression, yet it may or may not have served as reproduction copy for the offset plates used in later impressions, may or may not have been printed from the same plates as the first impression, may or may not have unique readings.

The uncertainty about whether certain impressions have been examined and collated creates uncertainty as well about the completeness of the lists of variant readings reported for each poem. At the listing for the first appearance of each poem, MacMahon records the textual variants that occur between the first appearance, usually in a periodical, and its later appearances in the American editions of Bishop's books. She does not list variants in the English editions, she says, because Bishop did not see proofs for them. Although limits must be set—and in providing such lists MacMahon has already set wider ones than most bibliographers—her justification for ignoring the English editions could easily mislead naive users of her work. Regardless of whether Bishop read English proofs, the texts of the

English editions may be significant. It is possible, for example, that the copy for them consisted of uncorrected proofs of the American editions and thus might reveal earlier states of the texts. Moreover, even if they lack authority, they are part of the history. As Bowers has said, textual criticism is concerned "with the transmissional history of the text" and not just "with the establishment of its most definitive form."[10]

The search for variants also stops short of "reprintings in anthologies." Yet variants, sometimes authoritative, are often found in anthologies and are an important part of a complete textual history. Here, for example, is the list of variants for Bishop's poem "Sandpiper" (C129) as reported by MacMahon:

   10 ocean] Atlantic QT[+]
   13 The world is marvellously] And then the world is QT[+]
   20 and mixed] mixed QT[+]

The lemma is the reading from the first appearance in the *New Yorker* (1962); the variants occur in *Questions of Travel* (QT, 1965) and, as the plus indicates, in later American books. But between 1962 and 1965, the poem also appeared in the anthology *Best Poems of 1962* (B22, 1963). If its readings were taken into account, the list would read like this:

   10 ocean] Atlantic B22[+]
   13 The world is marvellously] The world is uniquely B22, QT; And then the world is CP
   20 and mixed] mixed B22[+]

The revisions occurred earlier than MacMahon's list would indicate. Comparing the two lists also reveals another difficulty. The variant at line 13 is incorrectly reported in MacMahon's list. *Questions of Travel* and *Complete Poems* (CP) differ in their readings. (Or perhaps it is only the first impression of *Questions of Travel* that differs from the first impression of *Complete Poems*. Without collation of all impressions, one does not know.) Errors occur in other lists too. For example, at C44 ("The Man-Moth") the reading in *Life and Letters* should be 'of buildings', not 'of building'; at the same entry a substantive variant in line 39 is unreported: 'inherited] inherited the'; at C47 ("The Gentleman of Shalott") the reading in *Poems* should be 'Shalott', not 'Shalot' (the same error appears in the description of A2); at C124 ("Song for a Rainy Season") the reading in *Questions of Travel* should be 'map', not 'maps'. One wishes for an accuracy to match the industry. Because of errors and because many texts were not collated, the lists of variants must be used with caution.

Descriptive bibliographies are opportunities for error. That is especially true in quasi-facsimile transcription, in which what otherwise would be a matter of form becomes a matter of substance, with spelling, punctuation, and typography taking on added significance. MacMahon's use of photographs of title and copyright pages, besides providing more information than transcription, also reduces chances for error, though some confusion might be caused by the reversed order of the copyright-page photographs of *An Anthology of Twentieth-Century Brazilian Poetry* (A10).[11] But errors—or unrecorded states—such as the following appear in descriptions of bindings, contents, and so forth:

A2. The spine of the binding reads 'H•M•CO', not 'H.M.Co.'.

A4. The half title on p. i should be italic, not roman; the heading on p. vii should read *'INTRODUCTION'*, not 'Introduction'; the heading on p. xxxv should read *'AUTHOR'S PREFACE'*, not 'Author's Preface'; and the heading on p. xxxvii should be italic, not roman.

A8. The author's name and publisher's imprint on the spine should be italic, not roman.

A9. The dedication on p. 99 should read *'Que quanto'*, not *'que quanto';* the part titles on pp. 101 and 141 should be roman, not italic; the part title on p. 159 should have a line break after *'Translations';* the watermark should read 'WARREN'S', not 'WARRENS'; on the spine there should be a comma after *'Farrar'*.

A10. The title on the spine should be entirely capitalized.

A11. As the photograph shows, the title on the wrapper should read 'POEM', not 'Poem'.

A13. On the back flap of the dust jacket, the line break should occur after 'line', not before it.

B7. On the title page, *'AMERICAN DECADE'* should be italic, not roman; the colophon should read 'Four-hundred-seventy', not 'Four hundred seventy', and 'Press,', not 'Press'.

B12. On the title page, the title should be italic, not roman.

B16. The price of the paper issue should be 35¢, not $3.00.

B19. A line break should follow '*World*' on the title page.

In general, MacMahon's descriptions follow current practice. For some reason, though, instead of recording leaf measurements as height times width, MacMahon reverses the order when the leaf is wider than it is high (as in A8 and A11). The centroid color charts are cited for colors, but the color names themselves are often abbreviated, despite Tanselle's suggestion that "the ISCC-NBS abbreviations . . . should not be used, for they give essentially common terms an esoteric appearance."[12] At times the abbreviations confuse even MacMahon, as when she describes the buzzards on the title page of A8 as "d. Yellow (Centroid 85)." The problem is that "d. yellow" means dark yellow and is centroid 88 and that what MacMahon meant was deep yellow, which is indeed centroid 85. Elsewhere are such colors as brill.YG, s.Y, d.B, v.gY, gY, and s.gB., which are used quite accurately but which might cause some people to yearn for the days of cologne yellow, laundry blue, and blue jewel blue. MacMahon does not employ Tanselle's system—or the earlier systems of Sadleir, Blanck, and Hartzog—for designating binding cloth, probably because most of Bishop's books appear in unembossed calico. MacMahon's system of numbering entries, reflecting publishing practice rather than bibliographical findings, is probably not as useful as Bruccoli's, though MacMahon is careful to include the bibliographical designation in the headings for the entries. When the portion of the number reflecting a publisher's designation differs from her findings, she encloses it in square brackets, a measure that may confuse those who associate brackets with editorial correction or interpolation. In giving page numbers for anthology and periodical appearances, she sometimes cites inclusive page numbers, sometimes the initial number only. Like most bibliographers nowadays, she describes dust jackets; in fact, there is a hypertrophy of jacket description, more space being devoted to it than to descriptions of the books themselves. In his Styron bibliography, West quoted in full the dust jacket blurbs, thus providing texts often difficult to come by. MacMahon renders the entire jacket, including blurbs, in quasi facsimile. The result will seem to some a violation of the "proper sense of proportion" that Tanselle urges in his discussion of jackets.[13] The space might have better gone to describing the undescribed impressions.

In addition to describing and listing publications by Bishop, MacMahon lists works about her, which she splits into ten sections: book-length study (one item, because she does not list dissertations), journal issue devoted to Bishop, articles, reviews, current biography, notices of awards, works that mention Bishop, poems about or dedicated to her, and obituaries. These lists appear to be reasonably complete and accurate, except that the section on works that mention Bishop is an invitation to addenda if there ever was one.[14] Those who regret the splitting of secondary works into ten sections can find solace in MacMahon's comprehensive index, although they then might argue that such an index would allow lumping all the works into one chronological list better reflecting the development of Bishop's reputation.

Given their variety of needs and interests, it is difficult to please all users of a work like MacMahon's. But all will find this bibliography useful, if not definitive. Undergraduates grinding out what are called "research papers" will certainly discover more than they want. Book collectors and dealers, especially those whose interest is still limited to "first editions," will have a mostly reliable handbook against which they can compare their copies of Bishop's books and of books to which she contributed. Bishop critics will find descriptions of the forms in which Bishop's works appeared (and thus the sources of the texts that are the subject of their study), listings of previous criticism and scholarship, and the texts of often difficult to locate dust-jacket blurbs by such figures as Jean Garrigue, Randall Jarrell, Robert Lowell, Arthur Mizener, and Marianne Moore. Textual critics will find quoted at length correspondence between Bishop and her publishers and between Bishop and Marianne Moore concerning the publication of her work; they will find a faltering attempt to record some of the variations that it underwent during the course of its transmission. And bibliographers will find a partial but generally accurate map to a small but important area of twentieth-century printing and publishing as well as a bibliography that demonstrates the use of some recent advances in descriptive bibliography.

Notes

1. Bowers, "Bibliography Revisited," a paper presented in an abridged form before The Bibliographical Society on 17 October 1967 and printed in *The Library*, 5th series, 24 (1969), and reprinted in his *Essays in Bibliography, Text, and Editing* (Charlottesville: Univ. Press of Virginia for the Bibliographical Society of the Univ. of Virginia, 1975), pp. 181, 180.

2. Barnes, *A Bibliography of Elizabeth Barrett Browning* (Austin: The Humanities Research Center of the Univ. of Texas; Waco: The Armstrong Browning Library of Baylor Univ., 1967).

3. Bowden, *James Thurber: A Bibliography* (Columbus: Ohio State Univ. Press, 1968). See especially his treatment of *The Thurber Carnival* (A15).

4. Tanselle, "Some Remarks on Bibliographical Nonproliferation," *Proof,* 1 (1971), pp. 170, 178.

5. Bruccoli, *F. Scott Fitzgerald: A Descriptive Bibliography* (Pittsburgh: Univ. of Pittsburgh Press, 1972); West, *William Styron: A Descriptive Bibliography* (Boston: G. K. Hall, 1977).

6. See, for example, Tanselle's "A System of Color Identification for Bibliographical Description" (1967), "The Bibliographical Description of Patterns" (1970), and "The Bibliographical Description of Paper" (1971), which are reprinted in his *Selected Studies in Bibliography* (Charlottesville: Univ. Press of Virginia for the Bibliographical Society of the Univ. of Virginia, 1979); Tanselle's "Book-Jackets, Blurbs, and Bibliographers," *The Library*, 5th ser., 26 (1971), 91-134; "The Identification of Type Faces in Bibliographical Description," *PBSA*, 60 (1966), 185-202; "Tolerances in Bibliographical Description," *The Library*, 23 (1968); 1-12; "The Bibliographical Concepts of 'Issue' and 'State,'" *PBSA*, 69 (1975), 17-66; and James B. Meriwether and Joseph Katz's "A Redefinition of 'Issue,'" *Proof,* 2 (1972), 61-70. Many of the developments are not restricted to books of the machine-press period.

7. Bowers, *Principles of Bibliographical Description* (Princeton: Princeton Univ. Press, 1949; rpt. New York: Russell & Russell, 1962). Typical of those

bibliographies largely uninfluenced by Bowers and by more recent developments is Robert A. Wilson's *Gertrude Stein: A Bibliography* (New York: Phoenix Bookshop, 1974), which ignores Bowers's bibliographical definitions of such terms as *edition* and his recommendations on recording signature collations and describing dust jackets and which does not employ machine collation or Tanselle's methods of describing colors, bindings, type faces, dust jackets, and paper.

8. Bloomfield and Mendelson, *W. H. Auden: A Bibliography, 1924–1969*, 2d ed. (Charlottesville: Univ. Press of Virginia for the Bibliographical Society of Virginia, 1972), and Maynard and Miles, *William S. Burroughs: A Bibliography, 1953–73* (Charlottesville: Univ. Press of Virginia for the Bibliographical Society of Virginia, 1978), p. xv.

9. Tanselle, "Some Remarks on Bibliographical Nonproliferation," pp. 174–75.

10. Bowers, "Bibliography Revisited," p. 191.

11. In *Principles of Bibliographical Description*, pp. 135–37, Bowers discusses the advantages and disadvantages of photofacsimile and quasi facsimile.

12. Tanselle, "A System of Color Identification," pp. 159–60.

13. Tanselle, "Book-Jackets, Blurbs, and Bibliographers," p. 113.

14. To Section J (articles) may be added Marjorie Perloff, "Elizabeth Bishop: The Course of a Particular," *Modern Poetry Studies*, 8 (1977), 177–92, and David Shapiro, "On a Villanelle by Elizabeth Bishop," *Iowa Review*, 10 (1979), 77–81. To Section K (reviews) may be added, under K2, Donald Hall, *New England Quarterly*, 29 (1956), 247–52, and Anthony Hecht, *Hudson Review*, 9 (1956), 456; under K3, Padraic Fallon, *Dublin Magazine*, NS 32 (1957), 39–40; under K4, Ronald Hilton, *Hispanic American Report*, 11 (1958), 61–62; under K5, Ronald Hilton, *Hispanic American Report*, 15 (1962), 870; under K6, James Radcliffe, *Michigan Quarterly Review*, 6 (1967), 296–98; under K7, Penelope Palmer, *Agenda*, 6 (1968), 81–90.

Green Thought and Ideology

Annabel Patterson

James Turner. *The Politics of Landscape: Rural Scenery and Society in English Poetry, 1630–1660*. Cambridge, Mass.: Harvard University Press, 1979. xiii, 237 pp.

One of the signs of postmodernism in scholarly writing is self-consciousness. At the simplest level, and dictated by new rigors of publishing, academics are having to acquire new habits of self-presentation, to think in terms of audience and marketability. In addition, a decade of interest in "theory" by some of the profession's brightest minds is beginning to pay off, not so much in the quality or applicability of contemporary philosophies of literature (such as structuralism or literary phenomenology) as in a general alertness to the problem of method and stance. In an extreme form, this trend results in metacriticism—books that are explicit about their own critical assumptions, to the point of making them the real subject of inquiry.[1]

James Turner's *The Politics of Landscape* clearly participates in the postmodernist mode, at all three levels of sophistication. It has been shrewdly condensed from a dissertation into a manageable book and tactfully illustrated with landscapes, even on the endpapers. It addresses itself to an audience who think and argue, rather than doing research, and who will recognize the "hot issues" in recent theoretical discourse. And it contains a final chapter that, far from allowing us the old-fashioned privilege of recapitulation, demands more careful scrutiny than anything that precedes, because it is dense with self-analysis and theoretical legerdemain. No proper evaluation is possible without mastery of this chapter, because it makes large claims for the book's significance in the profession.

The opening gestures of this chapter are self-conscious to the point of being coy:

> Conclusion
> Beginning Theory
>
> . . . you will uncode all landscapes . . .
> (Seamus Heaney, 'The Peninsula')
>
> This will be a conclusion in which nothing is concluded. I would certainly like to make good after my labours, to landscape the ground I have chosen to build in. It would be satisfying to tie up loose ends, to make a decent closure or frame. . . . My conclusion would have the pleasant task of making dissent unthinkable.
> Instead I will offer a disclosure. The literary text is always both product and process, and my trick in this book is to force a wedge between the two in order to clarify their connection. . . . To reveal the processes to see how its traces make the product distinctive. I should therefore give some account of the influences and assumptions that have worked on this book, and of the contradictions it has attempted to conceal. [p. 186]

There could scarcely be a more explicit admission that the scholarly and critical text has become its own subject and lays claims to being itself "literature," of interest as much for what it is (and how it came to be so) as for the material it presents.

Yet the remainder of Turner's final chapter proposes something totally different and extroverted as the book's chief claim to our interest. It is to initiate a "theory of rural literature" that would in turn contribute to a new social theory of all literature. I am not sure whether Turner realizes the conflict between these two perceptions of his own work (the text as organic form vs. the text as conveyor of serious messages), but it is clear that he recognizes the primacy of the same conflict in the profession at large. In describing the evolution of his own theory from the transhistorical model of E. R. Curtius's *European Literature and the Latin Middle Ages* to a version of literary Marxism, Turner believes he has retained and combined the insights of each. By placing seventeenth-century landscape poems (or any poetic allusions to landscape) in their social and political context, he

Green Thought and Ideology

claims to be building a bridge between formalism and historicism.

Precisely because, if this were true, it would really be a significant achievement, this argument requires inspection. The importance of Curtius as a role model here lies in his use of topoi—motifs of conceptual density that are recognizable in works of different kinds and whose recurrence in literature at different periods stresses the continuity of Western culture. One of Curtius's most famous topoi has been that of the *locus amoenus*, the perfect landscape whose reminiscence, it need scarcely be said, connects to nostalgic theories of pastoral. Turner's original choice of landscape poetry as his *subject* might thus have been connected to his chosen *method* of collecting topoi and sorting them; a Marxist sensitivity for the mode of literary production might have pointed this out, along with the salient fact that the topical method is endemic to many types of dissertation.

At any rate, the transhistorical approach could not easily survive application to English poetry in the early seventeenth century. Turner's extremely wide reading and substantial research discovered a "world of historical change and class-consciousness" (p. 187) in the hundreds of references to landscape he collected;[2] and beyond proving that the idea of landscape painting was far more important at this date than had previously been allowed, he developed an account of its function in poetry. Between 1630 and 1660, as men struggled to hold off and then to survive a revolution in which land ownership was a crucial issue, landscape became a metaphor for conservative thought. The *formal* aspects of landscape as an ordered composition became a model of political stability and class hierarchy. All signs of actual agricultural labor were omitted from rural poetry, as landowners preferred not to look too closely at the rural poor. "Green thought" came out of its pastoral seclusion and became ideology.

The third stage in the evolution of *The Politics of Landscape* was, one may fairly surmise, discovery that this thesis resembled that of Raymond Williams, a trail that led ultimately to literary Marxism, to Terry Eagleton and Pierre Macherey.[3] But perhaps because he began where he did, Turner was unable to accept any simple equation of literature with ideological content. He believes that a valid theory of the social meaning of literature will have to be able to deal with the significance of form; and ideological form is to be perceived as something only made possible by "the social insitituion of Literature." The institution provides norms and expectations for a writer to accept, reject, or modify; it is those acts of choice that reveal his ideological position.

Potentially this argument is extremely important and is a considerable advance over orthodox Marxist conceptions of form. But what prevents *The Politics of Landscape* from really making a theoretical breakthrough is the extent to which it has been co-opted, *without* self-consciousness, by the very institution it proposed to study. Apart from its own decorative formalism (fine writing, fine art, final ironies) which it would be churlish to regret, the book has its own conservative bias. Its selection of texts for evidence, despite use of Digger poems and agricultural statistics, has clearly been influenced by the canonical decisions of "literary" scholarship: Denham, Marvell, Fanshawe, Herrick, Ben Jonson, and the country-house poems are still at the center of the argument.[4] This selectivity produces a stronger impression of royalist or gentlemanly solidarity than was probably the case, while at the same time Turner's idea of the function of literature is virtually narrowed to the single one of defensive restatement, shoring up the status quo. Turner does not see that Denham might, in *Coopers Hill*, have been *advising* the king about his options in 1642, or that Fanshawe's 1630 "Ode" in praise of country life was part of a public debate about peace with Spain, or that Jonson's "To Sir Robert Wroth" has a peculiar relationship to Horace's satirical second epode, which may well reflect Jonson's own feelings of having been co-opted by the Establishment. In Turner's thesis there is no room for the use of landscape in a dialectic to which both sides—the Establishment and the Opposition—have equal access; no room, either, for the more subtle manifestations of ambivalence and irony in men whose general political stance might be known but whose feelings on specific issues could not be simple.

Marvell, in *Upon Appleton House* (a poem from which the agricultural laborer had decidedly *not* vanished), was certainly aware of adapting the country-house poem to the retired general of a revolutionary army who had recently acquired a large estate by sequestration.[5] At the very least, this use of institutional conventions must have carried some ideological uncertainty.

It is certainly not my intention here to derogate *The Politics of Landscape* for not having pursued all of the possibilities. Turner's arguments have opened up the field in a way which should enable others to take up his challenge—to develop a social theory of rural literature—where a more conceptually balanced study might have deterred them from doing so. The generic boundaries of the problem can and should be expanded into drama and prose fiction, while the chronological boundaries can be widened forward and backward; forward to Wordsworth, and backward, of course, to Virgil.

What should, however, be regretted is that Professor Turner was not, in his final chapter, entirely candid about the evolution of his study, nor about the retroactive relationship of his theory to work begun with very different assumptions. *The Politics of Landscape* appears as a work still clearly in process of revision; and no amount of post-Romantic talk about the value of process can substitute for coherence. No admission of contradictions, finally, can charm them away.

Notes

1. "Baring of the device," or defamiliarization, has become one of the trademarks of Stanley Fish, who manipulates his readers by withholding his theoretical assumptions until the final chapter. See *Self-Consuming Artifacts* (Berkeley and Los Angeles: Univ. of California Press, 1972) and especially *The Living Temple: George Herbert and Catechizing* (Berkeley and Los Angeles: Univ. of California Press, 1978). The final chapter in Turner's book is entitled "A Conclusion In Which It May Appear That Everything Is Taken Back."

2. The phrase is actually used to define the counterinfluence of Erich Auerbach, here unfortunately referred to as "Ernst."

3. Raymond Williams, *The Country and the City* (New York: Oxford Univ. Press, 1973), especially pp. 22–45.

4. Cf. James Ackerman, "Toward a New Social History of Art," *New Literary History*, 4 (1973), 322: "We have gained from this [Marxist] enterprise some valuable new perspectives on the genesis of works of art, but the works themselves continue to be selected and interpreted according to principles entirely unrelated to those that justify concern for the social roots of art."

5. On the acquisition of royalist estates by Parliamentarians, see Margaret James, *Social Problems and Policy during the Puritan Revolution 1640–1660* (New York: Barnes & Noble, 1966), pp. 85–86. In 1647, Sir Thomas Fairfax received by parliamentary ordinance land to the value of £5,000 (*Journal of the House of Commons*, V, 162).

The Lees of Happiness: More Fitzgerald from Bruccoli

Veronica A. Makowsky

Matthew J. Bruccoli and Margaret M. Duggan, eds., with the assistance of Susan Walker. *Correspondence of F. Scott Fitzgerald.* New York: Random House, 1980. xxx, 640 pp.

Samuel Johnson had Boswell and F. Scott Fitzgerald has Matthew J. Bruccoli. Both Boswell and Bruccoli conducted prodigious research into the lives of their subjects, but the results are as different as a Gainsborough portrait from a Rauschenberg collage. Boswell portrayed Johnson in an integrated narrative of selected anecdote and action stamped with Boswell's own personality. Bruccoli presents us with more and more documents by and about Fitzgerald and leaves us to construe their meaning as we will. Bruccoli's approach to the study of a literary figure is characteristically modern, and in an age where biographies are often indiscriminate catalogues of facts and quotations, his method has the virtue of unpretentious honesty. Since F. Scott Fitzgerald could be considered the best-documented American writer of his age, a look at the four collections of his letters over the past two decades tells us a great deal about the trends in modern editing as well as an almost staggering amount about Fitzgerald.

Andrew Turnbull's 1963 edition of *The Letters of F. Scott Fitzgerald* is a textbook example of the faults and virtues of the traditional approach to editing letters.[1] Turnbull selected these letters for "readability, literary quality, and with an eye to displaying the variousness of their author's complex nature."[2] Turnbull succeeded admirably in meeting his first two criteria with the splendid letters to Fitzgerald's daughter, Maxwell

Perkins, Edmund Wilson, Gerald and Sara Murphy, and others. In keeping with his goal of readability, Turnbull presented the letters to each correspondent in a separate section, except for the miscellaneous collection at the end, which is in chronological order. We follow the turbulent yet loving course of Fitzgerald's directives to his daughter and the growth of his friendship with Max Perkins without having to hold a letter in mind over a series of unrelated ones. This method is less successful when there are only a few letters to a correspondent and little development to follow, as in the letters to Christian Gauss. It also has the drawback of making a letter more difficult to relate to the rest of Fitzgerald's life. Turnbull was somewhat hampered in this third goal by the discretion necessary at the time, as in his meager selection of letters to Zelda Fitzgerald.

"The whole job will have to be done over again," said Bruccoli in a scathing review of Turnbull's *Letters*. Speaking for a new generation of rigorous textual editors, he castigated Turnbull for his "bad editing": "disregard of textual procedure," silent emendations, failure to supply the location and source of his texts, faulty transcription, "inadequate" footnotes, and "inconsistent" identification of the recipients.[3] Bruccoli was absolutely right. To his list of citations one could even add the silent omissions of whole paragraphs, no physical description of the letter (typed, holograph, etc.), and errors in date and place of writing. As a research tool, Turnbull's *Letters* is an exercise in frustration. One can neither rely on the printed text nor find out where to consult the original. Turnbull's primary intention was not to produce an aid for scholars, but if he had avoided the failings described by Bruccoli the volume would have been just as pleasurable to read and much more useful.

Turnbull's traditional "readable" *Letters* was followed less than a decade later by two editions of Fitzgerald's correspondence which embody the modern desire for a faithful, unemended transmission of the text: *As Ever, Scott Fitz—: Letters between F. Scott Fitzgerald and His Literary Agent Harold Ober 1919–1940*, edited by Bruccoli, and *Dear Scott/Dear Max: The Fitzgerald–Perkins Correspondence*, edited by John Kuehl and Jackson R. Bryer.[4] In comparing both collections with Turnbull's *Letters* on the basis of "readability," the reader now finds no difficulty with unemended texts. The reader gains a reliable text and a sense of contemporaneity with the correspondents. Kuehl and Bryer, however, do not describe the letters in full bibliographical detail (holograph or typewritten, number of leaves, etc.) nor do they give the location of the letters, though one assumes they are in the Charles Scribner's Sons Archives at Princeton University. The pages of both editions are more cluttered with notes and brackets than those of Turnbull's *Letters,* but this is a small price to pay for greater accuracy.

As the titles indicate, both collections are also representative of the popularity of publishing the correspondence between two people, one or both of whom are famous. This type of volume succeeds only if the correspondents have a close or important relationship, are both good letter writers, and develop over the course of their correspondence. According to these criteria, *Dear Scott/Dear Max* is the more successful of the two. The friendship between Fitzgerald and Perkins has come to epitomize the relation of author to editor. Kuehl and Bryer maintain the "narrative," as they state in their preface, by deleting uninteresting or irrelevant portions (indicating the cuts by ellipsis) and omitting wires and brief letters of a like nature. The general reader and the scholar are served by two kinds of footnotes, those at the bottom of the page for information necessary to understand the letter and longer notes at the end of the book for further information. *Dear Scott/Dear Max* is a good example of an edition which is both readable and useful. The general reader gets an interesting book with necessary unobtrusive notes, and the scholar gets a faithful text, with full notes.

As Ever, Scott Fitz— is less successful, principally because Fitzgerald's relationship with Ober was of a more businesslike nature, often concerned with the price of a story or the status of Fitzgerald's debt to Ober. In his introduction, Bruccoli states that he finds it "regrettable" that the "economics of publishing" caused him to omit 362 pieces of the correspondence, mostly routine business letters and wires, because it "is impossible to understand Fitzgerald's career without understanding his feelings about money."[5] I believe *As Ever, Scott Fitz—* sheds sufficient light on Fitzgerald's attitude toward money (not a very subtle problem) and that 362 more items would constitute overkill. Bruccoli does provide the description and location of each piece, so that the scholar truly interested in a detail of Fitzgerald's finances can trace and consult the unpublished material. Beyond a certain point of general interest and significance, it is neither necessary nor desirable to print everything, which brings us to the most recent collection of Fitzgerald's letters.

When confronted with Bruccoli and Duggan's bulky *Correspondence*, it is natural to wonder if Bruccoli has indeed done "the whole job over again" as he suggested in his review of Turnbull's *Letters*. Unfortunately not. As the introduction states, "*Correspondence of F. Scott Fitzgerald* supplements the three published volumes of his letters. . . . None of the letters in those three volumes has been repeated here" (p. xv).[6] The book contains some new material which Turnbull probably had never seen, but since the source of most of the documents is the Princeton University Library, much of it must be material which Turnbull did not select (for reasons of discretion as well as space and quality). The question of the merits of these "leftovers" must be considered in relation to the three previous collections, the intrinsic worth of the new material, and Bruccoli and Duggan's editorial principles and performance.

The outstanding addition of this new volume to Fitzgerald scholarship is the publication of some eighty pieces of correspondence between Zelda and Scott Fitzgerald and some of Fitzgerald's letters to Zelda's family and doctors. Most of the letters are from Zelda to Fitzgerald, since, as the editors state in the introduction, many of Zelda's papers, which may have contained letters from Fitzgerald, were destroyed after her death. The extant letters from Fitzgerald are usually carbon copies or drafts. Most of the correspondence dates from 1930, when the Fitzgeralds were first separated by Zelda's breakdown. Although seven items appeared in *The Romantic Egoists* and some excerpts in Nancy Milford's excellent *Zelda*, this is our first prolonged opportunity to hear Zelda Fitzgerald's voice, the voice that so inspired and haunted Fitzgerald, telling her version of the most important relationship in his life.[7]

For all the Fitzgeralds' glamorous unity in the popular imagination, Zelda Fitzgerald's personality and interests appear quite different from those of her husband. Fitzgerald's letters are mainly about people, reflecting his novelist's concern with the analysis of character, whether his own or another's —an interest Zelda Fitzgerald did not share. She writes in one of the courtship letters: "People seldom interest me except in their relations to things. . . . Nothing annoys me more than having the most trivial action analyzed and explained" (p. 43). Instead she was mesmerized by metaphor, particularly when used in depicting a landscape: "I keep thinking of Provence and thin brown people slowly absorbing the deep shade of Aix—the white glare on the baking dust of a country pounded into colorless oblivion by an incessantly rotating summer" (p. 256). Many of her descriptions are striking in their novelty and precision, but often the words surge on and on with less and less regard for meaning as an abstract formality takes over: "Just at the point in my life when there is no time left me for losing, I am here to incapacitate myself for using what I have learned in such a desperate school—through my own fault and from a complete lack of medical knowledge on a rather esoteric subject" (p. 237). She says little about people and their concerns, but concentrates on description and abstraction as a refuge from feeling.

Perhaps because of Zelda Fitzgerald's lack of interest in describing character and feeling, her letters after her breakdown have a moving dignity. She rarely indulges in the self-pity and vituperation which are common in Fitzgerald's letters of the 1930s. Nostalgia is often her prevailing note, but the past she longed for was not Fitzgerald's novelistic world of assimilated, reconstructed human nature and growth, but a series of attractive word-pictures like the description of Provence quoted above. The one person who mattered in her world was Fitzgerald, and any interest she had in emotion and character was lavished on strengthening *his* morale. With the curious stoicism so characteristic of her, she counseled him from the Prangins

Clinic: "Stop looking for solace: there isn't any and if there were life would be a baby affair" (p. 267). When reviewers seemed inappreciative of *Tender Is the Night,* Zelda heaped praise on Fitzgerald in letter after letter from a New York sanitarium. Her outbursts of pain, usually triggered by a sense of being abandoned by him, are the more frightening because of her total isolation: "You didn't care: so I went on and on—dancing alone" (p. 250).

Fitzgerald was the center of Zelda's world, and without him she believed herself to be somehow incomplete. As early as their courtship, her letters are filled with protestations of devotion: "I'm absolutely nothing without you—Just the doll that I should have been born" (p. 51). In a long letter written during her hospitalization in Switzerland in 1930, she states repeatedly that she tried to make a new world in dance because she felt that Fitzgerald had lost interest in her: "You left me more and more alone" (p. 248). After her breakdown and the consequent end to her dancing, she tried once more to set Fitzgerald up as the arbiter of her destiny, but with a new ambivalence: "Stop thinking about our marriage and your work and human relations—you are not a showman arranging an exhibit—You are a Sun-god with a wife who loves him and an artist—to take in, assimilate and all alterations to be strictly on paper" (p. 268). When she attempted to construct her own world in *Save Me the Waltz,* she capitulated to Fitzgerald's fury and agreed to make revisions because she used material (her breakdown) which he considered "his." Possibly her acquiescence in this and other matters was dictated by fear, since Fitzgerald, the legally sane partner, controlled her life in and out of institutions. But the evidence of the letters shows that it also stemmed from the genuine need and love which caused her to write when he was away in Hollywood in 1931: "We are like a lot of minor characters at table waiting for the entrance of the star" (p. 270).

If Zelda believed herself a "doll" or a "minor" actress awaiting the life-giving cues of her "star," Fitzgerald reveals in his letters that he regarded himself as that godlike figure. In a long letter to his younger sister Annabel, written when he was about nineteen, he sounds like a latter-day Lord Chesterton as he advises her about dress, manners, and carriage with admonitions such as "In your conversation always affect a complete frankness but really be only as frank as you wish to be" (p. 15). Significantly, this letter became the basis for fiction, the short story "Bernice Bobs Her Hair." Fitzgerald was never happier than when playing Pygmalion, often with commendable results, as in his justly famous letters to his daughter, or in guiding Sheilah Graham's education in the "College of One." Zelda Fitzgerald's fundamentally dependent nature fed this tendency, which sometimes appears in its least attractive form in his letters about her.

Fitzgerald seemed to believe that character could be remolded in life as well as in fiction. After Zelda's breakdown, there are several references in the letters to her "re-education" (pp. 254, 292) by Dr. Oscar Forel at the Prangins Clinic. The only light shed on this intriguing notion comes in two letters from Fitzgerald to Dr. Adolph Meyer who later treated Zelda at the Phipps Clinic in Baltimore. In a letter of 10 April 1933, Fitzgerald writes approvingly that Forel "believes in the strictly teutonic idea of marriage" (p. 307). In a draft of a later letter he explains: "All I meant by the difference between the Teutonic +American ideas of marriage is expressed in the differences between the terms Herr+Frau and the terms Mr+Mrs" (p. 311). Herr Fitzgerald leaves no doubt about who should be in charge as he directs Meyer that Zelda's "will to power must be broken" (p. 311).

The letters to Zelda Fitzgerald and her doctors clearly show Fitzgerald trying out his favorite roles, parts which he played throughout the correspondence of the 1930s. One role is that of the tortured artist who needs drink for his health: *"The dark circles disappeared, the coffee didn't give me excema ... I looked forward to my dinner"* (p. 242, emphasis Fitzgerald's). Another favorite character was the romantic artist about to die of consumption, domestic sorrows, and public scorn: "By the time we reached the Rivierra I had developed such an inferiority complex that I couldn't fase anyone unless I was tight. I worked there too, though, and the unusual combination exploded my lungs" (p. 241).[8] Like his hero Napoleon, Fitzgerald saw himself as a general making tough but necessary decisions. He explains to Dr. Forel why he refuses to give up drinking: "Now when that old question comes up again as to which of two people is worth preserving, I, thinking of my ambitions once so nearly achieved of being part of English literature, of my child, even of Zelda in the matter of providing for her—must perforce consider myself first" (p. 243). The sense of artifice, or fiction-making, is reinforced by the fact that many of these letters were dictated to and typed by a secretary, sometimes from a corrected draft.

Although Fitzgerald's novelistic tendencies sometimes make him appear an insensitive poseur in his letters to and about his wife, those same writer's ways inspire some beautiful passages which show that he continued to love Zelda, if only in memory, as he supported her for the rest of his life. His reproaches for some accusations of homosexuality she made during her first breakdown are tempered with love: "I am hardened to write you so brutally by thinking of the ceaseless wave of love that surrounds you and envelopes you always, that you have the power to evoke at a whim—when I know that for the mere counterfiet of it I would perjure the best of my heart and mind" (p. 244). The novelist's ability to imagine himself in another's place allows Fitzgerald to feel Zelda's confinement during her decade in institutions. On 19 May 1938 he writes to Dr. Robert Carroll about the possibility of Zelda's spending more time outside of Highland Hospital: "Supposing Zelda at best would be a lifelong eccentric, supposing that in two or three years there is certain to be a sinking, I am still haunted by the fact that if it were me, and Zelda were passing judgment, I would want her to give me a chance" (p. 501). *Correspondence of F. Scott Fitzgerald* is worth having if only for these letters.

With the exception of the correspondence with and about Zelda Fitzgerald, *Correspondence* adds little to Turnbull's *Letters* in terms of important letters to Fitzgerald's principal correspondents. The twenty-five items to Fitzgerald's daughter in *Correspondence* include some charming postcards and humorous letters, but most of the moving, thoughtful letters to Scottie

More Fitzgerald Correspondence

appeared in *Letters*. The documents in *Correspondence* are more concerned with mundane details, like how much to spend on clothes or itineraries for Scottie's vacations from school. They reflect Fitzgerald's concern for his daughter, but no more so than those in *Letters,* and may have been included for information about Fitzgerald's whereabouts and mention of what he is writing.

Bruccoli and Duggan include approximately eighty items of correspondence (about a quarter of them wires) between Fitzgerald and Maxwell Perkins. For the most part, we are scraping the bottom of the barrel here. For example, a note from Fitzgerald to Perkins dated by the editors 13 May 1922, reads in its entirety: "By this time you have got the letter defending my title. The jacket is wonderful, the best yet and exactly what I wanted. I wouldn't change the title for anything now" (p. 106). A footnote identifies the book as *Tales of the Jazz Age*. The letter of 11 May to which Fitzgerald refers can be found on pages 58–60 of *Dear Scott/Dear Max*. Fitzgerald discusses the title through eight points for Perkins's consideration. Do we need more? Or is the note in *Correspondence* supposed to tell us Fitzgerald likes the dust jacket artwork? Or is it included merely to fill in one of the cracks (certainly not gaps) in the Fitzgerald-Perkins correspondence? Even one of the truly interesting letters from Fitzgerald to Perkins in *Correspondence,* the letter of 19 July 1939 in which Fitzgerald tries to justify his break with Harold Ober, is printed as a long note on pages 404–6 of *As Ever, Scott Fitz—*. Fortunately, only two pieces of correspondence with Ober are included, so a similar excess is avoided.

The rest of Fitzgerald's side of *Correspondence* is very much a mixed bag. The editors apparently value inclusiveness above all else. From the Hollywood years they include both letters to Hunt Stromberg containing film scenarios and scraps like the facsimile of a note to Budd Schulberg: "Am upstairs doing a sort of creative brood" (p. 528). Sometimes Fitzgerald makes important statements about literature to other writers, but quite often he is just indulging in reciprocal back-scratching of the I-like-your-book-so-please-like-mine variety. This is especially true for the inscriptions in books, usually printed as full-page facsimiles. In an inscription to H. L. Mencken in Hemingway's *Men without Women,* Fitzgerald particularly recommends two stories and describes Hemingway as "a great writer" and "the best we have" (p. 210). This inscription is a significant communication between two major writers about a third, but is a full-page facsimile of "For Gertrude Stien/with best wishes from/F. Scott Fitzgerald" (p. 163) of equal value? We learn that Fitzgerald gave *The Great Gatsby* to Stein (and misspelled her name in his constant trouble with "ei" and "ie"), but a list of such inscriptions would do just as well.

If the editors leave much chaff with the wheat of Fitzgerald's correspondence, they are more judicious in their choice of letters to Fitzgerald. Since so few of his own youthful letters survive, the letters of 1917–1918 from John Peale Bishop, Monsignor Cyril Sigourney Webster Fay, and Shane Leslie give us a rare glimpse of Fitzgerald's early character and interests as well as the evolution of *This Side of Paradise* (in embryo *The Romantic Egoist*). The many enthusiastic references to Compton Mackenzie's *Youth's Encounter* point up the moral of how an author so little read by posterity could have been a shaping influence in his day. As he contrasts *The Romantic Egoist* unfavorably with *Youth's Encounter,* John Peale Bishop gives Fitzgerald much excellent advice like "the way to get it ['the universal appeal'] is to have the usual thing done in an individual way" (p. 25). If all Monsignor Fay's observations were as percipient as this analysis of his own and Fitzgerald's characters, it would be easy to account for his great influence over Fitzgerald: "We have great faith, and we have a terrible honesty at the bottom of us, that all of our sophistry cannot destroy, and a kind of childlike simplicity that is the only thing that saves us from being downright wicked" (p. 24). Outstanding among the later correspondence are some very funny missives from Ring Lardner and some somberly beautiful letters from Gerald and Sara Murphy.

If the content is not as consistently interesting as that of Turnbull's *Letters,* Bruccoli and Duggan's editorial policy appears to be a great advance. They provide a description of the letter (ALS, TLS, TL(cc), etc.) and its length and location. When no date or place of writing is given in Fitzgerald's letter, the editors assign these in smaller type. (A little confusion can arise here because the typeface is not very different from the letter itself and the position is nearly the same.) The place of writing is not given for the other correspondents except Zelda Fitzgerald. The editors stress accurate transcription: "This edition retains the spellings and punctuation in Fitzgerald's holograph letters" (p. xix). Regularizations are minimal and dictated by common sense: punctuation within quotation marks, length of dashes, placement of insertions, and position of headings and signatures. Editorial deletions are indicated by ellipses and a word-count, an excellent idea since the reader can know what proportion of the letter is missing. A useful chronology of Fitzgerald's life is also provided.

Although the *Correspondence* is based on sound and helpful editorial principles, their execution leaves something to be desired. Since the letters appear in chronological order, there is no table of contents. Under a person's name the index does not differentiate between mentions within the text and items of correspondence, either by a bolder typeface or a list at the end of the entry (as in Turnbull). For example, the reader who wants to consult all of Zelda Fitzgerald's correspondence must wade through the long entry under her name and sort through the mentions and items of correspondence by checking the text. The problem is compounded here because the correspondence written before her marriage is under "Zelda Sayre" with no cross-reference under "Zelda Fitzgerald." There is no correspondence with Samuel Goldwyn, but the reader would have to check six references to ascertain this fact. The usefulness of *Correspondence* is seriously weakened by the lack of any sort of index of correspondents.

If this were not bad enough, the index is full of inconsistencies and inaccuracies. Aside from many ghost references, the reader cannot even be sure of finding all the letters by checking each reference under a given name. Two letters from Zelda Fitzgerald (pp. 388–89 and p. 390) cannot be found by checking page references under her name. There is no entry at all for Brooks Bowman, although a letter to him is on pages 399–400. A reference to "Don Stuart," Fitzgerald's version of Donald Ogden Stewart, is indexed under "Stuart," not with the rest of the references under "Donald Ogden Stewart." (No note in the text identifies him correctly for the reader.) An index entry, "Reminiscences of the Napoleonic Campaign (Marlot)," also picked up verbatim from an unannotated text, is probably a reference to *The Memoirs of Baron Marbot*. There are even more problems with Marlowes since the Elizabethan dramatist Christopher Marlowe, whose plays are mentioned in the text, turns into that fictional detective Philip Marlowe in the index. Would that we had his services to elucidate the contents of this volume!

Footnotes are doled out very sparingly. Apparently, the book is intended for reading straight through, not for random browsing or use as a research tool. People are identified only when they first appear, even if they are mentioned later by first name alone. For example, Essie Jackson is identified as a servant at La Paix on page 316. Zelda Fitzgerald mentions "Essie" on page 334. No identification is provided, and the index is no help without a last name. Another difficulty is that the footnotes sometimes tantalizingly cite the other editions of Fitzgerald's letters to develop or explain some point in the text, rather than providing the information right there in the note (pp. 23, 106 and 170, for example). Other than these problems of cross-referencing, the notes—while terse—generally conform to the good sense of the editorial note: "The policy on explanatory notes is to identify: (1) all of Fitzgerald's writings; (2) people or places important in his life; (3) references required for readers to understand the letters. Well-known figures are not identified, except to provide special information. Unidentifiable people are not so stipulated" (p. xx).

The transcriptions are much more accurate than Turnbull's *Letters*. I checked thirty-five items in the Princeton collections, trying to see examples of letters to and from Fitzgerald, holographs, typed letters including drafts and carbon copies, and wires. I found the rate of error to be about 0.5 per letter, or one error every other letter, counting only what the editors did not regularize. Most of the errors are very minor, like an apostrophe where the original had none. I will cite all the substantive differences so the reader may judge their degree of seriousness for himself. In an autograph letter from Louis Bromfield (pp. 341–42), the editors conjecture that part of the penultimate line reads "[my new] experience," which looks more like "one more experience" to me. A letter to Gene Buck (p. 561) is identified as a TL(cc). The letter I saw is a typed draft with corrections in Fitzgerald's hand, not a carbon. In a letter to Scottie Fitzgerald (pp. 446–47), a name is deleted in the third from last line in the second paragraph. The deletion is indicated by a long dash, not an ellipsis, and no word-count is given. In line 10 on page 447 of the same letter two words are deleted silently. In line 4 (p. 234) of a letter to Fitzgerald's mother, "dance" is actually "dinner." The word "development" is really "detachment" (line 12, p. 49) in an autograph letter from John Peale Bishop. A letter from John Galsworthy (p. 167) in a very difficult hand had the most errors. The first line reads "your your novel," not "your novel." Line 3 begins "I find," not "Find." In the last line "I write to you" actually reads "I write in bed," which is Galsworthy's explanation for his crabbed hand. My general impression is that typed letters are transcribed more accurately than holographs, and Fitzgerald's letters transcribed more accurately than those from his correspondents.

Two facsimiles are puzzlingly unidentified. A full-page facsimile of the drawing(?) of a fair young man appears on page 40. No identification or source is provided. One is left to wonder if that is the young Fitzgerald or Stephan Parrott, a letter from whom is on the facing page. On page 415 a facsimile of a four-page letter appears without identification. The reader is led to assume that the letter is in the hand of Zelda Fitzgerald since it is signed "Zelda" and faces a transcription of what seems to be this letter. The handwriting, however, does not look like that of Zelda Fitzgerald. Rather, it bears a striking resemblance to that of Harold Ober. A possible explanation for this curious phenomenon can be found on page 220 of Bruccoli's *As Ever, Scott Fitz*—. Fitzgerald writes to Ober in June 1935 that "on an impulse I'm sending you a letter from Zelda that came to day."

The letter from Zelda immediately follows Fitzgerald's letter and is the same letter which appears in *Correspondence*. One might assume Ober made a copy for himself before returning the letter to Fitzgerald. The letter in Zelda Fitzgerald's hand is listed in the catalogue of her papers in the Princeton University Library.

An examination of the *Correspondence of F. Scott Fitzgerald* does not suggest that "the whole job will have to be done over again," as Bruccoli said of *Letters*, although a corrected edition with a good index would be most welcome. Despite some problems of execution, Bruccoli and Duggan's editorial principles could stand as models with their sensible rules for transcription, descriptions, and locations of letters. If some stretches of *Correspondence* are tedious, it would be still easier to fault an editor for including too little, since it is impossible to tell where a bit of information may lead. I cannot, however, agree with Bruccoli and Duggan that the "letters constitute the most authoritative biography of F. Scott Fitzgerald" (p. xvii). We have most of the pieces assembled in a sort of collage, but we still await the finished portrait which only the biographer's unified sensibility can provide.

Notes

1. *The Letters of F. Scott Fitzgerald*, ed. Andrew Turnbull (New York: Scribners, 1963).

2. Ibid., p. xvii.

3. Matthew J. Bruccoli, untitled review in *American Literature*, 81 (March 1964), 102.

4. *As Ever, Scott Fitz—: Letters between F. Scott Fitzgerald and His Literary Agent Harold Ober 1919–1940*, ed. Matthew J. Bruccoli with the assistance of Jennifer McCabe Atkinson (Philadelphia: Lippincott, 1972); *Dear Scott/Dear Max: The Fitzgerald–Perkins Correspondence*, ed. John Kuehl and Jackson R. Bryer (New York: Scribners, 1971).

5. *As Ever, Scott Fitz—*, p. xxi.

6. Three letters which also appear in *Correspondence* can be found on pp. 515–16, 591, and 594–95 of Turnbull's *Letters*.

7. *The Romantic Egoists*, ed. Matthew J. Bruccoli, Scottie Fitzgerald Smith,

and Joan P. Kerr (New York: Scribners, 1974); Nancy Milford, *Zelda: A Biography* (New York: Harper and Row, 1970).

8. Fitzgerald had actual spots of tuberculosis on his lungs at various times, but he also used this tendency as an excuse for his poor state of health during and after drinking bouts.

Virginia Woolf and the Creative Critic

Harvena Richter

Maria DiBattista. *Virginia Woolf's Major Novels: The Fables of Anon.* New Haven: Yale University Press, 1980. xiv, 252 pp.

Leon Edel. *Bloomsbury: A House of Lions.* Philadelphia: J. B. Lippincott Company, 1979. 288 pp.

John Lehmann. *Thrown to the Woolfs.* New York: Holt, Rinehart and Winston, 1979. xx, 164 pp.

Perry Meisel. *The Absent Father: Virginia Woolf and Walter Pater.* New Haven: Yale University Press, 1980. xxii, 249 pp.

Roger Poole. *The Unknown Virginia Woolf.* Cambridge, England: Cambridge University Press, 1978. 285 pp.

Phyllis Rose. *Woman of Letters: A Life of Virginia Woolf.* New York: Oxford University Press, 1978. xxii, 298 pp.

Beverly Ann Schlack. *Continuing Presences: Virginia Woolf's Use of Literary Allusion.* University Park: Pennsylvania State University Press, 1979. xi, 195 pp.

Leonard Woolf. *The Wise Virgins.* rpt. New York: Harcourt Brace Jovanovich, 1979. xviii, 247 pp.

Anne Olivier Bell, ed., *The Diary of Virginia Woolf,* Vol. III: 1925–1930. New York: Harcourt Brace Jovanovich, 1980. xiii, 384 pp.

Nigel Nicolson and Joanne Trautmann, eds., *Letters of Virginia Woolf,* Vol. VI: 1936–1941. New York: Harcourt Brace Jovanovich, 1980. xviii, 556 pp.

Ralph Freedman, ed., *Virginia Woolf: Revaluation and Continuity.* Berkeley: University of California Press, 1980. vi, 299 pp.

During Virginia Woolf's sometimes tormented final year, she became obsessed with the idea of writing a history of English literature. One unrevised chapter remains, titled "Anon," a crystallization of her idea of the writer as an "anonymous I," a collective consciousness which links the creative mind with that of the common people. Having herself waged a constant battle between the critical element in her nature and the morbid fear of criticism of her writing, the concept of anonymity offered a certain solace. The audience is "undifferentiated," silent; the creator is faceless, nameless: "Anonymity was a great possession. . . . It allowed us to know nothing of the writer: and so to concentrate upon his song."[1]

Mrs. Woolf's concept of the "anonymous I," whether applied to herself or her method of depicting character in the later novels, surfaces in several of the books to be examined here. In contrast is the new breed of critical biographer who regards his work as an art form and impresses the sharp outline of his individuality upon it. In Woolf's essay "The Art of Biography" she warns of the perils of flouting the "limitations" that truth and fact impose. Rejecting the extremes of fact and fiction, she offers a mediating alternative that is very much her own: "the creative fact; the fertile fact; the fact that suggests and engenders."[2] Like the silent spaces in her novels in which the reader himself can move and create, the "creative fact" does not depart from truth but contains it even as it enlarges the scope of whatever the biographer touches.

Two recent works, *Bloomsbury: A House of Lions* and *Woman of Letters: A Life of Virginia Woolf*, avoid the pitfalls mentioned in "The Art of Biography." But they exhibit a different and less obvious tension than the one between life and art, and that is between biographer and subject. Far removed from the position of the "anonymous I," the personality of the biographer is not absorbed into his narration; he himself becomes "most subtly displayed."[3] In other words, it is the biographer's performance the reader watches rather than the life of his subject. In the case of *A House of Lions*, it is too simplistic to see Leon Edel as literary lion tamer, putting the gentle beasts of Bloomsbury through their hoops. His pentalogy of Henry James showed a biographer who, however skillful his technique of arranging his subject's life into a series of psychological and dramatic patterns, never intruded. Yet in *A House of Lions* Edel is always present, sometimes exhibiting his usual urbane elegance, other times taking himself too seriously as master biographer. There is occasional sentimentalism, such as the nativity scene of Angelica Bell's birth; and there is a puzzling indulgence of his characters as "our personages," characters that in spite of the author's attempts at intimacy manage to keep their distance. His skills are most evident in the psychological analyses of Leonard and Virginia Woolf, and of Lytton Strachey and Carrington, which form in their own way minibiographies; and in the uncommon insight into the almost incestuous relationship of Virginia and Vanessa with their brother Thoby. Edel is also particularly relaxed with the expatriate in Paris—Clive Bell, Desmond MacCarthy, Duncan Grant —terrain that Henry James knew well.

More than a collective biography shaped and textured like a novel, *A House of Lions* is a microcosm of time and place: intellectual England during the Edwardian era and the years of the First World War. The action unfolds on emotional, artistic, social, and political levels. As if the nine characters were one hero-heroine who changes name and costume, the viewpoint remains consistent: a story of self-emancipation.[4] That composite hero—man in search of himself—emerges most clearly in the figure of Leonard Woolf, the most complex of the nine. In a subtle way he dominates the biography as intellectually he dominated the group in life. Edel lends him the overtones of the existential hero, an outsider who surmounts a variety of handicaps and operates on several planes. Although a competent novelist, Leonard deferred to his wife and concentrated on political writing. His " 'invisible' presence" was felt at Versailles when the League of Nations covenant was drafted (p. 240). The reader is tempted to wish that Edel, who visited Leonard Woolf on several occasions, had focused on his story with the rest of Bloomsbury as background. Only one biography of Leonard, a political one by Duncan Wilson, has been published; more needs to be done to rescue Woolf from the rather desiccated picture of himself which his autobiographies present, and from the malice which some critics exhibit toward him.

One detects some of that malice in *Thrown to the Woolfs*. John Lehmann's account of his time as manager of the Woolf's Hogarth Press is negligent autobiography, giving a vivid scene of publishing during the Second World War and an occasional vignette of Leonard and Virginia (unfortunately, very little of the latter—she is mainly seen gliding by in further halls or offices), but not promising all the title would imply. Perhaps Lehmann gave that all in his earlier excellent volume *Virginia Woolf and Her World*. Perhaps nothing can quite compete with Richard Kennedy's *A Boy at the Hogarth Press* which Lehmann refers to as "slyly entertaining" (p. 11). The fascination of Lehmann's account of his own press experiences lies in his descriptions of the many quarrels he had with Leonard Woolf and his sense of being "on sacred ground, an initiate in a temple" (p. 11). But the sacred ground had its quicksands, the vestal virgin her quirks. Neither Leonard nor Virginia was in complete sympathy—at least so accuses Lehmann—with the younger poets and writers whom Lehmann wanted so much to push, with the exception of her nephew Julian Bell, of whom a charming glimpse is given. Lehmann lodges a complaint against two of Virginia's most famous essays, "Letter to a Young Poet" and "The Leaning Tower," for their contention that the modern poets were "'too introverted,'" too interested in their "'own limited experience,'" "'full of confusion & compromise'" (pp. 30, 110). Virginia's conciliatory answer to Lehmann regarding the earlier essay gives another picture of her unfailing modesty and tact (p. 31). It also serves as paradigm of Virginia and Vanessa's revolt against their own father who himself had broken with the Victorian world of his youth.

Far more malice surfaces in Roger Poole's *The Unknown Virginia Woolf*, a book which is little more than a repetitive series of quasi-psychological speculations on Virginia's madness, a condition which Poole regards not as true insanity but as unconscious revenge directed against a husband whose temperament was antagonistic to hers. The issues Poole raises are valid and have been raised before: Virginia's physical incompatability with Leonard, the trauma of her half brothers' erotic maunderings, the family deaths, the doctor's prescribed regimes, the prohibition of childbearing, even the rational and competitive atmosphere of Bloomsbury itself. But in attempting to deal with these emotional aspects of her life, Poole takes scenes and quotations out of context and often exaggerates or misreads a text to satisfy a particular theory. Moreover, he avoids any scientific inquiry into Virginia Woolf's mental problems and their manifest content, which even the scantiest clinical research could have yielded. Given the testimony of Septimus Smith's view of reality in *Mrs. Dalloway* and the modern knowledge of anorexia nervosa, which Woolf undoubtedly suffered from in addition to the schizophrenic episodes, to deny the existence of mental difficulties is itself irrational. Part of the problem is semantic, but it matters little whether the term *madness* or *insanity* or *abnormal behavior* is employed to describe a condition which periodically removed Virginia far enough from everyday reality that she was unable to function as a writer. If treatment in those days was primitive, that is no reason to castigate Leonard and to see him involved with the nurses and doctors whom Virginia at times believed to be conspiring against her.[5] Poole's espousal of the conspiracy notion appears to have been prompted by the eugenics theories of Dr. T. B. Hyslop whom Poole claims Leonard consulted before the marriage. Hyslop believed that in order to preserve the purity of the English race, women with family histories of mental disease *and* those involved in intellectual pursuits should not be permitted to have children. "'The departure of woman from her natural state to an artificial one involves a brain struggle which is deleterious to the virility of the race'" (p. 123)—an opinion on which Virginia, had she seen it, would have vented her fury in *Three Guineas*. Poole's accusation is not only cruel but ironical, since it charges Leonard Woolf with embracing Nazi-like concepts. Poole compounds the indignities by rearranging dates and facts so imaginatively that Anne Olivier Bell, editor of the Virginia Woolf diaries, wrote to the *Virginia Woolf Miscellany* about Poole's misreadings, setting the matter to rights and complaining about the portrait of Leonard as "a calculating, unsympathetic, and imperceptive Svengali—a view of his character totally at variance with all ascertainable evidence and informed opinion."[6]

One observes another major misconstruction in Poole's use of Leonard Woolf's novel, *The Wise Virgins,* as a diary. By calling it mere "fictional algebra" he gives himself leave to transpose patterns from fiction to life, impute ideas to the author that are only exigencies of the plot, even quote characters as if they were their counterparts in life. For example, the reader is apt to take as fact what Poole reports Vanessa as saying about Virginia, whereas in truth he is only quoting a speech of Katharine in the novel. Since *The Unknown Virginia Woolf* contains no notes, much less a bibliography, the reader is left in that gray area where he is unable to distinguish fact from fiction—in this case, both Leonard Woolf's and Poole's fiction. The reader also wonders why this book was ever published, although a responsible study of the relationship of Virginia's madness to both her marriage and her art would certainly be useful.[7]

Out of print for sixty-five years, *The Wise Virgins,* which Poole uses so discourteously, has fortunately now been reissued. Although the hero Harry Davis presents the author's "less pleasant characteristics,"[8] there is more of Leonard Woolf in the novel than the distorted self-portrait itself conveys, together with a depth of feeling which makes *The Wise Virgins,* especially in its second half, engrossing reading. Quentin Bell refers to Leonard in his Cambridge youth as "a strange wild man of powerful intellect,"[9] and some of that brooding strangeness inhabits Harry Davis, a young Jewish painter who attempts to cut through the barriers of middle-class Richstead and falls in love with Camilla Lawrence who is a class above him. Virginia would use Cam as her childhood self in *To the Lighthouse* some years later, and the name Camilla suggests a virgin not disposed to passion. Harry's own passion ensnares him in a middle-class marriage after Camilla rejects him. If this novel is only partially a *roman à clef,* as Ian Parsons says in his knowledgeable introduction, it nonetheless presents the despair Leonard Woolf must have felt during the first two years of his marriage when the novel was written.

Of the many Bloomsbury portraits in *The Wise Virgins*, that of Vanessa as Katharine Lawrence is closest to life. The picture of Camilla is less natural, and if certain tones of Virginia's conversation are captured, her self is not; the dreamlike and ephemeral qualities are exaggerated for the needs of the novel. But the ambience of the Lawrence household, transferred from the Stephen upper middle class to wealthy upper class, has unmistakable Bloomsbury inflections. And the novel's emphasis on breaking through to the "new world lying within" (p. 201) reflects the philosophy and actions of the group as a whole. Caste difference, the Jew as outsider, Leonard Woolf's own household (his mother never forgave her son for the portrait of Mrs. Davis), the various social worlds that Harry moves among, are shown with astringent humor balanced by often poetic sequences, such as the scene on Waterloo bridge (pp. 50–52), and by a piercing analysis of emotion. Even the title, suggesting an ironic twist on the New Testament parable, stresses the need to feel. Certainly the wise virgins are not Camilla and Gwen's spinster sister Ethel, who withhold their oil, but those who, like Gwen, are ready to give even before the bridegroom comes. Childlike, responsive to Harry's ideas, Gwen Garland may represent something which Leonard felt he had been denied.[10] And the reader wonders how Virginia herself reacted to the novel (the diary entry of 31 January 1915 reveals nothing) and how much it contributed, years later, to the depiction of Clarissa's sense of sexual failure in *Mrs. Dalloway*.[11]

Although Perry Meisel characterizes Leonard Woolf as "patriarchal in the Victorian mold" in *The Absent Father: Virginia Woolf and Walter Pater* (p. 35), it is against both Pater and her own father, Leslie Stephen, that Virginia is seen to rebel. Meisel's provocative thesis proposes that Virginia was attracted to Pater as essayist because her father so disliked him. In Leslie Stephen's eyes, Pater's life as well as his aestheticism was immoral; only one Pater volume, inscribed by Pater himself, was in the Stephen library. Yet if Virginia Woolf was influenced in a dozen ways by Pater's style and method, she never wrote a single essay on his work. This Meisel sees in turn as evidence of rebellion against parental authority—that is, Pater as "father" of her literary style. "Woolf's greatest anxiety about Pater has little to do with sexism, sexuality, or even Leslie Stephen. It lies in the infuriating knowledge that she had inherited modernism rather than created it herself" (p. 52). From this position Meisel attempts to prove that Woolf triumphed over Pater even while being indebted to him.

The first half of *The Absent Father* is a literary tale of ratiocination in which Meisel unravels Pater's influence, offering as proof the many themes, images, and stances which Woolf would take throughout her writing. "Pater's sense of perfect art as an ideal kind of 'integrity' or 'unity with one's self' " she would make her own (p. 54). Pater's Greek affinities likewise appealed to her (pp. 60 ff.). Questions of the artist as alchemist (p. 57), as martyr (p. 56), as a "smith" (p. 61), as a natural visionary (p. 71)—all Paterian concepts—surface in both Woolf's fiction and essays. The importance of the moment (p. 47), questions of ascesis (p. 63) and "organic wholeness" (p. 69) brought about by a perfect balance of opposites, underlie Woolf's concept of the novel. Images of imperialism, territory, maps, and property (pp. 181–82, 202), of the past as " 'a deep river' " (p. 166), of the room as personality (pp. 62–64), of the connective threads between people (pp. 175–78), of art as a chemical process (pp. 76–77)—these and many more Meisel claims to be of Paterian derivation. If Virginia Woolf drew her images from the whole spectrum of English literature —territory and maps and connective threads, for instance, run all through the verse of the metaphysical poets—Meisel does not acknowledge the fact.

The final Paterian influence on Woolf—the concept of selfhood as a negation of "I" and an affirmation of "the common life"—occupies the last and unfortunately longest chapter of the book. Although Meisel's understanding of the "anonymous I" seems clear enough, the connection with Pater is tenuous. Indeed, the scarcely anonymous personality of the critic seems to intrude uncomfortably in this chapter as he bends and shapes his material to intention rather than to fact; the parallels and arguments seem academic, the Paterian influence merely imposed. One can concentrate instead on the brief, excellent discussion of *Between the Acts* and on the sexism which Meisel accuses Woolf of showing and of which, by his very stance, he himself could be accused. In the final analysis, it is not important whether Woolf did or did not triumph over Pater. It is enough that the first part of the book burgeons with ideas and insights for anyone interested in art and literature.

Virginia Woolf's quest for anonymity is also pursued in Maria DiBattista's *Virginia Woolf's Major Novels: The Fables of Anon.* DiBattista stresses the theme in her competent introduction and in part of her section on *The Waves* but not sufficiently elsewhere. Lacking a unity of focus, her study is fragmentary, occasionally brilliant, always uneven. The opening chapters on *Mrs. Dalloway* and *To the Lighthouse,* although unrelated to Anon, are worth examining. But the following chapters lack the control and insight of the first two and offer novels which at times are unrecognizable as Woolf's. A confusion as to the main concerns of the novels (is *Orlando* proof that *"Amor Vincit Omnia"*? [p. 136]; is *The Waves* an attempt to "resurrect the literary 'figure' in the modern novel"? [p. 290]; is *Between the Acts* a "sexual tragedy"? [p. 198]) contributes to these failings as do several small but distressing misreadings of certain passages. For example, at the end of *Orlando* a wild goose, which DiBattista has identified as "natural desire" (p. 129), is seen "springing, like a burgeoning Athena, from the head of Shel in a moment of comic theophany . . . as much a cock and bull story as that ending *Tristram Shandy*" (p. 144). The truth is that the goose does not spring *out of* Shel's head but *over* it, and the goose, far from being either "natural desire" or a contrived bit of ectoplasm, is related to the image cluster of Shakespeare and goose-quill pen and writing which dominates the novel. A similar propensity to see comedy in more serious moments occurs in a discussion of *The Waves* when DiBattista calls Percival's fatal fall from a horse "burlesque" (p. 158). This misreading bypasses the rich symbolism of the horse image as well as the earlier reference in *Jacob's Room* to a riderless horse which gives Clara Durrant an unconscious premonition of Jacob's coming death. Since Percival and Jacob are modeled after Virginia's dead brother Thoby, the *Waves* episode becomes a "sequel image."[12]

It is in DiBattista's discussion of *The Waves* that the reader, anticipating an explication of the novel in terms of the chapter title, "The Epic of Anon," is most disappointed. She shows little of the epic thrust; and after a Freudian reading of the novel as a dream in which Woolf veils herself in the masculine personas of Bernard and Percival, thus achieving a kind of anonymity, DiBattista abandons her arguments by considering *The Waves* as "a comic romance in prose" (p. 189). Yet many other critics have floundered in the deceptive surfaces of *The Waves*. Considered by many, including DiBattista and Leonard Woolf, to be Virginia's masterpiece, *The Waves* seems to resist analysis; its depths have scarcely been intuited. *The Waves* has also fallen prey to what might be termed critical favoritism. Certain Woolf novels seem to be "in," such as *Between the Acts;* others are "out," like *The Waves* and *The Years*. The diversity of views points out how carefully the reader must select his own critic.

Phyllis Rose's negative assessment of *The Waves* in *Woman of Letters: A Life of Virginia Woolf* derives from her feeling that the 1930s were for Woolf a period of literary weakness. For Rose, *The Waves, The Years,* even *Three Guineas* are "out." *Flush* is not even mentioned. Woolf's biography *Roger Fry,* about to be rescued from critical oblivion, is hardly given a nod. The judgment of literary weakness seems based on an appraisal of Woolf's life during this difficult period rather than on the writings themselves. Apparently Rose is trying to establish a close correlation between Woolf's life and work for the purpose of dramatizing how wretched or satisfying certain periods of Woolf's life seemed to be. Continuing in this line of reasoning, Rose places Woolf's novels published during the second half of the twenties as "the most successful and invigorating of all her works. No accident, I think, that this was the time when Woolf engaged most actively in the kind of feminist activity she considered appropriate, writing about women, considering women in the context of culture" (p. 175). Yet however much

Rose wishes to exercise her transforming hand, life and art do not necessarily mirror each other. And the consideration of literature on the basis of biographical determinism can lead the unwary reader down a wrong path. Unfortunate in another way is Rose's admitted bias against poetry. Confessing that she finds "Time Passes" "the least interesting part of *To the Lighthouse*," she goes on to consider the poetic/lyric aspect of Woolf's art to be a manifestation of the irrational in her nature, "the most personal part of Woolf's gift, and the part she most mistrusted" (p. 137). So candid a statement seems calculated to appeal to the mass reader to whom a liking for poetry may be suspect and to whom Rose's book, with its strong feminist slant, is directed. Yet in the concluding chapter, which encapsulates Woolf's life as a woman of letters, the questions of Woolf's madness and its relation to her art are treated with wise understanding. That chapter redeems somewhat the shortcomings of the criticism and returns the emphasis to the real matter of the biography, Virginia Woolf herself.

The vagaries of personal taste which control the direction of *Woman of Letters* are absent from *Virginia Woolf: Revaluation and Continuity*, a collection of essays chosen to give a perspective on Woolf's work and to view an important facet of each of her nine novels. Particularly cogent is editor Ralph Freedman's introductory essay, stressing "the 'revolutionary' reappraisal of Virginia Woolf" in this country (p. 8) and commenting on the different ways Woolf is viewed here and abroad. If the British view her as novelist and poet, the Americans, concentrating on her persona, see a writer whose ideas are more important than her art, who acts as a spokeswoman or "soliloquist" for her own thoughts and those of our generation and as a "model" for "a more mature radicalism" (pp. 5–6). Freedman believes this emphasis on her persona to be a stimulation to American critics, making them look more deeply into her work and obtaining thereby a new angle of vision. At the same time, the new view blurs the line between "a writer's person and her artistic persona" as well as that between "narration and life." The trespassing of these lines, whereby the writer becomes more important than his work (as happens in Phyllis Rose's biography), leads to a further concentration on personality with a concomitant decline in the interest in fiction (p. 6).

There is no evidence of fiction's diminution in this lively and informative collection. The essays on perspectives concentrate on little-explored areas: the creative imagination (Harvena Richter), the relation between Woolf's narrators and art (James Hafley), the forms of the Woolfian short story (Avrom Fleishman). The essays on the novels likewise seek out fresh views. *Night and Day* is seen as a feminine echo of *The Magic Flute* (Jane Marcus); *To the Lighthouse* of Shakespeare's *The Winter's Tale* (Maria DiBattista). *Orlando* is an experiment in "Art, Love, and Sex" (Jean O. Love); a politico-historical vision informs *The Years* (James Naremore); *Jacob's Room* reconciles fact and fiction (Ralph Freedman). Several essays accent the dialectic Woolf exercises in so many novels: between chaos and order in *The Voyage Out* (Frederick P. W. McDowell); between Clarissa as "an object of social satire" and an existential heroine in *Mrs. Dalloway* (Lucio Ruotolo); between the spiritual and social self in *The Waves* (Madeline Moore); between the comic absurd and the tragic in *Between the Acts* (P. H. Fussell). The emphasis on the comic in Woolf's work is gratifying and does much to dispel the view that Virginia Woolf was a Terribly Serious Writer. And in the case of *Between the Acts,* the comic exegesis dispels the notion that this unrevised last novel is at times clumsy and inept.

In a scholarly sense, the most competent of the recent critical studies is Beverly Ann Schlack's *Continuing Presences,* an examination of Virginia Woolf's use of literary allusion in five radically dissimilar novels: *The Voyage Out, Jacob's Room, Mrs. Dalloway, Orlando,* and *The Waves.* Except for Avrom Fleishman, critics have made only the most random mention of literary allusion in Woolf's writing, as if its presence were decorative rather than functional, extending into the symbolic and thematic center of the work. As Schlack uncovers meanings heretofore unexplored or unsuspected, such as the negative emotions implied by Clarissa's reading of Baron Marbot's memoirs describing the retreat of Napoleon from Moscow ("a tale of agony, suffering, death and defeat," [p. 62]), the scope of the novel is enlarged.[13] Up to now, Virginia Woolf's voracious reading has not been taken seriously enough. This critical gap has resulted in misreadings, such as those pointed out by Schlack in her apt discussion of the passage from Milton's *Comus* quoted in the final chapter of *The Voyage Out*, and it is impossible to underestimate the importance of Woolf's knowledge of literature in any critical consideration of her work. Themes, characters, images, symbols, phrases, and concerns of other writers and poets find their way into her fiction in the least obtrusive manner, so that her novels are a palimpsest of everything she ever read. Reading was not simply a pleasure; like writing, it was a practiced activity which became part of her even as she became a part of what she produced. Her memory was more than associational; what she read was not stored but became, like experience itself, part of what might be termed the creative mix. As such, the images drawn from other writers are woven into the work in the same intricate fashion as her own. The multiplicity of allusions to Dante's *Inferno* in *Mrs. Dalloway*, for instance, or the references to Shelley in the five novels selected, show how "interlocked" that patterning can be.[14]

Thus in addition to presenting a comprehensive study of the allusions themselves (a useful concordance to those allusions is included), the text serves as an interpretive study of the novels and reveals something of the hidden world of formal relationships whose harmonies constitute the aesthetic aspect of Woolf's work. Still another bonus is offered the reader: the sense of being a spy in the house of creation—not only Woolf's organizing imagination, but that of Beverly Ann Schlack as she runs down a quotation, discovers a new meaning, clutches a bit of evidence to substantiate a view. Adventures in scholarship may be frequent, but the reader is not always allowed to share.

A similar joy is promised by Brenda Silver's forthcoming *Virginia Woolf's Reading Notebooks* from Princeton University Press, which I had a chance to scan in an early stage. The book's scholarly interest and painstaking thoroughness are reflected in Silver's notes and commentary to " 'Anon' and 'The Reader' " in *Twentieth Century Literature*. The manuscript of the *Reading*

Notebooks is a guide to the immense quantity of reading notes which Woolf made over a period of thirty-six years, furnishing a useful lead to her primary sources as well as an understanding of the background of her later writings, especially *The Years* and *Three Guineas*. The notebooks also reveal an unsuspected side of Mrs. Woolf as a scholarly researcher who undertook a staggering amount of reading for every article she wrote. Lively quotations from the notebooks themselves are contained in the preface and notes, and there are delightful notations, such as what color ink is used for each notebook, that make them spring to life. Little that Virginia Woolf wrote conveys so vividly a sense of the quick of her mind as do these spontaneous jottings. And surprises, such as learning that she read sixteenth-century treatises on witches, or finding out that she is "painting the diningroom pomegranate color," raises the level of Silver's book far above that of ordinary bibliography.

Eclipsing the critical and biographical work on Virginia Woolf, then, is the immense amount of material she herself wrote that is still coming to light. It is to be supposed that her complete reading notes will eventually be published in an edition comparable to that of Samuel Taylor Coleridge's *Marginalia*. Woolf was probably familiar with the nineteenth-century edition of *Marginalia,* and the fact that she was so methodical about binding her reading notes, even inserting an alphabetical table of contents for each volume, suggests that the possibility of future publication may have occurred to her. Certainly it was the case with her diaries, the third volume of which Anne Olivier Bell has recently published. As early as 1919, she imagined them refining and coalescing into "a work of art";[15] in 1926 she considered it as "rough material for that masterpiece," her memoirs, and wondered a few weeks later whether Leonard "should make a book from them" (III, 58, 67). As to her *Letters,* now in print through six volumes, she avidly read a bound typescript of her early letters to Violet Dickinson, and again considered using "some scenes and a few sentences" for her memoirs (VI, 87–90). Although she begs Violet not to show the originals to anyone, she must have realized at that late time that every scrap she wrote would be printed. The personal nature of that correspondence may have been what prompted her to ask Leonard in the suicide note to destroy all her papers. But even that uncharacteristic bid for anonymity can be discounted, for Woolf's essays on early women letter writers and diarists show how seriously she valued their particular arts.

Both diaries and letters were, for Woolf, much more than a convenient source for her memoirs. They gave her, as did her novels and essays, a sense of her own "proportions," indeed of her identity (III, 343). If Virginia Woolf is known in America more as a personality than as a writer, it is paradoxically her writing itself that gave shape to her fame. There seems scarcely the thickness of a transparent sheet of paper between Virginia Woolf, pen in hand, and the words she produced: She springs alive from every page of her memoirs, letters, diaries. The art of being able to convey the self so felicitously (the very foundation on which her life depended) makes it difficult to distinguish between Woolf and her writing persona, and the difficulty is increased by the existence of a diary self, a letter self, a memoir self, whose differences are based on the audience addressed. Yet all these audiences, including that of the faceless and nameless "common reader," seemed to be a basic necessity of Woolf's life. Terrified of literal mirrors, as her memoirs suggest, she used her audience as a substitute mirror which would reflect an image of herself with which she could live. Her times of madness, during which she must have felt herself surrounded by distorted funhouse mirrors, made it even more imperative that she have reflectors who would reassure and protect.[16] Seen in this light, both her morbid sensitivity to criticism of her writing and her urge for anonymity (no face in the mirror) are explained. Criticism, like the animal face she saw as a child in the looking glass, threatened her very identity.[17]

In spite of two quite different time spans being represented in volume III of the diary (1925–1930) and volume VI of the letters (1936–1941)—the earlier one of the happiest periods of her life, the later far more troubled—the sense of self varies little from that of the preceding volumes. *Diary* III is perhaps more relaxed and expansive than *Diary* II, more thoughtful regarding the creative process. The letters, in which she assumes a different actor's mask for each recipient, continue to be witty, improvisational, exaggerated specifically for audience response.[18] Because they are directed to one person only, Woolf can be in turn outrageous, malicious, charming, fawning (especially to Vita), chivalrously humble (to Vanessa), confident that never for a moment will her audience take her seriously, that they expect just such extravagance as she dispenses. Yet granite underlies the rainbow glitter; so do warmth, fidelity, concern. Her special delight in these last letters is her niece Angelica, the "Pixie" to whom she signs herself as "Witcherina Virginia." However grotesque the portraits of people sometimes appear —grotesque in the Mardi Gras manner rather than malicious —they are more than balanced by Virginia's fierce affection for Vanessa's children. The most tragic moment in Woolf's diary is her admission that "a little more self control on my part, & we might have had a boy of 12, a girl of 10" (III, 107). A similar abyss is glimpsed in Vanessa's final letter to Virginia begging her to rest and avoid collapse: "What shall we do when we're invaded if you are a helpless invalid—what should I have done all these last 3 years if you hadnt been able to keep me alive and cheerful. You dont know how much I depend on you" (VI, n.2, 485).[19] One has only to compare this with a note from Virginia's diary ("Mercifully, Nessa is back. My earth is watered again" [III, 186]) or a letter to Vanessa ("Oh what a joy to think you're coming back! I feel like a very old sponge that hears water dripping at the thought" [VI, 299]) to glimpse the sisters' symbiotic bond.

These last quotations suggest some of the ways in which the diaries and letters differ from Woolf's fiction. There is a stir of passion absent in the novels, a spontaneity and freshness of metaphor and image. "The greed of my eye is insatiable," she confesses in her diary (III, 130), and instead of the vagueness which mists over the images in her later novels—an attempt for a universal tone—there is a particularity that makes her descriptions of person, place, and scene seem cut from crystal. This visual concreteness—whether she's describing England during the Strike, her domestic battles with her servant Nelly, her in-laws, or a parade of titled, famous, or near-famous people from Yeats to Maugham, Edith Sitwell to Ethel Smyth—makes the autobiographical writings far more accessible than the fiction. So is Woolf herself: "an incorrigible outsider" (VI, 252), a fighter (III, 260), a "melancholiac" (III, 67, 235, 241) who can cry "Oh detestable time, that thus eats out the heart & lets the body go on" (III, 46) but retains until the end a gallant and insatiable appetite for life. Here is the immediacy and energy of *Jacob's Room,* filled with scores of "excited, talkative, friendly people,"[20] books crammed with life and enough of nature to link her with the earlier English romantic poets who were also tied to earth.

For Virginia Woolf's greatest gift was reporting life as she saw it.[21] And whenever she pins down life, in her biographical essays, in diaries and letters and memoirs, and in parts of *The Voyage Out, The Years,* and especially in *Jacob's Room,* she is at her incandescent best. Long after the present craze has worn away, she will be rediscovered, as was the Jane Austen she so admired, for her devotion to life, to people, and to a wit more eighteenth-century than twentieth. Today, sociological and psychological issues seem to blind us to Woolf's clarity; we use her as a mirror for our own malaise, pursue her down paths which are not hers but ours. An entirely new orientation is in order if we wish to give Virginia Woolf her critical due: which is to realize her as a chronicler not only of her times, as were Pepys and Dickens in their different centuries and different ways, but of life itself. Her *Diary* and *Letters* may well be Woolf's finest and most enduring works.[22]

Notes

1. "'Anon' and 'The Reader': Virginia Woolf's Last Essays," Introduction, Notes, and Commentary by Brenda Silver, *Twentieth Century Literature,* 25 (1979), 397.

2. *Collected Essays,* IV (London: Hogarth Press, 1967), 228.

3. Woolf, "The New Biography," *Collected Essays,* IV, 233.

4. The "nine characters in search of an author" (as Edel calls them in a blurb appearing on the book's dust jacket) are Clive Bell, Vanessa Bell, Roger

Fry, Duncan Grant, Maynard Keynes, Desmond MacCarthy, Lytton Strachey, Leonard Woolf, and Virginia Woolf.

5. Rose, *Woman of Letters,* p. 265.

6. Anne Olivier Bell's letter in the *Virginia Woolf Miscellany,* No. 14 (1980), p. 7, explains that Leonard consulted Hyslop five months after he and Virginia married, not before as Poole insinuates (p. 121). Hyslop also did not caution them against having children but thought they should wait for a year and a half.

7. Jean O. Love's *Virginia Woolf: Sources of Madness and Art* (Berkeley: Univ. of California Press, 1977) takes Virginia from childhood to 1907, five years before her marriage, and gives an excellent background of her immediate family. George Spater and Ian Parsons's *A Marriage of True Minds: An Intimate Portrait of Leonard and Virginia Woolf* (New York: Harcourt Brace Jovanovich, 1977) is intimate rather than psychological and focuses on a detailed account of the Woolfs' day-to-day life.

8. Spater and Parsons, p. 81.

9. Quentin Bell, *Virginia Woolf: A Biography* (New York: Harcourt Brace Jovanovich, 1972), p. 69.

10. See Spater and Parsons, p. 160, regarding Gwen, the girl with whom Leonard fell in love in Ceylon.

11. Poole partly blames *The Wise Virgins* and its "unflattering" picture of Virginia for "the outbursts of 'violent hostility' toward Leonard in 1915" in possibly her worst mental breakdown (see pp. 101–2).

12. The horse image is also connected to Virginia and Thoby's great-great grandfather, Chevalier de l'Etang, who was exiled to India—where he "ran a riding school, managed stud farms, traded in horses"—because of Queen Marie Antoinette's too open devotion to him (Love, pp. 51–52). Percival too goes to India and dies there. Thus an ancestral romance is linked with a Grail romance, the Arthurian knight Percival having gone to India in search of the holy vessel.

13. Rose suggests (p. 144) another meaning to this passage, that of Clarissa's "enjoyment of the pattern of aggressors repelled." Schlack's seems the more likely interpretation.

14. "Such is the unremitting, interlocked allusive structure of this novel," adds Schlack (p. 72). Some of the allusions to trees (p. 70) do not seem to come under her rubric but belong rather to other image-clusters.

15. *The Diary of Virginia Woolf,* Vol. I, 1915–1919, ed. Anne Olivier Bell (New York: Harcourt Brace Jovanovich, 1977), p. 266.

16. "Suppose one woke & found oneself a fraud? It was part of my madness—that horror" (*Diary* III, 136).

17. Woolf, *Moments of Being* (New York: Harcourt Brace Jovanovich, 1976), p. 69. See also pp. 67–68 for her feelings about mirrors and the fright of buying clothes which is connected with this; also *Diary* III, 132 ("I went to buy clothes today & was struck by my own ugliness") and p. 21 ("It is bad for me to see my own photograph").

18. Volumes II through V. In Vol. I Virginia has not yet found her letter voice.

19. The "3 years" refer to those following the death of Vanessa's older son, Julian Bell, killed in Spain on 18 July 1937. The invasion of England by Germany was expected at any moment.

20. *Jacob's Room* (London: Hogarth Press, 1960), p. 111.

21. "It is life that matters," a phrase Woolf used in *Night and Day*, in her essay on Montaigne, in *Diary* III, 8, and in *Letters* III, 1547 and 1550.

22. See *Letters* VI, 3192: "Letters and memoirs are my delight—how much better than novels!"

The Development of Hawthorne Primary Bibliography

Joel Myerson

C. E. Frazer Clark, Jr. *Nathaniel Hawthorne: A Descriptive Bibliography*. Pittsburgh: University of Pittsburgh Press, 1978. xxi, 478 pp.

The publication of Clark's Hawthorne bibliography is a major event. Its use to scholars is obvious; it fills not so much a gap as a canyon. But also, because it is the first descriptive bibliography of a nineteenth-century American author which uses modern bibliographical methodology and terminology, it is a book important to all bibliographers working in this period.

The history of Hawthorne primary bibliography is easy to recount. (Works aimed at dealers and collectors, such as those by P. K. Foley and H. S. Stone, and piecemeal exhibition catalogues will be ignored.) The first serious studies were Nina E. Browne's *Bibliography of Nathaniel Hawthorne* and Wallace Hugh Cathcart's *Bibliography of the Works of Nathaniel Hawthorne*, both published in 1905. These two compilations were useful during a period when bibliographical description consisted entirely of listing the title, place of publication, publisher, number of pages, and contents; but they are useless for obtaining satisfactory bibliographical descriptions. Also, since Browne and Cathcart did not have access to Hawthorne's manuscripts and to his publishers' records, the two bibliographies are severely restricted in what they can say about printing histories.

Jacob Blanck's monumental, multivolume *Bibliography of American Literature* (1955–) published the volume containing Hawthorne in 1963. Blanck lists nearly 200 separate editions and printings of Hawthorne's works and first appearances in collections or in works edited or written by others. Yet the *BAL*, important as it is, is inadequate for a full understanding of Hawthorne's publishing career. Blanck himself warned that the *BAL* was a "selective bibliography." Its omissions are not owing to Blanck's carelessness but rather are the result of his carefully stated scope. In dealing with all of American literature through 1930, Blanck had to be selective: accordingly he lists only first book or pamphlet appearances, revised editions, broadsides, significant reprints, and first appearances in collections or in works written or edited by others. Other subsequent reprints or collections are selectively listed. This approach provides, as Blanck knew it would, a fine starting point for future study, but not a comprehensive bibliography. Blanck's plan excluded contributions to periodicals and newspapers; a comprehensive account of Hawthorne material in collections edited by others; most subsequent reprintings within an edition; most separate editions and reprints of individual stories; and truly detailed publication information of any kind. There are also inconsistencies in the handling of material. For example, the *BAL* sometimes lists first printings of Hawthorne's letters in books by others, but silently omits many more such letters. Moreover, Blanck did his work before widespread use of the Hinman Collator made it possible to determine textual variations in printings from the same plates. Consequently the *BAL* is unable to distinguish between various states in many works and overlooks concealed printings. Since the Hawthorne volume of the *BAL* was published in 1963, fifteen years of productive scholarship and resulting editions of Hawthorne's writings are, of course, not accounted for. Finally, the *BAL*'s bibliography of Hawthorne is based upon reported examinations for a small number of libraries, mostly in the northeast, and a few private collectors. The examination of as many copies as possible, in order to discover variants, is essential. Blanck, because of the immense scope of the entire *BAL*, could not do this. Because of his concentration on one author, Clark can.

Clark can draw upon two enormous advantages that Blanck did not have: a superb private collection of over 30,000 items and the textual work of the Ohio State Centenary Edition.

Clark makes excellent use of both. Compare, for example, the entries for the first American edition of *The Scarlet Letter* in the *BAL* (7600) and in Clark (A 16.1). The *BAL* entry is three inches long; Clark's is five pages. The *BAL* states, "All examined copies of the first edition are textually identical"; Clark identifies two states and two substates within one of those states. The *BAL* uses contemporary publisher's advertisements for publication information; Clark uses extant manuscript publisher's records as well. The *BAL* notes that all copies examined have an inserted publisher's list dated "March 1, 1850," implying that copies with ads of this date are of the true first printing. Clark states "4 pp. of T[icknor]&F[ields] ads with various dates inserted . . . . Dates on ads have no bibliographical significance for the printing of the text bound with them" (p. 144). For the second American edition of *The Scarlet Letter,* the *BAL* lists two printings (7601), while Clark clearly identifies two separate editions (A 16.2, A 16.3). These examples—and there are many more—should be taken as a compliment to Clark's thoroughness and not as a comment on Blanck's omissions. The overall scope of the *BAL* is enormous and Blanck planned to compress all his work into eight volumes. But clearly all future bibliographical references in Hawthorne must be to Clark, not to the *BAL*. An examination of Clark's scope and format will indicate why.

Nathaniel Hawthorne: A Descriptive Bibliography is divided into eight sections: A. Separate Publications (pp. 1–337); B. Collected Works (pp. 339–76); C. First-Appearance Contributions to Books and Pamphlets (pp. 377–407); D. First-Appearance Contributions to Magazines and Newspapers (pp. 409–29); E. Special Material and Selected Ephemera (pp. 431–35); F. Selected Bibliographic Material (pp. 437–42); G. Prose Material Attributed to Hawthorne (pp. 443–50); and H. Verse by Hawthorne and Verse Attributed to Him (pp. 451–58). An eighteen-page comprehensive index completes the book.

Section A "lists chronologically all books, pamphlets, and broadsides wholly or substantially by Hawthorne, including all printings of all editions in English through 1883 and selected reprintings to 1975" (p. xv). Clark wisely chooses 1883 as the cutoff date for comprehensiveness, since that year saw publication of the Riverside Edition, with its subsequent myriad and almost untraceable reprintings. This section contains thirty-seven main entries and is the cornerstone of the book. Each entry contains photographs of bindings; facsimiles of the title and copyright pages, and a sample page of text; and reproductions of points of bibliographical interest, such as type batter and resettings. The illustrations of bindings provide a visual record of spine and cover stampings that would often be impossible to describe in words; see, for example, *True Stories from History and Biography* (A 12), where the spines on four copies are all goldstamped "TRUE STORIES | [rule] | HAWTHORNE" but with leaf-and-vine designs that are similar yet not the same. Facsimile reproductions of title and copyright pages are, of course, more accurate than quasi-facsimile transcriptions—all bibliographies should use this method. The sample page of text gives the reader a "feel" for the book. Clark's use of photofacsimiles for bibliographical points is especially pleasing; many variations are minute and must be seen to be fully understood. Thus Clark reproduces, among others, the three states of the frontispiece to *The Gentle Boy* (A 2.2); type batter and wrapper states for *Mosses from an Old Manse* (A 15); resettings causing different states in the first edition, first printing, and the second edition of *The Scarlet Letter* (A 16); type batter within the 1851 printings of *The House of the Seven Gables* (A 17); type batter within the second printing of the first edition of *The Blithedale Romance* (A 20); two forms of the wrapper for *Life of Franklin Pierce* (A 21); plate variants within the Tauchnitz edition of *The Marble Faun* (A 23); and distinctive characteristics of the first and second printings of *Passages from the American Notebooks* (A 26). For many of these examples, such as the difference between the third and the fourth printings of *The House of the Seven Gables,* where a distinguishing characteristic is a one-millimeter repositioning of a question mark, an illustration is essential.

Other information given in Section A includes pagination, collation, contents (with indications for the stories of first appearance in print, first collected appearance, and those attributed to Hawthorne), typography and paper (running heads and paper type), binding (color and material, and stamping, endpaper, flyleaf, edge gilding, and edge trimming information), publication (number of copies, date published, royalty statement), printing (from type metal or stereotype plates, by whom, and, for English works, from what form of the text—such as proof sheets), locations of examined copies, and locations of relevant manuscript material for the book. Various notes provide background information from previously published bibliographical studies and from unpublished manuscript sources. Later editions have quasi-facsimile transcriptions of title pages and selected publication information; here Clark draws heavily upon the manuscript costbooks of Hawthorne's publishers. Later printings within editions are grouped chronologically after the first printing within that edition, thus preserving a sense of textual transmission.

The relationship between English and American editions, printings, and issues is clearly stated. Clark gives full bibliographical treatment to major English editions (that is, photofacsimiles and complete bibliographical information). Where known, he states the source for the English text—such as the American proof sheets or American pages. Of course, when the English edition precedes the American, as in *The Transformation /The Marble Faun* (A 23), the English edition is listed first and full bibliographical treatment is given both.

Because Hawthorne published a number of short-story collections, Clark has to face the problem of what to do with separate editions of individual stories from a collection. His practical solution is to give full bibliographical treatment (as with the major volume) to all important contemporary separate editions, such as *The Gentle Boy* from *Twice-Told Tales* (A 2), and to quasi-facsimile the title pages and give selective bibliographical and publication information for later editions of individual stories or partial collections of stories.

One part of Section A—the listing of late nineteenth-century reprints—will prove to be of great value to future bibliographers of nineteenth-century American authors. Clark has made sense out of the apparent disorder of undated reprints by companies such as John B. Alden, Henry Altemus, H. M.

Caldwell, Samuel E. Cassino, Thomas Y. Crowell, Donohue, Home Book Company, Hurst, John W. Lovell, F. M. Lupton, David McKay, and Worthington. Clark's contribution to our knowledge of late nineteenth-century publishing practices is twofold: First, he is able to determine the order of these reprints—who leased, borrowed, or stole from whom; second, he indicates the various formats and series in which these publishers distributed their titles.

In Section B Clark organizes and describes the various collected editions of Hawthorne's works. Full publication information—number of copies printed, price, binding formats, deposit copies—is given. Clark identifies four major collected editions published by Ticknor and Fields and its successors. The Tinted Edition of 1865–1876 was the first collected edition of Hawthorne's works. Advertised but not identified as such, it apparently derives its name from its parchment-tinted paper. The Tinted Edition plates were used for the Illustrated Library Edition (1871–1882), The Globe Edition (1880), and the "New" Fireside Edition (1886). The second collected edition, the Little Classic Edition of 1875–1883, was also advertised but not identified as such, and its plates served for the Fireside Edition (1879–1882; advertised but not identified as such), the Popular Edition (1891), and the Concord Edition (1889). The Riverside Edition of 1883–1891 comes next, and its plates were used in the Kegan Paul issue of the Riverside Edition (1883–1891), the Wayside Edition (1884–1891), the Standard Library Edition (1891), the "New"Wayside Edition (1902; advertised as such but identified as the Wayside Edition), the Fireside Edition (1909), and the Jefferson Press edition (1913). Finally, plates of the Autograph Edition of 1900 were used in the Old Manse Edition (1903). This brief history does not include the other contemporary collected editions and various Large Paper Editions, all of which Clark describes as well. Also present in this section are "selected collected works and certain one-volume collections by other publishers through 1975, included because of their interest or for textual reasons" (p. 339). All bindings of major editions are fully illustrated by photographs.

The value of Section B to Hawthorne scholars is obvious: Now unlabeled collected editions can be identified and their place in the transmission of Hawthorne's texts can be established. To anyone else doing a bibliography of a Houghton, Mifflin author—and this includes most of the "New England authors"—this section is a godsend. Now books seductively —because only—identified as "Emerson's Works" or "Lowell's Writings" can be established as being parts of specific collected editions by comparing them with Clark's binding illustrations and other information. Also, since Clark has established the pedigree for collected editions of Hawthorne's works, and since Houghton, Mifflin tended to use similar formats during the same period for its other authors, Clark's bibliography serves as a starting point for similar examinations of other popular Houghton, Mifflin authors.

Section C lists first American and English publications in books and pamphlets. Also, "selected reprintings up through 1850 are noted to show the exposure and spread of Hawthorne's name and work prior to the publication of *The Scarlet Letter*" (p. 377). This last is an understatement, since Clark pulls in a large number of previously unrecorded newspaper and magazine reprintings.[1] Each entry contains a quasi-facsimile title page transcription, selected publication information, reviews and notices for the earlier books, a list of Hawthorne's contributions (cross-referenced to each work's appearance in other relevant sections of the bibliography), and information about contemporary reprintings of individual stories. Most entries are accompanied by photographs of bindings, especially wrappers. Clark has not only included the obvious—*Tokens, Æsthetic Papers,* various gift books—but also books containing quotations from Hawthorne's letters and manuscripts. There are eighty-nine entries in Section C.

Section D lists first American and English publication for Hawthorne items in magazines and newspapers. As in Section C, selected reprintings through 1850 are included. Clark provides complete bibliographical references and cross-references to subsequent appearances. Both prose and verse are included (even though verse publications are repeated as full entries in Section H). The 111 entries in Section D also include contemporary and posthumous serializations of Hawthorne's longer works, and posthumous printings of manuscript writings, journals, and letters through 1904. (Not included are twentieth-century printings of letters in scholarly journals, some of which are listed in Section C as offprints.)

Section E, "Special Material and Ephemera, " contains four items: Hawthorne's manuscript newspaper, "The Spectator" (illustrated), his manuscript Latin composition "De Patribus Conscriptis Romanorum," the sheet music for *The Ocean* (illustrated), and the *Address* of the American Copyright Club, of which Hawthorne was an associate member. Section F lists "Selected Bibliographic Material," twenty-five primary bibliographies and exhibition catalogues from Anderson's "Bibliography" in Conway's 1890 *Life of Nathaniel Hawthorne* to Clark's own *Nathaniel Hawthorne: The American Experience* in 1974. Section G discusses "Prose Material Attributed to Hawthorne," giving the reasons for and against attribution. Clark uses much previously unpublished material—especially J. E. Babson's ("Tom Folio") and P. K. Foley's notes—to trace the history of these mostly erroneous pieces. Included are attributed pieces collected in the Ohio State Centenary Edition. *Hawthorne's First Diary* is listed, and rejected, among the twenty-five items here. Section H, "Verse by Hawthorne and Verse Attributed to Him," lists thirty-seven items appearing in newspapers, magazines, and books by and about Hawthorne. Doubtful attributions are so indicated.

Clark's format follows that of other volumes in the Pittsburgh Series in Bibliography. Nearly everything is in chronological order, the sole exception being that printings within an edition are listed after the main entry for that edition. The numbering system for entries in Section A indicates the edition, printing, and, where applicable, state or issue. Thus for *Mosses from an Old Manse*, A 15.1.a "indicates that it is the fifteenth separate Hawthorne work published *(15)* and that the entry is for the first edition *(1)*, first printing *(a)*" (p. xv). States and issues are designated by subscripts.

Clark's terminology is also similar to other volumes in the

Pittsburgh series. An *edition* is "all copies of a book printed from a single setting of type—including all reprintings from the standing type or plates made from that typesetting"; a *printing* is "all copies of a book printed at one time (without moving the type or plates from the press)"; a *state* occurs "when some copies of a particular printing are altered *before* publication—that is, by stop-press correction or cancellation of leaves"; and an *issue* is "created by the alteration of some copies of a single printing *after* publication in a way that affects the circumstances of publication, sale, or distribution—frequently by alteration of the title page or other preliminary matter" (p. xvi). Clark applies the first three terms only to the printed sheets of a book but goes further with *issue,* using the term "to describe alterations of sheets and/or bindings created deliberately for the purpose of influencing the conditions of sale" (p. xvii). Clark gives as an example the English piracies sold in the Railway Library series, where the sheets of a work could be bound in paper wrappers, cloth, or leather (at different prices and often as parts of different "series"), or bound with sheets of another Hawthorne work to create a single volume containing two titles. These Clark describes as "binding issues because they represent deliberate alteration of some copies of a single printing *after* publication for the express purpose of changing the circumstances of publication, distribution, and sale" (p. xvii).

While Clark's use of *issue* may disturb some bibliographers, it is a practical one that comes to grips with the facts of nineteenth-century book publishing practices. Most bibliographical terminology derives from studies of Renaissance printing techniques. The mass-production period of the early and middle nineteenth century, however, introduced new techniques and eliminated old ones, and, therefore, the terminology based upon these earlier techniques often does not apply. The term *issue* is a good example, being derived from Renaissance practices when small printings on hand-run presses were made for local distribution. The sheets of the books were often sold unbound and therefore little attention was paid to the importance of bindings in bibliographical description or as a source of information. By the mid-nineteenth century, though, we see much larger printings on machine presses, often intended for international distribution. As a result, publishers would sometimes place a dual English and American imprint on the title page (for example, "Boston: John P. Jewett; London: Sampson Low, Son & Co."), bind one set of sheets in American casings and send another set of the same sheets to England where they would be bound in English casings (with the same title page). Clearly the English book's format indicates an attempt to affect the conditions of publication, but, because of the accepted definition of *issue*, it is usually identified only as a binding variant. Clark wisely calls such English importations of American sheets *issues*. The need for a reevaluation of *issue* also arises in cases where publisher B buys the sheets of a book from publisher A and binds them, with publisher A's title page, in publisher B's casings, as Little, Brown and Company did when they purchased Roberts Brothers' stock of Margaret Fuller's works. Clearly this is an important attempt to influence marketing and distribution, similar to a case in which an English publisher imports an American publisher's sheets. In general, Clark points the way toward a new, more comprehensive definition of *issue*, one that places the appropriate emphasis on merchandising or marketing, not merely upon sheets.[2]

Clark also discusses the relationship of publisher's advertisements to the book they are bound in. It is a sad comment on book dealers and collectors (and some bibliographers) that Clark has to state the obvious: *"only when the ads are an integral part of the text . . . can they have any bearing on determining the priority of the text"* (pp. xvii–xviii). In short, in nearly all cases, inserted ads have nothing to do with establishing printing priorities.

Binding cloth designations are based on G. Thomas Tanselle's "The Specifications of Binding Cloths" in *The Library* (September 1966).[3] Color specifications are taken from the *ISCC-NBS Color Name Charts Illustrated with Centroid Colors;* more on this later.

The University of Pittsburgh Press has produced a handsome book, lavishly illustrated. The type face leaves something to be desired, though, being a sans serif font which is hard on the eyes and hard to read—commas and periods are similar in appearance, as are lower-case *l*s, vertical lines, and brackets. Also, someone must have fallen asleep during printing, for the text for page 456 is repeated in full on page 458.

Any good bibliography should be accurate, and Clark's book meets this test superbly. I checked his descriptions against about three dozen copies and found no errors. As may be expected from a book this size, there are a few minor errors, such as a parenthesis instead of a bracket in A 16.50, the misspelling "Nonesense" in H 35, and the omission of Richard E. Peck's name from the index. The only serious omission I noted—and it is an important one—is Edward H. Davidson's *Hawthorne's "Doctor Grimshawe's Secret"* (1954).

As may be expected in a book of 478 pages, there are methods of handling materials that may be questioned. For example, Clark's *Hawthorne at Auction* (C 86), a facsimile reprinting of various auction catalogues, is included with "First-Appearance Contributions to Books and Pamphlets" because it contains "Facsimiles and transcriptions of material from previously unpublished letters, manuscripts, inscriptions" (p. 406). Yet what *Hawthorne at Auction* does is to *reprint* the first appearances; why, then, are not the original auction catalogues listed as separate Section C entries, and *Hawthorne at Auction* given only as a reprint source, not a major entry.

The handling of some Section G entries raises a question of consistency. Material not accepted as by Hawthorne rightly belongs in this section and this section only. But "David Whicher—a North American Story" (G 5), which has been attributed not only to Hawthorne but also to John Neal and Henry Wadsworth Longfellow and which is rejected by the Centenary Edition, is cross-referenced to its appearance in *The Token* for 1832 (C 2), where it is listed and tagged "Attributed. See G 5." This is a useful but unnecessary cross-reference, and it is also inconsistent, since first appearances in newspapers and magazines of items attributed to Hawthorne but subsequently rejected are not listed outside of Section G. More troublesome is the handling of items like "Graves and Goblins" (G 13) and

"A Visit to the Clerk of the Weather" (G 24). Both items were attributed to Hawthorne posthumously—the first by its inclusion in *The Dolliver Romance and Other Pieces* (1876), the second in Woodberry's *Nathaniel Hawthorne* (1902)—but are included in *The Snow Image, and Uncollected Tales* in the Centenary Edition. Both appeared first in magazines, but their magazine appearances are not listed in Section D. Why fail to list these accepted items in the appropriate first-appearance section when rejected works are so listed?

The inclusion of "offprints" or "separates" of Hawthorne material first published in scholarly journals in Section C ("First-Appearance Contributions to Books and Pamphlets") is a practice I strongly disagree with. Offprints of material first appearing in the *New England Quarterly* (C 69-C 71), *Papers of the Bibliographical Society of America* (C 74), and *Essex Institute Historical Collections* (C 82) are all listed as entries in Section C with quasi-facsimile transcriptions of the printed wrappers, which serve as cover titles. This custom of including offprints from scholarly journals (as the *BAL* also does) opens a can of worms, and it is a practice that future bibliographers would be wise to avoid. To begin with, if the offprints are worthy of inclusion, why are the original journal publications of these articles not listed in Section D, especially since journal publication nearly always precedes the printing and distribution of offprints? Another problem is format. Some journals place wrappers that serve as cover titles on their offprints, others merely insert a slug indicating the source of the offprint, and still others just send out guillotined pages from the number itself. Clark (and the *BAL*) describe only the first category; does not consistency demand that they also include and describe the other two? Moreover, what about journals, such as *American Literature*, which once used wrappers serving as cover titles on their offprints but have since discontinued (and then resumed) the practice? Does the bibliographer only include those items offprinted with wrappers, making binding rather than content the rationale for inclusion? Some journals such as the *New England Quarterly,* make offprints available without or—for an extra charge—with wrappers. Should the conscience-stricken bibliographer then describe "binding issues" for the offprint? There is also the problem of completeness. Can the bibliographer assume that offprints exist for all articles, or should he list only those he has seen? Finally, Clark's own *Nathaniel Hawthorne Journal,* listed five times as a major entry in Section C, provides offprints. If the bibliographer fails to list these offprints while he lists others, he is guilty of inconsistency; if he does list them, the confusing situation exists of two Section C main entries for the same item. This discussion should demonstrate that the inclusion of offprints creates enough problems to more than offset their usefulness. If an article is substantial enough to merit inclusion in a bibliography, then it should appear listed in its first-appearance form, whether in a book or journal, not in the secondary format of an offprint.

The handling of photofacsimile printings also raises problems. There are two photofacsimile reprintings of *The Scarlet Letter* (A 16.49, A 16.50) which are listed under the separate heading of "Facsimile Editions." Since Clark defines an edition as including "all reprintings from the standing type or plates made from that typesetting," his establishment of a separate category for modern photo-offset work is confusing, since these facsimiles are in reality later printings within an edition.

Other questions raised by Clark's handling of material stem directly from the *BAL*. Blanck did not intend the *BAL* to be the final word, and he lists some material he has not seen, if only to point out the possibility of its existence. This is expecially true of some of the entries in the "References and Ana" section and for English importations. For the latter, the *BAL* lists numerous contemporary advertisements for English imports or "new editions" of Hawthorne's works. Since Clark lists only works he has seen, and since he does not list all the *BAL*'s English references, are we to assume that they do not exist? Clark, of course, cannot do everything, but because of the *BAL* we still have these English "ghosts" to worry about. Similarly, some of the *BAL*'s "References and Ana" entries do not appear in Clark, leaving the questions raised by the *BAL* unanswered. More serious is the question raised by Clark's handling of the "Printed letter urging defeat of . . . 'A Bill to amend the Act respecting Copyrights,'" dated 25 April 1862, "signed by Hawthorne and many others." Clark does have a full entry for the 1843 *An Address to the People of the United States in Behalf of the American Copyright Club* (E 4), of which Hawthorne is listed as an associate member, and appends to this entry a note referring to the 1862 printed letter. Surely cosigning a letter is more important than being an associate member, and the importance and priority of the two should be reversed. (Also, it is impossible to locate the printed letter in the index.)

Not assigning *The Ocean* (E 3) and *Nathaniel Hawthorne: Poems* (C 83) Section A status is questionable. At least half of the *Poems* volume contains material either first published or newly edited from manuscript; as such, it certainly deserves Section A status as much as does Turner's *Hawthorne as Editor* (A 37). Hawthorne's poem "The Ocean" first appeared in the 26 August 1825 *Salem Gazette,* the earliest located newspaper publication of Hawthorne's work (D 1), and was reprinted in *The Garland* of August 1825, the earliest located magazine publication of Hawthorne's work (D 2). It was also reprinted in *The Mariner's Library* (1833; C 4) and *Autumn Leaves* (1837; C 9). Clark also lists it in Section H (H 19). So far so good. But "The Ocean" was also set to music by Edward L. White and printed as sheet music in 1836 (E 3), its first and only appearance as a separate publication. Why, then, is the sheet music edition of *The Ocean* not listed in Section A? Surely if *The Sunday School Society's Gift* (A 11), a slightly cut reprinting of the "Samuel Johnson" section of *Biographical Stories* (A 9), deserves full treatment, then the first separate appearance of *The Ocean* does as well.

Other matters of consistency are bothersome. Why is *The Yarn of a Yankee Privateer* (A 36), which Hawthorne edited, given Section A status, but the first publication of parts from it in seven installments in the 1846 *Democratic Review* not listed in Section D? And why is *The Sunday School Society's Gift* (A 11), reprinted from *Biographical Stories* (A 9), given a separate Section A listing while *The Gentle Boy* (A 2.2) is tucked away under the main entry for *Twice-Told Tales,* when the latter is certainly of greater personal and bibliographical interest? Also, why are *Carroll A. Wilson: Thirteen Author Collections of the*

Nineteenth Century (F 12) and Harwell's *Hawthorne and Longfellow* (F 19), both containing first appearances of letters and other manuscript material, in Section F and not in Section C?

My last query deals with the use of the *ISCC-NBS Color Name Charts Illustrated with Centroid Colors.* Tanselle's excellent discussion of how this system can be fully employed still leaves me unconvinced.[4] While the general color names ("very deep blue") are extremely useful, as soon as a Centroid number is attached, making one color and one color only acceptable, a false sense of precision is established. Oxidation, fading, wear, and nonuniform dyeing practices make precise color identification difficult, if not impossible. Besides, any time the human eye is used (rather than a spectograph) subjectivity is inevitable. One of the ironies of the Centroid system seems to be that in a desire to be precise, bibliographers are actually causing confusion: one man's "dark gray yellow brown" (Centroid 81) may become—in a different type of light with another copy of the book—another man's "dark gray brown" (Centroid 62). Attempts at using the ISCC-NBS charts as standard because they replace idiosyncratic color designations such as "banana yellow" or "apple red" are fine, but too much precision is misleading and will eventually lead to a whole series of book dealers' catalogues offering copies of Hawthorne's works for sale with binding colors "not in Clark."[5]

It is very easy to point out errors in bad bibliographies but hard to argue over points of interpretation in good ones. Clark is the first person to attempt a full-scale modern bibliography of a nineteenth-century American author, and he has had —mostly through trial and error—to set up his own procedures and rules in the absence of any before him. This takes courage, expecially when one knows that there are reviewers who will probably disagree. As the man who breaks the path, Clark becomes the scholar for all future bibliographers of nineteenth-century American authors either to agree or disagree with. As more work is done, the bibliographical methodology for this period will become refined. But it will be so because Clark was the first to give us a practical guide on which to base our own work.

Nathaniel Hawthorne: A Descriptive Bibliography, then, promises years of good use. On a lower plane it will—especially through its caveat on publisher's ads—help book sellers to be more accurate in describing and pricing. Catalogues that absurdly scream "not in *BAL*" to justify doubling prices will, one hopes, become fewer, while "not in Clark," with luck, will have real meaning. More important, Clark has given us the basic guide to Hawthorne's writings and—in reading between the lines—to his dealings with his publishers and to his popular reception, as measured in contemporary reprintings in newspapers and magazines and in the sales of his books. In fine, Clark's book is the best bibliography of a nineteenth-century American author we have. It will serve as a model for future studies and will be the high standard against which they will all be judged.

Notes

1. Clark has discussed the importance of newspaper reprintings to an author's reputation in "Origins of the American Renaissance: A Front-Page Story," *Studies in the American Renaissance 1977*, ed. Joel Myerson (Boston: Twayne, 1978), pp. 155–64.

2. For other discussions of the term *issue*, see James B. Meriwether and Joseph Katz, "A Redefinition of 'Issue,'" *Proof*, 2 (1972), 61–70, and the response by G. Thomas Tanselle, "The Bibliographical Concepts of *Issue* and *State*," *Papers of the Bibliographical Society of America*, 69 (2d Quarter, 1975), 17–66.

3. One should also consult Tanselle's expanded discussion "The Bibliographical Description of Patterns," *Studies in Bibliography*, 23 (1970), 71–102, an article that reproduces binding grains and patterns.

4. See Tanselle, "A System of Color Identification for Bibliographical Description," *Studies in Bibliography*, 20 (1967), 203–34.

5. James L. W. West III has recorded his difficulty in using the ISCC-NBS charts in his *William Styron: A Descriptive Bibliography* (Boston: G. K. Hall, 1977), pp. xxxii–xxxiii.

Foison Plenty: Nine Studies of Shakespeare

Thomas McFarland

Robert Grudin. *Mighty Opposites: Shakespeare and Renaissance Contrariety.* Berkeley and Los Angeles: University of California Press, 1979. 217 pp.

Bertrand Evans. *Shakespeare's Tragic Practice.* Oxford: Clarendon Press, 1979. xi, 327 pp.

Susan Snyder. *The Comic Matrix of Shakespeare's Tragedies.* Princeton: Princeton University Press, 1979. 185 pp.

Lawrence Danson. *The Harmonies of* The Merchant of Venice. New Haven: Yale University Press, 1978. 202 pp.

Darryl J. Gless. Measure for Measure, *The Law, and the Convent.* Princeton: Princeton University Press, 1979. xviii, 283 pp.

James L. Calderwood. *Metadrama in Shakespeare's Henriad: Richard II to Henry V.* Berkeley and Los Angeles: University of California Press, 1979. 234 pp.

Joseph A. Porter. *The Drama of Speech Acts: Shakespeare's Lancastrian Tetralogy.* Berkeley and Los Angeles: University of California Press, 1979. 208 pp.

Alice-Lyle Scoufos. *Shakespeare's Typological Satire: A Study of the Falstaff-Oldcastle Problem.* Athens: Ohio University Press, 1979. xvii, 378 pp.

Alvin B. Kernan. *The Playwright as Magician: Shakespeare's Image of the Poet in the Public Theater.* New Haven: Yale University Press, 1979. 164 pp.

In an essay called "Shakespeare and the Ideas of his Time," which appeared in *Shakespeare Survey 29* in 1976, J. W. Lever spoke of modern scholarship's "acceptance of opposed principles as the dynamic of Shakespearian tragedy," of "a latent dualism, an acceptance of multiple oppositions and polarities, at the roots of Shakespeare's response to thought and experience." He concluded that

> no approach of our time has done more to validate this unity than the remarkable rehabilitation of Renaissance culture by an inspired group of European-born scholars. Cassirer, Kristeller, Panofsky, Wind and others have brought back to light an artistic philosophy and a philosophical art, mutually interacting, alike sustained by the willing acceptance of contraries. Through paradox and irony, through antithetical images and myths, imaginative truth is shown to have broken from the grooves of scholastic logic to become an autonomous pursuit. Accordingly the way has been cleared for a new, more flexible historicism. To set Shakespeare's drama of dualities in its European context is to place him beside his peers of the Renaissance, instead of measuring him by the footrule or second-rate minds. . . . Hence the omnipresence in Shakespeare's plays of the comic and grotesque, effecting that *discordia concors* which the best minds of his age saw as the common aim of philosophy and art.[1]

Though Lever was here speaking of important matters, his lust for the au courant caused him to overlook in a rather striking way the historical truth that "the willing acceptance of contraries" is not the "remarkable rehabilitation" of our century; it is rather—and historical justice demands the correction—the very essence of the Romantic approach to Shakespeare. To Victor Hugo, true poetry existed only "in the harmony of contraries," and the "poetic summit of modern times" is Shakespearean drama: "Shakespeare is drama, and drama incorporates in the same breath the grotesque and the sublime, the terrible and the ridiculous, tragedy and comedy."[2] Somewhat earlier Coleridge too had said that "the true genuine modern poetry" is "the romantic; and the works of Shakespeare are romantic poetry revealing itself in the drama." Here also this view rests on the willing acceptance of contraries, for Coleridge says that Shakespeare is characterized by "signal adherence to the great law of nature that opposites tend to attract and temper each other"; the one great principle of dramatic illusion is "that ever-varying balance, or balancing, of images, notions, or feelings . . . conceived as in opposition to each other."[3] Hazlitt, again, insists that "Shakespeare's imagination . . . unites the most opposite extremes."[4]

Nor does Lever avail himself of theoretical statements propounded in our own day. As W. K. Wimsatt, for instance, has said in his *Hateful Contraries:*

> Metaphor is the holding together of oppositions. . . . All poetry . . . has something of that element of tension. . . . And through this tension poetry gives a fresh vision of reality. . . . It will be an experience that includes pain as well as pleasure, evil and ugliness as well as beauty and good, an experience where tragic and comic can be discriminated but where they show a complementary and an easily mixed relationship.
>
> But to present the argument of the critic in its necessary and I believe correctly guarded form: He will say that the human condition is intrinsically a material and mixed condition, where faith and love of God and fellow man can scarcely occur except in a milieu that is full of the possibility of their opposites.[5]

Having overlooked so much of the contribution of both past and contemporary criticism, Lever, it might be supposed, would instead summon an impressively full documentation of his thesis in modern Shakespearean study. Such, however, was not the case. The fullest exemplar of his statements available at that time, Norman Rabkin's 1967 study *Shakespeare and the Common Understanding,* was apparently too early to be included in the documents he was reviewing, and those he did mention are not decisive.

Would then that Lever had had in hand Robert Grudin's *Mighty Opposites: Shakespeare and Renaissance Contrariety,* for it answers his requirements in a more satisfactory way than do any of the other studies to which he was able to point. Grudin begins with an acknowledgment:

> The modern study of contrariety in Shakespeare is founded on three books which appeared more or less simultaneously in America during

the middle of the last decade. W. R. Elton's King Lear *and the Gods* (1966) speaks of Shakespeare's play as a philosophical pattern in which antithetical doctrines are interwoven dialectically, and ideas and tonalities are juxtaposed ironically. In Rosalie Colie's *Paradoxia Epidemica* (1966), Shakespearean paradox is seen in the context of an age which delighted in such devices, using them as means of expression and education. Norman Rabkin's *Shakespeare and the Common Understanding* (1967) is an effort to come to terms with Shakespeare's use of ideological and psychological forms of contrariety—his technique of setting up, in plays like *Hamlet* and *Troilus and Cressida*, dilemmas which baffle protagonists and seem to neutralize choices. To Rabkin, Shakespeare is a classic destroyer of certainties, whose "basic mode of vision" is one in which " 'opposed elements' are equally valid, equally desirable and equally destructive, so that the choice that the play forces the reader to make becomes impossible." Rabkin's argument is buttressed by an analogy to Niels Bohr's notion of *complementarity*—the theory that a physical phenomenon may evoke two equally valid but mutually contradictory explanations. [p. 13]

Grudin's book is different from Rabkin's in that it locates Shakespeare's practice within a historical tradition of philosophical theories of opposition. In its specifics the volume addresses itself to the permutations of contrariety in *The Merchant of Venice,* the "problem" comedies, the later tragedies, and *The Tempest.* (The author argues that Shakespeare progressed from the use of contrariety to illuminate ethical situations to an incorporation of it as a structural principle in the tragedies.) Yet these specific analyses are perhaps less useful than the historical backgrounds set forth in two preliminary chapters, "Shakespeare and the Function of Contraries" and "The Infant Rind: Contrariety and Shakespeare's Intellectual Milieu," where various Renaissance theorists, notably Paracelsus and Bruno, are discussed and where *Romeo and Juliet* is brought forward as embodying specifically Paracelsian elements.

The discussion of Renaissance theories of contrariety supplied by *Mighty Opposites* is the most explicit that has yet appeared in relation to Shakespeare, and by that fact alone Grudin's book should become, despite its relative brevity, a standard work in contemporary Shakespearean interpretation. Probably more could be done with the analysis of the modes of contrariety as they actually arise in Shakespeare's work, and certainly the historical sketches of Renaissance contrariety are far from exhaustive; still, they are fuller than any available to Lever, and I consider this a useful book that fills an important gap in the periodic table of Shakespearean elements.

A book that is in one sense related to Grudin's (and in another sense quite different) is Bertrand Evans's *Shakespeare's Tragic Practice*. Evans's book analyzes Shakespeare's tragedies, beginning at the beginning with *Titus Andronicus,* in terms of "Shakespeare's habit of creating and exploiting discrepant, or unequal, awarenesses as a means of producing various dramatic effects" (p. vii). Coleridge once said that "it is a common error to mistake the epithets applied by the *dramatis personae* to each other, as truly descriptive of what the audience ought to see or know."[6] Though Evans does not adduce this statement, it accords with his technique, which is to point out the difference between what the audience knows and what the characters know, as well as the differences between what one character knows and what other characters know. It is with this "special lens," as he calls it, that Evans embarks on a detailed examination of the tragedies.

It might be supposed that so simple a technique might yield results that would be very much of a piece. It does not. On the contrary, the "special lens" provides surprising insights into nuances of structure and emphasis. Perhaps two brief quotations will suggest something of the variety that Evans's examinations generate. The first is a summary statement about *Hamlet:* "If the allowance of some degree of ambiguity in the management of awareness in *Hamlet* is one deviation from the dramatist's normal practice of making important matters unmistakable, one other deviation is of at least equal significance: *Hamlet* is Shakespeare's sole tragedy in which the highest level of awareness, next our own, is occupied by the hero" (p. 78). The second is a statement about *Coriolanus:*

The decline in Shakespeare's use of unequal awareness to create dramatic effect has been noted in both *Antony and Cleopatra* and *Timon of Athens;* what had been a basic principle of his method earlier becomes, in these plays, a relatively unimportant element in a few scenes, a primary element in none. With *Coriolanus* the decline continues: if *Romeo and Juliet, Hamlet* and *Othello* represent the dramatist's fullest exploitation of gaps between awarenesses, *Coriolanus* represents his near abandonment of it. And if it is apt to call *Romeo and Juliet* and *Othello,* in particular, tragedies of unawareness, it is also appropriate to call *Coriolanus* a tragedy of awareness. [p. 298]

An idiosyncrasy of *Shakespeare's Tragic Practice* is that not only is its theoretical substructure a simple one, but also that it makes no reference to other Shakespearean scholarship or criticism. I have rarely encountered a book that exists so completely on its own terms. Yet the analyses are subtle, and indeed the book could easily be put forward as a particularization of the historical and theoretical elements contained in Grudin's discussion of contrariety. I wish to register only one caveat: the commonsensical simplicity of the "special lens" seems to hinder Evans from accounting very well for the greatness of Shakespearean tragedy. The discussions reveal nuance, but they are not intense. Still, this is a useful book, and it is a better one, I think, than Evans's earlier study, *Shakespeare's Comedies,* where the same mode of approach was utilized.

If *Shakespeare's Tragic Practice* is in some sense a documentation of Grudin's historical study of Renaissance contrariety in Shakespeare, so too, in a different context, is Susan Snyder's *The Comic Matrix of Shakespeare's Tragedies.* Indeed, the book is particularly pertinent to Hugo's insistence that Shakespeare incorporated "in the same breath the grotesque and the sublime, the terrible and the ridiculous, tragedy and comedy"; and it documents likewise Wimsatt's dictum about "the dramatic thesis" of tensional poetry: that such poetry provides an experience of reality "where tragic and comic can be discriminated but where they show a complementary and easily mixed relationship."[7]

Of the books examined in this review, this one, though the second shortest in length, is possibly the most complex in argument. In its analysis of the mixing of comic and tragic modes, it goes much beyond the traditional notion of "comic relief." To Snyder, comedy offers a view of human reality whereby alternative possibilities are constantly present, as opposed to tragedy, where an inexorable and unavoidable outcome defines the mode: "Tragedy . . . moves towards the inevitable, the chain of causality that denies or renders irrelevant all alternatives but one. Comedy always finds an alternative to break the chain. All its shifts and sleights can be seen as functions of an 'evitability' principle" (p. 41). From this fundamental understanding, which at least in the case of comedy is expanded by a subtle discussion based on a wide variety of historical and theoretical documentation, the author argues that Shakespeare was first and foremost at home in comedy —he "had thoroughly explored and mastered the comic mode while he was still finding his way in tragedy" (p. 4)—and that, in differing ways, the comic underlies the tragic in some of his most important plays. From *Romeo and Juliet* through *King Lear*, she argues, he moves through a sequence in which comedy and tragedy function "first as polar oppositions, later as two sides of the coin, and finally as two elements in a single compound" (p. 5). She treats *Romeo and Juliet* as a play that starts out as a comedy and reverses itself into a tragedy. *Othello*'s "action up until the reunion of Othello and Desdemona in Cyprus (II.i) is a perfect comic structure in miniature," and she sees "the tragedy of *Othello* developing from a questioning of comic assumptions" (p. 74). Hamlet incorporates in his character both the rigid *alazon* and the ironic *eiron* of comedy, as well as their characteristic opposition to one another, while Polonius's "longing for a central role in the action is finally fulfilled: not in the comedy he imagined but in the tragedy that is, not as the lively [comic] manipulator but as the last of the play's fathers to be killed and first to be avenged" (p. 110). In general, Shakespeare "projects a special kind of tragic disillusion in *Hamlet* by bringing into play an extraordinary amount of comic machinery only to subvert it" (p. 133), and this process culminates in the graveyard scene. In *Lear*, Shakespeare "sets comic order side by side with comic chaos, and out of the dislocation that results he develops a special, devastating tragic effect" (p. 137).

The brief remarks I have here made do not indicate the

unusual richness of *The Comic Matrix of Shakespeare's Tragedies*. The book is rich in its reference, in its use of secondary materials, and in the subtlety of its discussion. Indeed, perhaps the highest praise I can give it is to say that its merit ultimately depends even more on the quality of the author's sensibility at work on the plays than it does on her perceptive analysis of comic functions. I wish I did not have to report that this fine volume is slightly marred by repeated solecistic usages such as "debunking," "faking," and "ongoing."

One of the plays that Grudin found fruitful in terms of Renaissance contrariety was *The Merchant of Venice*. That single drama is the subject of Lawrence Danson's *The Harmonies of The Merchant of Venice*, and in this volume too motifs of contrariety loom large. The oppositions of law and freedom, justice and mercy, friendship and marriage, the Old Testament and the New, Jew and Christian, Venice and Belmont, are successively invoked by Danson and reconciled into a concording whole: "In each case, that of the caskets, the trial, and the rings, the antinomies—whether of law versus freedom, justice versus mercy, friendship versus marriage—resolve themselves in a more comprehensive whole" (p. 21). The book is therefore both an analysis and an expansion of C. L. Barber's judgment that "no other comedy, until the late romances, ends with so full an expression of harmony as that which we get in the opening of the final scene of *The Merchant of Venice*."[8]

The Merchant of Venice has traditionally posed problems of divergent interpretation; indeed, Danson argues not only for its inclusion in the canon of the designated "problem" plays (he says equably that the "slightest acquaintance with modern Shakespearean criticism convinces us that there is not one among the thirty-seven plays that is not, quite seriously, a 'problem' to some reasonable man or woman"), but terms it "the most scandalously problematic" of all Shakespeare's plays (p. 2). In terms of the realities of our own era, it can be taken as a document in anti-Semitism on the one hand, or as a kind of brief for Zionism on the other; as a satirical critique of Christian ideals, or quite the contrary, an affirmation of those ideals.

There are many lesser problems as well. Some critics, for instance, have raised the question of whether Antonio's melancholy implies a homosexual topicality in his friendship with Bassanio. Danson rejects this likelihood, but he does so with a reasonableness that characterizes his general approach to interpretational difficulties. Such reasonableness extends to the book's confrontation of the thorniest problem of all, that posed by the figure of Shylock, who, starting with Hazlitt's apotheosis of his character, has in the last two centuries grown so large as almost to step outside the play. Danson puts Shylock back into the play, and he does so with calm firmness and critical tact.

Critical tact, indeed, is a salient feature of Danson's book. Even so perspicacious a critic as Frank Kermode can become somewhat heated in the problem-charged atmosphere of this play: *"The Merchant of Venice . . .* is about judgment, redemption and mercy. . . . It begins with usury and corrupt love; it ends with harmony and perfect love. And all the time it tells its audience that this is its subject; only by a determined effort to avoid the obvious can one mistake the theme of *The Merchant of Venice.*"[9] But Danson coolly steers his argument between, through, and around the host of contesting judgments. He renders justice to all competing interpretations, but he refuses to forfeit the movement of the play to external ideological claims. He restores the drama as a comedy, with comedy's characteristic movement from schism and discord to harmony and happiness. Danson's is the best discussion I have encountered of *The Merchant of Venice;* it makes the play seem larger, more intricate, and more satisfying than I had previously thought it to be.

The play most closely related to *The Merchant of Venice* is *Measure for Measure* ("the ubiquitously problematic *Measure for Measure,*" as Danson calls it). All readers of Shakespeare are struck by the notable similarity of Portia's "The quality of mercy is not strain'd" speech, with its insistence that "in the course of justice, none of us/Should see salvation. We do pray for mercy," and Isabella's speech, in *Measure for Measure:* "How would you be/If He, which is the top of judgement, should/But judge you as you are? O, think on that;/And mercy then will breathe within your lips,/Like man new made." Both plays are in the largest sense about the competing relationship between justice and mercy, and both have exercised the judgment and ingenuity of diverse commentators.

Measure for Measure, however, is surely the greater play. Moreover, it generates its problems in a somewhat different way from *The Merchant of Venice,* which is no doubt why Boas included it in his original list of "problem" plays, and left out *The Merchant of Venice.* Where the latter drama tends to be thrown askew by external critical emphasis on the character of Shylock, *Measure for Measure* seems, more persistently than any other Shakespearean play except *The Tempest,* to suggest hidden meanings within its statement; it hints at anagogic overtones. Angelo, as his name implies, seems to suggest a fallen angel ("O, what may man within him hide,/Though angel on the outward side!"), and the "duke of dark corners" for many readers, including me, seems to correlate his function not only with that of King James, as David L. Stevenson's *The Achievement of* Measure for Measure persuasively argues (the suggestion was made as early as 1799), but also, as critics as diverse as E. K. Chambers and G. Wilson Knight suggest, with the agency of providence itself.

Darryl J. Gless's Measure for Measure, *the Law, and the Convent* finds this latter function the key to the play: "The master key to understanding the play's meaning and form is, as many have asserted, Duke Vincentio." Gless argues that the play has a "persistently theological milieu" and that the Duke intermittently represents Godhead; he "frequently and apparently" acts as "a little image of God" (pp. 53, 234). This is a rather long and very careful book—perhaps too much so on both counts—that argues for the interpretation of the play within a variety of Jacobean contexts, allegorical, theological, satirical, and sociological. Inasmuch as almost every possible position that could be maintained about the structure of *Measure for Measure* and the meaning of its characterizations has already been put forward by some critic or other, it is difficult to say that there is much really new here by way of interpretation, although a direct parallel would have to piece together arguments from a variety of commentators. What one has not encountered before is the variety of documentation about sociotheological attitudes in Shakespeare's time:

> By considering antimonastic satire . . . not simply as an element of Shakespeare's general intellectual background but as a type of language—a genre—that certain elements of *Measure for Measure* participate in, we can discover how the antimonastic elements of the Elizabethan background contribute directly to our perception of the details of the play. It is also possible to discover how the background allows us to perceive clearly implications that are hinted at but never made totally explicit in the text itself. [p. 10]

Gless sees two related Christian functions illustrated by the movement of the play, one the bringing of good out of evil, and the second a kind of shepherding of diverse characters into better lives, a continuing governance that is described at one point as "he hasteth unto every place, to govern and order all creatures." In general:

> The typical divine modus operandi, unceasingly bringing good out of evil . . . characterizes the Duke's ministrations throughout *Measure for Measure*. . . . He ensures that Angelo's legalism and Isabella's proud and merciless treatment of Claudio provide the latter a corrected attitude toward life. He arranges that Angelo's explosive lust for Isabella be used, first, to humble the deputy's pride by public revelation and shame, then to induce him to marry and thereby to mitigate appetites natural to the flesh. The Duke further arranges that Isabella's own rigid and prideful defense of her honor results not in Claudio's death but in her own public humiliation and consequent willingness to live the religion she had formerly parodied. [pp. 249–50]

Such a passage fairly represents, I think, the special critical achievement of Gless's book: the resolution in a unified pattern of diverse and seemingly heterogeneous or even contradictory dramatic actions. The high point of his interpretation, at least to me, comes in his analysis of the meaning of Isabella's perplexing role:

> Her marriage to God's imperfect earthly simulacrum symbolizes the marriage that awaits every flawed but endeavoring soul, all of whom

expect one day to become brides of the Lamb. . . . Isabella's marriage also confirms her rejection of monastic bondage and the puerile good intentions that had led her into it. In every way, then, this wedding is a fitting conclusion for a plot that endeavors throughout to lead its principal actors from private and public contentions bred of the flesh and the letter to the tranquil joy that follows love's true essence. [p. 255]

Two books quite different from those addressing themselves to contrariety and its resolutions are James L. Calderwood's *Metadrama in Shakespeare's Henriad:* Richard II *to* Henry V and Joseph A. Porter's *The Drama of Speech Acts; Shakespeare's Lancastrian Tetralogy.* Both of these books deal with the linguistic patterns of *Richard II, Henry IV, Parts I* and *II,* and *Henry V.* Indeed, both have as precursor Calderwood's fine volume *Shakespearean Metadrama* (1971). Porter, in fact, repeatedly salutes the earlier book:

One might say, then, that the overall action of the play [*Richard II*] is the decline and fall of this conception of language, of Richard's linguistic world.

James L. Calderwood, in the last chapter of *Shakespearean Metadrama,* in fact says approximately this, and very persuasively. In spite of differences in approach his view of Richard seems close to mine; and though he does not deal with the play as a larger unit, he does use two of the summary metaphors I shall be using for the action of the entire tetralogy. [p. 42]

To these two metaphors Porter adds a third, which is Tillyard's view that the tetralogy enacts the historical movement from the Middle Ages to the Renaissance. The two from Calderwood are the biblical story, much on people's minds in the late sixteenth and seventeenth centuries, of the building of the Tower of Babel and its fall, with the attendant proliferation of tongues —a theme that historically focused both the awareness of the breakdown of Latinate primacy into various vernaculars and the desire for a universal language; and, secondly, the biblical story of the Fall, which "summarizes a certain way in which Richard's linguistic situation is analogous to that of Adam in

Eden, with his privileges of talking with God and of assigning names to parts of creation" (p. 4).

Porter specifically utilizes the theory of speech acts propounded by the philosopher J. L. Austin and extended by John Searle, especially in the conceptions of "illocutionary force" and "explicitness," which he expounds effectively, though I shall not do so here. He eventually moves the direction of his argument, aided by Austin's distinctions, toward a rejection of G. Wilson Knight's belief that the form of drama is adventitious to Shakespeare's meanings. Porter points out that a "drama" is "a sequence of acts, verbal and nonverbal, done by a group of characters to or on each other" (p. 165); he argues that the "period of the Lancastrian tetralogy is the only time in Shakespeare's career for which we can be fairly sure that he was thinking of drama as a literary genre distinct from others" (p. 169); he concludes that "Shakespeare in writing the Lancastrian tetralogy was preoccupied with those attributes of drama which distinguish it from other literary genres. . . . The tetralogy's theme of language and speech in action is that of the idea of the genre of the drama" (p. 170).

The Drama of Speech Acts is a thoughtful and worthy book. It is the more regrettable, therefore, that its status as sequel to *Shakespearean Metadrama* involves it in direct comparison with Calderwood's own sequel, *Metadrama in Shakespeare's Henriad* (the Voltairean "Henriad" being Alvin Kernan's coinage), which Porter did not know was in progress. For the latter book is an unusually rich and successful study, a most rewardingly subtle and attentive reading of the four plays that unfortunately makes Porter's work seem almost heavy-handed.

Calderwood finds in *Richard II* "not merely the fall of a king but also the fall of kingly speech—of a speech conceived of as sacramental and logical, in which words are not proxies for things but part of the things themselves. With the fall of this King's English, there falls also a view of reality contained within it" (p. 13). The breakdown of the ontologically holistic language of divine-right kingship splits language into "lie," on the one hand, and metaphor on the other. (I would have been intrigued to see whether Calderwood's elegant discussion of the element of falsehood in metaphor could be accommodated to the analysis in Samuel R. Levin's recent and brilliant *The Semantics of Metaphor,* but Levin is not invoked.) "Exton kills a man who is, in his namelessness, already dead. Richard's world is dead too. It is a world conceived in metaphors that had died into names, as Richard discovered too late" (p. 19). Richard is replaced by Bolingbroke, the usurper and counterfeit king, and the ontological elements change accordingly: "If the king is a lie in the political realm, the lie is now king in the verbal world —and he who practices in that world must needs seem a liar" (p. 29). The changes Calderwood rings upon these themes are fascinating, and are almost uncannily supported by the texts of the plays. In *Henry V,* the ambivalent legitimacy of Hal eventuates in an ambivalent restoration of both kingship and language.

What makes Calderwood's book so unusually satisfying is finally, however, less his commitment to its themes than his own constitutional subtlety of critical vision. It is very difficult at this stage in Shakespearean criticism to say anything new without the severe risk of its being also foolish; this book says new things that are on the contrary true and revealing (it is disconcerting, therefore, to encounter in such a sophisticated discourse the use of the solecism "insightful"). I cannot resist an example: "Surely we are meant to see in Falstaff, the horsed knight hotly spurring toward Westminster, some comic likeness to Hotspur charging pell-mell into battle and a grave at Shrewsbury—each of them plunging myopically toward his separate doom dreaming on glories to come.... This parallel would imply of course that Hal kills Falstaff at Westminster as he did Percy at Shrewsbury" (p. 97). A single additional example may provide a more characteristic texture of Calderwood's discourse:

With speech degenerated to the status of money, Bolingbroke's verbal exchequer contains nothing but unredeemed promissory notes.... Even when Bolinbroke offers to pay off "with interest" before Shrewsbury (4.3.49), Hotspur is suspicious:

> well we know the King
> Knows at what time to promise, when to pay
> (lines 52–53)

It is for fear that the older conspirators "shall pay for all" (5.2.23) that Worcester intercepts and perverts Bolingbroke's one word of mercy before it can reach Hotspur's ears.

On the battlefield at Shrewsbury the man whose kingship is a lie is fittingly unrecognizable to Douglas:

> What art thou
> That counterfeit'st the person of a king?
> (5.4.27–28)
> I fear thou art another counterfeit.
> (5.4.35).

With no divine treasury backing up Henry's verbal currency, the kingly word is as counterfeit as the kingly person. And so as we turn to *2 Henry IV* it is not God or the divinely inspired Word in the mouth of an anointed king that binds the English together in Gaunt's lost paradise.... Instead, it is Rumor, "painted full of tongues" (Induction). Rumor, the counterfeit word— [p. 35]

Admirable though Calderwood's perceptions are, however, I must enter a certain stubborn reservation about the frame of analysis employed by him, as well as that of Porter. In a book of some years ago called *Tragic Meanings in Shakespeare*, I urged that "image-counting, metaphorical analysis, linguistic or textual approaches, can never be more than preliminaries to meaning," because "all tragic meaning depends on the *as if* assumption that dramatic creations are human beings."[10] At that time I thought the phenomenological analysis of human existence the best schematism for understanding Shakespeare's representations. I have since come to think that perhaps no schematism is required beyond the simple but difficult responsibility of thinking of dramatic representations as we think of other minds.

To be sure, comedy requires less rounded humanity than does tragedy, and doubtless history plays change the situation somewhat also. (As Calderwood cogently observes, "Having given hostages to English history, to his own tetralogy, and to the expectations of his English audience, Shakespeare might well have felt that writing *Henry V* was less an exercise in creative freedom than a discharge of obligations" [p. 149].) Nevertheless, the meanings of the drama must ultimately correspond to human emotions and experience. The burning core of these plays, the betrayal of Falstaff by Hal that brings to searing focus all those motifs of betrayal that, originating in the world of *Richard II,* eventually create the meaningless chaos of the world of *Henry VI* and the inhuman isolation of *Richard III,* is nowhere in these linguistic interpretations seen in its human dimension. Although Porter invokes Arthur Sewell's *Character and Society in Shakespeare* to argue for the indissolubility of character and action in Shakespearean drama, I would respond, stubbornly, that we must think of dramatic characters as human beings in the ordinary sense of our conception of human beings. In the approach of Porter, and the subtle readings of Calderwood, dramatic characters illustrate a pattern made out of something secondary to our human perception of life, and to that extent they do not in my judgment penetrate to the deepest meanings of Shakespearean art. In my own understanding these plays are first of all about human interactions, and only secondarily about kingship and the fall of language.

Another approach to the character of Falstaff seems to evacuate the human dimension in quite a different way. Alice-Lyle Scoufos's *Shakespeare's Typological Satire: A Study of the Falstaff-Oldcastle Problem* departs from an investigation of Renaissance theories of history, and it concludes that in the *Henry IV* plays Shakespeare rejected skeptical and nihilistic views of history, offering his allegiance instead to optimistic views of man's nature and destiny. Against this general background, the author projects the *Henry IV* plays, *The Merry Wives of Windsor,* and *Macbeth* as embodying an extended series of satires on the noble family of Cobham, to whose political activities Shakespeare was unsympathetic. The mode of entry for the author's argument is through the "Falstaff-Oldcastle crux," that is, the established fact that the character of Falstaff overlays the historical figure of Sir John Oldcastle, Lord Cobham, who was a Lollard martyr burned at the stake in the reign of King Henry

V. (I counterpose without comment Calderwood's contention that "Falstaff, whose origin is neither England's actual past nor Holinshed's pages, owes history nothing—not even if his name was once Oldcastle, 'for Oldcastle died a martyr, and this is not the man' [2 *Henry IV*, Epilogue]. Falstaff's origins are theatrical and literary: the Vice of morality tradition, the *miles gloriosus* and witty parasite of Plautine comedy, the clown-fool-butt-sponger-mocker-glutton of a thousand plays from Aristophanes to the anonymous author of *The Famous Victories of Henry the Fifth*" [p. 73].)

Scoufos's complex arguments about the ramifications of Shakespeare's dramatic presentations into political topicalities of his own day involve fascinating excursions into the kinds of materials familiar through the Chamberlain letters and the modern chronicles of scholars like G. P. V. Akrigg and G. B. Harrison. To some extent the book is also a contribution to the approach involved in David Bevington's *Tudor Drama and Politics*, although the author's specific topicality goes beyond what Bevington thinks feasible by way of interpretation. I myself am not wholly convinced by her arguments, to some extent because there are too many links of unaided speculation in the chain. Even if I were convinced, however, I should enter the same objection here that I do with reference to Calderwood and Porter. This is an honorable book: learned, rich in detail, and very probably at least to some extent correct in its contentions. But it is perhaps indicative of how far removed its approach is from the mode of character apprehension I espouse that in its three hundred and seventy pages there is not a single mention of Maurice Morgann's famous essay on the character of Falstaff.

The final book to be noticed in this review brings us back, in large sociohistorical contexts, to contrariety as the key to Shakespeare's achievement. Indeed, Alvin B. Kernan's *The Playwright as Magician: Shakespeare's Image of the Poet in the Public Theater* is itself an exemplar of the harmony of contraries: it is brief in length but extended in range; its style is one of elegant ease, but at the same time its arguments unobtrusively harvest a deep and comprehensive learning.

Kernan sees Shakespeare's image of the poet as suspended between opposing tensions: between a Sidneyan aristocratic amateurism and a work-a-day theatrical professionalism, between a Petrarchan idealism whereby art is a sacred vision of truth and a dissatisfaction with the status of plays as mere ephemeral entertainment. This conflict "between the ideal of who and what the poet was and the actual conditions in which the new poets lived and wrote would eventually be resolved by the creation of a new image of the poet" (p. 17). From an early anonymity as dramatic creator, Shakespeare increasingly began to merge his poetic idealism with his dramatic products, and, finally, in the character of Prospero, the dramatist who manages the events of a play becomes one with the magician who controls events on his island: the poet becomes magician. "In the ideal theater of *The Tempest*, the poet-playwright puts off his cloak of invisibility and emerges from behind his productions almost openly in the figure of Prospero" (p. 136). "The playwright who controls the 'sterile promontory' of his isolated island stage is a magician, almost limitless in his knowledge and in his ability to manipulate reality" (p. 138). But even in this final image of the poet, tensions still inhere, for "a magician is at once a mere trickster or sleight-of-hand artist and a philosopher who communicates with and commands spirits that control the universe" (p. 142). The great "Our revels now are ended" speech, which Dowden, I believe, may have been the first to point out as referring not only to Prospero but to Shakespeare the playwright, thus becomes a kind of absolute terminus ad quem for Shakespearean meanings, and Kernan's explication of this moment and its matrix is deep and satisfying. The book as a whole documents a continuing ambivalence on Shakespeare's part about his poetic role as playwright. There are intriguing chapters on "Actors and Audiences in Three Comedies and a History Play" (*The Taming of the Shrew, Love's Labour's Lost, A Midsummer Night's Dream*, and *1 Henry IV*), on "The Morality Play in *King Lear*," and most of all on "Politics and Theater in *Hamlet*."

I must interpose a rather stern objection to one aspect of Kernan's procedure, however. In interpreting the sonnets as a document in the sociology of patronage ("Shakespeare's *Sonnets* test the poetry of patronage against reality, find it untrue, and abandon the patron to the Dark Lady" [pp. 37–38]), Kernan, it seems to me, forfeits the essence of those poems. Even Coleridge, who recoiled from their homosexual implications, understood that "the sonnets could only have come from a man deeply in love." In Kernan's analysis, this central truth is obscured, and indeed what I take to be the burden of their statement is misconceived:

> The Poet of the *Sonnets* is extraordinarily adroit in phrasing the praises of the young man so that they seem to be no flattery but merely graceful compliment, or even the truthful description of a beauty of such extraordinary quality that it will not be believed by those who have not seen it:
>
> > If I could write the beauty of your eyes,
> > And in fresh numbers number all your graces,
> > The age to come would say, "This poet lies,
> > Such heavenly touches ne'er touched earthly faces."
> > [17]
>
> The Poet always manages to praise the young man's youth, beauty, and family extravagantly, even fulsomely, while always damping down the suggestion of flattery by the cleverness or gracefulness of the phrasing. [p. 28]

In line with such interpretation, Kernan can conclude, with what to my mind can be only a secondary or even tertiary relevance, that in the sonnets Shakespeare "was not so much writing a chapter of his own autobiography as depicting in a much more general way the experience of a transitional generation of poets from an amateur to a professional status, and from patronage to the marketplace for support" (p. 48).

If I cannot accept Kernan's way with the sonnets, however, I find myself continually in pleased agreement with his statements on a variety of other topics. In particular, his elucidation of *Hamlet* sheds rich light on the structure of that play. Arguing that in *Hamlet* Shakespeare undertook "a unique examination of the function of the dramatic poet and of theater in the political life of a kingdom" (p. 94), Kernan enters the play through the same gateway that the professional acting troupe of the player king does, and sees in that troupe's performance of the play-within-the-play an image of the whole of *Hamlet*. Scene after scene is approached in terms of "submerged or latent theater": "It is close to the surface in Hamlet's pretense of madness. . . . It is even closer to the surface when Hamlet enters his mother's room and holds up . . . the pictures of the two kings . . . presenting truth by means of a show. Similarly, when he leaps into the grave at Ophelia's funeral . . . he is acting out for Laertes. . . . The concluding scene of the play, the duel between Laertes and Hamlet, is another elaborately staged play-within-the-play" (pp. 102–3). Still another of the "internal plays" is that "in which Ophelia pretends to pray in order to draw Hamlet out, while Caludius and Polonius stand like directors and audience behind an arras" (p. 102).

Rather than pursuing the temptation to quote further from this variegated book, however, I must content myself with a concluding judgment. This study constantly brings to focus connections and emphases that have lain below the surface of one's cognition; when they are adduced by Kernan one tends to greet them with delighted recognition: I found myself repeatedly murmuring not "how new" but "how true." The book is remarkably successful in joining the functions of criticism with those of scholarship; it mingles with deceptive ease the sociological backgrounds of stage conditions and dramatic history, on the one hand, and the actual substance of the plays on the other. Standing behind Kernan's study, and sometimes invoked by it, are two seminal books: John Danby's *Poets on Fortune's Hill* and Patrick Cruttwell's *The Shakespearean Moment*. *The Playwright as Magician* is a richly satisfying addition to their select and significant genre.

Notes

1. J. W. Lever, "Shakespeare and the Ideas of his Time," *Shakespeare Survey 29*, ed. Kenneth Muir (Cambridge: Cambridge Univ. Press, 1976), pp. 89, 90–91.

2. Victor Hugo, *Théâtre complet*, ed. Roland Purnal, J.-J. Thierry, and

Josette Mélèze, Bibliothèque de la Pléiade (Paris: Gallimard, 1963–64), I, 425, 422.

3. Samuel Taylor Coleridge, *Shakespearean Criticism,* ed. Thomas Middleton Raysor, Everyman's Library (London: Dent; New York: Dutton, 1960), I, 175, 199, 181.

4. William Hazlitt, *Lectures on the English Poets* . . . , Everyman's Library (London: Dent; New York: Dutton, 1967), p. 53.

5. W. K. Wimsatt, *Hateful Contraries; Studies in Literature and Criticism* (Lexington: Univ. of Kentucky Press, 1965), pp. 41, 47.

6. Coleridge, I, 42.

7. Hugo, I, 422; Wimsatt, p. 41.

8. C. L. Barber, *Shakespeare's Festive Comedy* (Princeton: Princeton Univ. Press, 1959; rpt. Cleveland, 1963), p. 168; quoted in Danson, p. 11.

9. Frank Kermode, "The Mature Comedies," *Early Shakespeare,* Stratford-upon-Avon Studies, 3 (London, 1961), p. 224; quoted in Danson, p. 13.

10. Thomas McFarland, *Tragic Meanings in Shakespeare* (New York: Random House, 1966), p. 14.

Subtlety and Sabotage in *Piers Plowman*

Britton J. Harwood

David Aers. *Chaucer, Langland, and the Creative Imagination.* London: Routledge & Kegan Paul, 1980. xii, 236 pp.

Priscilla Martin. Piers Plowman: *The Field and the Tower.* London: Macmillan; New York: Harper & Row, 1979. ix, 172 pp.

Daniel Maher Murtaugh. Piers Plowman *and the Image of God.* Gainesville: University Presses of Florida, 1978. vi, 129 pp.

These three books can be distributed according to one of the most important antinomies in current *Piers Plowman* studies. For Daniel Maher Murtaugh, Lady Holy Church lays "the doctrinal groundwork for the whole poem" (p. 5), and he emphasizes the symmetries which Langland is held to create, in her speeches and later, within merged psychological and theological traditions. Murtaugh studies the richness of the dreamer's education and does not question its relevance. Like D. W. Robertson, Jr., B. F. Huppé, John Lawlor, and others, Murtaugh believes Will must be brought to understand the moral instruction he gets.[1]

To the contrary, David Aers and Priscilla Martin see the poem as turning critically against its own groundwork. Martin contends that the orthodox, optimistic theology of *Piers* is sabotaged in the very allegories and abstractions which elaborate it; "and the sabotage itself is part of the poem's meaning" (p. 37). In Aers's three chapters on Langland, he tries to show that the poet's imagination thwarts his ideology. Thus, Martin and Aers believe with Anne Middleton and Charles Muscatine (whom Martin quotes at length) that Langland's failure with "the great artistic schemes" he "attempts and abandons" suggests that these "had lost their meaning for him."[2] If so, regardless of the moral state in which Langland casts the dreamer, "we are meant, as readers, to stand with . . . Will . . . to the end, and not to regret having done so."[3] Will probes, in effect, for what gives meaning to morality itself.

Murtaugh's subject is the interanimation of psychological movement and social change, for Christian history comprises both. The poem, in Murtaugh's view, represents the revelation of God both in his creation and in human mental activity. Divine love can be discovered as cause of this activity; and when human love analogously impels man in his engagement with the world, the Incarnation is recapitulated. Divine love illumines knowledge of the moral law, in obeying which we are met by more divine love yet. Immanence opens into transcendent mystery. For Murtaugh, the dreamer has no essential problem which could not be overcome by his undertaking natural good works as Trajan did.

The human mind as somehow the image of God becomes the means of recovering the image of God in another sense. The thread of Murtaugh's argument may begin in his adducing the illuminationism of Augustine and Bonaventure. For Augustine, God is the reason why all people see the same truth in the same way. Next, Murtaugh seizes upon Randolph Quirk's identification of Inwit (in Wit's Castle of *Caro* allegory) as the agent intellect of Thomas Aquinas (p. 11), but a supernaturalized one, as if it fell within the Augustinian-Bonaventuran tradition (p. 15). Inwit is thus to be identified with "Treuþe," for Lady Holy Church "a kynde knowyng þat kenneþ in þyn herte/For to louen þi lord leuere þan þiselue" (B.I.142 f.).[4] Finally, Murtaugh sees "Treuþe" as knowing a fuller sense of love than just the moral law. "The idea of truth," Murtaugh writes, is "a natural knowledge of morality. . . . But we are also given a larger view. . . . Somehow our knowledge of the moral law implies the central events of redemptive history" (p. 8).

Of two difficulties here, the lesser is Murtaugh's imputing to Langland a conflation of the agent intellect (Inwit, in Murtaugh's account) and a habitual knowledge of the moral law. But the latter, as Francis Carnegy once suggested, is probably synderesis,[5] not a separate faculty but a perfection of the *ratio*, the knowledge immediately discoverable by every sane adult of the superior will of God the lawgiver.[6] Abstraction, as operated by the *intellectus agens*, has nothing special to do with this. When synderesis is understood in an older tradition as a faculty doubled by a habit,[7] a basic attachment to the sovereign good, leaving its mark on our other human powers,[8] then it includes Inwit as well, the constable of *Caro*.[9]

More seriously, Murtaugh's thesis leads him to suggest that the Incarnation can be known "kyndely." Rather, it is Holy Church who teaches that people know the natural law naturally, but who also knows that "þe fader" who is the donor of such knowledge "loked on vs wiþ loue and leet his sone dye/Mekely for oure mysdedes" (I.167 f.). "Truþe" is natural knowledge "þat loue is triacle of heuene;/May no synne be on hym seene þat vseþ þat spice" (I.148 f.). Anciently identified with *intelligentia*, linked with the angelic nature, and called by Wit "þe gretteste," second only to the grace of God (IX.60), this *kynde knowyng* merges *for Holy Church* with God the Creator (I.150). The church as magisterium knows what the gospels reveal; it knows, therefore, that the Creator also took "of þis fold flessh and blood" (I.155). Nevertheless, the fact that Holy Church makes "truþe" polysemous in this way does not mean that Will's own habitual knowledge of the moral law inevitably leads him to know Christ as well.

Groundlessly, then, Murtaugh maintains that knowledge in *Piers* begins and ends in love naturally. Imaginative will claim that Christ's love is the root of Clergy (XII.71), which Murtaugh defines as Learning *tout court*. It clearly is not, if for no reason other than the availability of the alternative, repudiated "science" of *kynde wit* (XII.128–38). Even if Clergy equaled *kynde knowyng*, however, Holy Church does not teach that the knowledge of Chirst comes *kyndely*, whatever the means of her own access to it. The thesis that knowing the natural law means knowing *deus caritas* may engender Murtaugh's unconvincing argument that, in the Pardon, the Redemption is "superimposed" upon the ordinary moral law" (p. 101).

For Murtaugh, "the soul's measured movement of love" (p.

97) reflects *deus caritas*. Moreover, this movement is met by something like sanctifying grace, which the Incarnation has brought to hand. For example, after Reason's sermon, the ideal form reached by society makes it an "apt subject for grace" (p. 108). Murtaugh likewise sees in the Pardon "a supernatural dimension" conferred upon "the ordinary goodness of man" (p. 107). Murtaugh appears to attribute to Langland a species of Pelagianism—one not supported by the poem. "Social love," "simple goodness," in his view, is a determinant of grace. Nouns, as we know from a C-text speech by Conscience that Murtaugh discusses at length, determine their adjectives. People control grace in a similar fashion. The performance of natural good works "is modified by the grace of the Incarnation just as a substantive is modified by an adjective." Piers the plowman "is the substantive sought by God" (p. 111).

Murtaugh's thesis that the image of God as a motive in the soul makes man "a god by þe gospel" when acts of social love are sanctified may have carried him into misreading several passages. In the directions given by Piers in Passus V to the blundering, frightened multitudes, the Ten Commandments come first, then a reference to Grace the gatekeeper (V.595).

> And if grace graunte þee to go in þis wise
> Thow shalt see in þiselue truþe sitte in þyn herte
> In a cheyne of charite as þow a child were. [V.605–7]

"The mystery of the Incarnation" (p. 10), Murtaugh writes of these lines, "seems to be implied in some immediate way by our good works." This is true enough: Obedience to the moral law, rather than made possible by grace, is itself the way to grace here. But critics have given too much weight at this point, I think, to Piers's claim to a knowledge of God (V.538–55) and not enough to the way this confidence is brought into question by the experience of the Pardon. The Pardon leaves him bent upon penance and (when he would otherwise have been working) upon weeping. It does not obviously confirm him in his mode of life.

Murtaugh perceives Langland wrestling with the question, "How can measurable hire reflect the infinite largesse of God?"

(p. 44). But God did not betake himself "into oure numbre" (C.IV.406)[10] because man had kept "relacion rect" between God and himself. If man had not violated the principle of *mercede*, "coueited / Alle kynne kynde" (C.IV.365 f.), there would have been no sins to sigh for or "harde penaunce" to suffer (403). Christ inflects himself after the manner of mankind (405–9), in Murtaugh's view, because of man's successes rather than his failures. The Redemption will provide a "divine endorsement" (p. 105) to the "maundement" by which Hope says he has saved thousands of people (XVII.21). But this boast of Hope's is reminiscent of Piers's short-lived claim that he and *Liberum-arbitrium* have successfully defended the fruit of the Tree of Charity. It is confounded by the "festred . . . woundes" of the man fallen among thieves (XVII.95). Finally, believing that social love is ultimately tinged with the transcendence of Eternal Love, Murtaugh reads Dame Study as subsuming all the branches of knowledge under the model of theology. Murtaugh thinks that theology, as Study sees it, progresses to its "confusion" (p. 69), the mystery of love, in which theology puts most stock (X.190). Only theology's good opinion of love, however, prevents Study from actually deploring theology (X.189), because she finds it inaccessible, like astronomy. She does not say *no* one gets no further in them than she, originate them though she did. Here, at least, Langland does not seem to mean either that theology ends in confusion or that Study would think of it as exemplary for that reason.

Of society as potentially somehow an image of God or man, Murtaugh writes that Langland tries to "pull the . . . world he sees about him into a coherent shape that will show him his face 'as . . . in a Mirour' " (p. 123). It is, of course, Christ whom Will is looking for, in those lines at least, and he has only his own guilty self to show for it (XV.151–64). But if it were his own image that he sought in society, what would that be? How can society reflect man in the way (for instance) that Augustine understood the relationship among memory, intellect, and will to reflect the Trinity? Murtaugh seems not to offer a clear explanation of this.

While I have been concentrating on Murtaugh's thesis,

because it relates to some serious difficulties I find in his book, I have perhaps insisted on it more than Murtaugh does; and his tact in arguing his principal points partly accounts for some fine things in his study. I do not agree that Will ends Passus X in "theoretical indeterminism" (p. 76). But Murtaugh does good service in introducing into *Piers Plowman* studies the questions argued by Ockham, Robert Holkot, Adam of Woodham, and others, which illuminate lines like these:

> Ther are witty and wel libbynge ac hire werkes ben yhudde
> In þe hondes of almy ʒty god, and he woot þe soþe
> Wher for loue a man worþ allowed þere and his lele werkes,
> Or ellis for his yeul wille and enuye of herte. [B.X.437–40][11]

Although he does not elaborate it enough for the reader to know how it arises from such local developments as Will's falling into the inner dream in Passus XI, Murtaugh offers a striking thesis for the whole movement of the *Vita:* He relates the tropological, allegorical, and anagogical senses of Christ's coming to the sections *Dowel, Dobet,* and *Dobest,* respectively; then suggests that this progression is countered by the logical priority of *Dobet* and its historical events to the moral reformation at the heart of *Dowel.* "The progress through 'Dowel' to the vision of the Redemption in 'Dobet' is . . . a tracing back of Langland's vision of individual and social goodness to its source and premise in the Redemption" (p. 56).

A number of minor disagreements and omissions may be recorded. I am not convinced that the parchment in Wit's analogy (IX.39) means "Man, or something involved exclusively in man's creation" (p. 17), rather than God as creative power as well as Logos; so Milton's epithets for Christ distinguished "Word" from "Effectual Might." It is not clear that the divine "fooles" who stand by Conscience at the end (XX.60–63) are simply the "lunatik lollers and leperes aboute" of C.X.107.[12] Wanderers, "aposteles," "disciples" behave in some respects as if they were insane without being madmen, who nevertheless seem to be treated by God as the apostles were. While Murtaugh writes insightfully about Langland's ambivalence toward the perfection of the social order, perfection spelling its end (pp. 60–62), he adduces little new evidence that the corruption of religious institutions in Passus XX is meant to mark the imminence of social perfection. The "Mirour þat hiȝte middelerþe" not so much "parodies a favorite title for both mystical and encyclopedic works of the Middle Ages" (p. 76), perhaps, as retains one function given the mirror of Scriptures in Augustine's commentary on Psalm 103, namely, to show you what you are, so that you may confess your deformity.[13] Murtaugh misreads Reason's horse (IV.20) as the virtue patience (p. 90), rather than the treacherous *Caro* ridden also by the Samaritan (XVII.110). Rather than the *Etymologiarum* of Isidore of Seville (p. 96), the source of Anima's description of the human soul (XV.23–36) seems to be the pseudo-Augustinian tractate *De Spiritu et Anima,* as Erzgräber pointed out (*William Langlands* Piers Plowman, p. 170). Imaginative appears to equate "cristes writyng" (XII.82) with the bread of the Eucharist, not the body of Christ or "Clergie" in itself: "Clergie" makes "goddes body" *of* bread, just as it is an interpretation *of* the written law.[14] Murtaugh may not quite do justice to the position of Howard Meroney, who would not have agreed that the Pardon scene "presents to us . . . the decalogue of Moses and the Redemption" (p. 101); for Meroney thought of "the role of Piers" here to be inconceivable without a "sequel."[15] Finally, in suggesting "the Epistle General of James, with its emphasis on the need for good works," as a gloss on the Pardon scene, Murtaugh ignores the substantial earlier work of Konrad Burdach.[16]

One turns from this book with a certain regret. Murtaugh seems to me a critic of uncommon honesty, intelligence, and perceptivity. He is widely and accurately informed. Yet in certain respects limitations inherent in his thesis have crippled his project. A very great deal of the poem does not seem to be interested in a notion of the *imago Dei* descending in the tradition of Augustine's *De Trinitate.* On *liberum arbitrium* as bearing the impress of the image of God, E. T. Donaldson has of course already done the exploratory work for *Piers Plowman* studies. And Murtaugh, like most other readers, is cool to

Edward Vasta's notion that *Piers* dramatizes "the soul's progress through the mystical way" to deification.[17] His own subtle alternative seems to me to account for the weaknesses of his book rather than its strengths.

Priscilla Martin's *Piers Plowman: The Field and the Tower* is a book of great sensitivity and considerable sophistication. Implicitly, she groups herself with those critics who "argue from their impression of the texture of the poem and the conduct of its argument . . . to theological uncertainty and vexation of spirit in the author" (p. 32). Her point of departure is Muscatine's description of certain formal traits of *Piers:* "the alternation of allegory and literalism, the violent changes of tone and temper, the peculiar equivalence of concrete and abstract terms." She holds that the poem proposes organizational schemes only to reject them, that it questions the reason for its own existence, that abstract and concrete words create difficulties through the poet's use of them as mutual correctives, that allegory functions to apprehend Christian truths simultaneously given as inaccessible, that such allegorical explorations frequently wreck upon "the literal mode," and that evasions of material history, whether through the *via contemplativa* or "spiritualizing metaphors" (as Martin calls them), leave the poet quite uneasy.

Like Aers, Martin believes that the "ideological statements" in *Piers* are often undercut "by poetic and dramatic techniques" (p. 39). Unlike him, she validates this position by concentrating on many of the traditional materials of literary analysis —allegory, diction, tone, form—and effects. For instance, of Piers's putting the penitent pilgrims to work on the half acre and Truth's evident endorsement of this, Martin comments: "Ideologically, it is right and satisfying that ploughing should be substituted for pilgrimage; yet, fictionally, it produces a sense of arrested purpose. The narrative structure and the structure of ideas contradict each other" (p. 51). Conversely, the dreamer's "self-inflicted frustrations" advance the movements but at the expense of gainsaying the Minorites, Thought, Wit, and others, whom Martin understands as "the essences of wisdom" (p. 49).[18] Martin points to a similar cancellation within the characters Recklessness (in the C-text, where he is free from anxiety about the necessities of physical life but also a figure of temptation) and Need, who both lends himself to abuses and "movingly" expresses the poverty of Christ (pp. 134 f.). Martin's point (of the antinomy of idea and technique) may have conduced to what seems a misreading of the "lered man," invited to table "to lere þee what our lord suffred" (XIII.444). While this figure rebukes, by implication, "the involutions and indirectness" (p. 66) of the poem's technique, Martin also understands the latter as making the Gospel lesson sound "very 'straight': . . . it tells Christians what they already know." One hesitates, nevertheless, to assimilate the "re-telling of a sacred narrative" to other advice Will gets. Other characters taking the higher end of a vertical dialogue with the dreamer matter for failing to give him what he thinks he needs; but the learned man, like the bedridden woman and blind man in the present passage and the "Plowmen and pastours and . . . lewed Iuttes" in an earlier one, may matter most to the dreamer for exciting his envy of their steadfast "bileue" (X.470).

The least satisfying element in Martin's book is her treatment of allegory—which unfortunately bulks very large in her work. To begin with, she believes that "the relationship between abstract and concrete vocabulary is obviously central to the allegorical mode" (p. 71), with abstraction apparently having to do with allegory and concreteness with the literal. But this is not at all self-evident. In Passus II, Simony and Civil ordain, of archdeacons and other officials,

> Lat sadle hem wiþ siluer oure synne to suffre,
> As deuoutrye and diuorses and derne vsurie,
> To bere Bisshopes aboute abroad in visitynge.
> [II.175–78]

In Passus XIV, Conscience will teach Hawkyn to be contrite, for

> That shal clawe þi cote of alle kynnes filþe:
> *Cordis contricio &c.*
> Dowel shal wasshen it and wryngen it poruȝ a wis confessour:
> *Oris confessio &c.*

> Dobet shal beten it and bouken it as bright as any scarlet
> And engreynen it wiþ good wille and goodes grace to amende þe,
> And siþen sende þee to Satisfaccion for to sonnen it after:
> *Satisfaccio.* [XIV.17–21]

These are diocesan officials; they are bribed, then they lead bishops harmlessly about the countryside. Contrition fulfills a necessary condition for an authentic confession as scraping does for washing; confession is completed by satisfaction as washing is by dying and drying. These passages I take to be allegorical, not simply because they are in some degree metaphoric, but because they attend especially to "a more or less definite *succession;* that is to say, the meaning of the allegory . . . is partly due to the succession in which the meanings of its constituents are combined and interpreted."[19] It is potentially interesting in Piers's directions to the pilgrims that he makes the Fourth Commandment a ford in the stream, prayers the bridge of manor house, grace the gatekeeper. But the distinctiveness of allegory seems to lie in its throwing a certain succession (here a puzzling one) into relief: Piers thinks you cannot get to grace until you have done the commandments.

In the first passage, silver and various fourteenth-century English officials might seem more concrete (less allegorical, in Martin's view) than the entities of the second—for instance, psychological states such as contrition and the desire to make amends. But many readers will find "abstract" and "concrete" not perspicuous. To think at all, it seems, is to abstract. "Abstractness," as Herbert Marcuse once pointed out, "is the very life of thought, the token of its authenticity."[20] No doubt there are discriminations to be made among represented objects—not only things and persons, but "all possible occurrences, states, acts performed by persons, etc."[21] And the manner of the constitution of these different objects in *Piers* —which it would be no mean task to specify—no doubt has much to do with Langland's intention and his intentionality. Distinguishing allegory as abstract, however, seems to me problematic in a way that Martin does not allow.

Martin further complicates matters by using "abstract" to

name quite different kinds of things. She sometimes means by it "idealization," in the sense of "clear-cut moral distinctions" (p. 112). This would be the sense of "idealized" in which a phoneme is an ideal, not an actual, sound, purged of regional traces. But Martin also uses "abstract" in the evaluative sense of "ideal" (p. 82): for example, "Law may be perverted by actual justices. . . . Only certain abstractions such as Truth, Conscience, Wit, and Wisdom are to be trusted" (p. 81). An abstraction then has the normative force of a Platonic type, a divine Idea. When Martin also denotes relationships by "abstract" ("measure," p. 82; "Peace," p. 114) and, furthermore, denotes psychological states (e.g., "Contrition," p. 127) by the same term, the stage is set for her to call the disturbance of these relationships or the loss of one of these states the widening of a gap "between the ideal and the actual" and therefore the "opposition of the allegorical and literal modes" (p. 128).

Situated within the critical tradition which may have begun with John Lawlor, Martin rightly apprehends Langland as showing "through his exhausted but indefatigable Dreamer that 'truth' must be felt as experience rather than learned as lesson" (p. 58). Will's search is represented as including empirical tests; and no one, to my knowledge, has done a better job than Martin of describing how these evaporate the consolations which the poem affirms. Nevertheless, her pervasive apparatus of "allegory," "abstract," and "concrete" seems to have obscured more than it has revealed.

Martin is fine at juxtapositions. She acutely contrasts Will's response to the Pardon scene, his "anxious hedging of bets," with Piers's "confidence" in tearing the document. One is left feeling "that Piers knew what he was doing" (p. 21). Will's "flabbiness" at the end of the *Visio* is replaced at the end of the A-text *Vita* by a decisiveness like the plowman's but (in Martin's view) of a desperate sort. The end of the B *Vita* elaborates this contention ironically:

> If B was meant to solve the problems left in abeyance at the end of A, it is strange that B's *Vita* should end as desperately as A's, and

> apparently with more cause for desperation. The whole poem has described a circle back to the world of the prologue. The B continuation seems also to have come full circle. Most Christians are, at the end of B, taking the cynical advice with which Will comforted himself at the beginning: 'Go confess þee to some frere' (XI.54). A broke off when a fallible narrator rejected Clergy; B closes when Conscience calls in vain for the help of Clergy and abandons the Church itself. In A the Dreamer loses faith in the significance of the actions of the individual; in B we feel the powerlessness of all activities and institutions. [p. 29]

Whether the poem ends in a disaster as complete as this passage of Martin's suggests surely depends in part on what *kind* of action this poem is meant to imitate. If the essential action is moral or political, then the ending makes one answer. But there may be another kind of action, and Martin may touch on it with her tantalizing reference to the poet's "theological uncertainty" (p. 32). No one, I think, has dealt more perceptively, comprehensively, or honestly with the kinds of tensions this creates within the poem and with the poet's evident ambivalence towards his own production. These critical achievements survive her unproved assertion that such "tensions . . . were exacerbated by his choice of mode" (p. 12).

Piers students will note a very few minor disagreements and omissions. Some discussion of Leo Spitzer's "Note on the Poetic and Empirical 'I' in Medieval Authors" (*Traditio*, 1946) might have been in order when Martin took up "the presentation of the self as both general and particular" (p. 7). Conscience is not ordinarily thought to be a virtue (p. 31). Also I do not see that the dreamer is "priding himself on his 'wit'" (p. 77) when he criticizes Reason at the end of B.XI. And not many will agree that XV.305–14 ("Ac god sente hem foode by foweles and by no fierse beestes") urges the laity to make a provision for friars so that the latter need not beg (p. 137).

Whereas Martin concludes that the poet's "trust in Christian concepts" is precarious, and spots the aporias in his heuristic, guilty attempts to learn from his own poem, David Aers, in a much less satisfactory book, sees the poet's beliefs as traditional enough, but thinks they are periodically challenged by "imagination." The time may be ripe for a Marxist reading of *Piers*, but *Chaucer, Langland, and the Creative Imagination* does not do the job. Aers believes that Langland's "conscious values and hopes" embrace the "ideology" held by the ruling class within the poet's society (p. 1). He is said to approve a "self-legitimating version of religion, rationality, and law" (p. 17), harmoniously hierarchical (p. 15), coherent (p. 24), inherited (p. 37), conventional (p. 42), feudal (p. 51), and traditional (p. 61). But English society is in transition, and Langland's brewers and bakers (in, for example, III.79–86) "represent small-scale commodity production for an impersonal market as it pressed most openly on poorer groups, especially in its control of food and rents" (p. 8). This "economic individualism" dominates such parts of the poem as the last passus (p. 57). The enterprise and pragmatic secularism of these primitive capitalists lay hold on Langland's imagination despite himself.

"Writing poetry," that is, "constantly released his imagination to embrace realities which pressed against received ideologies, his art putting these into solution" (p. 1). The "self-absorbed social practices" of his time, "in which there is no consciousness of any coherent order," "the revelling in processes of consumption and production which are an end in themselves" emerge in the poetry with such conviction that we realize "how extrinsic the major ideology has become" (p. 5). Repeatedly Aers asserts that the poet's "imaginative integrity" drives him to show, notwithstanding his own commitments, that "the traditional feudal ideology" cannot be frozen (p. 51).

Beyond the superficiality of Aers's tests for imaginative vitality ("Specificity," "engagement," "openness," "concreteness," "strenuous rhythms," "realization"), which leaves the suspicion that "the coherence . . . offered in the traditional model" may be an "imaginative insight" all its own, Aers's treatment fails particularly in its inadequate notion of ideology. Suppose he is right that *Piers* dramatizes a conflict between a dominant feudal ideology and images of a burgeoning, energetic capitalist economy. It is, nonetheless, an important error to think that the presentation of this conflict is not itself ideological. It will not do to say that Langland erects the "traditional" order with his right hand and paints with his left the skeptical brewers and bakers who ignore it to death. That gesture of the poet's needs to be dealt with (or would, if its status weren't fictional) as ideological. Aers believes that on the one side there are "ideologies" "through which self and world" are "perceived and understood" and that on the other there are imaginative realities. Conscience's "desperate resort to terror and physical afflictions" in Passus XX insubstantiates the latter, because it "cannot entail any particular set of moral values and social practices" (p. 35). But when we think of something not as an ideology but as a "fact" (the sharp practice of a London tavern owner, for instance, or Conscience's physical coercion), we mean only "that of the realities constituted by a variety of discourse conventions it is the most popular."[22] The account of Conscience's desperate behavior is not less ideological than the account of Truth's gloss on the Pardon. And where it is no news that, "in spite of its own claims, the [traditional] ideology is disclosed as historical" (p. 18), it may be news to Aers that what he takes to be an imaginative apprehension of history needs to be disclosed as historical too.

In a corollary error, Aers understands the dreamer to be "de-classed" (p. 201)—somehow privileged to wander among classes in conflict and to report the signs of dislocation. As Lukács pointed out of Flaubert and Zola, however, their conscious isolation as critical observers of capitalist society neither situated them outside the bourgeois class nor rendered their methods of presenting reality useless to the capitalist cause.[23] Similarly, there is no reason to think the poet's description of himself (wandering "wolleward and weetshoed . . . /As a recchelees renk") positioned him outside the classes of free peasant proprietors, wage earners, guildsmen, or primary accumulators.

The apocalyptic passages in *Piers*, which Aers believes to confess the inability of the traditional ideology to dam the river of material history, would not be apocalyptic if they contained the verifiable historical agents which he demands of them. Langland appears to believe that the world stands under judgment. The apocalyptic passages, through linguistic devices that perhaps have not yet been described, propose that it does. Complaining of historical vagueness in the threat that Daw the ditchdigger will die for hunger when a maid shall have the mastery (VI.327–31) is like finding psychotic speech unrealistic. Such passages remind us, however, that from the viewpoint of Marxist criticism, it is not enough to label imaginative literature a falsification. That would be gratuitous, for *Piers* gives itself to begin with as a dream. Narratives include a narrative action, however, despite Aers's having given scant attention to anything like plot. As George Huaco, perhaps the most promising of recent literary methodologists, has urged, until we describe what *happens* in the fiction, we cannot find an isomorphic pattern in material history—or, indeed, say how the fiction comes to operate on behalf of one economic class or another.[24]

Other shortcomings in Aers's three chapters on Langland are less important. The shift to capitalism is effected, not by the shift to individual profits as Aers suggests (pp. 8, 10), but by divorce of the worker from the means of production.[25] Aers believes that the eventual disappearance of the knight from Piers's half acre is a "social intuition" on Langland's part (p. 18), but this theory requires Langland to see a long way into the future, since not even the sixteenth century brought the end of the landed magnates as a critical force. While Aers makes much of religious "commodities" in *Piers,* the sale of forgiveness implies the preexistence of a bad conscience on someone's part; and Marxist criticism may be powerless to resolve into material history the phenomenology of fault. Curiously, where Aers will insist on Chaucer's Pardoner as a "reflexive" figure who questions "the grounds of discourse, values, and conventional practices" (p. 98), Aers hardly begins to deal with Will in the same way; nor does he modify (Will being part of the "contemporary church") his claim that Langland never attributes to the Christian church "any powers of self-criticism and self-transformation" (p. 51). Finally, one remarks a disjunction between Aers's footnotes—dense with the titles of the latest monographs on economic and social history—and his text, where one finds just the sparest use of economic or social detail. He does, however, make frequent use of such nonspecialized terms as "mediate" and "refract," which regrettably do not explain themselves.

While the style, scope, procedures, and the value of Aers's book differ from Murtaugh's and Martin's, it may be worth recalling that their studies share with his a preoccupation with features of *Piers* other than its narrative movement. In *The Anatomy of Criticism,* Northrop Frye wrote that "the form of a poem, that to which every detail relates, is the same whether it is examined as stationary or as moving through the work from beginning to end. . . . The *mythos* is the *dianoia* in movement; the *dianoia* is the *mythos* in stasis."[26] Since the appearance of R. W. Frank's Piers Plowman *and the Scheme of Salvation* (published, like the *Anatomy,* in 1957), critics for the most part have kept a cautious distance from the task that Frye implicitly set for them. And it is not that Frank has dispatched the job to everyone's satisfaction. The *mythos* of *Piers* remains one of the great open questions for criticism in the 1980s.

Notes

1. See Robertson and Huppé, Piers Plowman *and Scriptural Tradition* (Princeton: Princeton Univ. Press, 1951), p. 35; Lawlor, "The Imaginative Unity of *Piers Plowman,*" *Review of English Studies,* NS 8 (1957), 119; J. S. Wittig, "The Dramatic and Rhetorical Development of Long Will's Pilgrimage," *Neuphilologische Mitteilungen,* 76 (1975), 52, 75; and Murtaugh, pp. 7, 70, 72, 90.

2. Muscatine, *Poetry and Crisis in the Age of Chaucer* (Notre Dame: Univ. of Notre Dame Press, 1972), p. 107.

3. Middleton, "The Idea of Public Poetry in the Reign of Richard II," *Speculum,* 53 (1978), 109. Although Martin considers Langland's treatment of the dreamer generally unfavorable (pp. 44 f., 47, 50, 54, 77, 84, 89), she notes ambivalence as well: See esp. pp. 58, 89 f., 148.

4. Unless C is specified, I cite the B-text of *Piers,* using the edition by George Kane and E. Talbot Donaldson (London: Athlone Press, 1975).

5. See *The Relations between the Social and Divine Order in William Langland's* Vision of William concerning Piers the Plowman (Breslau: Priebatsch, 1934), pp. 4, 7.

6. See Thomas Aquinas, *Summa Theologica,* I.79.12, 13; I–II.90.1 *ad* 2.

7. See Odon Lottin, *Psychologie et morale aux XIIe et XIIIe siècles*, 2d ed. (Gembloux: Duculot, 1957–60), II, 230.

8. See ibid., pp. 143 f.

9. Cf. William Erzgräber, who, however, interpreted Inwit in B.IX only as a *habitus: William Langlands* Piers Plowman *(Eine Interpretation des C-Textes)* (Heidelberg: Carl Winter, 1957), pp. 60–62, 118 f.

10. I quote C from W. W. Skeat's edition, *The Vision of William concerning Piers the Plowman, in Three Parallel Texts* (London: Oxford Univ. Press, 1886; rpt. 1961).

11. Murtaugh emphasizes the fourteenth-century preoccupation with God's absolute power—his ability to do anything not including a contradiction—but virtually ignores the equal insistence on his *potentia ordinata*. God's "power to do something," as Ockham wrote, "is sometimes to be accepted according to the laws which he has ordained and instituted." Murtaugh cites H. A. Oberman's opinion that Gordon Leff, whose work on Bradwardine Murtaugh uses extensively, "laid too much stress on the skeptical elements in the thought of the Ockhamists" (p. 86); but Murtaugh overlooks Leff's own acknowledgment of this in his magisterial *William of Ockham: The Metamorphosis of Scholastic Discourse* (Manchester: Manchester Univ. Press, 1975), p. xiii.

12. See Murtaugh, p. 53.

13. See Ritamary Bradley, "Backgrounds of the Title *Speculum* in Mediaeval Literature," *Speculum*, 29 (1954), 102 f.

14. Cf. Murtaugh, pp. 94 f.

15. Meroney, "The Life and Death of Longe Wille," *ELH*, 17 (1950), 19.

16. Burdach, *Der Dichter des Ackerman aus Böhmen und Seine Zeit in Vom Mittelalter zur Reformation* (Berlin, 1926), pp. 220–26.

17. Vasta, *The Spiritual Basis of* Piers Plowman (The Hague: Mouton, 1965), p. 23.

18. The value of their advice must depend at least in part upon the dreamer's understanding of his own need. The same may be said about the value of Holy Church's instruction; this gives Will, as Morton Bloomfield pointed out, "a certain difficulty": Piers Plowman *as a Fourteenth-Century Apocalypse* (New Brunswick, N.J.: Rutgers Univ. Press, n.d.) pp. 20 f. (I am less sure than Martin [p. 36] that Bloomfield is an "undisturbed 'Christian' reader" of *Piers*.) Martin finds the Franciscans' advice to Will satisfactory. Because the exercise of "wit and free wil" is, in their account, the *cause* of sinning venially (falling down in the boat), their advice seems incoherent.

19. Gunnar Berefelt, "On Symbol and Allegory," *Journal of Aesthetics and Art Criticism,* 28 (1969), 207 (his italics).

20. Herbert Marcuse, *One-Dimensional Man* (Boston: Beacon Press, 1964), p. 134.

21. Roman Ingarden, *The Literary Work of Art,* 3d ed., tr. G. G. Grabowicz (1965 ; rpt. Evanston, Ill.: Northwestern Univ. Press, 1973), p. 219.

22. Stanley E. Fish, "How to Do Things with Austin and Searle: Speech Act Theory and Literary Criticism," *MLN,* 91 (1976), 1019. For a clear statement by Aers that Langland has no ideological alternative to what Aers calls the "dominant" one, see p. 16.

23. George Lukács, "Idea and Form in Literature" (1936), in *Marxism and Human Liberation* (New York: Dell, 1973), pp. 115, 117.

24. Huaco, "Ideology and Literature," *New Literary History,* 4 (1973), 421–36.

25. See Karl Marx, *Capital,* I, tr. E. and C. Paul (London: Dent, 1930), p. 792.

26. Frye, *Anatomy* (Princeton: Princeton Univ. Press, 1957), p. 83.

Correspondence

Dear Sirs:

Contrary to what is said in *Review*, I (1979), 190, the forthcoming Volume IX of the Northwestern–Newberry Edition of the Writings of Herman Melville, *The Piazza Tales and Other Prose Pieces 1839–1860,* will appear under the editorship of Harrison Hayford, Hershel Parker, and G. Thomas Tanselle.

I have not been associated with the Northwestern–Newberry Edition since October of 1978, when the component texts of Volume IX were in galley proof.

Sincerely yours,

Merton M. Sealts, Jr.
Henry A. Pochmann
Professor of English

The *Review* Association

Major funding for *Review* is provided by a grant from the Research Division and the College of Arts and Sciences at Virginia Polytechnic Institute and State University. Additional support is provided by The *Review* Association, a group of major universities which support the aims and purposes of the series. Member universities are as follows:

Columbia University
Duke University
University of Minnesota
Pennsylvania State University
Princeton University
University of Virginia

Contributors

CRAIG S. ABBOTT is Associate Professor of English at Northern Illinois University.
N.F. BLAKE is Professor of English at the University of Sheffield.
ROBERT C. BRAY is Associate Professor of English and American Studies at Illinois Wesleyan University.
JEROME H. BUCKLEY is Gurney Professor of English Literature at Harvard University.
WILLIAM E. CAIN is Assistant Professor of English at Wellesley College.
BRITTON J. HARWOOD is Professor of English at Miami University.
PETER HEATH is Professor of Philosophy at the University of Virginia.
JOHN DIXON HUNT is Professor of English Literature at Bedford College, University of London.
HUGH KENNER is Andrew W. Mellon Professor of the Humanities at The Johns Hopkins University.
THOMAS MCFARLAND is Murray Professor of English Literature at Princeton University.
VERONICA A. MAKOWSKY is Assistant Professor of American Literature at Middlebury College.
JOEL MYERSON is Professor of English at the University of South Carolina.
ROBERT L. PATTEN is Professor of English at Rice University and Editor of *Studies in English Literature*.
ANNABEL PATTERSON is Professor of English at the University of Maryland.
JOHN OLIVER PERRY is Associate Professor of English at Tufts University.
HARVENA RICHTER is Assistant Professor of English at the University of New Mexico.
THOMAS P. RIGGIO is Associate Professor of English at the University of Connecticut.

MARTIN ROTH is Professor of English at the University of Minnesota.

RONALD SCHUCHARD is Associate Professor of English at Emory University.

PHILIP H. SMITH, JR., is Professor and Director of the Arts Computing Office, Faculty of Arts, University of Waterloo.

MARK SPILKA is Professor of English and Comparative Literature at Brown University.

STANLEY WEINTRAUB is Director of the Institute for the Arts and Humanistic Studies, The Pennsylvania State University.